Dreamers, Scribes, and Priests

Supplements

to the

Journal for the Study of Judaism

Editor

John J. Collins
The Divinity School, Yale University

Associate Editor

Florentino García Martínez
Qumran Institute, University of Groningen

Advisory Board

J. DUHAIME — A. HILHORST — P.W. VAN DER HORST
A. KLOSTERGAARD PETERSEN — M.A. KNIBB — J.T.A.G.M. VAN RUITEN
J.SIEVERS — G. STEMBERGER — E.J.C. TIGCHELAAR — J. TROMP

VOLUME 90

Dreamers, Scribes, and Priests

Jewish Dreams in the
Hellenistic and Roman Eras

by

Frances Flannery-Dailey

BRILL

LEIDEN · BOSTON

2004

This book is printed on acid-free paper.

Library of Congress Cataloging-in-Publication Data

Flannery-Dailey, Frances, 1968–
  Dreamers, scribes, and priests : Jewish dreams in the Hellenistic and Roman eras / by Frances Flannery-Dailey.
    p. cm. — (Supplements to the Journal for the Study of Judaism, ISSN 1384-2161 ; v. 90)
  Includes bibliographical references and index.
  Contents: Dreams in the ancient Near East and Israel – Dreams in Greece and Rome – Dreams in Hellenistic Judaism: form, vocabulary and functions – Dreams in Hellenistic Judaism: creative transformations and elaborations – Reflections and implications.
  ISBN 90-04-12367-9
    1. Dreams—Religious aspects—Judaism. 2. Dreams—History—To 1500. 3. Dream interpretation—History—To 1500. I. Title. II. Series.

BF 1078.F54 2004
154.6'3'089924–dc22

2004050062

ISSN 1384-2161
ISBN 90 04 12367 9

PRINTED IN THE NETHERLANDS

For Sam

CONTENTS

ACKNOWLEDGEMENTS

I have many people to thank for their help and support on this project. A big thank you goes to my insightful and supportive editor, John J. Collins. His initial request to read my Ph.D. dissertation led to many fruitful discussions and the decision to pursue this investigation, with John generously giving me help every step of the way. I also received valuable feedback at crucial junctures from James Davila and Nicolae Roddy. I owe a tremendous debt to those who trained me at The University of Iowa and who shepherded me through my Ph.D. dissertation, which was the foundation on which this project was built. The expert guidance of my interdisciplinary dissertation committee, George W.E. Nickelsburg, Helen Goldstein, J. Kenneth Kuntz, Mary Depew, and Carin Green, is still apparent in parts of this manuscript. Above all, my graduate advisor George Nickelsburg sparked my initial interest in Second Temple Judaism with his passion for the material; for that and for his continued friendship I am grateful. Michael Stone also read my work on 4 Ezra at the dissertation stage and those discussions still frame much of my thinking on the ancient text. Of course, any mistakes in this project are my own.

I would also like to thank my colleagues in the Pseudepigrapha Group and Early Jewish and Christian Mysticism Group of the Society of Biblical Literature who have provided helpful comments on papers that eventually informed parts of this book. Also, Rachel Wagner has offered friendship and intellectual camaraderie, as well as insights on form criticism. A huge thank you goes to the people at Brill, especially Mattie Kuiper and Ivo Romein, who were considerate and patient throughout the development of this project.

I also had much practical help in putting together the manuscript. Beverly Bow prepared the indices and bibliography and also contributed most of the copy editing and humor. At earlier stages, I was fortunate to work with two former students of mine from Hendrix College. Lori McCullough helped with initial stages of research and copy editing, while Jonathan Jackson was an invaluable resource on languages, especially Akkadian and Ethiopic. I would also like to thank the Wabash Center for the Teaching and Learning of Theology and Religion as well as Hendrix College for generous grants that enabled me to pursue my research and writing. General but heartfelt thanks go to the entire Hendrix community, especially the following people who supported me in various ways: Peggy Morrison, Cathy Goodwin, Jay McDaniel, Joni Podschun, Shayna Simeone, Molly Moran, Courtney Jones, and Samantha Franklin. My colleagues and students have cheered me on, as have friends in the 'Goodgig' circle of AAR/SBL. I have been blessed with many friends whom I wish to thank for their continued support of not only my academic pursuits, but also my striving to live a life of artful balance. Although I cannot name everyone here, I hope I have thanked each of them personally.

Most of all, this book was made possible by the love and encouragement of my family, especially my husband Mike and our son Sam. Sam was dreaming in my womb during the genesis of this book, and he remains my inspiration. He was also my frequent companion as I wrote, which was admittedly difficult for him, requiring great fortitude and many crayons and puzzles. This book is for him, 21 months old today.

Conway, AR
December 19, 2003

ABBREVIATIONS

AB	Anchor Bible
ABD	*Anchor Bible Dictionary* (D. N. Freedman, ed.; 6 vols.)
AGJU	Arbeiten zur Geschichte des antiken Judentums und des Urchristentums
AJP	*American Journal of Philology*
ANET	*Ancient Near Eastern Texts Relating to the Old Testament*, 3rd ed. (J. Pritchard, ed.).
ANRW	*Aufstieg und Niedergang der Römischen Welt*
AOAT	Alter Orient und Altes Testament
ARM	Archives royales de Mari
ASOR	American Schools of Oriental Research
ATANT	Abhandlungen zur Theologie des Alten und Neuen Testaments
BAR	*Biblical Archaeology Review*
BDB	Brown, F., S. R. Driver and C. A. Briggs. *A Hebrew and English Lexicon of the Old Testament*
BHS	*Biblia Hebraica Stuttgartensia*
BZ	*Biblische Zeitschrift*
BZAW	*Beihefte zur Zeitschrift für die Alttestamentliche Wissenschaft*
CAD	*The Assyrian Dictionary of the Oriental Institute of the University of Chicago*
CP	*Classical Philology*
CTA	*Corpus des tablettes en cunéiformes alphabétiques découvertes à Ras Shamra-Ugarit de 1929 à 1939* (A. Herdner, ed.)
DJD	Discoveries in the Judean Desert
EJMI	*Early Judaism and its Modern Interpreters* (R. Kraft and G. W. E. Nickelsburg, eds.)
EncJud	*Encyclopedia Judaica*
ERE	*Encyclopedia of Religion and Ethics* (J. Hastings, ed.; 13 vols.)
FOTL	Forms of the Old Testament Literature
FRLANT	Forschungen zur Religion und Literatur des Alten und Neuen Testaments

HALOT	*Hebrew and Aramaic Lexicon of the Old Testament* (M. E. J. Richardson, ed.; 2 vols.)
HBMI	*Hebrew Bible and its Modern Interpreters* (D. A. Knight and G. M. Tucker, eds.)
HAT	Handbuch zum Alten Testament
HSM	Harvard Semitic Monographs
HSS	Harvard Semitic Studies
HTR	*Harvard Theological Review*
HTS	Harvard Theological Studies
IDBSup	*Interpreter's Dictionary of the Bible Supplementary Volume*
IEJ	*Israel Exploration Journal*
Int	*Interpretation*
JAAR	*Journal of the American Academy of Religion*
JAOS	*Journal of the American Oriental Society*
JBL	*Journal of Biblical Literature*
JJS	*Journal of Jewish Studies*
JQR	*Jewish Quarterly Review*
JRS	*Journal of Religious Studies*
JSJ	*Journal for the Study of Judaism in the Persian, Hellenistic, and Roman Periods*
JSNT Supp.	*Journal for the Study of the New Testament* Supplement Series
JSOT Supp.	*Journal for the Study of the Old Testament* Supplement Series
JSPSup	*Journal for the Study of the Pseudepigrapha* Supplement Series
KAR	*Keilschrifttexte aus Assur religiösen Inhalts* (E. Ebeling, ed.)
LSJ	Liddell, H. G., R. Scott, and H. S. Jones. *A Greek-English Lexicon*, 9th ed. with revised supplement.
NEAEHL	*The New Encyclopedia of Archaeological Excavations in the Holy Land*
NTS	*New Testament Studies*
OLD	*Oxford Latin Dictionary*
OTP	*Old Testament Pseudepigrapha* (J. Charlesworth, ed.; 2 vols.)
RB	*Revue biblique*
RevQ	*Revue de Qumran*
RSR	*Recherches de science religieuse*
SBL	Society of Biblical Literature
SBLEJL	Society of Biblical Literature Early Judaism and Its Literature
SBLSP	*Society of Biblical Literature Seminar Papers*
SBT	Studies in Biblical Theology
STDJ	Studies on the Texts of the Desert of Judah

SVTP	Studia in Veteris Testamenti Pseudepigraphica
TAPA	*Transactions of the American Philological Association*
TDNT	*Theological Dictionary of the New Testament* (G. Kittel and G. Friedrich, eds.; 10 vols.)
TDOT	*Theological Dictionary of the Old Testament* (G. Botterweck and H. Ringgren, eds.; 8 vols.)
TU	Texte und Untersuchungen
VT	*Vetus Testamentum*
WUNT	Wissenschaftliche Untersuchungen zum Neuen Testament
YCS	Yale Classical Studies
ZAW	*Zeitschrift für alttestamentliche Wissenschaft*
ZRGG	*Zeitschrift für Religions- und Geistesgeschichte*

INTRODUCTION

> The pre-scientific view of dreams adopted by the
> peoples of antiquity was certainly in complete
> harmony with their view of the universe in general,
> which led them to project into the external world
> as though they were realities things which in fact
> enjoyed reality only within their own minds … Our
> scientific consideration of dreams starts off from
> the assumption that they are products of our own
> mental activity.
>
> —Sigmund Freud, *The Interpretation of Dreams*[1]

> Jacob awoke from his sleep and said, 'Surely the
> LORD is present in this place, and I did not know
> it!'
>
> —Genesis 28:16

Ancient Mediterranean and Near Eastern peoples regarded dreams
quite differently than do those of us in post-Freudian modern society.
Whereas we tend to view dreams as unreal, interior, subjective phenomena, ancient peoples believed that some dreams were genuine visits from deities or their divine representatives. One did not 'have' a
dream; one 'saw' a dream, or a dream 'met' or 'visited' the dreamer.
Thus, the author of Genesis 28:10–22 depicts Jacob as dreaming that
the LORD was standing at the top of a stairway to heaven, whereupon
Jacob awakens and concludes that the LORD is actually present at the
spot where the dream occurred. Again, while modern dreamers tend
to hold that the value of dreams lies in their ability to yield information about the dreamers' past or present psychology, ancient peoples
believed that dreams impart knowledge of the future or knowledge of
events quite apart from the interior life of the dreamer. Today there

---

[1] S. Freud, *The Interpretation of Dreams* (8th ed.; trans. J. Strachey, New York: Basic
Books, 1965), 38, 80; first German Edition is *Die Traumdeutung* (Leipzig and Vienna:
Franz Deuticke, 1900).

exists a popular distinction between a 'dream' as a mental movie that
occurs during sleep and a 'vision' as a sort of hallucinatory experience
that occurs in a waking state.[2] By contrast, the ancients placed dreams
and visions along a thickly inhabited spectrum of hypnagogic phenomena. Some of these visionary experiences were likened to that nightly
experience we call a dream, although such 'dream' states often hovered
somewhere between sleep and wakefulness. Accordingly, the ancient
Egyptian texts use *rswt* for 'to see a dream,' which is written with the
determinative of an open eye and stems from the root 'to awaken.'[3]

This is a study of dreams in early Judaism or Hellenistic Judaism,
the period of Judaism between the Persian period and the late Roman
empire.[4] I examine diverse texts containing dreams in the Hebrew
Bible, Apocrypha, Pseudepigrapha, Dead Sea Scrolls, and Josephus.[5]
Many of the texts included in the study are early Christian in their

[2] Although these descriptions aptly capture the popular usages of the terms 'dream'
and 'vision,' scientific research on dream and visionary states indicates a complex range
of brain states for these activities. This was apparent well before the time of S. Freud,
who discusses studies on hypnagogic hallucinations by L.F.A. Maury and J. Müller in
The Interpretation of Dreams, 65. In more recent research it has become apparent that
even those experiences rightly called dreams in a scientific sense can occur at the onset
of sleep, in a semi-wakeful hypnagogic state, in non-REM states or in REM states;
see Sleep Research Society, *Basics of Sleep Behavior* (UCLA and Sleep Research Society,
1993), 57–60. Consider also that W.C. Dement, a pioneer in sleep research, states, 'At
some times the sleeping brain actually appears to be more active than it is while awake,
burning large quantities of sugar and oxygen as neurons fire rapidly. When dreaming,
the mind takes on a different consciousness, inhabits a new world that is as real as the
world it experiences when awake.' From W.C. Dement, *The Promise of Sleep* (New York:
Dell Publishing, 1999), 16, 292–311.
[3] Leo Oppenheim, *The Interpretation of Dreams in the Ancient Near East: With a Translation
of an Assyrian Dream-Book* (Transactions of the American Philosophical Society, vol. 46,
pt. 3; Philadelphia: American Philosophical Society, 1956), 226.
[4] M. Hengel has been largely responsible for illuminating the ways in which all
Judaism of the Hellenistic and Roman eras may rightly be called 'Hellenistic Judaism.'
Hengel, *Judaism and Hellenism: Studies in their Encounter in Palestine during the Early Hellenistic
Period* (2 vols.; trans. J. Bowden; Philadelphia: Fortress, 1974) and idem, 'Judaism and
Hellenism Revisited,' in *Hellenism in the Land of Israel* (Christianity and Judaism in
Antiquity 13; eds. J.J. Collins, G.E. Sterling; Notre Dame, IN: University of Notre Dame
Press, 2001), 6–37.
[5] The limits of this study exclude Philo, since his philosophical understanding of
dreams appears to constitute a trajectory so neatly distinct from those in the other
Hellenistic Jewish materials listed above. See R.M. Berchman, 'Arcana Mundi: Magic
and Divination in the *De Somnis* of Philo of Alexandria,' (*SBLSP* 26; ed. K.H. Richards;
Atlanta: Scholars Press, 1987): 403–428; and D.M. Hay, 'Politics and Exegesis in Philo's
Treatise on Dreams,' (*SBLSP* 26; ed. K.H. Richards; Atlanta: Scholars Press, 1987):
429–438.

extant form (e.g. *Testaments of the Twelve Patriarchs*,[6] *2 Enoch*,[7] and *Ladder of Jacob*[8]). In each case the arguments for a Jewish *Urtext* may be made, though not conclusively, and I have chosen to include these texts partially for their coherence with the rest of the Hellenistic Jewish dreams I survey.[9] Ultimately, then, this project might contribute some evidence towards an argument in favor of recoverable Jewish strata in these texts. I have also included the two texts in the New Testament that contain dreams (Gospel of Matthew; Acts), since both relate in significant ways to a Hellenistic Jewish context before the end of the first century, although they are patently Christian.

---

[6] Arguments on the composition of *T. Twelve* are numerous, but they have mostly fallen into two camps, the one based on R.H. Charles' classic theory that the testaments are Jewish with Christian redactions, the other following M. de Jonge's argument that a Jewish sub-stratum of *T. Twelve* is unrecoverable if it exists at all. See especially R.H. Charles, *The Greek Versions of the Testaments of the Twelve Patriarchs* (Oxford: Oxford University Press, 1908); idem, *The Testaments of the Twelve Patriarchs: Translated from the Editor's Greek Texts* (London: Blackwell, 1908); idem, *The Apocrypha and Pseudepigrapha of the Old Testament in English* (Oxford: Clarendon Press): II, 282–367; J. Becker, *Untersuchungen zur Entstehungsgeschichte der Testamente der Zwölf Patriarchen* (AGJU, VIII; Leiden: Brill, 1970); A. Hultgård, *L'eschatologie des Testaments des Douze Patriarches. II. Composition de l'ouvrage; texts et traductions* (Acta Universitatus Upsaliensis, Historia Religionum 7; Uppsala: Almqvist & Wiksell, 1982). Early on, A. Dupont-Sommer and M. Philonenko posited an Essene origin, noting resonances with Qumranic materials: M. Philonenko, *Les interpolations chrétiennes des Testaments des Douze Patriarches et les manuscrits de Qoumrân* (Paris: Presses universitaires de France, 1960) and A. Dupont-Sommer, 'Le Testament de Lévi (XVII–XVIII) et la secte juive de l'Alliance,' *Semitica* 4:33–53. For theories of Christian composition see M. de Jonge, *The Testaments of the Twelve Patriarchs: A Study of their Text, Composition and Origin* (Assen: Van Gorcum, 1975); H.D. Slingerland, *The Testaments of the Twelve Patriarchs: A Critical History of Research* (Missoula, MT: Scholars, 1977); H.C. Kee, 'Introduction,' *Testaments of the Twelve Patriarchs*, OTP 1:776–781; R. Kugler, *Testaments of the Twelve Patriarchs* (Guides to the Apocrypha and Pseudepigrapha; ed. M.A. Knibb; Sheffield: Sheffield Academic Press, 2001); cf. idem, *From Patriarch to Priest: The Levi-Priestly Tradition from Aramaic Levi to Testament of Levi* (SBLEJL 9; Atlanta: Scholars Press, 1996).

[7] Andersen and Böttrich both incline towards the theory of a Jewish *Urtext* of an early date (first or second century for Andersen; prior to 70 C.E. for Böttrich). F.I. Andersen, *2 (Slavonic Apocalypse of) Enoch*, OTP 1:91–100; C. Böttrich, *Das slavische Henochbuch* (Jüdische Schriften aus hellenistisch-römischer Zeit V,7; Gütersloh: Gütersloher Verlagshaus, 1996), esp. 812–813; idem, *Weltweisheit, Menschheitsethik, Urkult: Studien zum slavischen Henochbuch* (Wissenschaftliche Untersuchungen zum Neuen Testament 2; Tübingen: Mohr-Siebeck, 1992), esp. 108.

[8] H.G. Lunt notes that the date and provenance of *Ladd. Jac.* are uncertain, but he ultimately rests in favor of an originally Jewish work in Greek intended for a Palestinian audience in the first century. See Lunt, *Ladder of Jacob*, OTP 2:401–406.

[9] My title might have included the phrase *Jewish and Christian Dreams*, but since my accent is clearly on the former I have chosen rather to deal with this quandary by way of explanation.

Since modern and ancient views of dreams vary so drastically, I approach these ancient dreams as much as possible from the context of ancient expectations rather than in light of modern presuppositions about dreams. To this end, I use form criticism as well as other literary and historical methods to situate the corpus of early Jewish revelatory dreams within the context of antecedent and contemporary dream traditions of the ancient Near East, Greece, and Rome. This methodology allows me to illuminate what is typical as well as unique in the Jewish dreams. I also examine Hellenistic Jewish dreams in their social settings by employing methods from history and sociology and some findings from archaeology.

To be specific, this project analyzes numerous revelatory dreams in texts of varying genres from the third century B.C.E. to the second century C.E., including: *1 Enoch* 1–36, 83–90; Daniel; *Jubilees*; 2 Maccabees; Additions to Esther; *Pseudo-Philo*; *4 Ezra*; *2 Baruch*; *Ezekiel the Tragedian*; *Testament of Job*; *2 Enoch*; *the Ladder of Jacob*; *Testament of Abraham*; *Testament of Levi Greek*; *Testament of Naphtali*; *Testament of Joseph*; *Testament of Job*; *Jewish Wars*; *Jewish Antiquities*; *Life of Flavius Josephus*; *Against Apion*; and numerous texts from the Qumran Scrolls (*1Q Genesis Apocryphon, 1QJubilees, 4QEnoch, 4QBook of Giants, 11QTargum of Job, 4QApocryphon of Jacob, 4QAramaic Levi, 4QVisions of Amram, 4QVisions of Samuel, 4QPrayer of Nabonidus, 4Q and 11QPsalms*); as well as the Gospel of Matthew and Acts of the Apostles. Because of my emphasis on form criticism, I have not attempted to treat every general reference to dreams or visions in the early Jewish texts; instead, I have focused only on dreams for which some content is provided.

Divinely sent dreams are widely attested in texts from the ancient Near East, Israel (i.e., in the Hebrew Bible), Greece, and Rome, usually following patterns that remain surprisingly standardized for millennia. I find that when viewed cross-culturally, both literary and cultic materials understand divinely sent dreams to be genuine contacts with the divine that function to endow the dreamer with extraordinary knowledge, healing, or divine sanction (whether of the dreamer or of his/her activities).

The dreams of Hellenistic Judaism reflect and transform these dream forms and traditions, appropriating them for the situation of Hellenistic Jews living, with varying degrees of success, amongst pagan Hellenistic neighbors. This period of Judaism was one of rapid change and challenges posed by syncretism, the ravages of war, periodic rule by foreign empires, and tensions between various interpretations of

Judaism.[10] Moreover, shifting cosmologies seriously challenged the prevailing view of the structure of the cosmos. The Ptolemaic cosmos, with its seven concentric spheres of heaven,[11] was absorbed to different degrees into Jewish thought[12] such that God seemed to be transcendent, remote, and perhaps less involved in human life. The God of Genesis who walked in the Garden of Eden at the cool of the day, or even the Glory of God who rode in Ezekiel's *merkavah* chariot from Jerusalem to Babylon, now was viewed as residing firmly in heaven.[13] God's throne in the heavenly temple may have had wheels,[14] but it was not moving anytime soon.

Pagan peoples of the Hellenistic era responded to their greatly enlarged empires and cosmos by turning with increasing fervor to oracles, mystery cults, dreams, and divination of various sorts in an effort to procure divine contact and guidance.[15] I suggest that a similar phenomenon occurs in Hellenistic Judaism as Jews turn with renewed vigor to the dreams of the Bible, elaborating on these stories and creating new ones which they pseudepigraphically attribute to the sacred figures of past history. During this time of covenantal challenge, as the authors of our texts puzzle over the reasons for Israel's various plights and wonder whether righteousness would procure God's fidelity, the literary motif of divinely sent dreams gives expression to the need for inti-

---

[10] Hellenistic Jews faced a host of crises, some material and some perceptual. See the historical analyses in G.W.E. Nickelsburg, *Jewish Literature between the Bible and the Mishnah* (Philadelphia: Fortress Press, 1981), 9–17, 43, 71–73, 101–105, 195–203, 277–281; I. Gafni, 'The Historical Background,' *Jewish Writings of the Second Temple Period: Apocrypha, Pseudepigrapha, Qumran Sectarian Writings, Philo, Josephus* (ed. M.E. Stone, Philadelphia: Fortress Press, 1984), 1–27; M. Hengel, *Judaism and Hellenism*; and V. Tcherikover, *Hellenistic Civilization and the Jews* (New York: Atheneum, 1970).

[11] F. Cumont, *Astrology and Religion Among the Greeks and Romans* (trans. J.B. Baker; New York: Dover, 1960), 68; M.P. Nilsson, *Geschichte der Griechischen Religion* (2nd ed.; Munich: C.H. Beck), II: 702–711; E.R. Dodds, *Pagan and Christian in an Age of Anxiety* (New York: Norton, 1970), Chapter One.

[12] In the Jewish literature, seven heavens appear in *2 Enoch* and probably *4 Ezra* 7, but one and three heavens also appear. A.Y. Collins, 'The Seven Heavens in Jewish and Christian Apocalypses,' in *Death, Ecstasy, and Otherworldly Journeys* (eds. J.J. Collins and M. Fishbane; New York: SUNY Press, 1995), 57–92. J.R. Davila has recently suggested an explicit connection between the seven heavens and the seven concentric palaces of the *Hekhalot* literature, J.R. Davila, *Descenders to the Chariot: The People behind the Hekhalot Literature* (Leiden: Brill, 2000), 189.

[13] Martha Himmelfarb has made this point most convincingly in *Ascent to Heaven in Jewish and Christian Apocalypses* (New York: Oxford University Press, 1993).

[14] *1 Enoch* 14:18; Daniel 7:9.

[15] L. Martin, *Hellenistic Religions* (New York: Oxford University Press, 1987), 40–53.

mate contact with a transcendent God while also procuring assurance of the eventual hegemony of Israel and its leaders.

Thus, literary dreams, though fictional, function on both narrative and social levels. Dreams impart *divine knowledge* of Torah, eschatology, cosmology, and/or salvation history to characters within the narratives as well as to the audiences of the dream texts. Similarly, dreams impart *personal and national consolation* and assurance of *divine sanction* for pseudepigraphical community leaders, as well as for the audience and the leaders of real Jewish communities. In other words, we may glean insights into the social organization of Hellenistic Judaism by attending to the symbolic universes constructed in dream narratives, as well as to the ways in which the traditional dream functions of knowledge, healing, and divine sanction are reinterpreted.

In addition, I argue that the forms of dream narratives and the cultural expectations surrounding them provide for the imaginative suspension of constraints on reality that allows for the articulation of new worldviews, including apocalypticism[16] and mysticism. Without the constraints of space, a dreamer has access to heaven and the farthest reaches of earth in the form of otherworldly journeys. Angels from heaven mix freely with dreamers on earth, while earthly dreamers shoot up to the divine throne room in heaven or witness the realm of the dead. With the erasure of time, dreamers are able to gain knowledge of past and future, including the eschatological future. With the overcoming of ontological limits, dreamers may freely interact with

---

[16] The debate regarding proper use of 'apocalypticism' versus 'apocalypse' has proved extremely instructive. This study employs the definition of the genre apocalypse given in *Apocalypse: The Morphology of a Genre* (*Semeia* 14; ed. John J. Collins; Missoula, MT: Scholars Press, 1979), 9: 'a genre of revelatory literature with a narrative framework, in which a revelation is mediated by an otherworldly being to a human recipient, disclosing a transcendent reality which is both temporal, insofar as it envisages eschatological salvation, and spatial insofar as it involves another, supernatural world.' See also P.D. Hanson, 'Apocalypse, Genre,' in *IDBSup*, 28–34; K. Koch, *The Rediscovery of Apocalyptic* (SBT 2/22; Naperville, IL: Allenson, 1972); P. Vielhauer, 'Apocalypses and Related Subjects,' *New Testament Apocrypha* (eds. E. Hennecke and W. Schneemelcher; Philadelphia: Westminster, 1965), 2:581–607; E.P. Sanders, 'The Genre of Palestinian Apocalypses,' *Apocalypticism in the Mediterranean World and the Near East: Proceedings of the International Colloquium on Apocalypticism, Uppsala, August 12–17, 1979* (ed. D. Hellholm; Tübingen: Mohr-Siebeck, 1983), 447–459; C. Rowland gives definitions for the term 'apocalyptic' in *The Open Heaven: A Study of Apocalyptic in Judaism and Christianity* (New York: Crossroad, 1982), 14; also D. Hellholm, 'The Problem of Apocalyptic Genre and the Apocalypse of John,' *SBL Seminar Papers 1982* (SBLSP 21; Chico, CA: Scholars Press, 1982), 157–198.

angels or even the Glory of God, and they themselves may be transformed into angels. Thus, research on dreams impinges on the related topics of apocalypticism, early Jewish mysticism, cosmology, and ontological classifications in early Judaism.

Chapter Review

Part One establishes formal patterns and expectations surrounding dreams in dream traditions antecedent and contemporary to Hellenistic Judaism. I begin in Chapter One with a form-critical and historical overview of dreams in ancient Near Eastern texts and the Hebrew Bible. Drawing especially on the foundational work of Leo Oppenheim's *The Interpretation of Dreams in the Ancient Near East, With a Translation of an Assyrian Dream-Book*,[17] I address the question of what exactly constitutes a 'dream' in the literary and cultic sources. In Chapter Two, I turn to the Greek and Roman sources with the same form-critical and literary-critical approaches. In addition, since the Graeco-Roman material furnishes a contemporary parallel with the Jewish texts under consideration and since archaeological and historical evidence of the Graeco-Roman dream cults is relatively plentiful, I attend to practices from Hellenistic dream cults as a window on the lived background of literary expressions of dreaming.

By examining dreams cross-culturally over several millennia, I do not mean to imply the complete homogenization of these dream traditions.[18] Indeed, I notice some peculiar features in each dream tradition, arguing for instance that Greek poetry portrays women as dreamers more often than does Greek prose. However, such observations are not the focus of the present study, and thus I do approach this mass of materials in a somewhat reductionistic way, seeking to observe the overall set of common forms and expectations regarding dreams with an eye to my later study of early Jewish texts.

A broad analysis such as this one always owes a heavy debt to previous scholarship, and this is perhaps particularly the case in Part One.

---

[17] L. Oppenheim, *Interpretation*. See also idem, 'Mantic Dreams in the Ancient Near East' in *The Dream and Human Societies* (eds. G.E. von Grunebaum and R. Callois; Berkeley: University of California Press, 1966), 341–350; idem, 'New Fragments of the Assyrian Dream-Book' in *Iraq* 31 (1969): 153–165.

[18] Three influential cross-cultural studies of dreaming should be mentioned: *The Dream and Human Societies* (eds. G.E. von Grunebaum and R. Callois); *Dream Cultures:*

I review Oppenheim's categories of ancient Near Eastern dreams—
message, symbolic and psychological status dreams—and find them
illuminating for biblical and Graeco-Roman dreams as well. Although
a few scholars, including E.L. Ehrlich and W. Richter,[19] have developed
alternate categories for biblical dreams, most subsequent works on biblical dreams that attend to form-critical considerations have adopted
some variation of Oppenheim's classifications. Important works on biblical dreams include those by R. Gnuse, S. Bar, K. Seybold, and K.
Wood.[20] Oppenheim's work has of course been foundational for scholars of ancient Near Eastern dreams. In this area, notable studies have
been conducted on the following subjects: Mesopotamian dreams by
K. Bulkley, O.R. Gurney, and M. Leibovici; Egyptian dreams by S.
Sauneron, and J.D. Ray; Hittite dreams by M. Vieyra (as well as Gurney); Mari dreams by J. Sasson, as well as by H. Huffmon and A. Malamat in their work on prophecy; and ancient Israelite and Canaanite
dreams by J.R. Porter and A. Caquot.[21]

Explorations in the Comparative History of Dreaming (eds. D. Shulman and G. Stroumsa; New
York: Oxford University Press, 1999); and *Les songes et leur interprétation* (ed. S. Sauneron;
Sources Orientales 2; Paris: Seuil, 1959).

[19] E.L. Ehrlich, *Der Traum in Alten Testament* (*BZAW* 73; Berlin: Alfred Töpelmann,
1953); A. Resch, *Der Traum im Heilsplan Gottes: Deutung und Bedeutung des Traumes im Alten
Testament* (Greiburg: Herder, 1964); W. Richter, 'Traum und Traumdeutung im AT,' *BZ*
7 (1963): 202–220.

[20] For example, R. Gnuse, *The Dream Theophany of Samuel: Its Structure in Relation to
Ancient Near Eastern Dreams and its Theological Significance* (Lanham, MD: University Press
of America, 1984); idem, 'A Reconsideration of the Form-Critical Structure in 1 Samuel
3: An Ancient Near Eastern Dream Theophany,' *ZAW* 94 (1982): 379–390; S. Bar,
A Letter that Has Not Been Read: Dreams in the Hebrew Bible (Cincinnati: Hebrew Union
College Press, 2001), 9; K. Seybold, 'Der Traum in der Bibel,' in *Traum und Träumen:
Traumanalysen in Wissenschaft, Religion und Kunst* (eds. T. Wagner-Simon and G. Benedetti;
Göttingen: Vandenhoeck & Ruprecht, 1984), 32–54; K. Wood, 'The Dreams of Joseph
in Light of Ancient Near Eastern Divinatory Practice' (M.A. Thesis; Athens, GA:
University of Georgia, 1994), 40–45. See also F.H. Cryer, *Divination in Ancient Israel and its
Near Eastern Environment: A Socio-Historical Investigation* (JSOT Sup 142; Sheffield Academic
Press: Sheffield, 1994), esp. 267–272;

[21] K. Bulkley, 'The Evil Dreams of Gilgamesh: An Interdisciplinary Approach to
Dreams in Mythological Texts,' in *The Dream and the Text: Essays on Literature and Language*
(ed. C.S. Rupprecht; Albany: SUNY, 1993), 159–177; O.R. Gurney, 'The Babylonians
and Hittites,' in *Oracles and Divination* (eds. M. Loewe and C. Blacker; Boulder: Shamb-
hala, 1981), 142–173; M. Leibovici, 'Les songes et leur interprétation à Babylone,' in
Les songes, 63–86; S. Sauneron, 'Les songes et leur interprétation dans l'Égypte Anci-
enne,' in *Les songes*, 17–62; J.D. Ray, 'Ancient Egypt,' in *Oracles and Divination*, 174–190;
M. Vieyra, 'Les songes et leur interprétation chez les Hittites,' in *Les songes*, 87–98;
J. Sasson, 'Mari Dreams,' *JAOS* 103 (1983): 283–293; H. Huffmon, 'Prophecy in the
Mari Letters,' *Biblical Archaeologist* 31, no. 4 (1968): 101–124; A. Malamat, 'A Forerun-

By contrast, Oppenheim's work has hitherto had little influence on Classical scholars, who have paid much more attention to dreams than have scholars of the ancient Near East, and the Bible. The studies on Greek dreams are numerous and include significant monographs by B. Büchsenschütz, E.R. Dodds, W.R. Halliday, R.G.A. van Lieshout, and A.H.M. Kessels.[22] In addition, specialized studies have been conducted on the following genres: Homeric dreams by A. Amory, J. Hundt, W.S. Messer, and L. Pratt;[23] dreams in the Greek tragedians by C.A. Anderson, E.R. Cederstrom, G. Devereux, R. Lennig, W.S. Messer, K. Reckford, and G.S. Rousseau;[24] dreams in Herodotus and/or the historians by R. Crahay, P. Frisch, H.J.R. Hill, and

---

ner of Biblical Prophecy: The Mari Documents,' in *Ancient Israelite Religion: Essays in Honor of Frank Moore Cross* (eds. P.D. Miller P.D. Hanson, S.D. McBride; Philadelphia: Fortress Press, 1987), 33–52; J.R. Porter, 'Ancient Israel' in *Oracles and Divination*, 191–214; A. Caquot, 'Les songes et leur interprétation selon Canaan et Israel' in *Les songes*, 99–124. The brief entries in *TDOT* by J. Bergman, M. Ottoson, and J. Botterweck on dreams in Egypt, Mesopotamia, the Hittite Empire, Egypt, and amongst the West Semites are also useful, see '*chalam*' in *TDOT* (5 vols.; eds. J. Botterweck and H. Ringgren; Grand Rapids: Eerdmans, 1974–1990), 4:421–432. For helpful older treatments see also G. Foucart, 'Dreams and Sleep: Egyptian,' *ERE* 5:34–37; A.H. Sayce, 'Dreams and Sleep: Babylonian,' *ERE* 5:33–34; and A.D.F. Volten, *Demotische Traumdeutung* (Analecta Aegyptiaca 3; Kopenhagen: Einar Munksgaard, 1942). Finally, an often overlooked general treatment is by V. MacDermot, *The Cult of the Seer in the Ancient Middle East* (Berkeley: University of California Press, 1971).

[22] R. Berchman, *Mediators of the Divine: Horizons of Prophecy, Divination, Dreams and Theurgy in Mediterranean Antiquity* (Atlanta: Scholars Press, 1998); B. Büchsenschütz, *Traum und Traumdeutung im Altertum* (Wiesbaden: Dr. Martin Sändig O, 1967); E.R. Dodds, *Greeks and the Irrational* (Berkeley: University of California Press, 1968); W.R. Halliday, *Greek Divination: A Study of its Methods and Principles* (Chicago: Argonaut Inc., 1967); A.H.M. Kessels, *Studies on the Dream in Greek Literature* (Utrecht, HES, 1978); and R.G.A. van Lieshout, *Greeks on Dreams* (Utrecht: HES, 1980). See also J.S. Hanson, 'Dreams and Visions in the Graeco-Roman World and Early Christianity' in *ANRW* 23.2:1395–1427.

[23] A. Amory, 'The Gates of Horn and Ivory' in *Homeric Studies* (YCS 20; eds. G.S. Kirk and A. Parry; New Haven: Yale University Press, 1966), 3–57; idem, 'Omens and Dreams in the *Odyssey*' (Ph.D. Dissertation, Harvard University, 1958); J. Hundt, *Der Traumglaube bei Homer* (Greifswald: Hans Dallmeyer, 1935); W.S. Messer, *The Dream in Homer and Greek Tragedy* (N.Y.: Columbia University Press, 1918); L. Pratt, 'Odyssey 19.535–550: On the Interpretation of Signs in Homer' in *CP* 89 (April 1994): 147–152.

[24] C.A. Anderson, 'The Dream-Oracles of Athena, *Knights* 1090–1095,' *TAPA* 121 (1991): 149–155; E.R. Cederstrom, 'A Study of the Nature and Function of Dreams in Greek Tragedy' (Ph.D. Dissertation, Bryn Mawr, 1971); R. Lennig, 'Traum und Sinnestäuschung bei Aischylos, Sophokles, Euripides' (Ph.D. Dissertation, Universität Tübingen, 1969); W.S. Messer, *The Dream in Homer*; K. Reckford, 'Catharsis and Dream Interpretation in Aristophanes' *Wasps*,' *TAPA* 10, 7 (1977): 283–312; G.S. Rousseau, 'Dream and Vision in Aeschylus' *Oresteia*,' *Arion* 2 (1963): 101–136.

F. Loretto;[25] dreams in Plato and Aristotle by D. Gallop and H. Wijsenbeck-Wijler;[26] Artemidorus by R. White, L. Martin, and C. Walde;[27] incestuous dreams in Artemidorus and elsewhere by C. Grottanelli,[28] and Greek dreams and magic by S. Eitrem.[29] No monograph on Roman dreams in general exists as of this date. However, H. Cancik has recently offered an article on the subject and N. Berlin has contributed a study on dreams in Roman epic; also, a few articles explore selected Latin dream texts.[30]

The Greek and Roman dream cults have received extensive attention and are important to the present work. L. and E. Edelstein collected all extant references to the Asklepios cult, while P. Kavvadias and more recently L. LiDonnici have furnished translations of the Epidaurian inscriptions on dreams.[31] Other studies of the dream cults include those by R. Garland, M. Hamilton, U. Hausmann, R. Herzog,

---

[25] R. Crahay, *La littérature oraculaire chez Hérodote* (Paris: Société d'Édition 'Les Belles Lettres,' 1956); P. Frisch, *Die Träume bei Herodot* (Meisenheim am Glan, 1968); F. Loretto, 'Träume und Traumglaube in den Gesichtswerken der Griechen und Römer' (Ph.D. Dissertation, Graz, 1956).

[26] D. Gallop, *Aristotle on Sleep and Dreams: A Text and Translation with Introduction, Notes and Glossary* (Warminster, England: Aris and Phillips, 1996); idem, 'Dreaming and Waking in Plato' in *Essays in Ancient Greek Philosophy* (eds. J. Anton and G. Kustas; Albany: SUNY Press, 1971), 187–201; H. Wijsenbeeck-Wijler, *Aristotle's Concept of Soul, Sleep and Dreams* (Amsterdam: Hakkert, 1978).

[27] R. White, 'Introduction' in *Artemidorus: The Interpretation of Dreams* (Park Ridge, N.J.: Noyes Press, 1975); L. Martin, 'Artemidorus: Dream Theory in Late Antiquity' in *Second Century* 8 (1991): 97–108; C. Walde, 'Dream Interpretation in a Prosperous Age? Artemidorus, the Greek Interpreter of Dreams,' in *Dream Cultures*, 121–142; also see A.H.M. Kessels, 'Ancient Systems of Dream-Classification,' *Mnemosyne* 22 (1969): 389–424.

[28] C. Grottanelli, 'On the Mantic Meaning of Incestuous Dreams,' in *Dream Cultures*, 143–168.

[29] S. Eitrem, 'Dreams and Divination in Magical Ritual,' in *Magika Hiera: Ancient Greek Magic and Religion* (eds. C.A. Faraone and D. Obbink; N.Y.: Oxford University Press, 1991), 175–187.

[30] See H. Cancik, '*Idolum and Imago:* Roman Dreams and Dream Theories,' in *Dream Cultures*, 169–188; N. Berlin, *Dreams in Roman Epic: The Hermeneutics of a Narrative Technique* (Ph.D. Dissertation, University of Michigan, 1994); P. Aicher, 'Ennius' Dream of Homer,' *AJP* 110 (1989): 227–232; R.H. Feen, 'Nedyia {*sic*} as Apocalypse: A Study of Cicero's *Dream of Scipio*,' *JRS* 9 (1981): 28–34.

[31] Eds. L. and E. Edelstein, *Asclepius: A Collection and Interpretation of the Testimonies* (2nd ed.; 2 vols.; New York: Garland, 1975); P. Kavvadias, *Fouilles d'Épidaure* (Athens: Vlastos, 1891); L. LiDonnici, *The Epidaurian Miracle Inscriptions: Text, Translation and Commentary* (Atlanta: Scholars, 1995).

K. Kerényi, W.A. Jayne, C.A. Meier, R.A. Tomlinson, A. Walton, and T. Wagner-Simon.[32]

After having sketched the formal patterns and expectations of dreams in the ancient Near East (including Israel), Greece, and Rome, Part Two addresses the main focus of this study, the Hellenistic Jewish dream texts. My work builds on some important studies in this area, particularly that of R. Gnuse on dreams in Josephus, who also employs Oppenheim's categories in a diachronic fashion.[33] Dreams at Qumran also receive some attention from A. Lange, B. Dehandschutter, and M. Brayer.[34] A. Caquot and S. Niditch also include brief reviews of dreams in the apocrypha and pseudepigrapha their analyses of biblical dreams.[35] In addition, vital work has been conducted on select dreams within commentaries on individual texts. Those I have leaned on the most include M.E. Stone on 4 Ezra, G.W.E. Nickelsburg on *1 En.* 1–36 and 83–90, J.J. Collins on Daniel, R. Kugler on *4QAram. Levi* and *T. Twelve*, and M. Himmelfarb on dreams in the ascent traditions of *1 Enoch, 2 Enoch* and *T. Levi.*[36]

---

[32] R. Garland, *Introducing New Gods: The Politics of Athenian Religion* (Ithaca, NY: Cornell University Press, 1992); M. Hamilton, *Incubation Or the Cure of Disease in Pagan Temples and Christian Churches* (London: W.C. Henderson and Son, 1906); U. Hausmann, *Kunst und Heiltum: Untersuchungen zu den Griechischen Asklepiosreliefs* (Potsdam: Eduard Stichnote, 1948); R. Herzog, *Die Wunderheilungen von Epidaures* (Leipzig: Dieterich, 1931); W.A. Jayne, *The Healing Gods of Ancient Civilizations* (New Haven: Yale University Press, 1925); C. Kerényi, *Asklepios: Archetypal Image of the Physician's Existence* (trans. P. Manheim; N.Y.: Pantheon Books, 1959); C.A. Meier, *Antike Incubation und Moderne Psychotherapie: Mit Vier Kunstdrucktafeln und einer Abbildung im Text* (Zürich: Rascher & Cie.aG, 1949); R.A. Tomlinson, *Epidauros* (New York: Granada, 1983); A. Walton, *The Cult of Asklepios* (Ithaca: Cornell University Press, 1894); T. Wagner-Simon, 'Der Heiltraum,' in *Traum und Träumen*, 67–80.

[33] R. Gnuse, *Dreams and Dream Reports in the Writings of Josephus: A Traditio-Historical Analysis* (Leiden: Brill, 1996).

[34] A. Lange, 'The Essene Position on Magic and Divination,' in *Legal Texts and Legal Issues: Proceedings of the Second Meeting of the International Organization for Qumran Studies* (eds. M. Bernstein, F.G. Martínez and J. Kampen; Leiden: Brill, 1997), 377–436; B. Dehandschutter, 'Le rêve dans l'apocryphe de la Genèse,' in *La Littérature Juive entre Tenach et Mischna* (ed. W.C. Van Unnik; Leiden: Brill, 1974), 1–14; M. Brayer, 'Psychosomatics, Hermetic Medicine, and Dream Interpretation in the Qumran Literature,' *JQR* 60 (1970): 213–230; G. Brooke, 'Qumran Pesher: Towards the Redefinition of a Genre,' *RevQ* X, 10. 4 (1981): 483–504.

[35] A. Caquot, 'Les songes et leur interprétation selon Canaan et Israel,' in *Les songes*, 99–124 and S. Niditch, *The Symbolic Vision in Biblical Tradition* (HSM 30; Chico, CA: Scholars Press, 1980).

[36] M.E. Stone, *4 Ezra: A Commentary on the Book of 4 Ezra* (Hermeneia; ed. F.M. Cross; Minneapolis: Fortress, 1990); G.W.E. Nickelsburg, *1 Enoch: A Commentary on the Book of 1 Enoch, Chapters 1–36; 81–108* (Hermeneia; ed. K. Baltzer; Minneapolis: Fortress, 2001);

Despite the important contributions of these authors, the piecemeal nature of the treatment of early Jewish dreams has resulted in a lack of identification of what constitutes typical versus unique elements in these dreams, in both diachronic and synchronic contexts. By employing form criticism[37] and beginning with a broad view of dreams in antiquity, I am able in Chapter Three to sketch continuities of Hellenistic Jewish dreams with dreams in antecedent and contemporary cultures in terms of dream types, vocabulary, dream functions, and rituals. I find that these standard images are spun within an overarching *Weltanschauung* in which God sends dreams from the heavenly *hekhal*, with certain Jewish sacred sites, such as temples and altars, also figuring prominently. Accordingly, I note that many early Jewish dreams highlight priestly and scribal motifs in both heavenly and earthly contexts.

Next, in Chapter Four, I turn to a number of additional developments in Hellenistic Judaism, including borrowings and transpositions of motifs of the otherworldly journey / heavenly ascent, the portrayal of dream figures, and the character and abilities of dreamers. I also investigate the theme of dreams and death, which intertwine in Hellenistic Jewish dreams in fascinating ways that illuminate the artistry and imagination of individual authors.

In Part III, Chapter Five I reflect on implications of my project for several areas of study, including form criticism, the social roles of priests and scribes in early Judaism, and the rise of apocalypticism and early Jewish mysticism. In other words, one issue that my work bears upon is that of moving behind ancient literary texts to the social world of the individual authors and/or the communities that produced and circulated the texts, and perhaps again to the level of the authors' own ritualistic practices.[38] In forming my argument concerning societal roles

---

J.J. Collins, *Daniel: A Commentary on the Book of Daniel* (Hermeneia; ed. F.M. Cross; Minneapolis: Fortress, 1993); R. Kugler, *Testaments of the Twelve Patriarchs*; idem, *From Patriarch to Priest: The Levi-Priestly Tradition from Aramaic Levi to Testament of Levi*; M. Himmelfarb, *Ascent to Heaven*; R. Gnuse, *Josephus* and idem, 'Dream Genre in the Matthean Infancy Narratives,' in *Novum Testamentum* XXXII, 2 (1990): 97–120.

[37] Like all form critics, I owe a heavy debt to the methods inaugurated by Gunkel. H. Gunkel, *Genesis* (3rd ed.; trans. M.E. Biddle; Macon, GA: Mercer University Press, 1997); idem, *Die Psalmen* (5th ed.; Göttingen: Vandenhoeck & Ruprecht, 1968); idem, *Einleitung in die Psalmen* (completed by J. Begrich; 2nd ed.; Göttingen: Vandenhoeck & Ruprecht, 1966). My work has also been greatly enriched by the thoughtful collection of essays in *The Changing Face of Form Criticism for the Twenty-First Century* (eds. M.A. Sweeney and E. Ben Zvi; Grand Rapids, MI: Eerdmans, 2003).

[38] By contrast, M. Himmelfarb treats some of the texts I do and favors viewing

I am particularly indebted to works by E.P. Sanders, A.J. Saldarini, and C. Schams.[39] Also, although I do not always bring them into the discussion directly, my overall sociological orientation owes much to C. Geertz, M. Douglas and J. Turner.[40]

Since the issue of positing any kind of *Sitzen im Leben* behind literary texts is highly complex, let me be clear: I do not hold that the dreams related in early Jewish texts are the actual dreams that the authors or other real people have dreamt. Rather, I cautiously suggest that if form-critical methods illuminate a fairly standardized corpus of literary units understood as dreams, and if this corpus exhibits pervasive priestly and scribal motifs that consistently function within texts to confer or maintain authority for pseudepigraphic heroes (oftentimes in first-person narratives), these concerns shed some light on the social location of the authors and/or audiences. My conclusions do not, however, posit a single movement behind these widely varying texts, nor can I determine particular lineages of priests or specific social classes of priests and/or

---

heavenly ascents strictly as literature and not as practice, *Ascent to Heaven*, 109. This issue impinges on the debate concerning *Hekhalot* literature, with scholars such as D. Halperin and P. Schäfer maintaining it is impossible to get behind the *Hekhalot* texts to any practice of *merkavah* mysticism. D. Halperin, *The Faces of the Chariot: Early Jewish Responses to Ezekiel's Vision* (Tübingen: Mohr Siebeck, 1988); P. Schäfer, *Hekhalot-Studien* (Tübingen: Mohr Siebeck, 1988), esp. 294. In contrast to Schäfer, R. Lesses and J. Davila have strongly argued for the presence of actual mystical practice behind the *Hekhalot* texts, R. Lesses, *Ritual Practices to Gain Power: Angels, Incantations, and Revelation in Early Jewish Mysticism* (HTS 44; Harrisburg, PA: Trinity, 1998) and J. Davila, *Descenders to the Chariot*, esp. 12–16. Implicit in such debates is the larger problem of defining and understanding 'mystical experience.' See S. Katz, 'Language, Epistemology and Mysticism' in *Mysticism and Philosophical Analysis* (ed. S. Katz; New York: Oxford University Press, 1978), 22–74; Ed. R. Forman, *The Problem of Pure Consciousness: Mysticism and Philosophy* (New York: Oxford University Press, 1990); H. Smith, 'Is there a Perennial Philosophy?' *JAAR* 55 (1987): 553–566; S. King, 'Two Epistemological Models for the Interpretation of Mysticism,' *JAAR* 56 (1988): 257–279; S. Katz, 'On Mysticism,' *JAAR* 56 (1988): 751–761; J. Shear, 'On Mystical Experiences as Support for the Perennial Philosophy,' *JAAR* 62 (1994): 319–342; and F.S. Brainard, 'Defining "Mystical Experience,"' *JAAR* 64 (1996): 359–393.

[39] E.P. Sanders, *Judaism: Practice and Belief 63 B.C.E.-66 C.E.* (London: SCM Press, 1992); A.J. Saldarini, *Pharisees, Scribes and Sadducees in Palestinian Society: A Sociological Approach* (Grand Rapids, MI: Eerdmans, 2001, 1st ed. 1988 Michael Glazier); C. Schams, *Jewish Scribes in the Second-Temple Period* (JSOT Supp. 291; Sheffield: Sheffield Academic Press, 1998); S. Schwartz, *Josephus and Judean Politics* (Leiden: Brill, 1990).

[40] C. Geertz, *The Interpretation of Cultures* (New York: Basic Books, 1973); M. Douglas, *Purity and Danger: An Analysis of the Concepts of Pollution and Taboo* (London: Routledge & Kegan Paul, 1966); idem, *Leviticus as Literature* (Oxford: Oxford University Press, 1999); J.H. Turner, *Societal Stratification: A Theoretical Analysis* (New York: Columbia University Press, 1984).

scribes. However, since certain detailed rituals consistently appear that are also known in contemporary Graeco-Roman dream cults to be incubation rituals, it makes sense to posit that the authors were at least familiar with the idea of dream incubation. In some cases the knowledge seems detailed enough to suggest actual practice.

Finally, I suggest that it is the very forms of dreams, inherently flexible and allowing for the transcendence of spatial, temporal, ontological and perceptual limits of normal waking reality, which facilitate and/or catalyze the initial literary articulations of apocalyptic and mystical worldviews. In other words, if Hellenistic Judaism is the canvas, then dreams are the paint, and the resulting portraits of myriad dreams imagine access to otherworldly realms through a number of creative formulas, including apocalypses, mystical ascents, and ontological transformations.

PART ONE

CHAPTER ONE

DREAMS IN THE ANCIENT NEAR EAST AND ISRAEL

Thereupon Pharaoh awoke: it was a dream!

—Genesis 41:7

The ancient mind drew few boundaries between 'imaginary' and 'real.' Across the cultures of the ancient Near East and Mediterranean, numerous accounts of varying genres record divinely-sent dreams that mark important transformations for their dreamers. Oftentimes the dreams were incubated, or intentionally sought, for the purposes of healing and divine guidance in times of trouble. Whatever real dreams lay behind the myriad written accounts, the authors articulate divinely-sent dreams in surprisingly standardized patterns that transcend cultural, linguistic and geographic lines. Ishtar appears in much the same way and for many of the same purposes as Athena or Yahweh.

This chapter investigates the general literary forms, features, and functions of dreams in antiquity as found in ancient Near Eastern and biblical sources; Chapter Two continues this examination for the Greek and Roman sources. This endeavor is selective rather than exhaustive, with an eye to our later investigation of Jewish dreams, which draw extensively on these antecedent and contemporary dream patterns and cultural expectations. The aim of these first two chapters is to establish an understanding of what constitutes a 'dream' in antiquity. Our post-Freudian age views dreams as interior, subjective states expressing the wish-fulfillment of our unconscious—a view that is wholly incompatible with ancient expectations of divinely-sent dreams, which were held to be actual meetings with a transcendent reality. Moreover, in antiquity dreams and visions exist on a continuum and do not always neatly fall into categories of 'sleeping' or 'waking' states, although some individual cases do. Throughout this study, I am interested in that end of the visionary spectrum that articulates divinely-sent messages in terms of the nightly sleep experience we commonly call a 'dream.'

In an attempt to evaluate ancient dreams by their own standards, I utilize form criticism to determine those visionary episodes that qualify as 'dreams' by establishing baseline patterns and elements that ancient minds maintain clearly constitute the essence of dreams. Later in this study, form criticism enables me to identify some visionary episodes as 'dreams' even where the term is not used explicitly, as well as to explore individual dreams that vary slightly from given cultural paradigms.

I begin this chapter with a rather thorough review of Leo Oppenheim's form-critical classifications of dreams in the ancient Near East, which I utilize throughout the entire project.[1] With my later discussion of Hellenistic Jewish dreams in mind, I also take note of the typical vocabulary of ancient Near Eastern dreams and some important motifs associated with them, namely, the otherworldly journey and death. Next, I examine the social milieu of dreams by examining their connections to gender and social stratification, as well as the relation of dreaming to practices of divination, interpretation and incubation. Finally, I distill the basic functions of divinely-sent dreams in the ancient Near East. I then turn to dreams in the Hebrew Bible, again establishing the formal patterns of dreams and typical vocabulary, as well as the social setting and functions of dreams.

DREAMS IN THE ANCIENT NEAR EAST

Classifications of Ancient Near Eastern Dreams

The foundational work on dreams in antiquity is Leo Oppenheim's *The Interpretation of Dreams in the Ancient Near East: With a Translation of an Assyrian Dream-Book*.[2] His source material includes literary documents such as the *Epic of Gilgamesh* and royal inscriptions that purport to record actual dreams dreamt in cultic settings by or on behalf of kings.[3] In this wide-ranging work, Oppenheim identifies categories or patterns of

---

[1] Oppenheim, *Interpretation*. Special mention must be made of the work of Robert Gnuse, who uses Oppenheim's formal analysis of ancient Near Eastern dreams both to demonstrate that 1 Samuel 3 is properly understood as a dream and to investigate the dreams in Josephus. His works contain useful summaries of dreams in the ancient Near East, Bible, Greece, and Rome of the kind I offer in Part One. However, the differing foci of our projects lead me to emphasize certain aspects of dreams in antiquity that Gnuse omits. See R. Gnuse, *Samuel*; idem, *Josephus*.

[2] See also L. Oppenheim, 'Mantic Dreams,' 341–350; idem, 'New Fragments,' 153–165.

[3] The royal inscriptions include: Sumerian examples (from the end of the third millennium B.C.E.); Akkadian examples from the reign of Assurbanipal (seventh century B.C.E.) and Nabonidus (sixth century B.C.E.); a Hittite text of King Hattushili

dreams that occur in the literary and cultic sources across several cultures of the ancient Near East, including Sumeria, Akkad, Babylonia, Assyria, the Hittite Empire and Egypt. To a lesser extent, Oppenheim also treats dreams in the Bible and Greek literature, although not in any systematic fashion.

The three major categories or patterns of dreams that Oppenheim identifies are the *message dream*, the *symbolic dream*, and the *psychological status dream*.[4] Psychological status dreams are not divinely-sent; rather, they include dreams whose content reflects the psychological and/or physiological status of the dreamer.[5] Although at first glance such an understanding of dreaming seems to parallel some modern notions of dreaming, Oppenheim notes that peoples of the ancient Near East understood the psychological status and health of a person to be a general expression of that person's cultic standing or 'the extent to which [the person was] endowed with the protective deities who safeguard the life, success, and happiness of the individual.'[6] Psychological status dreams were sometimes '*pleasant dreams*,' but most were '*evil dreams*,' akin to our nightmares.[7] The remedy for evil dreams was the propitiation of the gods through ritual.[8] Perhaps to avoid fulfilling the dream, the content of these was almost never related; they are simply referred to as 'evil dreams.'[9]

Message dreams and *symbolic dreams* were viewed as direct communications from the divine realm worthy of the greatest attention, since they

---

(twelfth century B.C.E.); Egyptian inscriptions from Thutmose IV (fifteenth century B.C.E.), Pharaoh Merneptah (thirteenth century B.C.E.) and Tanutamon (seventh century B.C.E.); as well as Herodotus' account of Sethos and Plutarch's account of Ptolemy I Soter. In addition, Oppenheim translates the *Assyrian Dream-Book* and examines selected texts from the Hebrew Bible, the *Epic of Gilgamesh*, Homer and Hesiod, and some Demotic texts from Egypt. See Oppenheim, *Interpretation*, 186–187, 194. Most of these dreams are also found in *ANET* (3rd ed.; ed. J.B. Pritchard; Princeton: Princeton University Press, 1969).

[4] See Gnuse, *Samuel*; idem, *Josephus*.

[5] Oppenheim, *Interpretation*, 230; idem, 'Mantic,' 346. See also J. Bergman et al, 'חלם,' *TDOT* 4:421–432, 424. Cf. R. Gnuse, 'Dreams in the night—scholarly mirage or theophanic formula?: The dream report as a motif of the so-called Elohist tradition,' *B.Z.* n.s. 39,1 (1995): 28–53; also K. Seybold, 'Der Traum,' 32–54.

[6] Oppenheim, *Interpretation*, 232; idem 'Mantic,' 346.

[7] In the Akkadian, Hebrew, and Egyptian, 'evil dreams' always occurs in the plural. Oppenheim, *Interpretation*, 231–232; idem, 'Mantic,' 346.

[8] Oppenheim, *Interpretation*, 230–232; Sauneron, 'l'Égypte,' 33; Leibovici, 'Babylone,' 67.

[9] For a rare example of evil dreams in which some content is provided, see the thunderstorm dreams of the Hittite King Muršilis. Oppenheim, *Interpretation*, 230.

normally relayed predictions about the future and/or divine directives. In the *message dream*, a deity or a representative of the deity appears to the dreamer to impart revelation. By contrast, no clear message is imparted in the *symbolic dream*; rather, revelation consists of 'strange' symbols or figures that normally must be decoded, often by a professional.[10]

Message dreams and symbolic dreams exhibit reasonably predictable content as well as a typical frame that encompasses the dream itself, i.e., an introduction and conclusion. In addition, a passage indicating the fulfillment of the dream may also be present. Oppenheim points out that no dream contains all the formal elements that he identifies as occurring in message and symbolic dreams; rather, these elements form patterns that are typical for certain groups of dreams.[11]

Typical Patterns of Message and Symbolic Dreams

In the ancient Near East, a visionary episode may alternately be called 'dream,' 'vision of the night,' or 'vision.'[12] Within the possible range of these experiences, many episodes are articulated in terms of the nightly sleep phenomenon of dreaming. This association is made clear in the case of a message or symbolic dream by the INTRODUCTION, which depicts the person who is about to dream as being asleep or in bed, sometimes at night. To indicate a dream setting, the Assyrian texts simply use the verb *utūlu*, 'to be in bed', which most likely derives from *niālum/nâlum*, 'to lie down.'[13] If the dream is incubated, that is, purposefully sought, the INTRODUCTION also lists the various rituals of incubation. The basic ritual of incubation consists of sleeping in a temple or other sacred place, although fasting, mourning, praying, the offering of sacrifices, and purification rites are also sometimes attested.[14]

---

[10] Oppenheim, *Interpretation*, 186–190, 206–208. Oppenheim notes that the symbolic dream may be thought of as a type or sub-category of the message dream, but this only seems to cloud the classifications.

[11] Ibid., 186.

[12] Ibid., 225.

[13] W. Muss-Arnolt, 'niālum,' in *A Concise Dictionary of the Assyrian Language* (vol. 1; Berlin: Reuther and Reichard, 1905): 130; Oppenheim, *Interpretation*, 187.

[14] S. Ackerman, 'The Deception of Isaac, Jacob's Dream at Bethel, and Incubation on an Animal Skin,' in *Priesthood and Cult in Ancient Israel* (eds. G.A. Anderson and S.M. Olyan; JSOT Supp. 25; Sheffield: Sheffield Academic Press, 1991), 92–120, 108–112; E. Ehrlich, *Der Traum*, 57; Oppenheim, *Interpretation*, 188, 200; Vieyra, 'Hittites,' 90.

In the body of the *message dream* a deity appears, usually 'standing,' often by the head of the dreamer.[15] Whether the dream text is Hittite, Sumerian, Greek, or Egyptian, the verb 'to stand' describes the dream figure's action in both cultic and literary sources.[16] In the ancient Near Eastern texts, the dream figure is typically large, looming, and beautiful.[17] Rarely, the dream figure is not a divine being, but a deceased person. Living persons almost never appear.[18] The dream figure relates a spoken message to the sleeping dreamer that is ordinarily readily understood. Occasionally, a dialogue ensues between the dreamer and the dream figure, as in the dream of Thutmose IV from the Sphinx Stela.[19] Particularly in the Hebrew Bible and the Assyrian dream texts, the deity may exclaim, 'Be not afraid!'[20] Overall, the account stresses the objective reality of the dream as a genuine epiphany of a deity.

In addition to messages, some dream figures give objects to dreamers.[21] Thus, in an Egyptian dream, Ptah extends a sword to the Pharaoh Merneptah, saying, 'Take now this sword and banish from yourself your troubled heart!'[22] In the Greek sources, such *tokens* will remain in the waking world, testifying to the veracity of the encounter.

A variation on the message dream is the *auditory message dream*, in which a divine voice imparts a message, with no visible apparition. This dream type is most common in the Hittite texts, which identify the voices as those of divine beings or less frequently of living persons.[23] In only one case, in a Hittite text, the voice is identified as belonging to a deceased person.[24] In the ancient Near East, living and dead humans only rarely function as dream figures; dream messengers are typically divine.

---

[15] O.R. Gurney discusses how the phrase 'to stand at the head' may suggest to some that the apparition entered through the sleeper's head. Gurney, 'The Babylonians and Hittites,' 142–173, 143. I see no evidence of this, and am more convinced by Oppenheim's suggestion that the cultic setting of sleeping by a statue is in the background here, Oppenheim, *Interpretation*, 189–190.

[16] Ibid., 189.

[17] Ibid., 189.

[18] Ibid., 191, 193–195, 199, 200.

[19] 'A Divine Oracle through a Dream,' trans. J.A. Wilson (*ANET*, 449); Oppenheim, *Interpretation*, 203, 251, no.15.

[20] Oppenheim, *Interpretation*, 200.

[21] Ibid., 192.

[22] Ibid., 192; 251, no. 16.

[23] Ibid., 193.

[24] Ibid., 193.

Another variant of the message dream is the *Wecktraum*, in which the dream figure arrives and wakes the sleeping person, usually by saying, 'Are you asleep, NN?'[25] The dream figure then proceeds to tell the awakened dream recipient the divine message. For example, an account from the library of Ashurbanipal states, 'a *šabrû*-priest lay down and had a dream. He awoke with a start and then Ishtar caused him to see a nocturnal vision.'[26] Oppenheim explains that the *Wecktraum* is 'clearly meant to prepare the sleeper for the approaching … revelation,' that is, to provide some cushion for a waking revelation by the gradual appearance of the deity, first in a dream-state and then in a waking state.[27] Oppenheim rightly cites the quelling of human fear as a major function of dreams in general:

> The essential feature of the theophany … its dramatic, soul-shaking impact, the shattering inroad of the supernatural into the reality of this world, the terror-inspiring sight of the deity, etc., have disappeared in the transfer from consciousness to dream. The change of reality-level acts as a cushion to soften the contact between god and man.[28]

In other words, a message dream is a theophany that occurs in various states of consciousness, articulated in terms of sleep, which enables a person to withstand contact with the divine. A *Wecktraum* is a variant of the message dream that serves as a transition from the sleep state of consciousness to a waking visionary state.

In addition to the message dream and its variants, the other major category of divinely-sent dreams is the *symbolic dream*, in which the dreamer sees strange objects and 'a world which extends in sweep, variety and intricacy far beyond that to which the duller senses of man's waking consciousness grant him access,'[29] which always relates to the future. Although a symbolic dream is sometimes readily understandable, one normally needs an interpreter, who may be divine or human,

---

[25] Oppenheim, *Interpretation*, 189; cf. Dodds, *Greeks and the Irrational*, 105, n.13.

[26] 'An Oracular Dream Concerning Ashurbanipal,' trans. Robert D. Biggs (*ANET*, 606).

[27] Oppenheim, *Interpretation*, 190.

[28] Ibid., 192.

[29] Ibid., 206. Gnuse notes that Oppenheim originally attempts to distinguish between 'simple symbolic dreams' such as those in the Joseph cycle (Gen 37, 41–42) and more complex symbolic dreams like those in Daniel 2, 4, 7–11, which he labels 'mantic dreams.' The distinction proved complicated, and Oppenheim later labels the whole spectrum of dreams in which revelation comes in the form of symbols by the term 'symbolic dream.' Gnuse, *Josephus*, 38; Oppenheim, *Interpretation*, 237–245; cf. idem, 'Mantic,' 341–350.

male or female.[30] Ordinarily, the dreamer relates a symbolic dream to another person upon awakening since the act of *reciting the dream* is an important element in gaining an interpretation, bringing a good dream to fruition, or avoiding the negative consequences of a bad dream.[31] Leibovici stresses that the act of reciting a symbolic dream is itself an apotropaic ritual.[32] Accordingly, Sumerian and Akkadian texts use the same terms for the interpretation of a dream as for the apotropaic ritual of 'telling' an 'evil dream' to a lump of clay, which is then dissolved to avert negative consequences of the dream. Oppenheim concludes from this that a symbolic dream is considered an 'evil dream' as long as it remains without an interpretation.[33]

It should be noted that at times certain ancient Near Eastern and biblical dreams combine the previously mentioned dream types. A simple example occurs in the message dream of the priest of Ishtar, in which Ishtar appeared and spoke to the dreamer and then, in a *symbolic* gesture within the *message dream*, wrapped King Assurbanipal in a baby's sling.[34] Nested dreams, although rare, also occur. For example, King Nabonidus had a message dream in which the figures who appeared urged him to relate his earlier symbolic dream of an astral conjunction, which they interpreted favorably, all within the message dream itself.[35]

The CONCLUSION of both message and symbolic dreams describes the dreamer awakening, very often experiencing profound psychological and/or physical shock.[36] In Akkadian, the word used for ending a dream is *negeltû/nagaltû*, 'to wake up.'[37] The oldest recorded dream, the dream of Gudea, ends with the words, 'he woke up with a start, it was but a dream!'[38] The vividness of the dream is also sometimes mentioned as a measure of its authenticity.[39]

---

[30] Oppenheim overstates the case when he says that symbolic dreams without interpretations 'do not and cannot occur,' 'Mantic,' 349.
[31] Leibovici, 'Babylone,' 67; Oppenheim, *Interpretation*, 205–206, 219; idem, 'Mantic,' 349–350.
[32] Leibovici, 'Babylone,' 67.
[33] Oppenheim, 'Mantic,' 349–350.
[34] 'An Oracular Dream Concerning Ashurbanipal,' trans. Robert H. Pfeiffer (*ANET*, 451); Oppenheim, *Interpretation*, 201; 249, no. 10.
[35] Ibid., 250, no. 13.
[36] Ibid., 188.
[37] *CAD* 11 N II:106–107, 'nagaltû.'
[38] Oppenheim, *Interpretation*, 191.
[39] Ibid., 191.

Sometimes the FULFILLMENT of message and symbolic dreams is present as part of the overall formal pattern. If the dream message is a divine directive, the fulfillment may occur when the dream recipient acts on the directive. If the dream message concerns future events, the fulfillment may be implied by a statement that those events later came to pass as the dream had predicted.

Dreams or elements within dreams are often repeated in order to emphasize their veracity.[40] A variation of this theme is the *Doppeltraüme*, in which two people have a dream more or less simultaneously.[41] This motif is especially suited to love stories, in which the lovers both dream the same dream.[42] Another variation is mass dreaming, when numbers of people experience a certain dream. Assurbanipal, for instance, reports that the goddess Ishtar appeared 'in a dream' to his entire army. Similar occurrences are reported throughout the ancient Near East and Greece.[43]

Typical Dream Vocabulary

The vocabulary of ancient Near Eastern dream accounts sheds further light on ancient attitudes towards dreams. Many terms stress the visual aspect of dreams. The Egyptian texts use *rswt*, meaning 'to see a dream' or 'to see something in a dream.'[44] In Hittite texts, the verb *tešḫaniia*,[45] 'to appear in a dream,' describes the revelation of deities in dreams, again stressing the visual element.[46] Akkadian texts use *šuttu*, for 'dream,' from the same root as *šittu*, 'sleep,'[47] but also *tabrīt mūši*, 'vision of the night' or 'nocturnal revelation.'[48] A dream is not 'had,' rather, it is 'seen.' The verb *šubrû* means 'to show, to exhibit, to divulge, to

---

[40] Oppenheim, *Interpretation*, 208; see also F. Alexander, 'Dreams in Pairs and Series,' *International Journal of Psychoanalysis* 6 (1925, repr. 1953): 446–452.

[41] A. Wikenhauser, 'Doppelträume,' *Biblica* 29 (1948): 100–111.

[42] Oppenheim, *Interpretation*, 209.

[43] Guillaume, *Prophecy and Divination*, 49; Oppenheim, *Interpretation*, 209. Oppenheim cites examples from: Artemidorus; Plutarch's *Lives*, Alexander 24; *Ta'anith* 21b; and reports from World War I.

[44] Oppenheim, *Interpretation*, 226; Sauneron, 'l'Égypte,' 20; Bergman et al, 'חלם,' *TDOT* 4 422.

[45] Johannes Friedrich, 'tešḫaniia' in *Kurzgefaßtes Hethitisches Wörterbuch* (Heidelberg: Carl Winter Universitätsverlag, 1991): 222.

[46] Bergman et al, 'חלם,' *TDOT* 4:423.

[47] *CAD* S 17: 136, 'šittu.'

[48] *CAD* M 10, ii: 250, 'tabrīt mūši'; also Muss-Arnolt, 'tabrītu' in *Concise Dictionary* II, 1146.

reveal (in a dream or vision)' and stems from the verb *barû*, the meanings of which include 'to observe' as well as 'to inspect exta, to observe omens.'[49] Other verbs used for dreaming also stress seeing, including: *amāru* and *naṭālu*; also *naplusu* with the deity as the subject.[50] The root *ḥ.l.m.* gives rise to the word for dream in Hebrew, Aramaic, Ugaritic, Ethiopic and Arabic.[51] Similarly, Ugaritic texts often place *ḥlm*, 'dream,' in conjunction with *ḥdrt* 'revelation, vision,' pointing to the intimate relationship between these ideas.[52]

Other vocabulary illuminates the understanding that dreams are objective phenomena existing independently of the dreamer. In Sumerian, the word for 'dream' and 'sleep' is ᵈMA-MÚ or ᵈMA-MÙ, a term that also denotes the 'god of dreams,' as do ᵈ*Zaqīqu* and ᵈ*Ziqīqu*, which are suggestive of wind.[53] That is, sometimes the term 'dream' refers both to a dream event as well as to the god who appears to the dreamer or who carries the dream along, like the wind. In fact, some Assyrian dreams are accompanied by the verb *abālu*, 'to carry or bring,' further underscoring the objective nature of the dream or dreamer as things that are transported, as in the following phrases: 'this dream which was brought to me' (*Assyrian Dream-Book*), 'my dreams will bring to me' (*Old Babylonian letter*); or the Dream-God 'who carries [dreamers] around' (*KAR* 58: rev. 1 ff.).[54] Cognate meanings apply to pregnant women who 'carry' a baby and to the dying.[55] The underlying connection here seems to be that the soul is transported, whether in utero, by the Dream-God, or in death.

Finally, certain terms describe dreams as a liminal state that entails something other than ordinary sleep. For instance, the Akkadian term *munattu* possesses a range of meaning, including 'early morning,' 'sleep,' and 'dream.' Oppenheim notes that this term appears to allude to the belief maintained in numerous classical sources that the early morning hours in which one hovers *between sleep and wakefulness* yield the most

[49] *CAD* B 2: 115–118, 'barû.'
[50] Bergman et al 'חלם,' *TDOT* 4:423; also Oppenheim, *Interpretation*, 226.
[51] *BDB* 'חלם,' 321; also Oppenheim, *Interpretation*, 226.
[52] G. del Olmo Lete and J. Sanmartín, *Diccionario de la Lengua Ugarítica*, (Barcelona: Editorial AUSA, 1996) 1:164; Bergman et al, 'חלם' *TDOT* 4:426; *CTA* 14 [I K], I:26; III:50.
[53] *CAD* Z 21:58–61; Bergman et al, 'חלם,' *TDOT* 4:423–424; Oppenheim, *Interpretation*, 232.
[54] Bergman et al, 'חלם,' *TDOT* 4:426; Oppenheim, *Interpretation*, 226.
[55] *CAD* 1 A I:16–17, 'abālu.'

veridical dreams.[56] Similarly, the Egyptian *rswt*, 'to see a dream,' stems
from the root 'to awaken.' Written with the determinative of an open
eye, the term 'apparently represent[s] dreaming as a special state of
consciousness, something like "watching during sleep."'[57]

Two Motifs of Ancient Near Eastern Dreams

The Otherworldly Dream Journey

Some ancient Near Eastern dream episodes describe soul journeys, a
motif that will become important in dreams of Hellenistic Judaism.
One form of the notion is that the dreamer experiences him/herself
as appearing in a far-away place, as the Egyptian Sinuhe expresses in
the following simile: 'It was just like a dream, as when a native of the
Delta sees himself in Elephantine or a man of the [Delta] lagoons in
the land of Nubia.'[58] Robert Wilson dubs this phenomenon 'soul migra-
tion,' and notes that it is the major mechanism for non-possession theories explaining the experiences of divine-human intermediaries such as
shamans, prophets, diviners, and so forth.[59]

In the *otherworldly journey*, the dreamer is transported to an otherworldly realm, much to his/her shock. W. Bousset has examined
ancient examples of ecstatic otherworldly journeys through heaven and
has concluded that this theme ultimately derives from Persian beliefs
about the fate of the soul after death.[60] He maintains that a Persian
schema in which the soul journeys through three heavens influenced
Greek sources by way of Mithraism, which also absorbed Babylonian
ideas about a seven-heaven cosmological structure.[61] Bousset's study
makes an important contribution to the attempt to locate the roots of

---

[56] Bergman et al, 'חלם,' *TDOT* 4:425; *CAD* 1 A I:10–31, '*abālu.*'

[57] Oppenheim, *Interpretation*, 226; Sauneron, 'l'Égypte,' 20; Bergman et al, 'חלם,'
TDOT 4:422.

[58] Oppenheim, *Interpretation*, 228; 'The Story of Sinuhe,' trans. J.A. Wilson (*ANET*,
18).

[59] R. Wilson, *Prophecy and Society in Ancient Israel* (Philadelphia: Fortress, 1980), 41–42.
For some anthropological examples of this trance phenomenon see I.M. Lewis, *Ecstatic
Religion: A Study of Shamanism and Spirit Possession* (2nd ed.; London: Routledge, 1971, repr.
1989), 40–50.

[60] W. Bousset, *Die Himmelreise der Seele* (Darmstadt: Wissenschaftliche Buchgesellschaft, 1960), 38, 43–50.

[61] Ibid., 57–58.

the otherworldly soul journey, but his findings should be considered alongside the evidence of otherworldly journeys taken from ancient Near Eastern dream texts which may predate the Persian materials. In these materials, the otherworldly journey motif most often appears as a descent of the soul to the netherworld.

The earliest Mesopotamian netherworld soul journey takes place after death, when King Ur-Nammu tours the underworld during his funeral. However, most ancient Near Eastern netherworld journeys occur in dreams and visions, including Enkidu's visionary experience in the *Epic of Gilgamesh*.[62] As Enkidu tells it:

> this night I had dreams ... There came a griffin with gloomy mien ... holding me (by the hand) he led me down to the Dark Mansion, the abode of Irkalla/ *To the house which he who enters it will not leave any more/ Upon a road on which there is no way back,/* To the house whose inhabitants are bereft of light,/ Where earth is their fare and clay their food ... To the House of Dust ... I entered (now) myself ...[63]

Enkidu then sees Ereshkigal, Queen of the Netherworld, seated on her throne. The main function of this literary journey motif is to impart to Enkidu knowledge about an otherworldly realm from which a person may normally never return, as well as to grant a vision of deities. In return, Enkidu relates what he has learned to Gilgamesh and to the audience of the epic, who are now privy to extraordinary information.[64] Such texts suggest that in dreams the normal constraints of time, space, ontology, and knowledge are erased.

Dreams and Death

The previous examples of netherworld journeys are one expression of the ancient Near Eastern association between death and dreams, an idea expressed in many forms.[65] For instance, in Babylonia and ancient Israel, both dreams and spirits of the dead are able to convey mes-

---

[62] S. Kramer, 'Epic of Gilgamesh' in *ASOR Bulletin* 94:6, n. 11; Leibovici, 'Babylone,' 76–80; Oppenheim, *Interpretation*, 214, 248–249, no. 7.

[63] Oppenheim, *Interpretation*, 248–249, no. 7.

[64] See Oppenheim, *Interpretation*, 214. Also see the Akkadian 'Vision of the Netherworld,' trans. E.A. Speiser (*ANET*, 109–110). Also see 'Descent of Ishtar to the Nether World,' trans. E.A. Speiser (*ANET*, 106–108), and 'Inanna's Descent to the Nether World,' trans. S.N. Kramer (*ANET*, 52–55).

[65] Leibovici, 'Babylone,' 65; Sauneron, 'l'Égypte,' 19–20.

sages concerning the future.[66] The Mesopotamian divinatory professional called *ša'ilu / ša'iltu* was primarily responsible for the interpretation of dreams, but also engaged in necromancy.[67] In fact, *ša'ilu / ša'iltu* comes from *moushelou* or *mušêlû* meaning 'one who raises the spirit of the dead.'[68] As we have seen, *abālu* may be used in the sense of a dreamer being carried by the Dream-God or of dying.[69] In the *Epic of Gilgamesh*, Gilgamesh digs a hole in the earth, the typical ritual for communicating with the spirits of the dead, and his dream arises 'out of a hole like a *zaqiqu* {*dZaqīqu*}' a word that can mean 'spirit,' 'demon,' 'wind,' or 'god of dreams.'[70] In this case, it appears that the dream and underworld spirits originate from the same realm, the subterranean earth.[71] Therefore, Babylonian dreams are said to be under the influence of both the moon and the psychopompic sun, guide of the dead, as it travels at night through the netherworld.[72]

   The association between death and dreams is also expressed in the common motif of one who is close to dying seeing his/her death foretold in a dream,[73] as Enkidu does in the *Epic of Gilgamesh*. These death-dreams are at times accompanied by a moralising tale or a warning to the living;[74] this seems to be a forerunner to the testamentary genre in Hellenistic Judaism. The underlying assumption of death-dreams as well as of dream journeys to the netherworld appears to be that dreams make it possible for the soul to overcome the ontological constraints of a living, physical body, which cannot abide in the realm of death. The similar appearance of sleep and death may have also contributed to the notion that dreamers' souls are freed to access the realm of the dead, resulting in extraordinary knowledge.

---

[66] F. Schmidtke, 'Träume, Orakel und Totengeister als Kunder der Zukunft in Israel und Babylonien,' in *BZ*, N.F. 11 (1967): 240–246.

[67] Oppenheim, *Interpretation*, 223; Gurney, *Babylonians and Hittites*, 146; Leibovici, 'Babylone,' 68.

[68] Leibovici, 'Babylone,' 68.

[69] *CAD* 1 A I:16–17, '*abālu*.'

[70] Leibovici, 'Babylone,' 66, 81; Oppenheim, *Interpretation*, 234–235.

[71] Leibovici, 'Babylone,' 65–6.

[72] Ibid., 65.

[73] Bergman et al, 'חלם,' *TDOT* 4:424–425.

[74] Oppenheim, *Interpretation*, 214.

Social Milieu of Ancient Near Eastern Dreams

Dreams and Social Stratification

Anyone can dream, and Oppenheim notes, 'A person's social position in Mesopotamia has no effect upon the validity or the interpretation of his dreams.'[75] At Mari, ordinary persons regularly had dreams that contained prophecy intended for kings.[76] This leads Oppenheim to state that dreams 'in no way establish the social or cultic standing of the person who experiences them.'[77]

Yet, it is clear from the evidence that some dreams and dreamers were, in fact, held in higher esteem than were others. The majority of recorded dreams are by males, typically a king, priest, or hero.[78] Moreover, as we have seen, the dreams of kings often legitimated royal undertakings such as war, political succession, and the rebuilding of religious monuments, all of which ultimately secure the power of the king by implying divine sanction. Other than at Mari, the dreamers were typically royalty, officials, or professional dream intermediaries, who were cultic or non-cultic priests that dreamt on behalf of important males.[79] According to R. Wilson, cultic dream intermediaries usually functioned to maintain the status quo, whereas those intermediaries on the periphery or outside of the state cult normally dreamt subversive dreams that effected societal change.[80]

In general, there also seems to be a rough ranking of message dreams as being more valuable than symbolic dreams, which engender a 'certain uneasiness and a more or less voiced feeling of distrust.'[81] This makes sense given that message dreams entail actual appearances of the deity and clear messages, whereas symbolic dreams must be decoded.[82]

---

[75] Oppenheim, *Interpretation*, 240.

[76] Huffmon, 'Mari Letters,' 114–120; Malamat, 'Forerunner,' 43–44; also Bergman et al, 'חלם,' *TDOT* 4:424.

[77] Oppenheim, *Interpretation*, 185.

[78] Sauneron, 'l'Égypte,' 32; Leibovici, 'Babylone,' 81; Vieyra, 'Hittites,' 92; cf. Caquot, 'Canaan et Israel,' 106; Oppenheim, 'Mantic,' 347; idem, *Interpretation*, 186. This is true in not only the royal inscriptions but also in the *Epic of Gilgamesh*, in which the hero is a king.

[79] Huffmon, 'Mari Letters,' 116–122; Oppenheim, *Interpretation*, 239, n. 10.

[80] Wilson, *Prophecy and Society*, 97, 109, 112–113.

[81] Oppenheim, 'Mantic,' 349.

[82] Oppenheim, *Interpretation*, 349–350.

It is perhaps not surprising given the patriarchal social structure of
ancient Near Eastern societies that, according to the written records,
men are generally thought to have message dreams, whereas women
typically have less clear symbolic dreams.[83] Exceptions to the rule are
present only in scant Hittite and Mari materials. In the former, the Hittite queen Poudahepa receives a message dream of Ishtar plus numerous auditory message dreams,[84] and the Hittite princess Kassoulawijas
has a message dream of the goddess Lelwani.[85] At Mari, women figure
predominantly among the untitled lay prophets[86] who received many
of their oracles in dreams, which were primarily message dreams and
auditory message dreams. However, the dreams of lay prophets were
considered unreliable unless confirmed by a divinatory 'hem and hair'
test.[87]

Thus, overall, the sources appear to consider the message dreams
of public persons, who are most often males, to be the most important kinds of divinely-sent dreams. The perception that mostly women
received symbolic dreams may explain the need for female dream interpreters to serve them.[88]

In establishing the social setting of dreaming in the ancient Near
East, I turn now to practices associated with dreaming: divination,
dream interpretation and incubation.

Dreams and Divination

The belief that message and symbolic dreams foretell the future is best
viewed against the widespread belief in and practice of divinatory arts
in the ancient Near East.[89] As R. Wilson states, 'Mesopotamians saw
all aspects of reality as an interlocking totality.' Thus, dreams convey

---

[83] Oppenheim, *Interpretation*, 190.
[84] Ibid., 193, 197; Vieyra, 'Hittites,' 92–94.
[85] Vieyra, 'Hittites,' 92.
[86] The period of rule under King Zimri-Lin seems to mark an important exception
to the rule of gender inequality amongst prophets.
[87] For an example of Mari women who have message dreams, see Malamat, 'Forerunner' 37, 44; *ARM X* 50, 100.
[88] T. Frymer-Kensky, *In the Wake of the Goddesses: Women, Culture and the Biblical Transformation of Pagan Myth* (NY: Fawcett Columbine, 1992), 41; Oppenheim, *Interpretation*, 222,
225.
[89] F.H. Cryer, *Divination in Ancient Israel*, 124–186; Wilson, *Prophecy and Society*, 90–97;
H. Ringgren, *Religions of the Ancient Near East* (Philadelphia: Westminster, 1973), 93–99;

divine messages, as do the livers of animals and the flight of birds.[90] The Akkadian *šaʾilu/šaʾiltu* priest or priestess appears to have been responsible not only for dream interpretation, but also for libanomancy, necromancy, augury, and probably other forms of divination as well. The etymology of the title simply means 'to ask (of the gods).'[91]

However, divine revelation imparted through dreams, whether sought or unsought, appears to have been viewed as a less technical and perhaps less reliable form of divination than professional practices such as hepatoscopy, extipiscy, and astrology.[92] According to R. Wilson, oracular intermediaries, including those who obtained oracles through dreams, usually possessed a more peripheral social standing in Mesopotamia than did other diviners.[93] At Mari, for example, divinatory dreams came mainly to non-technical and non-cultic lay persons.[94] Although their messages were meant to be relayed to the king, the dreamers' low standing and lack of cultic expertise necessitated that the messages be verified by divinatory means, including augury and/or a test of the dreamer's lock of hair and hem.[95] It would seem that non-tangible oracles, such as symbols and words, carried less weight than did divination through material substances.[96] Where material divination appears in conjunction with dreams, such as in the 'Dream of Nabonidus' which contains astrological portents, the divinatory means are mutually confirming.[97]

Leibovici, 'Babylone,' 66; Gurney, *Babylonians and Hittites*, 245; Porter, 'Ancient Israel,' 201; and Ray, 'Ancient Egypt,' 175.

[90] Wilson, *Prophecy and Society*, 92; Leibovici, 'Babylone,' 66.

[91] Gurney, *Babylonians and Hittites*, 146; Oppenheim, *Interpretation*, 221–224; Guillaume, *Prophecy and Divination*, 40–41.

[92] Wilson, *Prophecy and Society*, 90–97; Ringgren, *Religions*, 93–99; Vieyra, 'Les songes,' 87–98, 89; Caquot, 'Canaan et Israel,' 102; Guillaume, *Prophecy and Divination*, 40–1.

[93] Wilson, *Prophecy and Society*, 133–134.

[94] Huffmon, 'Prophecy in the Mari Letters,' 116; A. Malamat, 'A Forerunner of Biblical Prophecy,' 44.

[95] Huffmon, 'Mari Letters,' 116–122; A.15, 222, 455; VI.45; X.7–8, 50, 81; XIII.112 (for editions of the Mari letters see the Appendix in Huffmon, 'Mari Letters,' 124); Malamat, 'Forerunner,' 46–47.

[96] Two 'intangible' divinations are better than one; thus kledonomancy, or the technique of interpreting overheard chance utterances, did sometimes serve to confirm an interpretation of a dream or to provide one. Oppenheim, *Interpretation*, 211, 229.

[97] Oppenheim, *Interpretation*, 205.

Dream Interpretation

The available evidence attests that ancient Near Eastern peoples considered the proper interpretation of symbolic dreams to be vitally important.[98] Various cultures used different means to interpret dreams,
whether by intuition, by using an oracular apparatus through which the
god made his/her will known, (e.g., provoking a dream or vision that
interprets the prior dream), or by using collections of dream-omina.[99]
These dream books, found in Egypt, Babylonia, the Hittite Empire,
and Assyria, were most likely used by professional dream interpreters
to provide the mantic meaning of simple dream symbols.[100] The Egyp-
tians were particularly well known for their skillful dream interpretation
and dream books,[101] but Babylonians and Assyrians also had highly specialized dream interpreters and dream books.[102] The Egyptian dream
books have the peculiarity of considering factors such as the dreamer's
health, wealth, social status, character, and gender in arriving at an
interpretation.[103] Whatever the mode employed, proper dream interpretation testified to the intelligence of the interpreter as well as of the
dreamer who first recognized the dream as significant.[104]

The Semitic root *p.š.r* means 'to interpret' or 'to solve' a dream or
a difficult passage in a text, as well as 'to dissolve' and 'to absolve,'
suggesting that negative consequences might be avoided with a sound
interpretation. The Sumerian *bur* and Akkadian *pašāru* both carry the
meanings of 'interpret' as well as 'undo,' paralleled by the Egyptian
wḥᶜ meaning 'to untwine a rope,' 'to explain a difficult passage,' 'to
remove sins,' or 'to heal afflictions.'[105] Accordingly, interpreters often
performed or prescribed apotropaic rituals.[106] The *Assyrian Dream-Book*

---

[98] Oppenheim, *Interpretation*, 220.

[99] Sauneron, 'l'Égypte,' 32; Oppenheim, *Interpretation*, 221.

[100] Sauneron, 'l'Égypte,' 33–35; Leibovici, 'Babylone,' 70–72; Vieyra, 'Hittites,' 89;
Bergman et al, 'חלם,' *TDOT* 4:422; Oppenheim, *Interpretation*, 238, 256–258; idem, 'New
Fragments of an Assyrian Dream-Book,' *Iraq* 31 (1969): 153–165; Caquot points out that
no dream books have been found in Canaan or Israel, 'Canaan et Israel,' 101.

[101] See Volten, *Demotische Traumdeutung*, and the Middle Kingdom hieratic 'Book of
Dreams' in Papyrus Chester Beatty III.

[102] *Assyrian Dream-Book*, trans. L. Oppenheim, in *Interpretation*, 256–334; also 238–239.

[103] Volten, *Demotische Traumdeutung*, 8–10; Sauneron, 'l'Égypte,' 33–35.

[104] Oppenheim, *Interpretation*, 207; Caquot, 'Canaan et Israel,' 102.

[105] Bergman et al, 'חלם,' *TDOT* 4:425.

[106] Wilson, *Prophecy and Society*, 95; Sauneron, 'l'Égypte,' 20–21, 33; Leibovici, 'Babylone,' 67.

describes rituals for averting bad outcomes of dreams, including 'telling' (*pašāru*) the dream to a lump of clay that is in turn 'dissolved' in water or 'telling' it (*pašāru*) to a reed that is then burned in the fire on which the dreamer blows.[107] Other apotropaic rites included prayers, sacrificial offerings, and libations.[108]

It is clear that some women acted as dream interpreters in ancient Mesopotamia, e.g. the *ensi* priestess interpreted dreams in Sumer and among the Hittites[109] and at Ebla the daughters of king Ibbisipiš, Zaase and Tarkabbi were *ša'iltu* dream interpreters in the temple.[110] Goddesses act as dream interpreters for both men and women in epic, as when Gilgamesh has his dreams interpreted by his divine mother in the *Epic of Gilgamesh* and the Sumerian god Tammuz has his interpreted by his sister.[111] Women and goddesses are also depicted as helping others to incubate dreams.[112]

The role of female dream expert might have translated into a high social status for a few individual females. Frymer-Kensky hypothesizes that the role of female dream interpreters developed from mothers comforting their children after nightmares and/or explaining their children's dreams to them, thus testifying to women's traditional skill in the learned cultural arts.[113] I suggest that the close association between females and dream interpretation may stem from the collective societal presumption that women typically see symbolic dreams, which are unclear, while men usually see message dreams, which need no interpretation.[114] In fact, only one message dream of a woman is recorded in all of ancient Near Eastern literature—the wife of Hittite King Hattushili has a dream of Ishtar—and even then the dream concerns the

---

[107] Leibovici, 'Babylone,' 67; Oppenheim, *Interpretation*, 219, 302–303; *KAR* 252 I:51–78.

[108] Ackerman focuses on sacrificial offerings, 'Deception of Isaac,' 116–117.

[109] Oppenheim, *Interpretation*, 222.

[110] In Gnuse, *Josephus*, 52; Lorenzo Vigano, 'Literary Sources for the History of Palestine and Syria: The Ebla Tablets,' *Biblical Archaeologist* 47 (1984): 10; Oppenheim suggests that only women sought their services, *Interpretation*, 222.

[111] Frymer-Kensky, *In the Wake of the Goddesses*, 38–39, 41, 115; see also Oppenheim, *Interpretation*, 246–247, nos. 2–4.

[112] In 'Song of the Plowing Oxen,' translated by M. Civil, the goddess Nanshe helps a farmer incubate a dream, in *Kramer Anniversary Volume*, (ed. Barry Eichler; *AOAT* 25; Kevelaer/Neukirchen-Vluyn: Verlag Butzon und Bercker/Neukirchener Verlag, 1976), 83–95; according to Frymer-Kensky, *In the Wake of the Goddesses*, 38.

[113] Frymer-Kensky, *In the Wake of the Goddess*, 40–41.

[114] Oppenheim, *Interpretation*, 190, 240.

king and is in fact related by him.[115] The presence of any female dream
interpreters, which in any case is one of the lesser esteemed divinatory arts,[116] then ironically serves on a broader social level to reinforce
the cultural association of women with non-verbal, associative, mud-
dled thinking. These cultural constructions stand in tension with the
contents of the Egyptian dream books, which indicate that in reality
both men and women had symbolic dreams and sought the advice of
interpreters.[117]

Dream Incubation

Incubation, or the attempt to provoke divinely-sent dreams, is attested
in ancient Near Eastern sources, although it is rare in comparison with
Greek and later Near Eastern sources.[118] In the ancient Near East,
kings or priests were the major practitioners of incubation, which was
conducted by sleeping in temples or at other sacred sites, normally
beside the statue of the god. Oppenheim, with others following, has
argued that the practice of temple incubation may have inspired the
idea of the message dream since sleeping at the base of a statue suggests
to the dreamer the appearance of a looming deity.[119] Other rituals
of incubation may include: prayer, mourning, fasting, abstaining from
sex and/or wine, laying out special clothes, ritual nakedness, sacrificial
offerings, libations, self-abasement, crying, or special preparations for
the sleeping place.[120] Leibovici has also noted at least one case of the use
of necromancy in provoking dreams.[121] Examples of incubated dreams
include the dreams of the Sumerian King Gudea, the Hittite King
Murshili, the Babylonian King Nabonidus, the Akkadian King Narâm-
Sin, a priest of Ishtar on behalf of the Assyrian King Assurbanipal,

---

[115] Oppenheim, *Interpretation*, 197; 254, par. 8, no. 27.

[116] If the *ša'iltu* priestess conducted dream divination, she functioned outside and
below the domain of the official, temple-centered religious life. Oppenheim, *Interpretation*, 222.

[117] Volten, *Demotische Traumdeutung*.

[118] Oppenheim, *Interpretation*, 187.

[119] Ibid., 190; idem, 'Mantic Dreams,' 348; E. Ehrlich, *Der Traum*, 17; R.G.A. van
Lieshout, *Greeks on Dreams*, 44–45.

[120] Oppenheim, *Interpretation*, 188. For examples of prayer and mourning in dream
incubation see the dreams of Assurbanipal and Sethos in Oppenheim, *Interpretation*,
249, no. 10; 252, no. 22. See also Ehrlich, *Der Traum*, 14–15; Ackerman, 'Deception of
Isaac,' 92–120.

[121] *Epic of Gilgamesh*; Leibovici, 'Babylone,' 80–81.

and the dream of the Egyptian King Sethos.[122] In the case of Egypt, it is unclear when incubation began to be practiced; it may have been introduced only in Ptolemaic times.[123]

Functions of Ancient Near Eastern Dreams

Whether incubated or not, divinely-sent dreams recorded in literary and cultic sources serve three main functions: to impart knowledge; dispense healing or infirmity; or convey divine sanction or the reverse, divine punishment. These functions hold whether the dreamer is a hero in an epic, an historical person in a royal record, or a common person in a dream-book.

The knowledge that dreamers gain is extraordinary knowledge beyond normal human ken. For example, King Ptolemy Soter dreams of the colossus of a god's statue in an unknown land that gives him directions to bring it to Alexandria.[124] Later, the King tells the dream to his friends, who find a well traveled man named Sosibus who recognizes the description as that of an actual statue of Pluto in Sinope, although the account stipulates the king had never been there. The statue is brought immediately to Alexandria, where Pluto's cult is erected. The logic of the account confirms the veracity of the information relayed to the king, although he had no conventional means of knowing these facts. However, more often, dream knowledge concerns the future.[125]

---

[122] Oppenheim, *Interpretation*, 188–189, 191, 199, 205, 224, 245–246, 249–250; Leibovici, 'Babylone,' 80–81.

[123] Bouché-Leclerq argues that incubation probably did not reach Egypt until the creation of the Hellenistic Sarapis cult. H. Magnus maintains incubation was common from the earliest days of ancient Egypt, and Volten believes Egyptian incubation to be pre-Ptolemaic. See A. Bouché-Leclerq, *Histoire de la divination dans l'antiquité* (4 vols.; Paris: Bruxelles, 1979–1881), 2:251–260; H. Magnus, *Abhandlungen zur Geschichte du Medicin* (vol. 1; Breslau, 1902), 6–8, as cited in E. Thrämer, 'Health and Gods of Healing,' *ERE* 6:540–556; Volten, *Demotische Traumdeutung*, 44, n. 3. Also see Sauneron, 'l'Égypte,' 40–1; Ray, 'Ancient Egypt,' 184; G. Foucart, 'Dreams and Sleep: Egyptian,' *ERE* 5:34–37; Oppenheim, *Interpretation*, 188, 252. See the possible 'accidental' incubation of Thutmose IV in Oppenheim, *Interpretation*, 187, 191, 251.

[124] Oppenheim, *Interpretation*, 252, no. 21.

[125] Examples abound in both the historical and epic sources, e.g. Thutmose's dream that is also a dream of divine sanction, 'A Divine Oracle through a Dream,' 449; Djoser's Dream in 'The Tradition of Seven Lean Years in Egypt.' trans. John A. Wilson (*ANET*, 32); or the dream of Tammuz in Oppenheim, *Interpretation*, 246, no. 2.

Divinely-sent dreams may also impart physical or psychological healing; conversely, suffering may be inflicted. A short example from a Hittite text should suffice:

> A dream of the queen: Somebody said again and again to me in a
> dream: 'Make a vow to the goddess Ningal as follows: If that (disease)
> Fire-of-the-Feet of His Majesty will pass quickly I shall make for Ningal
> ten *talla* (oil flasks) of gold set with lapis lazuli!'[126]

Obviously, the King had a foot ailment and the dream reveals to the
Queen which god could cure him, as well as what gift would induce
the god to do so. Annunciation dreams fulfill this healing function and
are therefore oftentimes incubated.[127] In these dreams, a deity appears
to a childless husband or wife and announces that a child, especially
a preeminent child, will soon be born.[128] Sometimes the name of the
child is provided by the dream figure.[129]

Finally, dreams often grant divine sanction to the dreamer, another
person or a project; conversely they may serve as divine chastisement
or punishment. Not surprisingly, this function is prominent in royal
dreams. For example, the Egyptian Pharaoh Tanutamun dreamt of
two serpents, a dream which was interpreted to mean, 'Upper Egypt
belongs to you; take for yourself Lower Egypt [also]. The Two Goddesses appeared on your head. The land is given to you in its length
and in its breadth.'[130]

In noting the function of divine sanction, I also have in mind divine
directives, which implicitly suggest sanction of the dreamer who is the
executor of the god's wishes.[131] Frequently, the command is to rebuild
ruined sanctuaries[132] and the temple plan is given within the dream.[133]
Similarly, when dreams commission artwork or literary endeavors, the
dreamer is shown the completed product in the dream.[134] For example,
the Akkadian poem 'Epic of Erra,' from the first millennium B.C.E.,

---

[126] In Oppenheim, *Interpretation*, 255, no. 32.
[127] For an Egyptian example, see Vieyra, 'Les songes de Méhitousket et de son mari Satni' in *Les songes*, 41.
[128] Oppenheim, *Interpretation*, 194; 252, no. 20.
[129] Ibid., 194.
[130] In Oppenheim, *Interpretation*, 251, no. 17; cf. 'A Divine Oracle through a Dream,' trans. J.A. Wilson (*ANET*, 449).
[131] See A. Caquot, 'Canaan et Israel,' 107 and the examples in Oppenheim, *Interpretation*, 248, nos. 1, 12, 18, 19, 21, 23, 25, 30, 33.
[132] Oppenheim, *Interpretation*, 203, 209.
[133] See particularly the Dream of Gudea, in Oppenheim, *Interpretation*, 245, no. 1.
[134] Oppenheim, *Interpretation*, 193.

states that the poem itself was shown exactly as is to the poet by a god 'in a nocturnal vision' and that the poet did not miss or add a single line.[135]

Summary of Ancient Near Eastern Dreams

Unlike modern dreams, message and symbolic dreams were thought to be communications from the divine realm that concern the future.[136] Oppenheim's category of *message dream* entails a visit from a deity and is an actual epiphany that imparts a clear message. The *symbolic dream* is, by contrast, a coded message from the divine realm that requires interpretation. The typical vocabulary associated with dreams underscores the idea that dreams are objective phenomena seen by the dreamer in a receptive state, which is described in terms of an unusual, wakeful sleep.

Some important literary dream motifs include otherworldly dream journeys and a pervasive association between death and dreams. The latter idea is expressed through many formulas, including netherworldly dream journeys, the netherworld as the source of dreams, dreams by the dying and testamentary dreams. However, the deceased only rarely appear in dreams.

The social setting of dreaming expresses and reinforces the patriarchy of the ancient Near East, since those dreams deemed most worthy are message dreams seen by important males such as kings, officials and priests. Symbolic dreams, which were viewed with some suspicion, are more widely attested for women than for men; perhaps for this reason, women as well as men functioned as dream interpreters. Dream interpretation operated both within and outside of the official cult and in general was considered a lesser example of the divinatory profession. Still, the proper interpretation of dreams was considered crucial, and great emphasis was placed on the act of telling symbolic dreams, not only to secure an interpretation, but also to avert any negative effects of the dream through magico-apotropaic rituals. The practice of evok-

---

[135] Oppenheim, *Interpretation*, 193. Similarly, the claim in the Egyptian wisdom text 'Instruction of King Amenemhet' is that the whole of the poem was revealed to the king in a dream by his deceased father, Oppenheim, *Interpretation*, 193–194.

[136] By contrast, modern dream analysis focuses on the dreamer's interior psychological world in relation to the past and present.

ing divinely-sent dreams through temple incubation is attested for kings and priests, usually in response to times of political or religious crisis.

Overall, divinely-sent dreams function in three ways: to impart extraordinary knowledge, dispense healing or sickness, and convey divine guidance and sanction or the opposite, divine punishment.

DREAMS IN ANCIENT ISRAEL

I have treated ancient Israel as a special case in this chapter since dreams in the Hebrew Bible are obviously particularly pertinent to the discussion of dreams in Hellenistic Judaism. I begin with an examination of the formal patterns, typical vocabulary and motifs of biblical dreams.[137] Applying Oppenheim's categories to biblical dreams allows me to compare them directly to ancient Near Eastern dreams so that the peculiar contours of biblical dreams emerge. Next, I explore the social milieu of dreams in ancient Israel with attention to social stratification, gender and power relations and also investigate the relationship of biblical dreams, divination and biblical prophecy. Finally, I analyze the functions of biblical dreams and find that they follow those of ancient Near Eastern dreams, with some important differences.

Classifications of Biblical Dreams

Before turning to Oppenheim's patterns of dreams, a survey of other systems of dream classification in the Hebrew Bible is in order. Major works on biblical dreams include the following: monographs by E.L. Ehrlich, A. Resch, S. Bar and R. Gnuse; general articles by W. Richter, S. Zeitlin, A. Caquot, K. Seybold and J. Priest.[138] Most use Oppenheim's categories, but Ehrlich proposes a different set of classifications,

---

[137] Dreams in the New Testament derive from the cultures of Hellenistic Judaism and early Christianity and will be dealt with in a later chapter. Also, I mention the biblical book of Daniel here, but as it is a Hellenistic Jewish work, (which draws on earlier traditions), it receives a much fuller treatment in Part Two.

[138] Ehrlich, *Der Traum*; Resch, *Der Traum im Heilsplan*; Bar, *A Letter that Has Not Been Read*; Gnuse, *Samuel*; idem, *Josephus*; W. Richter, 'Traum und Traumdeutung'; S. Zeitlin, 'Dreams and their Interpretation from the Biblical Period to the Tannaitic Time: An Historical Study,' *JQR* 66 (1975): 1–18; Caquot, 'Canaan and Israel,' 99–124; Seybold, 'Der Traum'; see also J. Priest, 'Myth and Dream in Hebrew Scripture,' in *Myths, Dreams and Religion* (ed. J. Campbell; New York: Dutton, 1970), 48–67.

as follows: symbolic dreams, dreams in which God transmits commands/orders, dreams in which divine revelation (other than commands) is imparted, and dreams as simile.[139] Since some of these categories are based on form, while others reflect content, Ehrlich's system is less consistent than is Oppenheim's. Also, both Ehrlich and Resch draw an untenable distinction between 'dream' and 'night vision.'[140] While Ehrlich recognizes the difficulty in distinguishing between dreams and visions, he ultimately misconstrues the evidence by maintaining that visions are clear and dreams are confused.[141]

Both Gnuse and Bar rely on Oppenheim's classifications, with minor changes. Gnuse labels Oppenheim's 'message dream' the 'auditory message dream,' which I find misleading since he applies the term both to dreams in which a visual apparition of the deity occurs along with the spoken message and to dreams in which only a divine voice is heard.[142] Bar renames Oppenheim's 'message dream' the 'prophetic dream.'[143] I have chosen not to follow his lead since in early Jewish literature this distinction would prove untenable vis-à-vis symbolic dreams, which may also be prophetic.

In their brief studies, Richter, Zeitlin, Caquot, Seybold and Priest do not attempt a comprehensive system of dream classification.[144] However, Richter does apply form criticism to selected biblical dreams and some ancient Near Eastern dreams to arrive at the following useful pattern of some biblical dreams: *Anzeige, Traumeröffnungsformel, Traumkorpus, Deutung, Erfüllung.*[145]

Typical Patterns of Message and Symbolic Dreams

Overall, I find Oppenheim's form-critical patterns to be most useful in identifying and categorizing the dreams in the Hebrew Bible, since they contextualize biblical dreams in relation to the broader ancient Near Eastern understandings of dreams. Using this lens, it is evident

---

[139] Ehrlich, *Der Traum.*

[140] Ibid., 55; Resch, *Der Traum,* 131.

[141] Ehrlich, *Der Traum,* 1–12.

[142] Gnuse, *Josephus,* 37–38, 40–41; idem, 'Dreams in the Night,' 32.

[143] Bar, *A Letter That Has Not Been Read,* 9. See also F. Flannery-Dailey, 'Review of *A Letter that Has Not Been Read,*' in *JBL* 121, 3 (Fall, 2002): 536–537.

[144] B. Long elaborates somewhat on Richter, and examines dreams in the wider context of visions, 'Prophetic Call Traditions and Reports of Visions,' *ZAW* 84 (1972): 494–500.

[145] Richter, 'Traum und Traumdeutung,' 202–220.

that biblical dreams adhere very well to the conventional 'frame' of
ancient Near Eastern dreams, as is easily illustrated using the example
of Jacob's dream in Genesis 28:10–22:[146]

> I. INTRODUCTION: It was night (v. 10), Jacob took a stone, put it
> under his head and 'lay down in that place to sleep' (v. 11).
>
> II. DREAM: 'And he dreamed' (חלם v.12).
> > a. Symbolic dream of ladder to heaven, angels ascending and de-
> > scending (v. 12).
> > b. Message dream: יהוה 'stood' נצב above it and related promises of
> > future progeny, land and blessing (v. 13).
>
> III. CONCLUSION: 'Then Jacob awoke … and he was afraid, and said,
> "How awesome is this place!"' (vv. 16–17); 'So Jacob rose early in the
> morning …' (v. 18)

The INTRODUCTION is typical for ancient Near Eastern dreams; it
establishes a setting in which the dreamer lies down and goes to sleep at
night (Gen 28:11).[147] Although not all the settings of ancient Near Eastern dreams stress it is night, many do (28:10).[148] The DREAM begins
like a symbolic dream, if the ladder is a symbol that bridges earth and
heaven, signifying that the divine realm is accessible from earth (28:12).
However, the dream continues as a stereotypical message dream, in
which the deity appears and imparts a message of divine sanction, predicting future progeny, land, and blessings (28:13–15). Although angels
are visible, the messenger of the theophany is not an angel, but יהוה
who is 'standing,' (ויעמד), as deities typically do in ancient Near Eastern
dreams.[149] However, unlike the description of those deities, the physical appearance of God is never mentioned. The CONCLUSION is
normal for ancient Near Eastern dreams: Jacob awakens and registers the psychological and emotional impact of the experience (28:16–
7).[150]

The FULFILLMENT of this dream, which imparts divine sanction
to Jacob and his descendants, is not immediately stated. However, the

---

[146] Ackerman considers this to be a case of dream incubation, 'Deception of Isaac,'
92–120; Cf. Gnuse, 'Dreams in the night,' 40–41, for a slightly different form-critical
analysis of Gen 28.

[147] Ackerman, 'Deception of Isaac,' 114–115; Oppenheim, *Interpretation*, 186–187.

[148] See Oppenheim, *Interpretation*, 274, nos. 5–7, 1, 17.

[149] Oppenheim, *Interpretation*, 189.

[150] Ibid., 188.

fulfillment is implied and understood as occurring over the course of Israel's sacred history, since as the biblical epic progresses Jacob's descendants do become a nation that controls the land in which Bethel is located. From the reader's point of view, this portion of the message has already come to pass, thereby reinforcing the expectation that the remainder of the message will likewise be fulfilled, namely: 'by you and your descendants shall all the families of the earth bless themselves' (28:14). Thus, the fulfillment of the dream has implications for the Israelite readership, and Jacob's erection of a stone pillar and the renaming of Luz as 'Bethel' or 'House of God' marks the location as the sacred space wherein these promises were received.[151]

Niditch has rightly stressed the importance of the experience of the divine realm in ancient Israelite religion, stating that 'Israelites were acutely and passionately concerned with the experiential dimension ... The numinous is experienced in a personal, strongly visceral manner, down to the very bones of one's body.'[152] Biblical dreams speak directly to the idea that contact with the divine has a profound effect on the dreamer.[153] This is evident in Jacob's reaction to the dream at Bethel: he is afraid, makes an awestricken remark, and sets up a pillar to mark the location of the dream as sacred space (Gen 28:16–18; cf. Gen 26:24).

Symbolic dreams also abound; the brief account of Pharaoh's symbolic dream in Genesis 41:5–7 is paradigmatic:

I. INTRODUCTION: He fell asleep and dreamed וייׁשן ויחלם (v. 5)

II. DREAM: symbolic dreams of seven healthy and unhealthy ears of grain

III. CONCLUSION: 'The Pharaoh awoke: it was a dream!' (v. 7) וייקץ פרעה והנה חלום

As throughout the ancient Near East, message dreams and symbolic dreams are the standard forms for divinely-sent dreams in the Hebrew Bible.

---

[151] J.K. Kuntz, *The Self-Revelation of God* (Philadelphia: Westminster Press, 1967), 125–127; Seybold, 'Der Traum,' 43.

[152] S. Niditch, *Ancient Israelite Religion* (NY: Oxford Univ. Press, 1997), 35.

[153] Ibid., 34–49. Experiential events which Niditch cites are covenant making, annunciation, encounters with the deity, transportation to the heavenly realm, and encounters with the dead.

Table of Biblical Dreams

Applying Oppenheim's form-critical patterns to the entire corpus of visionary episodes results in the following table of dreams in the Hebrew Bible, which lists each episode according to dream type. I omit visionary episodes that, according to vocabulary and form-critical standards, are completely lacking in dream characteristics (e.g. Ezekiel 1:1–3:15). The following table is exhaustive for biblical dreams and allows me to arrive at some general conclusions.[154]

Table 1: Dream Types in the Hebrew Bible

Dream Episode	Content	Dream Type and Special Features	Dream Vocabulary
Gen 15:12–21	Abraham's dream of the covenant between the pieces	auditory message dream (the Lord), symbolic dream	–
Gen 20:3–7	Abimelech's dream about Sarah and Abraham	auditory message dream (the Lord)	חלום vv.3, 6
Gen 26:24	the Lord appeared to Isaac by night וירא אליו יהוה	message dream (auditory?)	–
Gen 28:10–22	Jacob's dream of the ladder	symbolic dream (of the ladder), message dream ('the Lord stood' יהוה נצב)	חלום v. 12
Gen 31:10–13	Jacob's dream of the goats	auditory message dream (the angel of God)	חלום vv. 10, 11
Gen 31:24	Laban's dream	message dream (auditory?) '*God came … and said*' ויבא אלהים	a dream by night חלום הלילה
Gen 37:5–7	Joseph's dream of the wheat sheaves	symbolic dream	vv. 5–8, (cf. 42:9) חלום; vv. 5, 6, 8 חלם
Gen 37:9	Joseph's dream of sun, moon and eleven stars	symbolic dream, forms a pair with Gen 37:5–7	37:9.10, 20 (cf. 42:9) חלום 37:9, 10 (cf. 42:9) חלם
Gen 40:9–15	Dream of Pharaoh's cupbearer	symbolic dream interpreted by Joseph	40:5, 8, 9, 41:11, 12 חלום; 40:5, 8; 41:11 חלם
Gen 40:16–19	Dream of Pharaoh's baker	symbolic dream interpreted by Joseph, forms a pair with Gen 40:9–15	40:16, 41:11, 12 חלום; 41:11 חלם

---

[154] The table includes all dreams in the Hebrew Bible for which some content is provided. References to dreams devoid of content have not been included in the table, including Gen 37:19; Num 12:6; Deut 13:1, 3, 5; 1 Sam 28:6, 15; Job 7:14, 20:8, 33:15; Ps 73:20, 126:1; Eccl 5:3, 7; Isa 29:7, 8; Jer 23:25, 27, 28, 32, 27:9, 29:8; Dan 1:17; Joel 2:28; Zech 10:2.

Gen 41:1–4	Pharaoh's dream of the seven sleek and fat cows	symbolic dream, interpreted by Joseph (41:14–45)	41:7, 8, 15, 17 חלום 41:1, 5, 15 חלם
Gen 41:5–8	Pharaoh's dream of the seven fat and withered ears of grain	symbolic dream, interpreted by Joseph, forms a pair with 41:1–4 (41:14–45)	41:7, 8, 15, 22, 25, 26, 32 חלום
Gen 46:2	Jacob's dream of God assuring him of prosperity in Egypt	'visions of the night' auditory message dream?	במראת הלילה
Numbers 22:9–13	Balaam's dream (see vv. 8, 13)	message dream, probably auditory message dream (God came and said) ויבא אלהים	–
Numbers 22:20–21	Balaam's second dream (vv. 20, 21)	message dream, probably auditory message dream (God came and said) ויבא אלהים	–
Judges 7:13–14	A Midianite's dream predicting Gideon's victory	symbolic dream, a *kledon* (cf. v. 9, a dream?)	vv. 13, 15 חלום; v. 13 חלם
1 Sam 3:2–5	God calls young Samuel at night	auditory message dream (the Lord), a *Wecktraum* (incubation, sleeping in the temple with the ark of God)	–
1 Sam 3:5b–6	God calls young Samuel at night, a second time	auditory message dream (the Lord), a *Wecktraum* (incubation)	–
1 Sam 3:6b–15	God calls Samuel a third time	message dream, a *Wecktraum* (God came and stood there ויבא אלהים ויתיצב)	3:15 המראה
1 Kings 3:5–15	Solomon's dream and request for wisdom	message dream (type?) (the Lord *appeared to Solomon in a dream* נראה יהוה אל שלמה בחלום	vv. 5, 15 חלום
1 Kings 19:5–7	An angel wakes Elijah and gives him food and drink	two *Wecktraümen* (messenger is an angel)	–
Zech-ariah 1:8–4:2	Zechariah has a series of oracular night visions	elements of message dreams (I saw a man, standing), symbolic dreams (of multi-colored horses, etc.), and a *Wecktraum* in 4:1 also identical to a 'word of the LORD' (1:7) דבר־יהוה	I saw in the night ראיתי הלילה (1:8); ועירני כאיש אשר־יעור משנתו woke me as a man is wakened from sleep (4:1)
Job 4:12–21	A spirit (an angel?) appears in a dream to (Eliphaz) (cf. 7:14–15)	message dream, (a spirit glided past my face, it *stood* יעמד still ... then I heard a voice)	'visions of the night' מחזינות לילה (v. 13)
Daniel 2:31–35	Nebuchadnezzar's dream of the great statue	symbolic dream, interpreted by Daniel (2:24–45)	vv.1–3 חלם חלום; vv. 4–9, 26, 28, 36, 45 חלם

Daniel 4:4–18	Nebuchadnezzar's dream of the tree felled by the watcher	symbolic dream, interpreted by Daniel (4:19–27, fulfillment in vv. 28–37)	vv. 5, 6, 7, 8, 9, 18, 19 חלם
Daniel 7:1–28	Daniel's dream of the animals representing Gentile kingdoms and the throne room vision	symbolic dream (7:1–8) and a symbolic dream with elements of an otherworldly journey (7:9–14), interpreted by angelic attendants (7:15–27)	v.1: 'Daniel saw a dream and visions of his mind' דניאל חלם חזה וחזוי ראשה and חלמא v. 2: 'in my vision at night' בחזוי עם־ליליא
Daniel 8:2–27	Daniel's dream of the ram and goat	symbolic dream (8:1–14), with elements of auditory message dream (8:13–14), interpreted by the angel Gabriel (8:15–26)	v. 1, 15, 17, 26, 27 ואראה בחזון (v. 2)
Jeremiah 30:1–31:26	Jeremiah is given an oracle against Israel	auditory message dream, instructions to record it	—

In some cases of biblical dreams, it is unclear from the phrases, 'God/the Lord came (ויבא)' or 'God/the Lord appeared (נראה)' whether a physical epiphany or an auditory message dream is implied (i.e., whether some divine presence is manifested, but without any visual aspect). Zechariah's night visions in 1–3 and 4 are a difficult, liminal case.[155] The night settings of 1–3 seem to indicate a dream, and 4:1 is a classic *Wecktraum*; however the visions that follow the prophet's awakening do not differ markedly from those that come earlier. The oracles are also called a 'word' or 'matter' of the LORD (דבר־יהוה).

Several general observations may now be made regarding biblical dreams. First, on the basis of form-critical elements, mostly concerning setting, several episodes may qualify as 'dreams' even when no specific term for 'dream' is used: Genesis 15:12–21, 26:24; Numbers 22:9–13, 22:20–21; 1 Samuel 3:2–15.[156] Second, it is evident that the message dream, the auditory message dream, the *Wecktraum*, and the symbolic dream are each well represented in the Bible. Third, like their ancient Near Eastern counterparts, several of the biblical dreams exhibit the characteristic repetition that lends veracity to the dream's message (Gen

---

[155] By contrast, C.A. and E.M. Meyers hold that this is not a dream, maintaining that Zech 4:1 'expresses the prophet's awareness that his visionary experience is as different from normal experience as wakefulness is from slumber,' C.A. and E.M. Meyers, *Haggai, Zechariah 1–8: A New Translation with Introduction and Commentary* (Anchor Bible; Garden City, N.Y.: Doubleday, 1987), 229.

[156] For a detailed study of 1 Sam 3 as a dream see Gnuse, *Samuel*.

37:5–7 and 37:9; Gen 40:9–15 and 40:16–19; Gen 41:1–4 and 41:5–8; 1 Sam 3:2–5, 3:5b–6, 3:6b–15).[157] Fourth, the Hebrew Bible does not contain a record of a woman's dream.[158] Fifth, dead or living persons do not appear in biblical dreams. Sixth, it is quite clear that the dreams of the Daniel 7–8, which stem from the 2nd c. B.C.E., combine dream types in a more complex way than do earlier dreams, including Daniel 2 and 4, which were probably independent tales collected during the Hellenistic period.[159]

Seventh, as in the example from Genesis 28 above, the messenger in biblical dreams is normally יהוה and not the angel of the Lord (e.g. Ex 33:20, 1 Kings 19:13; Isa 6:2; cf. Gen 3:8). Although the idea that God cannot be seen might lead us to presume the latter is implied in יהוה, this is our importation into the text.[160] Despite the fact that angels commonly function as dream messengers in Hellenistic Judaism, there are no clear cases of biblical message dreams containing an angelic epiphany, except in the case of Daniel 7–8, which stems from the Hellenistic period.[161] Some marginal cases include: Genesis 31:10–13, an auditory message dream in which an angel is heard but not seen; 1 Kings 19:5, in which an angel appears in a *Wecktraum* but delivers no message;[162] and possibly Job 4, in which a wind or spirit that may be an angel imparts an auditory message in a dream.[163] That is, even though angels frequently appear and function as messengers elsewhere in the Hebrew Bible, they generally do not do so in dreams. Surprisingly, dream epiphanies are reserved for יהוה. The angels in Zechariah's night visions in Zech 1–6 and in Daniel's dreams in Dan 7–8 represent a new development in that they do not relay the main revelation, which occurs in the form of visual symbols; rather, they function as inter-

---

[157] Bergman et al, 'חלם,' *TDOT* 4:425; Wikenhauser, 'Doppelträume'; Alexander, 'Dreams in Pairs.'

[158] K. Seybold maintains Song of Solomon 3:1–2 is a dream. Despite the elements of a bed and night, I find Seybold's conclusion unconvincing since the woman appears to be waiting anxiously in the bed for her lover; see Seybold, 'Der Traum,' 46–47.

[159] Collins, *Daniel: A Commentary on the Book of Daniel*, 35–36.

[160] For the issue of the corporeality of God as it relates to both the Elohist tradition and dreams, see Gnuse, 'Dreams in the night,' 50–52.

[161] Cf. Gospel of Matthew 1:20–24.

[162] J. Lindblom understands the angel's appearance to occur in a dream since Elijah lies sleeping under a broom bush, *Prophecy in Ancient Israel* (Philadelphia: Muhlenberg, 1965), 56–57.

[163] The dream is odd for several reasons and could be an example of an 'evil dream,' the content of which is provided. See Oppenheim, *Interpretation*, 230.

preters for the visions that the dreamer sees. This motif will become
standard for Hellenistic Jewish dreams and we will investigate it more
thoroughly in Part Two.

Typical Dream Vocabulary

The biblical Hebrew root ח.ל.מ from whence stems the word for dream,
חלום, does not seem to share the meaning of 'sleep' associated with
other ancient Near Eastern words for dream, such as the Sumerian
ᵈMA-MÚ or ᵈMA-MÙ, meaning 'dream' and 'sleep,' or the Akkadian
šuttu, from the same root as šittu, 'sleep.' Rather, ח.ל.מ may ultimately
stem from the Ugaritic root meaning 'to see,'[164] and other biblical terms
for dreaming place a similar stress on the visual aspect. The Hebrew
roots for 'see', ה.א.ר, (Gen 46:2, 1 Sam 3:15) and 'vision', ח.ז.נ, (Job 4:13,
Dan 7, 8) are used with formal elements that indicate a חלום is meant.[165]
The dream itself is usually introduced with והנה.[166]

The etymology of ח.ל.מ remains obscure. It occurs in other Semitic
languages, including various dialects of Aramaic (Jewish, Christian-
Palmyrene, Samaritan, Mandaic), Ugaritic, Arabic and Ethiopic.[167]
TDOT and *BDB* suggest two roots, one with a semantic meaning of
'be strong' or 'be healthy' and the other meaning 'to dream' as well
as 'attain puberty,' 'experience an emission of the seminal fluid,' and
'come of age' (Arabic and Tigré).[168] *HALOT* sees a link between the
attainment of puberty and sexual dreaming, which *TDOT* rightly notes
seems forced and may also come from separate roots.[169]

Biblical message dreams express God's appearance in terms that
describe His activity and that emphasize a certain embodiment. That
is, God is said to have 'come,' 'appeared,' 'made Himself known,' 'spoken,' or 'stood beside' the dreamer.[170] However, unlike in non-Israelite
dreams, the Hebrew God's physical appearance is never described.[171]

---

[164] Oppenheim, *Interpretation*, 226. S. Bar also covers the etymology of חלום and other
related terms, 10–13, 79–80, 144–145.

[165] Bergman et al, 'חלם,' *TDOT* 4:422–423.

[166] Ibid., 4:427.

[167] Ibid., 4:427.

[168] *BDB*, 'חלם,' 321; Bergman et al, 'חלם,' *TDOT* 4:427.

[169] Bergman et al, 'חלם,' *TDOT* 4:427; L. Koehler, W. Baumgartner, J.J. Stamm,
'חלם,' *HALOT* (2 vols.; ed. M.E.J. Richardson; Leiden: Brill, 2001), 1:320.

[170] Bergman et al, 'חלם,' *TDOT* 4:427.

[171] See Gnuse's discussion of the issue of corporeality in the Elohist dreams, 'Dreams
in the Night,' 50–52.

In sum, rather than associating dreams with sleep, the vocabulary of biblical dreams emphasizes the visual aspect of dreaming, the similarities between dreams and waking visions, and the reality of the divine visit.

Social Milieu of Biblical Dreams

Biblical Dreams, Interpretation and Social Stratification

As mentioned earlier, ancient Near Eastern epic literature as well as royal records portray message dreams as coming mainly to male national and religious leaders—kings, officials and priests—while symbolic dreams are dreamt by women.[172] Although the Hebrew Bible certainly cannot be taken as an historical record of dreaming in ancient Israel, as sacred literature it is in some way an important barometer of what that culture valued. Thus, it is striking that in the Hebrew Bible, there is not a single instance of any kind of dream coming to a woman,[173] nor is there a female dream interpreter, despite women's prominence in this role in other ancient Near Eastern texts.

The absence of women in the biblical dream traditions is all the more noteworthy when one considers that message dreams and dream interpretation both function to increase social power in the Bible. One important example must suffice to illustrate that biblical message dreams usually impart divine sanction to male dreamers. The patriarchs receive their covenantal blessing via message dreams in Genesis 15:12–21, 26:24 and 28:10–22. The similarity of the dreams suggests the ancient Near Eastern motif of dream repetition to underscore the veracity of the promises, emphasizing even further the patriarchs' special status in comparison to other characters in the sacred history.

In addition, the two prominent dream interpreters in the Bible are males, Joseph and Daniel, and their divinely inspired interpretations of royal dreams result in a sharp increase in their political authority and social status. Joseph's ability to interpret correctly the dreams of

---

[172] Oppenheim, *Interpretation*, 185.

[173] Hasan-Rokem, 'Communication with the Dead in Jewish Dream Culture,' in *Dream Cultures*, 213–232, 214.

the royal cupbearer, the royal baker, and the Pharaoh results in his elevation from a prisoner to an official in Pharaoh's royal court:

> Pharaoh said to his servants, 'Can we find anyone else like this—one in whom is the spirit of God?' So Pharaoh said to Joseph, 'Since God has shown you all this, there is no one so discerning and wise as you. You shall be over my house, and all my people shall order themselves as you command … See, I have set you over all the land of Egypt' (Gen 41:37–41)

Joseph's ability to interpret the Pharaoh's dreams demonstrates that God is on Joseph's side, resulting in real political power.[174] This extends the scope of the authority accorded to interpreters in the ancient Near East; here correct interpretation demonstrates not only the intelligence of the interpreter, but also divine favor.[175]

Similarly, Daniel is able not only to interpret King Nebuchadnezzar's dream, but he is also able, miraculously, to know its content as well (Dan 2:17–45). As in the Joseph cycle, this means that God is on the side of the Israelite: 'No wise men, enchanters, magicians, or diviners can show to the king the mystery that the king is asking, but there is a God in heaven who reveals mysteries …' (Dan 2:27–28).[176] Like Joseph, Daniel's abilities earn him a promotion and he is made 'ruler over the whole province of Babylon and chief prefect over all the wise men of Babylon' (Dan 2:46–49). Even more remarkable than the exaltation of a Jew in a foreign court is Nebuchadnezzar's proclamation: 'Truly, your God is God of gods and Lord of kings and a revealer of mysteries, for you have been able to reveal this mystery!' (Dan 2:47). The Joseph and Daniel dream cycles thus link dreaming and religious/political authority and power. When viewed against the roles of female dream interpreters in the ancient Near East, males clearly form the locus of social power in the biblical dream tradition.

Oppenheim generalizes that in the Hebrew Bible, message dreams only come to Israelites, and symbolic dreams only come to Gentiles.[177] Were this correct, it might imply a ranking of message dream over symbolic dream. However, Oppenheim's statement is erroneous since Jacob and Joseph receive symbolic dreams (Gen 28:10–22; Gen 31:10–

---

[174] See C. Westermann, *Joseph: Eleven Bible Studies on Genesis* (Minneapolis: Fortress Press, 1996), 33–52.

[175] Oppenheim, *Interpretation*, 207.

[176] L. Rosenthal, 'Die Josephsgeschichte, mit den Büchern Ester und Daniel verglichen,' *ZAW* 15 (1895): 278–284.

[177] Oppenheim, *Interpretation*, 207.

13; Gen 37:5–9; also Dan 7–8), while Abimelech, Balaam, and possibly Eliphaz receive message dreams (Gen 20:6–7; Num 22:9–21; Job 4:12–21).[178] Rather, in the Hebrew Bible, the type of dream does not appear to correspond to whether a person is Israelite or Gentile, and there is no clear hierarchy of types of dreams, unlike in ancient Near Eastern sources.

Finally, G. Hasan-Rokem has argued that the fact that the dead do not appear in dreams of the Hebrew Bible, taken together with the absence of dreams by women, implies a correlation of dreams of the dead with female necromancy of the sort related in the account of the witch of Endor (1 Sam 28).[179] Supporting evidence includes the fact that the *ša'iltu* dream interpreter also engaged in necromancy, obtaining her name from *moushelou*, 'one who raises the spirit of the dead.'[180] However, we have seen that the dead rarely appear in any ancient Near Eastern dream accounts. Thus, Hasan-Rokem may be more on target when she states: 'That there are no dead in dreams in the Bible stems from a general apprehension toward the dead, which permeates the cultural registers of ancient Israel ...'[181]

Biblical Dreams, Divination and Prophecy

Mantic dreams of the ancient Near East were part and parcel of a general atmosphere of divination, but the biblical critique of divination makes the relationships of dreams, divination, and prophecy more complex.[182] Most biblical dreams are presented as communications from God containing information about the future, and they therefore retain a divinatory aspect in function if not in name. Not only are mantic dreams accepted in the Bible as legitimate revelation, certain biblical dreams clearly contain prophetic oracles intended for transmission to

---

[178] In an extra-Biblical Aramaic inscription at Deir 'Alla, Balaam is called *ḥzn 'lhn*, 'seer of the gods,' and it is said that the gods came to Balaam by night (see Wilson, *Prophecy and Society*, 132–133).

[179] Hasan-Rokem, 'Communication,' 214–215.

[180] Oppenheim, *Interpretation*, 223; Gurney, *Babylonians and Hittites*, 146; Leibovici, 'Babylone,' 68.

[181] Hasan-Rokem, 'Communication,' 216. However, it cannot be maintained that there is no dream that speaks of death in the Bible since Gen 15 promises a good death to Abraham.

[182] M. Weinfeld, 'Ancient Near Eastern Patterns in Prophetic Literature,' *VT*, Vol. XXVII, Fasc. 2; 178–195.

someone other than the dreamer (Num 22:9–13, 22:20–21; 1 Sam 3:2–
15; Jer 30:1–31:26; Dan 7:1–8:27; cf. Joel 2:28–29).[183]

However, some biblical texts reflect a negative view of dreams stemming from their association with pagan divinatory practice. At least one
biblical text directly equates dreaming with evil divination (Zech 10:2).
Other biblical texts speak negatively of dreams (Job 7:14, 20:8, 33:15; Ps
73:20; Eccl 5:3, 7; Isa 29:7), and Jeremiah 29:8 and Deuteronomy 13:1–5
associate some dreaming with false prophecy.

Deuteronomy 13:1–5 represents the extreme since it requires a test
for 'a dreamer of dreams' that clearly associates dreaming with pagan
divination: if the dreamers urge the worship of pagan gods, they are
to be put to death, even if their prophecy comes true (cf. Deut 18).[184]
However, this passage does not necessarily imply an outright objec-
tion to all dream revelation, but only to dreamers who urge apostasy.
The text's concern is that the 'prophet like Moses' should be the legitimate intermediary through which Israel communicates with God (Deut
18:14–15).[185]

The Book of Numbers has a slightly different understanding since it
connects dreaming not with pagan practice, but with a lower level of
prophecy than that experienced by Moses:

> If there is a prophet among you, I the Lord make myself known to him
> in a vision, I speak with him in a dream. Not so with my servant Moses;
> he is entrusted with all my house. With him I speak mouth to mouth,
> clearly, and not in dark speech; and he beholds the form of the Lord.
> (Num 12:6–8).

Dreaming is legitimate since it comes from God, although it is not
the preferred channel of communication with the divine. It is clearly
inferior to a waking theophany of the sort Moses received, but it is
prophecy nonetheless.

Jeremiah is often cited as a prophet who condemns dreaming,[186] but
he actually only condemns *false prophets who use dream revelations for their
own ends*:

---

[183] The appropriation of divination by the prophets is illustrated by Amos, regarding
whose message Niditch states 'God's pronouncement, set within the language and
mechanism of divination, gains extra strength and penetration,' *Symbolic Vision*, 3.

[184] Cf. Zech 10:2, which equates false divination with dreamers who tell false dreams.

[185] Lindblom, *Prophecy*, 201; Wilson, *Prophecy and Society*, 162.

[186] Gnuse, *Josephus*, 93; Ehrlich, *Der Traum*, 158–159.

> For thus says the Lord of hosts, the God of Israel: Do not let the prophets and the diviners who are among you deceive you, and do not listen to the dreams that they dream, for it is a lie that they are prophesying to you in my name; I did not send them, says the Lord. (Jer 29:8; cf. 23:23–32)

It is not clear from this passage that Jeremiah necessarily rejects the idea that some dreams are divine revelations, only that *false* prophets wrongly claim to have had dreams from the Lord.

In fact, Jeremiah himself has a prophetic dream. After receiving an oracle, the prophet declares: 'Thereupon I awoke and looked, and my sleep was pleasant to me' (Jer 31:26). This is the paradigmatic CONCLUSION for an ancient Near Eastern dream.[187] Although the dreamer is startled upon awakening, a pleasant dream leaves the dreamer with a happy feeling, as when after his dream Djoser declares, 'Then I awoke refreshed, my heart determined and at rest …'[188] Also, as we have seen, the theme of being instructed to write down an oracle imparted in a dream is a standard feature in ancient Near Eastern dreams.[189]

Thus, a careful reading of biblical texts suggests to me that nowhere does the Bible reject outright the idea that the God of Israel sometimes communicates to prophets through dreams.[190] Rather, these texts seem to suggest that since dreams are so characteristic of divination throughout the ancient Near East, one must ensure that the dreamer has really dreamt a dream from the God of Israel, rather than from another god (which is apostasy) or from himself (i.e. the dream lacks a divine source altogether). Also, one must guard against those false prophets who fabricate dream accounts.

R. Wilson points out a geographical difference in ancient Israelite attitudes towards divination that may explain some of the varying biblical opinions regarding dreams as revelation.[191] He notes that in Judah

---

[187] Oppenheim, *Interpretation*, 191.

[188] Ibid., 251–252, no. 19.

[189] Ibid., 193–194.

[190] Bar correctly notes that texts such as Zechariah and Job do not actually reject dreams as a legitimate channel of communication from God, but his evaluation of Jeremiah appears to waver on this point, as when he states: 'Hence it is clear that Jeremiah shares the negative evaluation of Deuteronomy, which views dreamers [not "some dreamers"] as prophets who incite the people to idolatry,' Bar, *A Letter that Has Not Been Read*, 113, 140–141.

[191] Niditch connects the waxing and waning of visions and dreams in the Hebrew Bible to the rise and fall in popularity of mythic traditions, at times appropriated into monotheistic Israelite religion and at other times associated with destructive for-

various types of diviners operated within the central social structure before the Exile and were accepted by some Jerusalemite prophets.[192] The Southern receptiveness to divination may explain why Judahite prophetic sources cite dreams and/or visions as the primary mechanism for prophetic revelation.[193] In fact, the most common prophetic title in the Judahite sources is *ḥozeh*, a participle of the verb *ḥazah*, meaning 'to see' or 'to have a vision,' a term used in reference to dreaming.[194] By contrast, the northern or Ephraimite prophetic traditions thoroughly condemn divination of varying kinds, considering it to be pagan practice. According to Wilson, the northern prophet or *nabiʿ* receives verbal messages by way of 'spirit possession' rather than by dreams and visions.[195]

Biblical Dreams and Incubation

The Hebrew Bible contains a few examples of dream incubation, suggesting the practice was at least known in ancient Israel. The clearest example occurs in the episode of King Solomon in Gibeon when he sleeps near the altar and has a divine dream (1 Kings 3:5; 2 Chron 1:5).[196] Other dreams may be examples of 'accidental incubation' in a holy place. The child Samuel dreams when he is asleep near the Ark of the Covenant at Shiloh (1 Sam 3:2–15).[197] Jacob's dream at Bethel is clearly connected to the place where he saw the dream: 'Surely the

---

eign cults that threatened monotheism, *Ancient Israelite Religion*, 4, 12–19. Gnuse notes that overall, dreams are positively evaluated in the epic (Pentateuchal), historical, and apocalyptic literature of the Bible, while they are negatively evaluated by the prophets, Psalms, and Wisdom literature. Gnuse asserts that this trend developed from a conflict with false prophets who used dream revelations, *Samuel*, 63.

[192] Wilson, *Prophecy and Society*, 256–257.

[193] Ibid., 144–146, 254–257, 260–261.

[194] Ibid., 254–255. Using role theory, D.L. Petersen reaches similar conclusions as Wilson. First, he finds that Judahite prophecy uses the term *ḥozeh*, whereas Northern Israelite prophecy uses the title *nabiʾ*. Second, while the prophetic mechanism of the *nabiʾ* stresses the word (in the context of the Deuteronomic covenant), the *ḥozeh* utilizes visions. D.L. Petersen, *The Roles of Israel's Prophets* (JSOT Suppl. 17; Sheffield: JSOT Press, 1981), 53, 63, 86.

[195] Wilson, *Prophecy and Society*, 144. Samuel forms an interesting exception to the rule that Ephraimite prophets are called *nabiʾ*. In 1 Sam. 9:9, *nabiʾ* is set in parallelism with *ro'eh* or 'seer,' the etymology of which suggests one who receives revelation in the form of dreams or visions. See Wilson, *Prophecy and Society*, 140.

[196] C.L. Seow, 'The Syro-Palestinian Context of Solomon's Dream,' *HTR* 77, 2 (1984): 141–152.

[197] Seybold, 'Der Traum,' 42–43.

Lord is in this place; and I did not know it … How awesome is this place! This is none other than the house of God, and this is the gate of heaven' (Gen 28:16–17).[198] In fact, Jacob erects and anoints the stone on which he slept and dreamt as a pillar to mark the place as sacred (Gen 28:18).[199] Some scholars have argued that Jacob sees not a ladder, but a Babylonian ziggurat that anticipates the future temple at Bethel; this would then be a variation on temple incubation.[200] The concept that divinity resides in certain places with such particular power that the place itself induces dreaming or contact with the numinous is in view in these biblical texts. Put another way, a person is more susceptible to communication with the divine realm in the state of sleep, and some spaces are so saturated with divinity that a dream is very likely to occur there.

Functions of Biblical Dreams

Like many ancient Near Eastern dreams, biblical dreams relay messages from the divine realm that impart extraordinary knowledge and divine sanction. However, the function of healing is seriously attenuated.

Biblical dreamers gain knowledge of the future or other extraordinary information. Several examples make this point: Abimelech learns the truth about the secret relationship between Abraham and Sarah (Gen 20:6–7); a Midianite foresees Gideon's victory (Judg 7:13–14); and Nebuchadnezzar gets a glimpse of future history, both his own and that of his nation (Dan 2:31–35, 4:4–18). Like the Mari dream oracles, some biblical dreams also contain prophetic oracles intended for someone other than the dreamer (1 Sam 3:2–15; Num 22:8–20; Jer 30:1–31:26).[201]

As we have seen, by and large, most biblical dreams function to impart divine sanction to male dreamers and/or Israel. The covenants

---

[198] Seybold, 'Der Traum,' 42–43.
[199] Similarly, altars are erected at other theophanic sites in Genesis 12:7, 13:18 and 26:25. See Kuntz, *Self-Revelation of God*, 115.
[200] See Ibid., 125; Seybold, 'Der Traum,' 43.
[201] To avoid confusion, I mention A. Malamat's article on prophecy and dream oracles at Mari, in which he defines the 'message dream' as 'a dream in which the message was not intended for the dreamer himself but rather for a third party.' Malamat, 'Forerunner,' 33–52, 44. I have chosen instead to abide by Oppenheim's use of the term 'message dream,' along with the terms 'auditory message dream' or '*Wecktraum*' when those sub-types are indicated.

with the patriarchs are received in dreams (Gen 15:12–21, 26:24; 28:10–22), and like the dreams of ancient Near Eastern rulers from Ashurbanipal to Tanutamun, they promise numerous descendants, land, and divine protection.[202] In addition to these sweeping statements of divine sanction, several dream episodes depict God as orchestrating smaller events on the patriarchs' behalf, such as when Laban's dream warns him to treat Jacob well (Gen 31:24). Even in those cases where non-Israelites dream, the dream episode as a whole functions to increase the standing of a male Israelite. For instance, when Pharaoh is warned about upcoming years of famine, God orchestrates events so that only Joseph can correctly interpret the dream, which results in a rise in his status (Gen 41:1–8). Again, when Balaam, a non-Israelite, is summoned to dream a message from God *against* Israel, the situation turns and results in a blessing from God upon Israel (Num 22:9–21).[203]

The following cursory list confirms that most biblical dreams function to demonstrate God's providential care for Israel and for the major characters of Israelite history:[204]

Gen 15:12–21	God establishes a covenant with Abraham in a dream.
Gen 20:3–7	Abimelech's dream prevents Sarah and Abraham from coming to harm.
Gen 26:24	God makes a covenant with Isaac in a dream.
Gen 28:10–22	God makes a covenant with Jacob in a dream.
Gen 31:10–13	The dream enables Jacob to succeed over and against Laban.
Gen 31:24	The dream warns Laban that God is looking out for Jacob.
Gen 37:5–7	The dream predicts Joseph's future exaltation over his family.
Gen 37:9	The dream predicts Joseph's future exaltation over his family.
Gen 40:9–19, 41:1–8	Joseph's ability to interpret the dreams correctly leads to his political exaltation.
Gen 46:2	God assures Jacob of prosperity in Egypt through a dream.
Num 22:9–13	Balaam is told in a dream that Israel is blessed.
Judg 7:13–4	The dream predicts Gideon's victory over the Midianites. Gideon hears of the dream and is spurred to action (a *kledon*).

---

[202] See also Cryer, *Divination in Ancient Israel*, 265.
[203] Zeitlin, 'Dreams,' 1.
[204] Cryer, *Divination in Ancient Israel*, 265.

| I Kings 19:5–7 | An angel provides food and water for Elijah when he wishes to die. |
| Jer 30:1–31:26 | The conclusion of Jeremiah's dream oracle against Israel promises the eventual restoration of blessings to the nation. |

Thus, the function of divine sanction is amply attested in biblical dreams. Biblical dreams testify to Israel's future blessing (Genesis 15:12–21, 26:24, 28:10–22, 46:2; Numbers 22:9–13; and Jeremiah 30:1–31:26), predict the downfall of the enemies of Israel and favored Israelites, (e.g. Gen 31:10–13; Num 22:20–21; Judges 7:13–14; Dan 2:31–35, 4:4–18), and demonstrate God's special care for individual male heroes of Israel's sacred history, including Abraham, Isaac, Jacob, Joseph, and Elijah (Gen 20:3–7, 31:10–13, 31:24, 37:9, 40:9–19, 46:2; I Kings 19:5).

By contrast, there is little biblical evidence of healing dreams. In I Kings 19:5–7, the angel wakes Elijah and then gives him food and drink to revive him; this could be construed as a healing *Wecktraum* in a loose sense. The reverse may be found in Job 4:15–21: if the purpose of this dream is to instill psychological terror in the dreamer, we may have a divinely-sent dream that brings suffering. Neither case is as clear cut, however, as the cases of ancient Near Eastern healing dreams. In addition, since the Hebrew Bible contains no dreams by women, there are no annunciation dreams to women. Instead, the annunciation dreams have been transmuted into promises of many descendants made to the patriarchs.

Summary of Biblical Dreams

In searching for influences on the dream traditions of Hellenistic Judaism, the most obvious source is the biblical dream traditions. This review of the dream traditions in the Hebrew Bible has demonstrated their general continuity with ancient Near Eastern dream traditions regarding form, vocabulary and thematic content. Biblical dreams relay knowledge about the future and sometimes are intended as prophecy for a larger audience. Just as many ancient Near Eastern dreams demonstrate the deity's sanction of male royalty, biblical dreams testify to God's special care for Israel and for the male characters central to Israel's sacred history, especially the patriarchs.

Biblical dreams do diverge in some important ways from the ancient Near Eastern traditions. The function of healing in dreams is attenuated in the Bible. There are no otherworldly dream journeys, nor any dreams of living or deceased persons. The typical dream messenger is the God of Israel, but no physical description is provided. Strikingly, there are also no female dreamers, no genuine annunciation dreams, and no female dream interpreters. Interpretation becomes a male action that results in the rise of the interpreter's social position, as in the cases of Joseph and Daniel. Annunciation dreams are transmuted into the covenantal promises made to the patriarchs, even when they concern extraordinary conception by the matriarchs.

There are some examples of biblical dream incubation. Like ancient Near Eastern dream incubation, these episodes presuppose the idea that particular spaces, especially temples, are places in which contact with the divine is more easily attainable. However, the incubatory ritual is not complex and does not include typical ancient Near Eastern practices such as fasting, mourning, sacrifice, or eating certain foods.

The idea that dreams are communications with the divine realm that foretell the future takes on special contours in light of biblical prophecy. Since attitudes towards divination differ amongst biblical sources, including between Judahite and Ephraimite prophetic traditions, dream revelation may be viewed as genuine prophetic revelation (Num 22, 1Sam 3, Dan 7–8, Joel 2:28–29) or, conversely, may be viewed with suspicion, associated with pagan divination, false prophecy, or prophecy of a lower caliber than Mosaic-type prophecy. However, there is no clear rejection of the concept that the God of Israel sometimes communicates to men through dreams.

CHAPTER TWO

DREAMS IN GREECE AND ROME

> Now it occurred to the grey-eyed goddess Athena
> to make a figure of dream in a woman's form –
> Iphthimê ... So, passing by the strap-slit through the door,
> the image came a-gliding down the room
> to stand at her bedside and murmur to her ...
>
> —Odyssey 4.848–855[1]

The investigation in Chapter One demonstrated remarkable agreement in the forms, vocabulary, social milieu and functions of divinely sent dreams in the ancient Near Eastern sources, including the Hebrew Bible. As we turn to the Graeco-Roman world, understandings of dreams become more diversified, with Greek philosophy giving rise to an enduring skepticism concerning the divine origin of dreams. However, in those sources that do accept the notion of divinely-sent dreams, we again find continuity in dream forms, vocabulary and functions. In addition, certain important literary innovations arise that bear on our later discussion of dreams in Hellenistic Judaism, particularly the Greek motif of the *oneiros*, the dream messenger of the gods, and the Latin development of the otherworldly dream journey. The social setting of dreaming also takes on new contours in the Hellenistic world, as the phenomena of dream incubation and interpretation explode in popularity.

In the sections that follow I continue to sketch the antecedent and contemporary dream traditions of Hellenistic Judaism by applying Oppenheim's classifications to a selective but broad sampling of Greek and Roman dreams. I attend both to literary sources, including poetry and prose, and to cultic sources. Since Greek and Roman dreams are not the focus of my study, I do not attempt an exhaustive survey, but rather employ a synchronic approach that notes formal patterns, vocabulary, important motifs, and attitudes towards dreaming. The Greek and

---

[1] From the translation by R. Fitzgerald, *Homer: The Odyssey* (New York: Vintage Books, 1990), 76.

Roman literary sources for dreams are vast, encompassing epic, short poems, drama, comedy, histories, philosophy, and scientific and medical writings. Moreover, cultic evidence of dream interpretation and incubation, including Artemidorus' dream-books and archaeological and epigraphic remains, provides an important window into how ordinary citizens understood dreams, shedding further light on the social dimensions of dreams in terms of societal stratification, gender and functions.

DREAMS IN ANCIENT GREECE

Classifications of Dreams in Greek Poetry

Although Oppenheim's classifications of dreams have been adopted almost universally by those working on ancient Near Eastern and biblical dreams, they have not attracted the attention of scholars working with Greek and Roman materials. Thus, a survey of other classification systems proposed for Greek dreams is in order.

J. Hundt's early study on Homeric dreams divides them into the categories of *Innenträume* and *Aussenträume*, according to their origin from within or without the psyche.[2] This division has rightly been criticized as imposing modern views on antiquity since Homer does not distinguish between dreams on this basis.[3]

Alfred Wikenhauser proposed a complex system of classification of Greek dreams, as follows: 1) symbolic message dreams, 2) non-symbolic message dreams announcing fortune or the reverse, 3) dreams in which deities speak about the neglect of their cult, 4) deities who appear in order to give messages, 5) deceased persons who appear, 6) frightening dreams, 7) warning dreams and 8) Christian dreams that reveal the divine will.[4] Since they are not clearly based on either form or content, these categories prove awkward and inadequate, particularly as they unnecessarily lump all Christian dreams together.

---

[2] For Hundt, the *Innenträumen* include *Il.* 2.6ff.; *Il.* 23.65ff.; *Od.* 4.795ff.; *Od.* 6.20ff.; the *Aussenträumen* include *Il.* 22.199ff.; *Od.* 19.535ff.; *Od.* 20.87ff. J. Hundt, *Der Traumglaube bei Homer*, 11, 43.

[3] For criticism see Kessels, *Studies on the Dream*, 3, n.8.

[4] A. Wikenhauser, 'Die Traumgesichte des Neuen Testaments in religionsgeschichtlicher Sicht,' in *Pisciculi: Studien zur Religion und Kulture des Altertums* (eds. T. Klauser and A. Rücker; Münster: Aschendorff, 1939), 325–332; see R. Gnuse, *Josephus*, 103.

R.G.A. van Lieshout has proposed the division of Greek dreams into passive/enstatic, active/ecstatic, and subjective dreams.[5] These categories stem from a consideration of the dreamer's point of view. Thus, a passive/enstatic dream is one in which:

> a. dream and dream-apparition coincide; b. the dream announces itself as 'genuine,' 'in the flesh'; c. the terminology for coming, standing and going is local and anthropomorphic; d. the message is conveyed orally, by means of words; e. the dream often leaves an 'apport' behind … f. the dream is primarily a visual perception and this takes place in a sort of border-region between waking and sleeping; e.g. it is impressed upon the dreamer that he is asleep.[6]

His criteria for this dream type emphasize the relative *passivity* of the dreamer, in contrast to the *activity* of the dream itself, which consists of a theophany of a dream-being who imparts a revelatory message (i.e., Oppenheim's 'message dream'). Van Lieshout uncritically lumps symbolic dreams within the general discussion on the passive/enstatic dream. Although the dreamers of both message and symbolic dreams are relatively 'passive,' the content of such dreams is sufficiently differ-ent to warrant a distinction, which Van Lieshout never makes. Another difficulty arises in the slippery slope between the 'subjective dream' in which the dreamer engages in dialogue and then action in the dream,[7] and 'passive dreams' in which these activities also occur.[8]

As an alternative, Kessels proposes the division of Greek dreams into two categories: allegorical/symbolic dreams, and message-dreams (or 'theorematical dreams,' from Artemidorus, i.e. those consisting of direct revelations).[9] Kessels' categories also need further clarification. He dis-tinguishes between the 'allegorical dream' and the 'symbolic dream' by stating that the former is a 'direct fabrication by some author' the 'constituent parts [of which] are closely connected with, in fact depen-dent on, the situation,' whereas the latter 'has an existence of its own in that the symbolism of the constituent parts remains valid whatever the actual situation.'[10] Kessels' distinction is highly inadequate, in that it is difficult to imagine the case in which a symbolic dream in Greek

---

[5] Van Lieshout, *Greeks on Dreams*, 12–33.

[6] Ibid., 13.

[7] Ibid., 33–34.

[8] Van Lieshout himself acknowledges this problem, *Greeks on Dreams*, 33–34.

[9] Kessels, *Studies*, 3.

[10] Ibid., 168, n. 9.

literary sources might *not* represent the creation of an author; even
Herodotus highly stylizes purportedly real dreams according to literary
conventions.

The systematic overviews of Greek and Roman dreams found in
John Hanson's foundational article on dreams in early Christianity and
Gnuse's monograph on dreams in Josephus are much more helpful.[11]
Although these two studies are exemplary in many ways, I hope to
improve on some deficiencies in their approaches and systems of classi-
fication in a cross-cultural context.

As Hanson's title indicates, his article conflates dreams and visions;
noting that terminology for dreams and visions is sometimes inter-
changeable, he concludes the two are practically indistinguishable.[12] His
caution is well-taken, yet there *are* instances in which authors take pains
to note that a visionary episode either occurs in sleep *or* in a waking
state, as in the following example from the *Oxyrhynchus Papyri* XI, 1381
(lines 91–145):

> ... she perceived—*it was no dream or sleep* (οὖτ᾽ ὄναρ οὖθ᾽ ὕπνός), for her
> eyes were open immovably, though not seeing clearly, for a divine and
> terrifying vision came to her, easily preventing her from observing the
> god himself or his servants, whichever it was.

Precisely for this reason, my approach seeks to identify the part of the
visionary spectrum that explicitly connects revelatory episodes to the
common occurrence we call dreaming.

Hanson's form-critical divisions of dreams and visions accord well
with some of Oppenheim's: 1) his 'audio-visual dream-vision
proper' with Oppenheim's message dream, 2) the 'auditory dream-
vision proper' with the auditory message dream, and 3) the 'visual
dream-vision proper' with the symbolic dream.[13] However, for the purposes of a broad cross-cultural examination, some difficulties arise with
Hanson's descriptions, based as they are on sensory reception. Symbolic dreams often contain sounds, voices, and, in early Jewish dreams,
an angelic dream interpreter who often appears and speaks. This makes
the distinction between 'audio-visual' and 'visual dream-vision proper'
quite difficult. Also, the *Wecktraum* and psychological status dream do
not neatly fit any of Hanson's three categories, but are important dream
types in the Graeco-Roman world.

---

[11] Hanson, 'Dreams and Visions'; Gnuse, *Josephus*.
[12] Hanson, 'Dreams and Visions,' 1408.
[13] Ibid., 1410–1413.

R. Gnuse's superb treatment of dreams in Josephus, which includes an examination of Graeco-Roman dreams, is distinguished by his attention to ancient Near Eastern dreaming and to Oppenheim's magnum opus. Gnuse notes that Hanson's three categories somewhat parallel his own, which in turn draw on Oppenheim's and include: 'dream image dream reports, auditory message dream reports and visual symbolic dream reports.'[14] For the purposes of this study, I again note the absence of the *Wecktraum* and psychological status dreams, but otherwise have little quarrel with Gnuse's system.

Overall, I submit that Oppenheim's classifications of the message dream, (including sub-types of the *Wecktraum* and auditory message dream), the symbolic dream, and the psychological status dream accurately classify the range of Greek dreams, illuminate important form-critical elements, and permit appropriate cross-cultural assessments.

Oppenheim's Classifications of Dreams and Greek Poetry

All of Oppenheim's classifications of dreams except the auditory message dream appear in Homer. *The Iliad* and *The Odyssey* contain message dreams (*Il.* 10.496–497; *Od.* 4.795 ff., 6.19 ff.), *Wecktraümen* (*Il.* 2.1 ff., 23.62 ff., 24.678 ff.; *Od.* 20.30), a symbolic dream (*Od.* 19.534 ff.), and psychological status dreams (*Il.* 22.200; *Od.* 20.87).[15]

Other Greek poets replicate Homeric dream patterns, with the ancient Near Eastern style auditory message dream again missing.[16] Apollonius Rhodius' *Argonautica*, a Homeric style epic, contains Medea's psychological status dream (3.616–635) as well as the symbolic dreams of Circe (4.663–672) and Euphemus (4.1731–1745). Callimachus' *Aetia* contains an important *soul journey*, in which the poet is transported in a dream to Mt. Helicon, where he converses with the Muses.[17] Dreams or important descriptions of dreams also occur in Hesiod (*Theog.* 211–225); Sappho (fr. 63, 134); Alcaeus (fr. 406, 444); Alcman (fr. 1.49, 47); Pindar (*Ol.* 13.61–80, *Pyth.* 4.156–165, 8.95–100); and Herodas 8.[18]

---

[14] Gnuse, *Josephus*, 107.

[15] Compare the outline provided by Kessels, which nicely matches Oppenheim's pattern. Kessels, *Studies*, 134–135.

[16] I have not found a clear example of an auditory message dream in Greek literature. Hanson proposes it is not a genuine type, but results from an author failing to mention the visual component. Hanson, 'Dreams and Visions,' 1410–1411.

[17] This dream inspires Ennius. See G.O. Hutchinson, *Hellenistic Poetry* (Oxford: Clarendon Press, 1988), 43 ff., 237, 278–279.

[18] For a more detailed survey of the Greek and Roman dream materials see Frances

The false generalization is often made that tragedies lack Homeric type message dreams and contain only symbolic dreams.[19] In fact, however, a message dream occurs in Euripides (*Hec.* 1–97, cf. 702–706) and there are references to message dreams in both Aeschylus (*Prom. Bound* 645–657) and Euripides (*Orestes* 618–620; *Alcestis* 349–356). A classic *Wecktraum* also occurs in Aeschylus' *Eumenides* 94–178. However, the tragedians do mostly depict symbolic dreams of women, as follows: Aeschylus (*Pers.* 176–230; *Cho.* 520–550; *Eum.* 94–178), Euripides (*Iph. Taur.* 42–64; *Hec.* 87–97), and Sophocles (*Electra* 410–425; message dream containing a symbolic dream). Euripides' *Rhesus* 780–789 is an exception, since a male sees a symbolic dream.

In comedy, Aristophanes reveals through parody his familiarity with psychological status dreams (*Nub. 1*-35), message dreams (*Eq.* 1012ff., 1090ff.; *Ran.* 1331–1344), and symbolic dreams (*Vesp.* 13–54). He also mocks the incubation oracle of Asklepios, discussed below (*Plut.*).[20]

Typical Vocabulary and Patterns of Message and Symbolic Dreams in Greek Poetry

No verbs are used for 'dreaming' until Plato. Homer uses the nominal terms τὸ ὄναρ, ὁ ὄνειρος, τὸ ὄνειρον and τὸ ἐνύπνιον, and these are standard in Greek sources thereafter.[21] Each term refers to a thing or vision seen in sleep and not to a waking vision, e.g.: οὐκ ὄναρ ἀλλ᾽ ὕπαρ ἐσθλόν (*Od.* 19.547, cf. 29.90).[22]

In Homeric and other Greek message and symbolic dreams, the INTRODUCTION usually consists of references to sleep or night. In the message dream, a divine dream messenger of the gods, an *oneiros*, comes or stands by the head of the dreamer (στῆ δ᾽ ἄρ᾽ ὑπὲρ κεφαλῆς) and relays a message (*Il.* 2.20; cf. 10.496).[23] The CONCLUSION of the dream stresses the materiality of the dream messenger, often describing

Flannery-Dailey, 'Standing at the Heads of Dreamers: A Study of Dreams in Antiquity' (Ph.D. diss., The University of Iowa, 2000), 78–123.

[19] Messer, *Dream in Homer*, 65, n. 253; Kessels, *Studies*, 200. In his list of passive dreams, Van Lieshout lists only Aeschylus' *Eumenides* 94–178 as a passive dream (i.e. a message dream) in the tragedians, Van Lieshout, *Greeks on Dreams*, 13–14.

[20] Aristophanes mocks the concept of mantic dreams in general (*Eq.* 809–810; *Vesp.* 121, 1039–1042, 1218; *Ran.* 48–52). See also *Vesp.* 90–94 for a possible reference to the soul journey.

[21] Kessels, *Studies*, 186–195, 198; see Hanson's thorough list of terms for dreams and visions in Greek poetry and prose, 'Dreams and Visions,' 1408, n. 51.

[22] 'ὄναρ,' 'ὄνειρος,' 'ὄνειρον,' and 'ἐνύπνιον,' LSJ 1230–1231.

[23] Kessels, *Studies*, 199.

its departure in terms of wind.[24] In a symbolic dream such as Penelope's dream of the eagle and the geese, the body of the dream consists of visual symbols and no clear dream message, with an INTERPRE-TATION following the CONCLUSION (*Od.* 19.535).[25] Both message and symbolic dreams make a profound psychological and/or physical impact on the dreamer, whose reactions upon awakening are described in detail, ranging from a strange calm (*Od.* 4.840) and joy (*Od.* 20.87–90) to bewilderment (*Od.* 6.49–50) or amazement (*Il.* 23.101).[26]

In Homer, the FULFILLMENT of the dream normally follows the dream itself. In some cases this fulfillment takes place when the dream-er acts as the dream messenger has directed, for example when Nau-sicaa obeys the dream's instructions to take her laundry to the river to be washed (*Od.* 6.57ff.). In other cases the fulfillment occurs over the course of the plot, as when Telemachus returns home safely after the dream has promised Penelope he would (*Od.* 4.824ff.). A strange instance of the fulfillment of a dream transpires when King Rhesus dreams that Diomedes is standing over him, just as Diomedes slays him in his sleep like an 'evil dream' (*Il.* 10.496ff.).[27] In that instant, the dream world and the waking world merge into one reality.

A compact example from Pindar illustrates the Greeks' familiarity with numerous dream features already discussed in relation to the ancient Near East and the Bible. In Pindar's *Olympian Ode* 13.61–80, Athena gives Bellerophon a golden bridle, saying, 'Are you asleep, prince of Aiolo's race?' (13.67).[28] This greeting is typical of a message dream that is also a *Wecktraum*. Upon awakening, Bellerophon 'leapt to his feet' and picked up the bridle that remained in his waking world (13.72–73). This is a classic example of the *dream token* left behind that 'really' exists in the waking world, beautifully illustrating the *shifting borderline between dream-world and waking-world* present in Greek dreams.

This passage may also shed light on similar cultural settings of dreams in Greece and the ancient Near East, since after his dream Bellerophon immediately seeks out the local seer, attesting to the impor-tance of receiving the proper *interpretation* of dreams (13.73–77). More-

---

[24] Kessels, *Studies*, 143–144.
[25] Ibid., 93–94.
[26] Ibid., 151.
[27] Ibid., 44–49.
[28] *Pindar* (Loeb; ed. and trans. W.H. Race; Cambridge, MA: Harvard University Press, 1997); Oppenheim, *Interpretation*, 189.

over, Bellerophon declares he saw the dream while he 'slept the night on the goddess' altar' (75–77), testifying to knowledge of temple *incubation*. Finally, this incubation was done 'at the bidding of that seer's oracle,' which commands him to make sacrifices to the gods, testifying to the *interdependency of dreams and other forms of Greek divination and religion*.

Literary Motifs of Dreams in Greek Poetry

The Oneiros

In Greek literary dreams, the gods often send a dream messenger, the *oneiros*, who comes to the dreamer and imparts a message.[29] The *oneiros* is a liminal being, traversing the boundaries between dream-world and waking-world, spirit and matter. Kessels notes that the meaning of the term *oneiros* in Homer '[ranges] from almost total deification to a mere psychic state,' encompassing the ideas of 'dream-figure,' 'dream-experience,' 'dream' as a (mythical) being, and perhaps, 'god of dreams.'[30] These semantic meanings evoke the concept of the ^{d}*Zaqīqu*, a Mesopotamian god of dreams who is also 'spirit' and 'wind.'[31] However, the substance of the *oneiros* is something between solid matter and airy phantom. On the one hand, it is likened to wind, moves from heaven and earth, and passes through bolted doors; on the other it must fit through keyholes, is a 'black-winged phantom of night,'[32] and stands by the heads of dreamers. Message dreams are sometimes said to be marked by ἐνάργεια, as in the phrase 'ὥς οἱ ἐναργὲς ὄνειρον ἐπέσσυτο' (*Od.* 4.841).[33] Van Lieshout maintains the term conveys the idea that the ὄνειρος is 'real,' 'bodily,' and 'in the flesh.'[34]

---

[29] E.g. *Il.* 2.1 ff., 10.496–497, 23. 62 ff., 24.682–689; *Od.* 4.795 ff., 6.19 ff.

[30] Messer, *Dream in Homer*, 8–9, 108; Messer calls the *oneiros* a 'genuine dream daimon,' *Dream in Homer*, 7–8. Kessels arranges the understanding of *oneiros* from 'almost total deification to a mere psychic state' in the following order: *Il.* 2.8; *Od.* 24.12; *Od.* 19.562; *Il.* 2.56; *Il.* 2.80; *Il.* 5.150; *Od.* 6.49; *Od.* 4.841; *Od.* 20.87; *Il.* 22.199. Kessels, *Studies.*

[31] *CAD* Z 21:58–61.

[32] Euripides, *Hec.* 31–32, 702–706; cf. Aristophanes, *Ran.* 1331–1344. Other references in Homer include *Od.* 6.21, 4.801–803, 838; *Il.* 2.20, 23.68; Kessels, *Studies*, 155–162; Messer, *Dream in Homer*, 3, 7, 10, 24–25.

[33] Van Lieshout, *Greeks on Dreams*, 16

[34] Ibid., 16.

In fact, in Greek literary dreams, the god or *oneiros* disguises itself as an *eidolon* or image of a person.[35] This device first appears in Homer.[36] The *oneiros* generally takes on the guise of someone familiar to the dreamer, such as Nestor (*Il.* 219), Iphthime (*Od.* 4.795 ff.), or Dymas' daughter (*Od.* 6.19). The logic behind the convention of disguise, particularly of someone known to the dreamer, is apparently to soften the impact of the divine world meeting the human realm.[37]

The dreamer herself dwells in a liminal state, which van Lieshout calls the 'visual borderland-experience' of Greek dreams.[38] He explains, 'Though the nature of the perception seems much closer to the dream-perception than to the waking experience, it seems to differ from both.'[39] This paradox is captured in the *Odyssey* when Penelope, 'slumbering sweetly in the gates of dream,' speaks with the *oneiros* who is really in her room, having slipped in through the doorbolt (*Od.* 4.801 ff.). Van Lieshout notes that this strange 'reality-awareness of dreams' is marked by the use of δοχεῖν, a term first found in *Odyssey* 20.93, which thereafter frequently introduces Greek dreams in both literature and cultic epigraphic evidence.[40]

The figure of the *oneiros* represents a distinct departure from ancient Near Eastern dreams in which gods themselves typically figure as messengers. Even in the Bible the messenger is usually said to be Yahweh and not an angel. By contrast, as will become evident, in early Jewish message dreams an angel almost always appears who acts as guide, interpreter or messenger.

Greek Dreams and Death

To a much greater degree than in the ancient Near East, Greek poets and tragedians associate dreams with death. Hesiod's brief mention of dreams in the *Theogony* links dreams with the realm of death, darkness, and pain: 'And Night bare hateful Doom and black Fate and Death,

---

[35] Kessels, *Studies*, 158.

[36] Van Lieshout, *Greeks on Dreams*, 16. Somewhat similarly, angels are often not recognized initially in the biblical traditions. See Judges 13:3–21; Genesis 18:1 ff.; Tobit 5:4.

[37] By contrast, Patroclus' *psyche* appears to Achilles as himself to lament that his body has not received a proper burial because there is no need to disguise the non-divine (*Il.* 23.63 ff.).

[38] Van Lieshout, *Greeks on Dreams*, 24–27.

[39] Ibid., 24.

[40] Ibid., 26.

and she bare Sleep and the tribe of Dreams' (*Theog.* 211–213).[41] In
Homer the land of dreams and the tribe of dreams are located near
Hades (*Od.* 24.12), recalling the underworld source of some ancient
Near Eastern dreams. Another expression of the association between
dreams and death occurs in a *Wecktraum* in which Patroclus' ψυχή
appears in a dream to Achilles and complains that his body has not
received a proper burial (*Il.* 23.62 ff.).[42] The ψυχή resembles an *oneiros*,
taking the customary stance at Achilles' head and waking him with the
formulaic question, 'Are you sleeping ... Achilles?' before vanishing like
a wisp of smoke (*Il.* 23.69, 99).

Homer and Hesiod's association of death with dreams had a last-
ing influence on the tragedians, who frequently portray the shades
of deceased people as dream messengers. Rare in the ancient Near
East and absent in the Bible, these dreams of the dead represent
a new accent. In Sophocles' *Electra*, Agamemnon's shade appears to
Clytaemnestra in a dream (410–425), and in Euripides' *Hecuba* the
ghost of Polydorus hovers around his mother's head for three nights
(1–97). A deceased Agamemnon appears to Electra in *Orestes* (618–620),
and Admetus hopes to receive dreams of his deceased wife in *Alcestis* (349–356). Aeschylus' *Eumenides* contains a striking dream of death:
Clytaemnestra's ghost appears to the sleeping Furies and rebukes them
by inquiring how they can sleep while the grievous injustice of her
death goes unavenged (94–104; cf. 155).[43] This episode connects death
and dreams on several layers, for the Furies themselves are the chthonic
goddesses who avenge matricides (74–78; 120–178).

Yet another variation on the association between tragic dreams and
death is expressed in the theme of foreseeing death in a dream, as
when Xerxes' mother sees his death in a symbolic dream (Aeschylus,
Pers. 175–200). Several dreams in Herodotus predict a person's death
and are interwoven with the motif that the fate is inescapable (*Hist.* I.
34–45, 209; III. 124–125; V. 55–6).[44]

A comedic passage in *Frogs* demonstrates by way of parody how
deeply ingrained was the association of dreams and death in Greek

---

[41] Moreover, the siblings of Dreams include Blame, Woe, the Destinies, Nemesis,
and Age (*Theog.* 211–225).
[42] Kessels, *Studies*, 53–58.
[43] For the rebuke in Homer, see Kessels, *Studies*, 134, 141.
[44] P. Frisch, *Die Träume bei Herodot*, 28–35.

thought. The dream contains exaggerated and comical references to night, death, and the gory oneiric world:

> What vision of dreaming, Thou fire-hearted Night,
> Death's minion dark-gleaming, Hast thou sent in thy might?
> And his soul was no soul, and the Murk was his mother,
>   a horror to sight!
> Black dead was his robe, and his eyes all blood,
>   and the claws of him great;
> Ye maidens, strike fire and arise; Take pails to the well by the gate
> Yea, bring me a cruse of hot water, to wash off this vision of fate.
>
> (*Ran.* 1331–1344)[45]

The dream messenger is 'Death's minion'; moreover, he is so real that he steals the dreamer's rooster, giving rise to a florid prayer for vengeance (*Ran.* 1331–1344)!

Dreams in Greek Prose

A dichotomy exists in the attitudes of prose writers regarding dreams. On the one hand, the historian Herodotus frequently records dreams, and these dreams show continuity with the forms and functions of dreams in the Greek traditions examined thus far. In fact, the psychological status dream, the message dream, and the symbolic dream all appear in Herodotus.[46] Like Homer and the tragedians, Herodotus understands message dreams to be real visits by *oneiroi*. He also views message and symbolic dreams as mantic messages from the gods that should be trusted.

On the other hand, beginning in the 5th c. B.C.E., the pre-Socratic philosopher-scientists began to doubt the divine origin of dreams, and they sought to explain the dream experience in rational, physical, and scientific terms. This viewpoint continued to exert influence on subsequent philosophers and scientists, including Plato, Aristotle, and the physician-scientists such as pseudo-Hippocrates.

---

[45] Aristophanes, *Frogs* (trans. G. Murray; London: George Allen & Unwin Ltd., 1908, repr. 1946).

[46] Frisch also uses Oppenheim's formal criteria to examine dreams in Herodotus. Frisch, *Heredot*, 66–71.

Typical Vocabulary of Dreams in Greek Prose

Most Greek sources continue using the Homeric terms for 'dream' as a noun: τὸ ὄναρ, ὁ ὄνειρος, τὸ ὄνειρον and τὸ ἐνύπνιον.[47] Plato and Aristotle are the first to speak of 'dreaming' as a verb: ὀνειροπολέω (*Rep.* 534c; *Tim.* 52b; Ar. *Nu.* 15).[48] Aristotle and other later sources also use ἐνυπνιάζω (*Insom.* 459a21; *Somn.Vig.* 453b19).[49] The magical papyri speak of sending a dream or getting one sent, ὀνειροπομπέω,[50] and of dream revelations, ἡ ὀνειραιτησία.[51] Artemidorus, speaking of the actual dreams of persons seeking professional dream interpretation, distinguishes amongst five categories of dreams: 1) ὄνειρος, a puzzling dream, 2) ὅραμα, a prophetic vision, 3) χρηματισμός, an oracle, 4) ἐνύπνιον, a nightmare, and 5) φάντασμα, an apparition.[52] In the fourth century, Macrobius distinguishes between three kinds of dreams: the symbolic dream, the ὅραμα or vision, and the χρηματισμός oracle.[53] Overall the semantic ranges of meaning for 'dream' and 'dreaming' evoke associations with sleep, visions, divination and otherworldly appearances.

Herodotus

Herodotus records twenty accounts of dreamers, only three of whom are female (*Hist.* III. 124–125; VI. 69; VI. 131). Moreover, in these three cases, the dreams themselves pertain to male rulers. The lack of female dreamers hinges on the issue of authority since Herodotus is concerned with depicting international leaders, who are usually non-Greek males.

In the *Histories*, Xerxes' uncle Artabanus describes psychological status dreams or *Angsttraümen*: 'Those visions that rove about us in dreams are for the most part the thoughts of the day.'[54] This understanding of

---

[47] Kessels, *Studies*, 186–195, 198.

[48] 'ὀνειροπολέω,' LSJ, 1231.

[49] 'ἐνυπνιάζω,' LSJ, 579.

[50] E.g. *P. Mag. Lond.* 46.488; *P. Mag. Par.* 1.1869, 2077; *P. Mag. Berol.* 1.329; *P. Mag. Leid.* V.4.16; *P. Mag. Par.* 1.2500, 2.163; *P. Mag. Lond.* 121.916; *P. Mag. Leid.W.* 7.45; 'ὀνειροπομπέω,' LSJ, 1231.

[51] *P. Mag. Berol.* 1.329, *P. Mag. Par.* 1.2077, *P. Mag. Leid.*V.6.15, *P. Mag. Lond.* 121.222, 250; 'ὀνειραιτησία,' LSJ, 1231.

[52] See especially 1.1–7 and the introduction to Book 4; in R. White, *Artemidorus*, 7; see also Dodds, *Greeks and the Irrational*, 107.

[53] Ambrosius Aurelius Macrobius, *Commentary on the Dream of Scipio* (trans. H. Stahl; New York: Columbia University Press, 1952); Dodds, *Greeks and the Irrational*, 107.

[54] VII. 16. All quotations are from *Herodotus* (4 vols.; Loeb; trans. A.D. Godley;

dreams mirrors the modern view of dreams as an inner psychological experience and represents some departure from the 'evil dreams' of the ancient Near East, which reflect a person's cultic standing as well as the psychological and physiological status of the dreamer.[55]

However, Artabanus' attitude does not represent point of view in the *Histories* as a whole, which records at least twenty divinely-sent message and symbolic dreams.[56] A god appears once in a dream (II.141), gods send three dreams (I.45, 210; III.65), and gods send *oneiroi* in numerous dreams (I.34–45; II.139, 141; III.30; V.55–56; VI.69, 131; VII.12, 14, 17).[57]

The message dreams in Herodotus exhibit the typical pattern we have seen, as is illustrated by a passage in Book VII. 12:

> I. INTRODUCTION: it is night-time, Xerxes 'fell asleep' (κατύπνωσε)

> II. DREAM: 'then it would appear ... that in the night he saw this *vision*: (ὄψιν) ... *It seemed* (ἐδόκεε) to Xerxes that a tall and goodly man *stood* (ἐπιστάντα) over him and said ...'

> III. CONCLUSION: 'thus the vision spake, and *seemed to Xerxes to vanish away* (ἐδόκεε ὁ Ξέρξης ἀποπτάσθαι) ... when day dawned the king took no account of this *dream* (ὀνείρου) ...'

> IV. FULFILLMENT: worked out over the course of several dream visions

The usual formal elements present in message dreams of the ancient Near East and in the Greek poets are easily recognizable in Herodotus.[58] The INTRODUCTION establishes that it is night and that the dreamer is asleep. The dream itself consists of an epiphany of a divine dream figure, an anonymous man, described as 'tall and goodly' in typical ancient Near Eastern fashion.[59] The figure's appearance is introduced by a form of δοκέω and the figure is said to have *stood* over him (ἐπιστάντα). After relaying the message, a directive concerning divine sanction, the *oneiros* seems to vanish, as in Homer.[60] The CONCLU-

---

Cambridge, MA: Harvard, 1971; 1st ed. 1922).

[55] Oppenheim, *Interpretation*, 232; idem, 'Mantic,' 346.

[56] Frisch links the fact that gods do not appear as regularly in Herodotus as in Homer to a rise in rationalism. Frisch, *Heredot*, 48. However, compared to the philosophers, Herodotus is an ardent believer in divinely-sent dreams.

[58] Hundt, Frisch and others have noted the similarity of this dream with *Il.* 2.6. Frisch, *Heredot*, 14–15.

[59] The tall and handsome anonymous man appears in II.139; V.56; VII.12ff. See Frisch, *Heredot*, 50; Oppenheim, *Interpretation*, 189.

[60] Frisch labels this and other dreams 'Auftragsträume,' *Heredot*, 36–38, 53–54.

SION of the dream establishes that it is morning and provides an account of the dreamer's reaction.[61] Normally, Herodotus also skillfully interweaves the FULFILLMENT into the plot, stressing that the fate decreed in dreams is inescapable.

Xerxes' dreams provide a powerful illustration of several dream features noted in our investigation of ancient Near Eastern, biblical, and Greek poetic dreams.[62] In the dream of Xerxes outlined above, the messenger imparts a *divine directive* that Xerxes should not abort his plan to send an army against the Greeks (VII. 12). At first, Xerxes ignores the message (VII. 13), and thereafter he sees a second message dream that upbraids him severely (VII. 14). Although Xerxes 'took no account of [the first] dream,' the second dream appearance leaves him 'greatly affrighted by the vision' (VII. 15), demonstrating *the repetition* that underscores the veracity of divinely-sent dreams.

Next, in a passage that displays Herodotus' understanding of the reality of the dream visitation, Xerxes asks his uncle to pose in his clothes and to sleep in his bed, saying, 'Now if it be a god that sends the vision, and it be his full pleasure that there be this expedition against Hellas, that same dream will hover about you and lay on you the same charge as on me' (VII. 15). No other passage in Greek literature so aptly illustrates the view that *a dream messenger is a real being* and not a projection of a dreamer's mind. Since it possesses an objective reality and is known to visit that spot, Xerxes believes the *oneiros* can be tricked into relaying the same message to his uncle Artabanus. He in turn protests by saying that the majority of dreams are simply the result of a person's state of mind (VII. 16), but later concludes that if the dreams are indeed divinely sent, the dream figure is not so dumb as to be tricked. After Artabanus finally consents to Xerxes' plan the message dream does appear to him, and it indeed knows his identity (VII. 17).

Finally, the dream ends with the *oneiros* saying, 'But neither hereafter nor now shalt thou go scatheless for striving to turn aside that which must be' (VII. 17). Herodotus repeatedly stresses the theme that *the predictions of dreams should and must be trusted*, because this fate is unavoid-

---

[61] Frisch calls such a reaction 'ein psychologisch-nüchternes Gewand' and links this to a rise in rationalism. However, our survey of dreams in the ancient Near East, the Bible, and Greek literature has demonstrated a similar emphasis on the dreamer's reaction. Frisch, *Heredot*, 49–52.

[62] In light of Herodotus' emphasis on the fulfillment of dreams, Frisch labels several dreams 'Schicksalträume' (I.34, 107–108; II.139; III.30; VII.12–14, 17, 19), *Heredot*, 3–24.

able.[63] In fact, as a result of these three repetitive dreams, Xerxes follows the dream directive and thus fulfills the dream (VII. 19 ff.), whereupon he has a fourth confirmatory symbolic dream (VII. 19). When dreamers do attempt to avert a dream prediction, they almost inevitably fail.[64] In several of these cases, a misinterpretation of the dream's true meaning results in catastrophe for the dreamer since the dream is fulfilled regardless.[65] Thus, *proper interpretation* is crucial and the dream must be told to another person, often to professional Magis (ὀνει-ϱοπόλοι) of the ancient Near East (I.107, 108; 209; III.124–125; VI.107–108, 131; VII.19 ff.).[66]

Pre-Socratics

In stark contrast to the Greek poets and Herodotus, the Pre-Socratic philosopher-scientists doubted that dreams were communications from the divine world. Rather, as part of an overarching effort to rationalize myth, they sought to explain dreams, along with divination and oracles, in rational, physical, and psycho-physiological terms.[67]

The regular Greek terms for dreams (ὄνειϱος and ὄναϱ in the literary sources previously examined, and ἐνύπνιον and ὄψις in the cultic evidence treated later), do not appear in the extant fragments of Heraclitus. However, he does refer to knowledge gained while sleeping, which apparently connotes dreaming.[68] Heraclitus provides a biological explanation, postulating that dreams result when the senses are cut off from the exterior world during sleep and a person sees his 'inner walls,' which he mistakenly perceives to be reality.[69] The information gained in

---

[63] See Frisch, *Heredot*, 3–24, 64–65.

[64] I. 34–45, 107, 108, 209; III. 30,124–125. Only one exception does not record the failure that results from the attempt to dodge a dream predication, II. 139.

[65] For example, see the dream of Astyages in I.107–128. In Herodotus, not only are symbolic dreams misinterpreted, (I. 107, 108, 209) but message dreams, which normally contain clear and incontrovertible disclosures, are misinterpreted at least twice (I. 34–45; III. 30; possibly V. 55–56).

[66] Frisch distinguishes between 'allegorisch' and 'theorematisch' dreams, *Heredot*, 59–60.

[67] Although the reconstruction of the Pre-Socratics is tentative since they are preserved as scattered quotations in later ancient authors, enough remains of Heraclitus and Democritus to mark their divergence from traditional Greek attitudes on dreaming. G.S. Kirk and J.E. Raven, *The Presocratic Philosophers: A Critical History with a Selection of Texts* (Cambridge: Cambridge University Press, 1963), 1–3.

[68] Van Lieshout, *Greeks on Dreams*, 67.

[69] Ibid., 67–85; Heraclitus, 237 in Kirk, *Presocratic Philosophers*, 207. As Van Lieshout

sleep is unreliable and deceptive in that it is 'a private illumination that
supplants the real illumination of the Logos which is common to all.'[70]

The only resonance between Heraclitus' view of sleep and traditional Greek views is the association between death and sleep. However, while in the latter case this association is based on myth—for
instance, on the proximity of the land of dreams to Hades in Homer—
Heraclitus' conclusions are based on rational and physiological explanations. According to Heraclitus, sleep is a halfway point between
life and death in which a person's soul-fire is nearly extinguished.
The sleeper remains in contact with the exterior world only through
his breath, which acts against the watery state he acquires in sleep.[71]
Dreams are a light kindled in the night, when a person's 'vision is
extinguished.' Thus, '[the dreamer] is in contact with the dead, when
asleep.'[72]

Unlike Heraclitus, Democritus posits that dreams are caused by
external, objective phenomenon, the result of the action of atomic εἴδωλα particles that break off of objects and/or living beings, including
the gods, entering the body through the pores during sleep.[73] Dreams
may also be caused by residual εἴδωλα that enter the pores before sleep
and are later remembered as dreams.[74] These minute particles can ran-
domly combine in freakish images in dreams, or they can convey some
true knowledge of their source to the dreamer.[75] Since he maintains that
dream images ultimately stem from a physical source and are sometimes accurate reflections, particularly when the εἴδωλα come in great
numbers from tumid and heated bodies,[76] Democritus does not go as
far as his predecessor Xenophanes, who rejects the idea of divination
completely.[77] In fact, Democritus sometimes seems to speak of message

---

puts it, sleep and dreams form a 'closed monad of internal sensorial activity,' *Greeks and Dreams*, 85.

[70] Heraclitus, 197 (fr. 1), 198 (fr. 2), 237 in Kirk, *Presocratic Philosophers*, 187–188, 207–208.

[71] Kirk, *Presocratic Philosophers*, 208; Heraclitus, 232–234 (frags. 36, 118, 117) in Kirk, *Presocratic Philosophers*, 205.

[72] Heraclitus, 236 (fr. 26) in Kirk, *Presocratic Philosophers*, 207.

[73] Van Lieshout, *Greeks on Dreams*, 86–97

[74] Ibid., 86–97.

[75] Ibid., 88.

[76] Ibid., 97.

[77] A. Meijer, 'Philosophers, Intellectuals, and Religion in Hellas,' in *Faith, Hope and Worship: Aspects of Religious Mentality in the Ancient World* (ed. H.S. Versnel; Leiden: Brill, 1981), 216–263.

dreams: 'When they strike the recipient thus accompanied, they speak to him, as if they were alive, and report to him the thoughts, reasoning and impulses of those from whom they escape.'[78] However, these messages are not sent by the gods on purpose and their reception is affected by physical circumstances, such as the quality of air or by what the dreamer ate before sleep.[79] In the end it is clear that in his emphasis on the physiological causes of dreaming, Democritus is closer to Heraclitus than to Homer.

Plato and Aristotle

At times, Plato reflects the traditional ideas of the dream found in Homer and the playwrights; at other times he seems to partake of the rational, scientific approach towards dreaming found in the pre-Socratics. On the one hand, Plato mentions Socrates' belief in prophetic, divinely sent dreams; he even describes a prophetic message dream that portends the time of Socrates' death (*Apol.* 33c; *Phaed.* 60d–61c; *Crito* 44a-b; *Symp.* 202e–203a).[80] By contrast, however, Plato also provides rational, psycho-biological explanations for dreaming that suggest it is not a valid source of knowledge.

Somewhat like Heraclitus, Plato understands dreaming to be the result of the irrational part of the soul's perception of the motions of internal residues reflected off the smooth part of the liver (*Tim.* 46a, 52b-c). Thus, dreaming is for Plato an internalized process, rather than an external visit or message sent from the gods. Plato does credit God with making the liver the seat of divination (*Tim.* 70c–72b). However, while the possibility for divination in sleep is thus opened, Plato clearly derides such dream divination or prophecy as inferior to philosophical knowledge. It has 'no share in mind or reason' as it is only apprehended in an altered state and not by any man 'in his wits,' that is, not by any rational means. Thus, such prophecy is 'not to the wisdom, but to the foolishness of man' (*Tim.* 71c–72b). In fact, Plato explains, dream interpreters are necessary precisely because the dreamer cannot interpret his own dream 'while he continues demented' (*Tim.* 72a; cf. 571c–572b).[81]

---

[78] Plato, *Sympos.* VIII, 10.2.; Van Lieshout, *Greeks on Dreams*, 95.
[79] Van Lieshout, *Greeks on Dreams*, 97.
[80] Gallop, 'Dreaming,' 187–201.
[81] Cf. Gallop, 'Dreaming,' 188–189.

Plato's low view of dreaming also appears in his use of the dream as a metaphor to represent madness and disease (*Theaet.* 157e–158b, *Phileb.* 36e) as well as that which is unrealized, illusory, or unreal (*Theaet.* 208c, *Soph.* 266c, *Pol.* 278d, 290b, *Tim.* 52b-c, *Resp.* 576b, *Leg.* 746a, 969b).[82] Finally, Plato sometimes uses the concept of the dream as an epistemological metaphor for various states of inferior, irrational, or impermanent knowledge (*Symp.* 175e; *Theaet.* 190b; *Pol.* 277d; *Parm.* 164d; *Resp.* 414d).[83]

Even more than Plato, Aristotle disallows any possibility of divinely sent dreams, speaking of dreaming strictly in psycho-physiological terms. In three essays within the *Parva Naturalia*, 'De Somno et Vigilia,' 'De Insomniis,' and 'De Divinatione per Somnum,' Aristotle defines a dream as a wholly inner apparition (*phantasma)* that occurs during sleep (459a 19–20; 462a15).[84] Aristotle explains that sleep is a necessary psycho-physiological condition and dreaming is a by-product of that condition.[85] Sleep occurs in all animals and is the necessary incapacitation of the perceptual powers—the disabling of the primary sense-organ, the heart—which allows for active perception when awake (454a11–454b9; 455b2–13). It is brought on by the rising and falling of hot matter, such as happens after eating (456a30–456b28; 457a33-b6). Dreams occur when the movements arising from sense-impressions are perceived, somewhat like Plato's theory of the motion of internal residues (460b28–461a8):

> … the movements arising from sense-impressions, both those coming from outside/ and those from within the body, are present not only when people are awake, but also whenever the affection called sleep comes upon them, and that they are especially apparent at that time. For in the day-time, while the/ senses and the intellect are functioning, they are pushed aside or obscured … By night, however, owing to the inactivity of the special senses and their/ inability to function, because

---

[82] Gallop, 'Dreaming,' 190.

[83] Ibid., 187–201. Admittedly, the dream sometimes stands for an unrealized ideal and even for the *Republic* itself (*Charm.* 173a-c, *Resp.* 443b, 520c). However, this usage does not outweigh the clearly negative understanding of dreams outlined above. Gallop, 'Dreaming,' 194–201.

[84] D. Gallop, *Aristotle on Sleep and Dreams*, 9; *Aristotle*, vol. 8 (Loeb; 23 vols.; trans. W.S. Hett; Cambridge, MA: Harvard University Press, 1975). According to Gallop, although Aristotle states that the dream is 'daemonic' and 'not divine' (463b14–15) he seems to mean that, despite their uncanny character, dreams are not the workings of a divine agent. Gallop, *Aristotle*, 46.

[85] *Hylemorphism*, which views the soul and the body as inseparable, marks Aristotle's thought throughout *De Somno*. See Gallop, *Aristotle*, 19.

of the reversed flow of heat from the outer parts to the interior, they are carried inward to the starting point of perception, and become apparent as the disturbance subsides.

The information gotten through dreams is only a fragmented reflection of the source, and thus the job of a dream interpreter is to try to reconstruct the original source of the reflection (464b5).

As for the question of mantic dreaming, Aristotle explains that dreams that appear to come true may cause the events they portend (462b26, 463a21), may portend illness in the dreamer simply because medical conditions are more noticeable in sleep (463a3), or may simply be a coincidence (463a31). In fact, he believes the latter is the case with most cases of so-called dream-divination. Even when he admits the possibility of a rare precognitive dream, he explains the phenomenon in rational, physical terms. He likens dreams to ripples made in air or water that resemble the εἴδωλα particles theorized by Democritus:

> ... In this way it is possible that some sort of movement/ and perception reaches the souls of dreamers, coming from the objects whence Democritus derives his images and emanations. And wherever they arrive, they may be more perceptible at night, because those carried by day are more easily dissipated ... It would be these movements that cause appearances (*phantasmata*) from which people have previsions of what is going to happen ...   (463b31).

Moreover, Aristotle does not value such precognition since unlike philosophy *it does not come from God* and comes to random people, who in fact are not the most intelligent (464a19). Overall, then, it appears he does not believe dreams are divinely sent, nor that dream messengers really appear to people.

The rational, scientific approach to dreaming initiated by the pre-Socratics and continued by Plato and Aristotle desacralizes dreams and diminishes the value of the knowledge imparted through them. This denigration of dreams as a reliable source of knowledge continues in the Greek philosophical tradition, as exemplified by Aristotle's student Theophrastus. He equates the superstitious man with the one who trusts in dreams: 'Whenever he has a dream, he visits the dream analysts or the prophets or the omen-readers to ask to which god or goddess he should pray' (*Char.* 16.11).[86] Since the superstitious man is

---

[86] *Theophrastus, Herodas, Cercides and the Choliambic Poets* (Loeb; ed. and trans. J. Rusten; Cambridge: Harvard University Press, 1993), 48–166.

considered alongside such ignominious characters as the coward, the
shameless man, the obnoxious man, and the boor, Theophrastus' view
of dream divination is clearly derogatory.[87]

Physician-Scientists

The physician-scientists continue to explore rational, physiological explanations of dreaming. The author of *On the Sacred Disease* plainly states
that there is no divine cause behind dreams (ps. Hippocrates, *Morb.
Sacr.* 2.1–3).[88] Rather, the author explains that nightmares result from
the abnormal heating of the head by blood.[89]

Similarly, the author of *On Dreams*, an essay within the Hippocratic
or pseudo-Hippocratic *On Regimen*, provides an extensive physiological
explanation of dreaming.[90] This author believes the soul can function
independently of the body, and does so in sleep when it takes over the
activities of seeing, hearing, walking, touching, and so forth; this phenomenon is the cause of dreams (*On Reg.* IV.86). The author does seem
to consider the possibility of divine dreams, recommending professional
dream interpreters in this case (*On Reg.* IV.87), but he leaves the matter
uninvestigated. At the very least, this essay exhibits a shift from traditional, non-philosophical Greek views of dreaming in that divinely-sent
dreams garner little concern in comparison with dreams as a natural
physiological process.

Functions of Dreams in Greek Literature

As in the ancient Near East and Hebrew Bible, dreams in Greek poetry
and prose impart unusual *knowledge, healing* and *divine sanction* or their
opposites. However, there are some new accents.

Mantic knowledge of the future relayed in a dream often intertwines
with themes of death and/or murder, e.g.: Penelope learns of the Suit-

---

[87] *Theophrastus*, 48–166.
[88] H. Grensemann dates the essay to the last quarter of the fifth century B.C.E.,
Grensemann, *Die hippokratische Schrift 'Über die heilige Krankheit'* (Berlin: Walter de Gruyter,
1968), 18.
[89] Van Lieshout, *Greeks on Dreams*, 99–100.
[90] See 'Des Reves,' in R. Joly and S. Byl, *Hippocrates: Du Regime* (Berlin: Akademie,
1984), 219–231. The treatise stems from the late fifth or the early fourth century
B.C.E. Joly and Byl, *Hippocrates*, 49.

ors' future murder by Odysseus in the symbolic dream of the geese (*Od.* 19.534), Clytaemnestra foresees that Orestes will kill her in the symbolic dream of the suckling snake who bites her (*Cho.* 510–550), Xerxes sees his mother's death in a dream (*Pers.* 176–230) and Circe learns in a symbolic dream that a murder will consume her house, just as Jason and Medea come to visit (*Argon.* 3.616). Sometimes the dead visit dreamers to bring about remembrance of their own concerns, such as when Patroclus reminds Achilles that he has yet to be buried (*Il.* 23.62), or when Clytaemnestra spurs the Furies to avenge her matricide (*Eum.* 94–178).

In an unusual twist on the death theme, Admetus hopes for a dream of his deceased wife specifically for the sake of comfort, a type of *psychological healing* (Euripides, *Alc.* 349–356). This kind of healing is also in view in Penelope's dream of Iphthime (really an *oneiros)*, which Athena sent to soothe her (*Od.* 4.795). The concept that dreams are supposed to bring *physical healing* is mocked by Aristophanes in his parody of the Asklepios cult in *Plutus*, but is clearly part of popular religion.

Divine sanction and the withdrawal of divine sanction also function in new ways in Greek literature. Oftentimes the gods use dreams to manipulate those they favor or disfavor into fulfilling divinely decreed schemes. This is perhaps clearest in Homer, where dreams are obvious tools the gods use to affect human affairs, resulting in the destruction or salvation of whomever they choose. Using dreams, Zeus spurs Agamemenon to attack Troy (*Il.* 2.1), Hermes urges Priam to leave (*Il.* 24.678) and Athena places Nausicaa where she can meet Odysseus (*Od.* 6.19).[91] In each case, the humans are puppets of the divine as they act on dream messages to their appointed end.

In Herodotus' *Histories*, dreams function overwhelmingly to bestow *divine sanction or divine punishment* on male leaders. Several dreams illustrate the point by *imparting knowledge* to the dreamer of the future rule of another leader (I. 107, 108, 209; III. 30). Herodotus uses the motif of the annunciation dream, familiar in the ancient Near East as well as in Greece, to predict the future greatness of the child to be born: Pericles' mother dreams she gives birth to a lion, an overt symbol of Pericles (VI. 131) and the mother of Demaratus dreams that a hero, a deceased person of semi-divine status, comes to her in the guise of her husband, impregnates her, and leaves her a visible token of garlands

---

[91] Additional dreams of divine sanction include Euphemus' dream in the *Argonautica* 4.1731 and Bellerophon's dream in Pindar's *Olympian Ode* 13.61–80.

(VI. 69).[92] Whereas annunciation dreams are typically healing dreams in the ancient Near East, their overwhelming function here is to facilitate the divine sanction of a future, eminent, male child.

Finally, another new emphasis is belief in *psychological status dreams*. Although the fact was known in the ancient Near East that dreams may reflect the dreamer's state of mind, the theme gains new prominence in Greek epic poetry and tragedy. Medea's dreams in the *Argonautica* provide a sterling example: 'Dreams assailed her, deceitful dreams, the nightmares of a soul in pain.'[93] Psychological status dreams reflect the anxieties of the dreamer, but in strange ways they also seem to bring about the deserved fate of the dreamer and are therefore closely linked to the conveyance of divine sanction and knowledge.[94]

Social Milieu of Dreams in Ancient Greece

This typology of Greek dreams has shown both continuity and discontinuity with the dream traditions of the ancient Near East and the Bible. On the one hand, the Greek poets and historians display forms, functions and attitudes towards dreaming similar to those in the ancient Near Eastern and biblical sources. On the other hand, beginning in the fifth century B.C.E., there is a tendency in the philosophers and the physician scientists to disbelieve the divine source of dreams, which are newly explained in rational and biological terms. Skeptics such as Xenophanes dismiss all forms of divination, including mantic dreams, and Theophrastus places belief in divinely sent dreams firmly within the arena of superstition. However, although philosophy will continue to scorn the idea of divine messages through dreams, the dream cults soar in prestige in Hellenistic times, a phenomenon that I will investigate more fully at the close of this chapter.

In those literary sources that accept the divine provenance of dreams, we see some social contours that differ markedly from the ancient Near East and Israel with respect to gender. In fact, my examination overturns two widely held positions concerning gender and dreams in Greece. First, many Homeric scholars, including Hundt and Messer,

---

[92] See Frisch, *Heredot*, 42–46.
[93] *Argonautica* III.614–647; from Apollonius of Rhodes, *The Voyage of the Argo: The Argonautica* (trans. E.V. Rieu; London: Penguin, 1959, repr. 1971), 126.
[94] E.g. *Agam.* 880–885; *Nub.* 1–35; *Il.* 10.496, 22.200; *Od.* 14:590.

maintain that in the *Iliad* only men dream, while in the *Odyssey* only women dream.[95] This assertion is false, since in the *Odyssey*, Odysseus tells a story in which he fabricates having been sent a dream from the gods (*Od.* 14.495),[96] challenging the idea that men are not portrayed as dreamers in the *Odyssey*. Moreover, *Odyssey* 20.22–55 contains a complex passage which, by form-critical standards, describes the simultaneous dreams of Odysseus and Penelope.[97] Second, Van Lieshout and others have argued that from the *Odyssey* onward only women dream.[98] Such an imprecise statement ignores the obvious evidence in tragedy (*Rhesus* 780–789; *Alcestis* 349–356) and in Herodotus, who records seventeen males as having dreams.

What I do find is a striking gender division between poetry and prose when it comes to dreaming. Homer, Apollonius Rhodius, Aeschylus, Euripides, and Sophocles each portray women and men dreaming, and many women are given long and memorable dream scenes. By contrast, women are largely absent as dreamers in the prose of Herodotus, Diodorus Siculus, the Pre-Socratics, Plato, Aristotle, and the physician scientists. Although the subject matter of the *Histories* may account for some of this scarcity of female dreamers, this is not a wholly satisfactory explanation.

Since in reality everyone dreams,[99] the literary evidence sheds light on the social constructions of gender and dreaming. My understanding of the issue is shaped by two trends discussed in Chapter One: 1) female dreamers are absent in the Hebrew Bible, wherein dreams generally convey social power, and 2) the ancient Near Eastern sources generally maintain that women mainly see symbolic dreams, while men see clearer message dreams, which are more greatly esteemed. In Greek tragedy, there is also a marked tendency to associate symbolic dreams with women rather than men, e.g.: Aeschylus (*Pers.* 176–230; *Cho.* 520–

---

[95] Hundt, *Der Traumglaube*, 42, n. 7; Messer, *Dream in Homer*, 27–28.

[96] Kessels, *Studies*, 163.

[97] Odysseus' dream is a classic message dream of a disguised *oneiros*: 'it seemed to his heart that she knew him and was standing by his head' (*Od.* 20.90–93). Other factors secure the interpretation of the event as a dream: it occurs at dawn, the typical conclusion of a dream is present (namely, that Odysseus rose from his bed), and the episode occurs in close temporal proximity to Penelope's dream, suggesting the motif of simultaneous dreaming. See Wikenhauser, '*Doppelträume*,' 100–111; Alexander, 'Dreams in Pairs and Series,' 446–452; Oppenheim, *Interpretation*, 208.

[98] Messer, *Dream in Homer*, 65, n.253; Van Lieshout, *Greeks on Dreams*, 16; Kessels argues against this notion, *Studies*, 163–165.

[99] All mammals except the echidna dream.

550; *Eum.* 94–178), Euripides (*Iph. Taur.* 42–64; *Hec.* 87–97) and Sophocles (*El.* 410–425). There are exceptions where women appear to see
oneiroi,[100] but there is only one case where a male sees a symbolic
dream (Euripides, *Rhes.* 780–789). Given that most Greek prose represents philosophical and scientific concerns, I conclude that a societal
presumption again appears to be at work that links males with linear
rationality and females with non-rational, intuitive, associative forms of
knowing and modes of expression.

    Earlier I noted that Herodotus records twenty divinely-sent dreams
that convey divine sanction of males. These 'historical' dreams are
patently fictional to some degree, as their marked stylization betrays.
However, the Greek historian Diodorus Siculus, writing in Rome in
the 1st c. B.C.E., records an event that is particularly noteworthy for
the light it sheds on the ancient social function of dreams. Diodorus
describes the life of a Syrian slave by the name of Eunus who led a successful slave-revolt and was eventually named King of Sicily around 135
B.C.E.[101] Eunus 'had an aptitude for magic and the working of wonders' and 'claimed to *foretell the future by divine command, through dreams*'
(ἐξ ὀνείρων ἐμαντεύετο) (XXXIV/XXXV.2.5). Eventually, he claimed
that the Syrian goddess Atargatis appeared to him in an ἐπιφαινο-
μένην, a message dream or a vision, telling him that he should be
king (XXXIV/XXXV.2.7, cf. 2.6). Apparently, this divine sanction had
currency for other slaves, since Eunus was able to mobilize them to
revolt successfully (XXXIV/XXXV.2.14). Although Diodorus Siculus
himself does not accept Eunus' claims, sarcastically noting that 'of his
many improvisations [predictions] some by chance turned out true'
(XXXIV/XXXV.2.6), the slave revolt is an excellent example of the
way in which dreams of divine sanction could provide persons with
actual social authority. That these persons are normally males is noteworthy.

---

[100] In Aeschylus, *Prometheus Vinctus* 645–657, Io gives a classic description of message
dreams 'coming into my maiden chamber and exhorting with winning words.' In fact,
in *Eumenides* 94–178 the Furies have a collective message dream of Clytaemnestra,
containing a nested symbolic dream, ending in a *Wecktraum*.
[101] Diodorus of Sicily, Books XXXIV/XXXV (vol. XII; trans. F.R. Walton; London:
Heinemann, 1967).

Greek Dreams and Divination

As in ancient Near Eastern sources, Greek texts associate dreams with divination.[102] The first reference to dreams in Homer illustrates this well: 'let's ask a soothsayer or a priest or some interpreter of sacred dreams who can tell us why that god is angry ...' (*Il.* 1.62–65). The interconnectedness of Greek divinatory arts and dreams is nowhere better expressed in tragedy than in Prometheus' claim to have taught mortals all forms of divination:

> It was I who arranged all the ways of seercraft, and *I first adjudged what things come verily true from dreams*; and to men I gave meaning to the ominous cries, hard to interpret. It was I who set in order the omens of the highway and the flight of crooked-taloned birds, which of them were propitious or lucky by nature ... also I taught of the smoothness of the vitals and what color they should have to pleasure the Gods and the dappled beauty of the gall and the lobe ... It was I who made visible to men's eyes the flaming signs of the sky that were so dim.
>
> (Aeschylus, *Prom. Vinc.* 480–505)

Prometheus claims to be the teacher of the interpretation of mantic dreams as well as of seercraft, omina, augury, extispicy, hepatoscopy, and astrology.

Apotropaic rituals figure prominently in the dreams of several tragedies. When one received an unwanted message in a dream or a negative interpretation of a symbolic dream, one would make libations, offerings, and prayers to the gods, Earth, or the dead, in order to avoid any negative consequences (Aeschylus, *Agam.* 998–1000; *Cho.* 525–551; cf. 37–41; *Pers.* 200–205, 214ff., 520ff., *Prom. Vinc.* 660; Sophocles, *El.* 405–410; Euripides, *Iphig. Taur.* 60–65, *Hec.* 87–89, 709–711). Clytaemnestra therefore makes a sacrifice to Apollo, praying: 'Grant, Lycian lord, that if the visions in two dreams that I saw last night are favourable, they may be accomplished, but if they are inimical, send them back upon my enemies!' (Sophocles, *El.* 645–647).

In Herodotus, some dreams occur in conjunction with oracles (II.139, VI.118), and there is at least one attestation of incubation, a type of divination. In that account, King Sethos of Egypt, who was also a priest of Hephaestus, 'went into the temple shrine and there bewailed to the god's image the peril which threatened him. In his lamentation

---

[102] J. Pollard, 'Divination and Oracles: Greece,' in *Civilization of the Ancient Mediterranean: Greece and Rome* (2 vols.; eds. M. Grant and R. Kitzinger; NY: Charles Scribner's Sons, 1988), 2:941–950.

he fell asleep, and dreamt that he saw the god standing over him …' (II. 141).[103] Herodotus also describes the incubation oracles of Trophonius and Amphiaros (I. 46, 49, 52, 92; IV. 172, VIII.133), and Aristophanes mocks the cult of Asklepios in *Plutus*, thereby showing his familiarity with its workings.

Summary of Dreams in Ancient Greece

My use of Oppenheim's classifications has illuminated both continuities and ruptures with ancient Near Eastern and biblical dream traditions. Attention to formal patterns demonstrates that even records of purportedly 'historical' dreams in Herodotus and Diodorus Siculus follow highly standardized patterns that accord well with Greek literary dreams, as well as with dreams in ancient Near Eastern and biblical sources. However, differences also emerge. Fewer gods appear in Greek dreams than in ancient Near Eastern and biblical dreams, and when they do appear, they are in disguise. More often, they are replaced by the spirits of the dead and by the *oneiroi*, winged, semi-material intermediaries who bridge the divine and human realms and who also often appear disguised. Only rarely does the dreamer move; the otherworldly journey is not a prominent theme except in Callimachus. Also, the auditory message dream, so important in Hittite sources, is rare or absent.[104]

Generally, dreams in both poetry and prose function to relay unusual knowledge, healing or divine sanction, and they tend to uphold societal constructions of gender roles. Women dream in murky ways, while men dream clear messages from the gods that function to increase male power. Dreams may also inflict torment and divine punishment and are oftentimes tools of the gods to manipulate humans' fate. Belief in psychological status dreams increases in prominence, but is not necessarily incompatible with belief in divinely decreed fate or even in divinely-sent dreams. Finally, the pre-Socratics initiate an enduring

---

[103] The comfort the god provides Sethos leads Frisch to label this a 'Beruhigungstraum,' *Heredot*, 39–41.

[104] Oppenheim, *Interpretation*, 193. As his only example of a possible Greek auditory dream report, R. Gnuse mentions the case of Zoilos of Aspendos. A letter from 257 B.C.E. mentions that in a *chrematismos* Sarapis directs a Ptolemaic finance minister, Zoilos, to erect his temple and establish his cult. R. Gnuse, *Josephus*, 109; Gregor Weber, 'Traum und Alltag in hellenistischer Zeit,' *ZRGG* 50, 1 (1998): 22–39.

skepticism towards the entire idea of divinely-sent dreams, influencing the philosophers, later scientists and physicians, urging them to find psychological and physiological causes for dreaming.

DREAMS IN ANCIENT ROME

A fitting metaphor for the influence of Greek dream traditions on Latin literature is Ennius' dream in which he learns that Homer has been reincarnated in him, thereby enabling him to write in the personage of Homer for the glory of Rome.[105] Roman culture was in many respects an appropriation and transformation of Greek culture, and this is readily apparent in Latin dream texts.[106] Oppenheim's classifications are mirrored in Latin counterparts, including psychological status dreams, message dreams, *Wecktraümen*, symbolic dreams, and even a few auditory message dreams.[107] Greek innovations also appear, including the *oneiroi* and deceased shades who serve as dream messengers. The Greek philosophers' rational suspicion towards divinely-sent dreams is manifest as well. Since the Latin traditions follow the Greek ones so closely, I provide only a brief, selective sketch of Latin literary dreams from the third century B.C.E. through the second century C.E., a period roughly contemporaneous with the early Jewish texts of Chapter Three, concentrating my attention on new emphases in the Roman dream tradition such as the otherworldly journey. I then turn to the social milieu of dreaming in the Graeco-Roman world, including the practices of interpretation and incubation.

---

[105] O. Skutsch, *The Annals of Q. Ennius* (Oxford: Clarendon Press, 1985), 147; *Cambridge History*, 60; *Annals*, lines 2–10 in *Remains of Old Latin: Ennius and Caecilius* (Loeb; 3 vols.; ed. and trans. E.H. Warmington; MA: Harvard University Press, 1935, repr. 1956), I:5.

[106] This idea is captured in the phrase '*Graecia capta ferum uictorem cepit*,' or 'captive Greece led her rough conqueror captive,' (Horace, *Ep.* 2.1.156), *Cambridge History of Classical Literature* (2 vols.; ed. E.J. Kenney; Cambridge: Cambridge University Press, 1982), II:5.

[107] Gnuse cites the following possibilities for auditory message dreams: Livy, *History* 2.36.2–3; Plutarch, *Lives*, Alexander 24.3; Suetonius, *Lives*, Caligula 57.1–2, Vespasian 5.5 and 5.6. Gnuse, *Josephus*, 109.

Classifications of and Attitudes toward Dreams in Latin Poetry

Quintus Ennius (239–169 B.C.E.) is often said to be the father of Latin literature,[108] but Greek was most likely his first language.[109] Nowhere is the influence of Greece clearer than in the fragmentary *Annals*,[110] in which Ennius finds that he is Homer reincarnated. However, this message dream entails both a soul journey plus an auditory message dream, two dream types that find little resonance in Greek literature.[111] Ennius' *Alexander* also contains a standard symbolic dream.[112]

Some fragments of Ennius indicate that he may have exhibited skepticism towards professional dream interpreters; some or all, we cannot tell since we are dealing with fragments out of context.[113] Cicero quotes Ennius as mocking various types of diviners including 'village-trotting gut-gazers … star-readers from the circus … and interpreters of dreams,'[114] holding that such diviners are 'averse to work, or mad, or ruled by want … from those to whom they promise wealth they beg a coin.'[115] A compromise attitude towards dreams may be evident in another fragment from Ennius: 'Some dreams are true; but it does not follow that all are so.'[116]

Virgil's Homeric style epic, the *Aeneid* (30–19 B.C.E.) contains eight detailed dream reports. There are references to Dido's 'nerve-wracking dreams,' probably psychological status dreams,[117] but the dreams reported are message dreams in which the messenger is either a deceased person's shade or a god.[118] Many of the message dreams are *Weckträu-*

---

[108] *Cambridge History*, 5. Since his poetry and tragedy are only extant in fragmentary form, any theory of Ennius' treatment of dreams must remain tentative.

[109] P. Harvey, *Oxford Companion*, 158; H.D. Jocelyn, *The Tragedies of Ennius: The Fragments Edited with an Introduction and Commentary* (Cambridge: Cambridge University Press, 1967), 43.

[110] For a more detailed survey of the Latin dream texts, see Flannery-Dailey, *Standing*, 124–155.

[111] *Annals*, lines 32–48; cf. lines 229–230 and 480 in Warmington, *Remains*, 15–6, 82–3, 180–181.

[112] *Alexander*, lines 38–49, in Warmington, *Remains*, 235–236.

[113] Ennius' leanings towards skeptical rationalism are evident in his work *Euhemerus*, which explains the origins of the gods in non-mythic and rationalistic terms.

[114] Warmington attributes the phrase to Cicero, *Remains*, 341, but W.A. Falconer attributes it to Ennius, in *Cicero: De Divinatione* (London: Heinemann, 1923), I.lviii.132.

[115] *De Div.* I.lviii.132.

[116] In Warmington, *Remains*, 379.

[117] *Aeneid* IV.1–26; IV.62–92; IV.461–494.

[118] Message dreams in the *Aeneid* include: I.341–372; II.264–294; III.134–204; IV.525–

men, in which the dream figure either tells the dreamer to wake or to rise up, or chides him/her for sleeping, such as when Mercury says to Aeneas, 'Goddess-born, can you go on sleeping at such a crisis?'[119]

Ovid's *Metamorphoses*, completed in 8 C.E., also displays a healthy interest in dreams and contains the following dream types: psychological status dreams (*Metam.* VIII.817–865; IX.454–483, an example of pleasant dreams), message dreams of gods (IX.649–687; XV.587–761), message dreams of *oneiroi* disguised as the dead (XI.628–699), and a possible symbolic dream (VII.634–664).[120] Notably, several of the dreamers in Ovid are women; for instance, there is an annunciation dream in which Isis comes to Telethusa shortly before the birth of her child with instructions on preserving the child's life (IX.649–687). Overall, then, a range of dream types and attitudes towards dreams is evident in Latin poetry.

Classifications of and Attitudes toward Dreams in Latin Prose

A variety of opinions towards dreams is likewise present in the prose writers, with Cicero, Juvenal, and Suetonius spanning the spectrum. In fact, Cicero himself seems to embody this ambivalence. On the one hand, the *De Republica* contains one of the most elaborate message dreams and otherworldly journeys in all of antiquity, the *Somnium Scipionis*.[121] On the other hand, in the dialogue *De Divinatione* Cicero speaks in his own voice against belief in dream divination, which he calls a superstition that should be torn up by the roots (*Div.* II.lxxii.148).

In *De Divinatione*, Cicero clearly partakes of the skeptical attitude of the Greek philosophers and scientists, using the philosophical method of the New Academy to argue that 'it must be admitted that God con-

---

590; V.705–739; V.838–871; VII.386–482; and VIII.27–68. There are no symbolic dreams in the *Aeneid*.

[119] *Weckträumen* in the *Aeneid* include III.134–204; IV.525–590; VII.386–482; and VIII.27–68.

[120] King Aeacus' dream of the ants who become the human Myrmidons is a difficult dream to classify since it bridges the dream-world and waking-world so tenuously. Is it a *symbolic dream* symbolizing the industry, loyalty and cooperative spirit of the people or do the events actually occur since upon awakening he sees the human forms of the Myrmidons (*Aen.*VII.634–664)?

[121] The translations of Cicero used here are *Cicero: De Republica, De Legibus* (trans. C.W. Keyes; London: William Heinemann, 1928) and *Cicero: De Senectute, De Amicitia, De Divinatione* (trans. W.A. Falconer; London: William Heinemann, 1923).

veys no information by means of dreams' (II.lx.125), which he explains
in terms of biology (II.lxvii.139-lxviii.141). The influence of the Greeks
is not univocal, however since his brother Quintus applies Stoicism and
physiological arguments in support of his belief in divinely sent dreams,
drawing selectively from Plato, Aristotle and Crattipus (I.xxix.60;
I.xxxii.70–71; I.l.113; I.li.115). Still, Cicero's position in the dialogue and
as author provides overall point of view, which could hardly be clearer:

> ... do the immortal gods, who are of surpassing excellence in all things,
> constantly flit about, not only the beds, but even the lowly pallets of
> mortals, wherever they may be, and when they find someone snoring,
> throw at him dark and twisted visions, which scare him from his sleep
> and which he carries in the morning to a dream-expert to unravel?
>
> (II.lxiii.129)

Regardless of his skepticism, the debate between Marcus Tullius Cicero
and his brother Quintus illustrates the author's familiarity with the
dream types and features we have sketched for other cultures. The
following are mentioned: commissioning dreams that command the
rebuilding of temples (I.ii.4; I.xliv.99), healing dreams (I.xxv.53), annunciation dreams (I.xx.39; I. xxiii.46), soul migrations (I. xxiv.49; I.xxv.53;
I. l.114), dreams of impending death (I.xxx.63–65), and prophetic
dreams by the dying (I.xxx.63–65). In terms of formal types, there
are symbolic dreams with their interpretations (I.xx.39; I. xxii.44–45;
I. xxiii.46–47; I.xxviii.59), message dreams (e.g. I.xxv.54; I.xxvi.55), an
auditory message dream (I.xxiv.50), and combinations of message and
symbolic dreams (I.xxiv.48–51). In addition, Cicero knows the motif
that dream repetition underscores the veracity of the prediction
(I.xxvi.55), and he is familiar with the practice of dream incubation
(I.xliii.96). Cicero's thorough acquaintance with nearly every aspect of
the Greek and ancient Near Eastern dreams is illustrative of the extent
to which these traditions were shared by Roman society.

Like Cicero, Juvenal seems skeptical of dreams. In a satire that mocks
women in general, he mocks a female Jewish dream interpreter:

> ... a palsied Jewess ... comes begging to her secret ear; she is an inter-
> preter of the laws of Jerusalem, a high priestess of the tree, a trusty go-
> between of highest heaven. She, too, fills her palm, but more sparingly,
> *for a Jew will tell you dreams of any kind you please for the minutest of coins (aere*
> *minuto qualiacumque voles Iudaei somnia vendunt).*   (*Sat.* VI.542–547)

Although disparaging, this passage is illuminating for this study since
this passage testifies to the fame of Jewish dream interpretation ca. 98–

138 C.E., as well as to the activity of female dream interpreters who claim to function as interpreters of Torah.

In addition, Juvenal seems to believe that gods use dreams to punish criminals, which accords with the function of many literary dreams we have seen. In *Satire XIII* he states that a criminal will see the temple of a god and then will see the god in his dreams, which will wring out a confession (XIII.217–222). He also discusses a would-be criminal who is punished by the oracle at Delphi for his meditations on crime (XIII.192 ff.).

If Cicero and Juvenal manifest complex attitudes towards dreams, Suetonius is straightforwardly accepting. Dreams form a vital part of Suetonius' *Lives of the Caesars*,[122] written around 120 C.E., foretelling their births, deaths, and the acquisition of power as well as its loss. The overarching theme that ties together all this dream lore is the imparting of divinely sanctioned authority, or its withdrawal.

The biographies of Caesar, Augustus, Tiberius, Caligula, Nero, Galba, Otho, Verspasian, and Domitian each contain references to dreams or full dream reports. The form of the dreams conforms to the classifications seen already: message dreams (II.91; III.63; VII.18; VII.7; VIII.7; VIII.15), symbolic dreams (I.81; II.94; IV.50, 57; VI.46; VIII.23), and evil dreams or psychological status dreams (I.45; II.91; IV.50).[123] In addition to formal patterns, several features common to ancient Near Eastern and Greek dreams are also present. There are two *token dreams*, one in which Augustus' mother Aitia is left with a child and a body mark that prove a serpent copulated with her in her sleep (II.91), and another in which a bronze statue is left behind to prove that the Goddess Fortune visited Galba in a dream (VII.4). *Lives* also contain several *annunciation dreams* that announce the greatness of the child to be born (I.94), and numerous *death dreams* (discussed below). Some *repeated or simultaneous dreams* occur, reinforcing the veracity of the message (I.81; II.94; perhaps VIII.7 [*Vesp.*]). Suetonius also displays familiarity with *dream incubation*, evident in his record that Serapis appeared in dreams to two persons and instructed them to go to Vespasian to be healed (VIII.7 [*Vesp.*]).[124]

---

[122] Also called the *Twelve Caesars*.

[123] The editions consulted are *Suetonius* (2 vols.; trans. J.C. Rolfe; London: William Heinemann, 1920) and *The Twelve Caesars: Gaius Suetonius Tranquillus* (trans. R. Graves; Baltimore: Penguin, 1957).

[124] This may be interpreted as another dream that secures authority since Vespasian is able, much to his own surprise, to heal miraculously the blind man and the deaf man.

Typical Vocabulary and Patterns of Message and Symbolic Dreams in Latin Poetry and Prose

From Ennius onward, the poets and prose writers alike use both *somniō* and *somnium* to denote 'dream' as an activity as well as a noun.[125] *Somnus* or 'sleep' is often used in reference to dreams[126] and the term may also refer to the god of Sleep and Dreams. *Somnium* may be used interchangeably with *uīsum*, 'vision.'[127] In accordance with the skepticism towards divinely-sent dreams evident particularly in prose, many of the uses of *somniō* are derogatory, as in 'to have a remote conception of'[128] or 'to indulge in idle fancies' or 'to have delusions.'[129] Similarly, *somnium* can carry the meaning 'dream' or 'vision' as well as 'an idle hope or imagining, fantasy, delusion, day-dream.'[130]

A simple dream account from Virgil suffices to show that Latin dreams follow the patterns established by Oppenheim for dreams in the ancient Near East:

> I. INTRODUCTION: 'Aeneas slept.'
>
> II. DREAM: 'To him in a dream there appeared the shape of the god.'
>
> III. CONCLUSION: 'He spoke, and vanished in the darkness. Then, startled by the shock of the apparition, Aeneas snatched himself out of sleep ...'   (IV.525–590)

In the whole of Latin literature there are fewer symbolic dreams than one might expect, given their popularity in Greek tragedy. There are no symbolic dreams in the *Aeneid*, but they occur in Ennius' *Alexander* 38–49 and Ovid's *Metamorphoses* VII.634–664.

---

[125] Ennius, *var.* 45, *scen* 42; Virgil, *Aen.* 5.840; Ovid. *Ep.* 18(19).196, *Metam.* 11.614; *Oxford Latin Dictionary* (8th ed.; ed. P.G.W. Glare; Oxford: Clarendon Press, 1982, repr. 1983), 1790–1791.

[126] 'Somnus,' 'somnium,' *OLD*, 1791.

[127] 'Uīsum,' *OLD*, 2077–2078.

[128] Plautus, *Mer.* 257; Cicero, *Att.* 13.19.5, Petrarch 74.13; *OLD*, 1790.

[129] E.g. Plautus, *Mer.* 950, *Mos.* 955, *Rud.* 1327; Cicero *Nat. D.* 1.18, *Att.* 9.13.6 and many more; 'somniō' *OLD*, 1790.

[130] 'Somnium,' *OLD*, 1791.

Literary Motifs of Latin Dreams

The Otherworldly Journey

It is ironic that despite his efforts in *De Divinatione* to discount divination of all sorts, Cicero's 'Somnium Scipionis' in *De Republica* profoundly influenced the 4th c. Macrobius, whose commentary fed medieval interest in dream divination.[131] For our purposes, the 'Dream of Scipio' is interesting for the otherworldly dream journey it contains, which is more developed than earlier extant ancient Near Eastern and Greek otherworldly journeys and which parallels those in the early Jewish works.

'Somnium Scipionis' is an otherworldly dream journey modeled in part on Plato's 'Myth of Er,' an otherworldly journey that occurs in a near death experience.[132] Scipio's dream is a standard message dream with a familiar formal structure:

> I. INTRODUCTION: Scipio 'fell immediately into a deeper sleep than usual' (*Resp.* VI.x.10)
>
> II. DREAM: 'I thought that Africanus stood before me ...' (*Africanus se ostendit ea forma*) (*Resp.* VI.x.10). Africanus imparts a message, and takes him on an otherworldly journey the universe.
>
> III. CONCLUSION: 'He departed, and I awoke from my sleep' (*Resp.* VI.xxvi.28–29).

The dream figure is, as in many Greek dreams, a deceased person known to the dreamer.[133] The dreamer registers psychological shock and terror upon seeing the deceased Africanus (VI.x.10), but the dream messenger in usual fashion comforts him, saying 'have no fear.'[134] Next, the dream figure relates a message that predicts the future, in this case a detailed prediction of the younger Scipio's involvement in political events, thereby legitimating his political authority as destiny (VI.xi.11-

---

[131] See W.H. Stahl, *Macrobius: Commentary on the Dream of Scipio* (New York: Columbia University Press, 1952, 1990), esp. 39–55.

[132] Both tales convey the idea that people obtain the afterlife appropriate to their lives on earth. In Plato, the afterlife may consist of various forms of reincarnation or astral immortality. In Cicero, the just person who was loyal to Rome in his lifetime receives the reward of an afterlife in the heavenly spheres. However, while there are broad thematic similarities between the two accounts, only Cicero's version is presented as a dream. Plato, *Resp.* X: 613–620.

[133] Kessels, *Studies*, 53–8; *Il.* 23.62ff.

[134] Oppenheim, *Interpretation*, 200.

xii.12). He then takes Scipio on an otherworldly journey in which he
meets his deceased father. Like the netherworld dream journeys of
Enkidu and Kummaya, the dream gives Scipio special access to the
realm of the dead, here heaven.[135] He also learns that 'a path to heaven
... is open to those who have served their country well' (VI.xxii.24-
xxiv.26). Thus, in addition to knowledge of his political future, Scipio
learns about divine realities that are interwoven with the divine sanction of Rome. The CONCLUSION to the dream contains the typically
Greek emphasis on the messenger's departure and the statement that
the dreamer awoke (VI.xxvi.29).[136]

This otherworldly tour is more complex than any other we have seen
in ancient Near Eastern or Graeco-Roman sources.[137] Scipio is escorted
by a guide throughout the heavenly regions and also sees remote places
on the earth (VI.xvi.16-xx.22). Looking ahead to our investigation of
dreams in Hellenistic Judaism, it is noteworthy that R.H. Feen points
out numerous parallels between Cicero's *Dream of Scipio* and Jewish
apocalyptic literature. These parallels include an otherworldly journey
conducted by a guide, the seer's response of awe followed by a word of
comfort, the foretelling of events, and astrological and cosmological elements.[138] Feen rightly does not go so far as to posit the direct influence
of Jewish apocalyptic literature on Cicero, but he does argue that the
similar sociological crises of each setting contributed to the similarity in
style, structure, and themes.[139] Feen concludes that just as apocalypticists emphasize rewards in the world to come, Cicero 'is calling out to
the faithful to endure, as they will have the "final" reward.'[140]

Latin Dreams and Death

Judging from the dream traditions in both Latin poetry and prose,
one might think that Romans were obsessed with death. In the *Aeneid*,
Virgil develops in complex ways the association between death and

---

[135] *Epic of Gilgamesh* in Oppenheim, *Interpretation*, 248–249, par. 8, no. 7; 'A Vision of
the Nether World,' trans. by E.A. Speiser (*ANET*, 109–110).
[136] Oppenheim, *Interpretation*, 188.
[137] This does not, however, imply a Roman innovation in the otherworldly journey,
as the journey most closely resembles that of Enoch in *1 Enoch* 1–36, which predates
Cicero by over two centuries.
[138] Feen, 'Nekyia,' 28–34.
[139] Ibid., 33.
[140] Ibid., 32.

dreams that exists in the ancient Near Eastern, Greek, and earlier Latin writers. Several of the messengers in dreams are deceased spirits,[141] and several spirits of deceased persons who appear in explicitly waking visions are likened to the winged *oneiroi* figures in dreams (II.765–801, VI.684–717).[142] In a hitherto unseen twist on the trope of dreams and death, the god of dreams lulls Palinurus into a deep sleep so that he may kill him (V.838–871).[143] Also, Mercury is portrayed as a god who commands both the dead and dreams. With a wave of his magic wand, he 'summons wan ghosts from Orcus and consigns others to dreary Tartarus, gives sleep or takes it away, seals up the eyes of dead men' (IV.227–261).

The most important elaboration of the theme of death and dreams occurs in the extended *catabasis* of Book VI, in which Virgil describes in remarkable detail the dwelling of dreams near the entrance to the Underworld.[144] Past the porch and entrance way to Orcus, and past the dwelling places of such beings as Grief, Anxiety, Old Age, Death, Agony, Sleep, the Furies and various monsters, Aeneas spies a clearing with a huge dark elm tree, on which 'Roost the unsolid Dreams, clinging everywhere under its foliage' (VI.273–308).[145] The close association between death and sleep is clear in the description of sleep as 'Sleep ... which is the cousin of Death' (VI.273–308) as well as in Charon's cry, 'This is the land of ghosts, of sleep and somnolent night ...' (VI.376–408). Although the entrance to the Underworld is open night and day

---

[141] These occur in both dreams and dream-reports. See I.341–372; II.264–294; IV.326–360; V.705–739.

[142] Cf. V.616–644 in which a similar phrase is applied to a conjured wraith that looks like Aeneas.

[143] This episode fits the formal definition of a dream in that Palinurus is asleep during the appearance and conversation with the Sleep-God.

[144] For a discussion of the *catabasis* of Book VI in light of similar descents in ancient Near Eastern and Greek traditions, without, however, a focus on dreams, see R.J. Clark, *Catabasis: Vergil and the Wisdom-Tradition* (Amsterdam: B.R. Grüner, 1979) and H. Cancik, 'Der Eingang in die Unterwelt: Ein religionswissenschaftlicher Versuch zu Vergil, Aeneis 6, 236–272,' in *Der altsprachliche Unterricht* (Stuttgart, 1983), 55–66. Also see S.J. Huskey, 'Ovid's *Tristia* I and III: An Intertextual Katabasis' (Ph.D. diss., The University of Iowa, 2002).

[145] It is interesting that in the Underworld these entities, dreams included, are 'unsolid' and 'incorporeal Existences,' whereas dreams and monsters do have a corporeal existence on earth (VI.273–308). This corresponds to the states of humans on earth and in the Underworld as well. Compare also 'the substance of [Juno's] heavenly body' which causes the threshold of the Underworld to groan (IV.449–479), with the 'unsubstantial dreams' who live there (XI.565–699).

(VI.95–127), the exit—at least for Aeneas and the Sibyl, his guide—is through a gate of dreams (VI.863–901).[146]

In *Metamorphoses*, Ovid continues to develop the Homeric-Virgilian motif of the Underworld lair of dreams.[147] Ovid gives the location of Sleep's home as a labyrinthine cavern under a Cimmerian mountain (XI.565–699). Ovid describes the residence in some detail: it is marked by eerie silence, except for the Lethe stream that murmurs 'sleep,' while poppies bloom in profusion before the open doorway, one of Night's tools (XI.565–627). Inside, Sleep slumbers on a dark couch, surrounded by the dreams, whom Ovid describes as real beings:

> … around [Sleep] lie, in various forms, the unsubstantial dreams, as numerous as the wheat-ears of the harvest, the green leaves of the wood, or grains of sand along the shore.   (XI.596–627)

Like their leader, the dreams are asleep, and the goddess Iris who wishes to consult Sleep must part the dreams with her hands to clear a path to the god.[148]

Ovid greatly elaborates on the Greek *oneiroi* traditions and delights in the descriptions of dreams, even exploring their ontology. He explains that Morpheus is best at imitating the exact likeness, gait and speech of humans, while Icelos imitates beast, bird, or serpent and Phantasos 'wears shapes of earth, rocks, water, trees' (XI.628–662). That is, Ovid speculates that the numerous dreams each have specialized functions and personal identities replete with names. Moreover, he states, 'There are dream-gods here who show themselves by night to kings and rulers only, and there are others who come to common people,' indicating a hierarchy of dreams. He further describes Morpheus' flight and 'noise-less wings,' as well as the manner in which he assumes the form of Ceyx in a message dream seen by Alcyone (XI.565–662).

The Latin prose authors exhibit a similar preoccupation with dreams and death. Suetonius' *Lives* includes several death dreams in which the

---

[146] Virgil quotes Homer's tradition about the gate of horn, through which genuine dreams pass, and the gate of ivory, through which false dreams pass (VI.863–901, cf. *Od.* 11). Curiously enough, Anchises leads Aeneas and the Sibyl out through the gate of ivory, for which no satisfactory explanation has yet been provided. H. Clarke calls this 'one of the great enigmas of classical literature.' H. Clarke, *Vergil's Aeneid and Fourth ('Messianic') Eclogue in the Dryden Translation* (University Park: Pennsylvania State University Press, 1989), 178, n. 1235.

[147] *Od.* 24.1–16; *Aen.* Book VI.

[148] Iris' visit must be brief, because even goddesses' are susceptible to the somnolent surroundings (*Metam.* XI.628–662).

dreamer foresees his own death or a dreamer foresees someone else's death (I.81; III.74; IV.57), or in which the shades of deceased persons appear in dreams (VII.7). Rather like Juvenal's idea that criminals will be tortured by their dreams, Nero begins to have the nightmares after his matricide:

> … it seemed to him that he was steering a ship in his sleep and that the helm was wrenched from his hands; that he was dragged by his wife Octavia into thickest darkness, and that he was now covered with a swarm of winged ants, and now was surrounded by the statues of the nations which had been dedicated in Pompey's Theatre and stopped in his tracks. A Spanish steed of which he was very fond was changed into the form of an ape in the hinder parts of its body, and its head, which alone remained unaltered, gave forth tuneful neighs. The doors of the Mausoleum flew open of their own accord, and a voice was heard from within summoning him by name …   (VI.46; see also IV.50).

The last image clearly portends Nero's own death.[149]

Functions of Dreams in Latin Literature

As we have already seen, Latin texts interweave the functions of knowledge, healing and divine sanction, frequently with the accent on sanction as it relates to the glory of Rome. In Ennius, many dreamers gain knowledge of the future,[150] and the poet's transmigration dream, a standard commissioning dream (familiar from Callimachus and Hesiod, but known also in the ancient Near East[151]), provides him with Homer's knowledge and skill[152] so that he might compose the national epic of Rome.[153] Thus, divine sanction of the city as well as of the poet

---

[149] From the translation by Rolfe, *Suetonius*. It should be noted that Oppenheim claimed that symbolic dreams left uninterpreted were considered evil dreams, 'Mantic,' 349–350.

[150] E.g. Aeneas' daughter, Ilia, learns from her deceased father that she will face hardships and then bounty, *Annals*, lines 32–48.

[151] Skutsch, *Q. Ennius*, 148; Hutchinson, *Hellenistic Poetry*, 278–279; Oppenheim, *Interpretation*, 193.

[152] As Skutsch notes, this allows him to circumvent the Callimachean ban on Homeric style epic by writing not in the style of Homer, but as Homer himself, Skutsch, *Q. Ennius*, 148.

[153] P. Aicher explains that the theme of Pythagorean transmigration shows not only is the boundary between Greek and Latin fluid, the boundary between individuals is fluid as well, 'Ennius' Dream of Homer,' 230.

is intertwined with the receipt of knowledge. Again, Hecuba's symbolic dream of giving birth to a burning firebrand is noteworthy as an
annunciation or healing dream that bears on national concerns, since it
predicts the suffering of the Trojan-Greek war.[154]

In Virgil's *Aeneid*, dreams typically function to impart hidden knowledge to the dreamer, especially about the future (VII.386–482; I.341–
372; II.264–294; IV.525–590; cf. IV.326–360). Again, dreams serve above
all to demonstrate the divine sanction of Aeneas and of Rome (III.134–
204; V.705–739; VIII.27–68).[155] This motif is most vividly illustrated in
Virgil's departure from the Greek dream tradition that gods appear
in dreams while disguised.[156] Here, the gods appear in true form only
to Aeneas, whose epithet 'Goddess-born' indicates not only his divine
descent, but also his ability to easily interact with divinity.[157] The poet
stresses that Aeneas sees the striking likeness of Mercury down to the
last detail: 'To him in a dream there appeared the shape of the god
… Mercury's very image, the voice, the complexion, the yellow hair
and the handsome youthful body identical' (III.134–204; VIII.27–68;
IV.525–590). By contrast, gods who appear in dreams to mere mortals
continue the Greek tradition of disguise (V.838–871). In Turnus' dream,
a goddess alters her appearance, but out of anger metamorphoses back
into her original form of a Fury before the close of the dream (VII.386–
482). The dreamer's stark terror at seeing the true appearance of the
goddess, evidenced in a sweat that soaks him head to foot, seems to
support the conclusion that the motif of disguise helps to cushion the
shock of theophany (*Aen.* VII.386–482). For this reason, the *absence* of
this motif in the dreams of Aeneas is noteworthy and adds dimension
to his heroic stature and, in turn, to the glory of Rome.

Compared to Ennius and Virgil, Ovid seems less interested in using
dreams to testify to the divine sanction of Rome. For example, Suetonius uses the annunciation dream to predict the future greatness of
the child, who is always a Roman leader, but Telethusa's annunciation
dream functions as a healing dream that saves an ordinary, female child
from death (*Metam.* IX.649–687). One exception is the story of Ascle-

---

[154] *Alexander*, lines 38–49.

[155] Hundt, *Der Traum Glaube*, 133.

[156] Kessels, *Studies*, 158; Van Lieshout, *Greeks on Dreams*, 16.

[157] At one point Aeneas even chides his mother Venus for appearing in disguise
during a daytime meeting, saying: 'Must you too be cruel? Must you make game of
your son with shapes of sheer illusion?' (*Aen.* I.407–444).

pius' arrival in Rome, in which a message dream establishes the god's sanction of the 'capital of the world' (XV.597–761).[158]

The constellation of dreams, divine sanction and the glory of Rome is even more pronounced in Latin prose. Suetonius' *Lives of the Caesars* links divinely sent dreams and the acquisition of authority in several ways. First, annunciation dreams tell of the future greatness of a child, such as Octavius' dream that the sun rose from between Augustus' mother's thighs (*Aug.* II.94).[159] Second, some dreams foretell that a child already born will be great, as in the dreams in the biography of Augustus which explicitly portray him receiving divine authority from Jupiter, or even being arrayed as Jupiter himself (II.94 [*Oct.*]). Third, certain dreams signal that divine favor has been withdrawn, such as when Minerva appears to Domitian to inform him that she can no longer offer him divine protection (VIII.15 [*Dom.*]). Finally, two dreams from Serapis, a god of an incubation cult, portray Vespasian as a healer (VIII.7 [*Vesp.*]), thus linking the function of healing with divine sanction of a ruler.

Overall, the way in which dreams repeatedly and consistently function to dispense divine favor on the heroes and leaders of Rome finds a close parallel in biblical dreams, which usually demonstrate God's sanction of the patriarchs and other important males in Israel's sacred history.

Summary of Latin Dreams

Although the rational skepticism of the Greek philosophers towards dreams is also evident, the Latin sources mostly maintain that some dreams are divinely-sent. These reports closely reflect the patterns, vocabulary, and features of dreams found in traditional Greek literary sources.

The Latin sources also extend and develop the Greek dream traditions in distinct ways. There is a heavier accent on dreams functioning to bestow or withdraw divine sanction of Roman leaders and

---

[158] Another exception is the story of the deification of Caesar, which predicts the future deification of Augustus at his death and closes off the work (*Lives*, XV.734–761 [*Jul.*]). Still, Ovid is mostly interested in the personal level of love and tragedy, as is evident in his treatment of heroic characters of the *Aeneid*.

[159] In fact, II.94 contains three annunciation dreams, two by Atia and one by Octavius.

of Rome itself. The associations between death and dreams expand greatly, resulting in full-blown otherworldly dream journeys to the netherworld and to heaven (Virgil, *Aen.* VI; Ovid, *Metam.* XI; Cicero *Resp.*). Moreover, Virgil and Ovid both speculate further on the nature of the *oneiros* itself (Virgil, *Aen.* VI; Ovid, *Metam.* XI). Thus, overall the Latin dreams illuminate Roman interests in authority, death, and otherworldly realms and beings.

SOCIAL MILIEU OF DREAMING IN GREECE AND ROME

Literature is only a reflection of society, but we can gain from it glimpses of the social constructions of dreaming. As is the case for Greece, a curious gender split between prose and poetry is present in Rome: Ennius, Virgil, and Ovid portray several women as dreamers, whereas there are far fewer female dreamers in prose writers such as Cicero, Juvenal, and Suetonius. In fact, when Juvenal has occasion to mention a female dream interpreter, he does so mockingly, and Suetonius' few female dreamers all dream about the fate of male rulers. It may be that the construction of gender in Graeco-Roman antiquity—females as imprecise, irrational, and liminal; males as precise and rational—lends itself to portraying women as dreamers in poetry and men as dreamers in prose. Moreover, since dreams normally confer divine sanction, the hegemonic associations amongst men, dreams and social power cannot be missed.

The actual dreams of people in antiquity lie outside of our reach, except as they are expressed through social and literary constructions of dreaming. The historians Herodotus, Diodorus Siculus, and Suetonius purport to record the real dreams of leaders, but the whole breadth of dream reports in antiquity, from the epigraphic records of Assurbanipal to Suetonius' *Lives of the Caesars*, tightly conforms to the form-critical patterns that are in place from Sumer onward.

With this in mind, I turn now to the best available window onto the dreams of ordinary people in Greece and Rome: the professional dream-books of Artemidorus and the evidence of the dream cults, particularly those of Asklepios.

Dream Interpretation: Artemidorus

Artemidorus' five book manual *Oneirocritica*[160] furnishes us with a different kind of material than the Greek and Latin poetry and prose examined thus far. It was meant to be a professional guide explaining the
principles of dream interpretation. In fact, the author clearly means to
pass Books 4 and 5 on to his son, also a dream interpreter, and warns
him to keep the books secret lest he lose his competitive edge. Although
as H. Cancik notes, 'dreams were not an element of Roman state religion in their own right,' Romans frequented dream interpreters in their
private religion, 'to the great annoyance of the official cult functionaries.'[161] The examples of dreams that Artemidorus provides are those
of private citizens, but they are selective and do not cover the range
of real dreaming: only those *oneiroi* he deems to be *allegorical*, i.e. symbolic and in need of interpretation, merit his attention. Their content is
often ordinary and uninspiring; for example, in one case Artemidorus
provides interpretations of a dream depending on the qualities of the
dreamer's hair, i.e., whether it is long, disheveled, made of hog's bristles
or wool, missing, or cut by a barber. Such examples may be multiplied
(1.18–22).

The chief value of the *Oneirocritica* for us is the insider's look it provides for professional dream interpretation, which balances the critiques that Ennius, Cicero, and Juvenal level against dream interpreters.
Artemidorus' work exposes the reader to a long Greek and Roman
oneirocritical tradition spanning at least the fourth century B.C.E. to
the second century C.E. He claims to have 'taken special pains to procure every book on the interpretation of dreams' as well as to have
'consorted for many years with the much-despised diviners of the mar-
ketplace' (1.1).[162]

Artemidorus distinguishes five categories of dreams: 1) ὄνειρος, a
puzzling dream, 2) ὅραμα, a prophetic vision, 3) χρηματισμός, an oracle,
4) ἐνύπνιον, a nightmare, and 5) φάντασμα, an apparition.[163] The basic

---

[160] White, *Artemidorus.*
[161] H. Cancik, 'Idolum and Imago,' 169–170.
[162] Artemidorus claims to include the works of Antiphon of Athens, Aristander of
Telmessus in Lycia, Demetrius of Phalerum, Alexander of Myndus, Panyasis of Hali-
carnassus, Nicostratus of Ephesus, Apollonius of Attalia, and Apollodorus of Telmessus;
White, *Artemidorus*, 6–7.
[163] See especially Artemidorus' Dream Book 1.1–7 and the introduction to Book 4; in
White, *Artemidorus*, 7; see also Dodds, *Greeks*, 107.

principle of Artemidorus' interpretations depends on the relationship
between content and signification as determined by either similarity
or dissimilarity, which he calls 'interior,' corresponding in kind to the
impression of the dream-event, or 'exterior,' appearing to contradict
the mood or tone of the dream-event (1.5). Another principle involves
the 'generic' or 'specific,' that is, whether many images in a dream
proclaim many things or a few things, and whether few images in
a dream pertain to many things or few things (1.3, 4). In addition,
he suggests that interpreters judge dreams as a complete whole and
gives examples of false interpretations that were derived from only
considering individual symbols in dreams (3.66).

Many particular factors influence these general principles. Artemidorus takes into account the individual circumstances of the dreamer
including: occupation, economic status, age, birth, health, and so forth
(1.9). He notes that kings, magistrates, and other public officials tend
to have dreams that have public implications, whereas this is not true
of private citizens (1.2), a presupposition Latin authors clearly reflect.
Also, time of night might be a factor, with the post-midnight period and
dawn producing the most veridical dreams (1.7). Whatever a dreamer
has eaten might also influence dreams (1.7). In Books 4 and 5, Artemidorus urges his son to learn local customs to aid in proper interpretation (4.4). He also discusses the concept of 'similarities,' which interprets
a symbol in accordance with the character of the dreamer. For example,
a prophet's daughter dreamt she gave birth to a serpent, and her child
became a hierophant because the serpent is a sacred animal, whereas a
wanton prostitute had the same dream and her child turned out to be
sneaky and wanton, like a serpent (4.67). While in Book One Artemidorus discussed the technique of transposing the letters of objects in
a dream (1.11), he admits to his son in Book Four that this technique
is unreliable and should only be used when he desires to make a big
impression on someone (4.23). He also reminds his son that recurrent
dreams merit the most attention, a theme we have also seen in literary
sources (4.27).

In summary, Artemidorus preserves the mundane content of the
dreams of ordinary citizens and provides an insider's peek at professional dream interpretation, which enjoyed widespread popularity in
the Greek and Roman eras. His profession testifies to the ancient view
that dreams have meaning that can be decoded, usually foretelling the
future and the will of the gods. In his stress on the role of the personal history of the dreamer and environmental factors, he also reflects

ancient understandings that some dreams reflect the dreamer's state of mind and body.[164]

Dream Incubation

Although the Greek philosophers initiated a rational and skeptical view of dreams that several Greek and Latin authors embrace, the activity of the dream cults testifies to widespread belief in divinely-sent dreams throughout Greek, Hellenistic, and Roman times.[165] Ordinary people throughout the Hellenistic and Roman Empires frequented the cults and dreamt dreams that they in turn articulated in the stylized forms known from literature. The question of whether and to what extent private citizens attending the temples actually dreamt according to this pattern cannot be definitively answered. However, the literary patterns and typical dream vocabulary do shed light on cultural expectations of dreams, e.g.: they are visits or messages from real beings, occur in a liminal state, and function to bestow unusual knowledge, healing or divine sanction.

Dream incubation had long been practiced in the ancient Near East. It is reasonable to assume that the importation of incubation to the Greeks occurred through this route, perhaps from the cults of Babylonia by way of Lydia.[166] By the 5th–4th c. B.C.E., incubation was one of the most popular modes of divination and religious practice in Greece. A possible reference to dream incubation is found as early as Homer in his reference to the Selloi as 'The prophets of Zeus of

---

[164] The Egyptian dream books also consider the dreamer's personal information. Kessels, *Studies*, 158; Van Lieshout, *Greeks on Dreams*, 16. Contrast the argument by Walde that Artemidorus 'occupies an intermediate position between antiquity and modern times' for his rational and systematic approach that takes into account the client's history and the intuition of the researcher. Walde also compares his system to Freud and finds some correspondence, Walde, 'Dream Interpretation,' 135.

[165] This divergence in attitudes towards dreaming is especially interesting since, as Garland points out, the growth in the Asklepios cult at the beginning of the fifth century parallels the rise of the Hippocratic tradition of systematic medical inquiry. R. Garland, *New Gods*, 116, 134. Note, however, that Cancik argues the cult of Asklepios was incidental in Roman religion, 'Idolum and Imago,' 170.

[166] So argues Thrämer, 'Health and Gods of Healing,' 541–542. The two main pieces of evidence he cites for the Babylonian influence on Greek incubation are a preference for a time towards morning (Philostratus *Vit. Apoll.* ii. 36; cf. Artemidorus, *Oneir.* I.7) and incubation on behalf of another person, 542.

Dodona, who sleep on the ground and wash not the feet' (*Il.* 16.235).[167] Dream cults were sites of healing and/or oracles and were associated with numerous gods and heroes. Such cults included the numerous Asklepieia, especially at Trikka, Epidauros, Pergamon and Kos, the Plutonion near Nysa, a Dionysian dream-shrine at Amphikleia, the cult of the Dioscouroi at Byzantium, the oracle of Trophonios at Livadia in Boeotia, the oracle of Amphiarous at Oropos, the hero Achilles' dream shrine at Leuce, and in Hellenistic and Roman times the many scattered temples of Sarapis and Isis.[168] Other gods and goddesses who are not specifically known as having dream cults are also attested as providing oracular dreams and/or healing by dreams including Athena, Pan, and Demeter.[169]

By far the most popular dream cult was that of Asklepios, god of dreams and healing, whose temple sites numbered over 400 throughout Greece, the Hellenistic world, and the Roman Empire.[170] The oldest cult center of Asklepios may have been Trikka in Thessaly[171] or perhaps Epidauros, which became the most famous incubation site.[172] This successful cult quickly attained Panhellenic status, reaching Attica by 420 B.C.E. and spreading throughout the Mediterranean world, reaching the Tiber Island in Rome by 293 B.C.E. upon the advice of the Sibylline books.[173]

For this project it is quite important to note that archaeology has turned up Asklepieia in Palestine. C. Dauphin has found an Archaic Greek or Hellenistic Asklepieion built over a subterranean *adyton* (or 'holy of holies') underneath the basilica at Dor.[174] E. Shenhav notes that evidence of a Roman era octagonal Asklepieion has been found at Shuni (including the cult statue from ca. 3rd c. C.E.), just north of Cae-

---

[167] Thrämer, 'Health and Gods of Healing,' 542, 545; see also M. Hamilton, *Incubation*, 7.

[168] Thrämer, 'Health and Gods of Healing,' 543, 549, 552; W.A. Jayne, *Healing Gods*, 201–202; R.J. Clark, 'Trophonius,' *TAPA* 99 (1968): 63–75.

[169] For Athena see Plutarch, *Pericl.* 13, Pliny xxii.43; for Pan see Pausanias, ii.32,6; for Demeter see Artemidorus, ii.39; in Thrämer, 'Health and Gods of Healing,' 545–549.

[170] Thrämer, 'Health and Gods of Healing,' 550. Edelstein, *Asclepius*, 1:370–441.

[171] Strabo, *Geogr.* 437.

[172] Garland, *New Gods*, 117.

[173] C. Kerényi, *Asklepios*, 9, 48; Hamilton, *Incubation*, 9, 63, 74, 75; Thrämer, 'Health and Gods of Healing,' 550.

[174] C. Dauphin, 'Dor,' *IEJ* 29 (1979): 235–236, 31; idem, *IEJ* 31 (1981): 117–119; idem, *IEJ* 34 (1984): 271–274; see also C. Dauphin, 'Dora-Dor: A Station for Pilgrims in the Byzantine Period on their Way to Jerusalem,' in *Ancient Churches Revealed* (ed. Y. Tsafrir; Jerusalem: Israel Exploration Society, 1993), 90–97.

sarea Maritima.[175] Moreover, as P. Xella has shown from archaeological altar inscriptions, the chief deity of Sidon, Eschmun, was identified with Asklepios from at least the 2nd c. B.C.E. if not earlier.[176]

The cult mythology varied over time and with location. Homer describes Asklepios as an ordinary mortal ruler with knowledge of the healing arts (*Il. 2.729–732*). In the best attested myth, Asklepios' father, Apollo, kills his mortal mother Koronis while she is still with child (*Hom. Hymn for Askl.* III 207–213; Pindar, *Pyth.* III 1–58, Ovid, *Metam.* II 542–648).[177] Apollo then regrets his action, takes Asklepios from the womb of his dead mother, and entrusts him to the care of the centaur Cheiron, who teaches Asklepios the arts of healing and hunting.[178] Zeus eventually kills Asklepios for raising Hippolytus from the dead, but thereafter raises Asklepios himself as a chthonic healing deity.[179] Thus, the appearance of Asklepios in a dream draws on the traditions of the appearance of the deceased as well as of gods.

The cult sponsored both public and private worship. The festival of Asklepios was celebrated in Epidauros nine days after Poseidon's festival at the Isthmian Games, which helped attract worshippers from all over Greece who stopped at Epidauros on their way home.[180] In the formal procession to the sanctuary, thousands of worshippers chanted hymns of praise to Asklepios. Upon arriving, they underwent a purification at a well just inside the Propylon, brought certain animals for sacrifice, and dined on the sacrifices at a banquet within the sanctuary precincts. Artistic and athletic contests were also a part of the festival.[181]

The Asklepieia were most famous for their private dream cults. Set in a beautiful valley flanked by graceful mountains, Epidauros was a sort of ancient spa to which one would retreat for healing, after which

---

[175] E. Shenhav, 'Shuni' in *Excavations and Surveys in Israel* 7–8 (1988/1989): 166–168; also idem, 'Shuni' in *NEAEHL* 4:1382–1384.

[176] P. Xella, 'Eschmun von Sidon: Der phönizische Asklepios,' in *Mesopotamia Ugaritica Biblica: Festschrift für Kurt Bergerhof zur Vollendung seines 70. Lebensjahres am 7. Mai 1992* (Neukirchen-Vluyn: Neukirchener Verlag and Verlag Butzon and Bercker Kevelaer, 1993), 481–498.

[177] Garland, *New Gods*, 117. In some versions of the myth, Artemis kills Koronis, see R.A. Tomlinson, *Epidauros*, 13; Edelstein, *Asclepius*, 1:1–7, 24–5.

[178] Tomlinson, *Epidauros*, 13.

[179] Garland, *New Gods*, 117; Tomlinson, *Epidauros*, 13; Hamilton, *Incubation*, 8; Cicero, *Nat. d.* II.24, 62.

[180] Tomlinson, *Epidauros*, 16; for sources see Edelstein, *Asclepius*, 1:285–319.

[181] Tomlinson, *Epidauros*, 16–17. For a wrestling contest at the Epidaurian festival, see Pindar, *Vth Nemean Ode*; for the artistic contests see Plato, *Ion* 530a.

one might stay on in the hotel for a short period of sacrificing and shop-
ping. Incubants first underwent purification in ritual baths[182] and then
conducted a preliminary sacrifice.[183] Although fasting was required at
many other dream oracles, especially the Plutonion, Amphiaron, and
Trophonion, this is not attested for the Asklepieia.[184] Following the preliminary rituals at Epidauros, the incubant slept on a *klinê*, or couch, in
the *abaton*, a place reserved for incubants.[185] The *abaton* itself lay within
a relatively small *temenos* that excluded most of the major buildings at
the site. Within this area, strict purity rules were maintained.[186] The
rituals of purification and sacrifice as well as the restricted nature of
the sacred area served to heighten the incubants' expectations.[187] In
addition, some incubants may have had to make their way through
the Epidaurian *tholos*, a dark, underground, circular labyrinth that may
have housed snakes.[188] Such a ritual would certainly have aroused their
emotions and may have contributed to some interesting dreams! Whatever its exact function, the structure reflects the chthonic nature of the
deity.

Part of the preparatory ritual also included reading the *iamata*, stelae
near the entrance of the sanctuary attesting to miraculous cures by
Asklepios, most often in the form of dream cures. Archaeology has
shown these stelae were likely displayed within the *abaton* as well.[189]

---

[182] Hamilton, *Incubation*, 11.

[183] Aristides, *Oratio* XLVIII. 27 (Edelstein, *Asclepius*, 1:286–287). See Hamilton, *Incubation*, 11–12; Tomlinson, *Epidauros*, 60–67; LiDonnici, *Epidaurian Miracle Inscriptions*, 11–12;
Meier, *Antike Incubation*, 69–83.

[184] Strabo *Geogr.* xiv.650; Plato *Symp.* viii.10; Kratinos, *Trophonios*; in Hamilton, 85,
89–90; see also Meier, *Antike Incubation*, 87–111.

[185] Meier, *Antike Incubation*, 57–68; idem, 'The Dream in Ancient Greece and Its
Use in Temple Cures (Incubation),' in *The Dream and Human Societies* (eds. G.E. von
Grunebaum and R. Caillois; Berkeley: Univ. of California Press, 1966), 303–319, 315;
LiDonnici, *Epidaurian Miracle Inscriptions*, 19.

[186] LiDonnici, *Epidaurian Miracle Inscriptions*, 12–14, 19.

[187] See J.W. Hewitt, 'The Major Restrictions of Access to Greek Temples,' *Transactions
of the American Philological Society* 40, 1 (1909): 83–91.

[188] There also appears to be a small, round labyrinth at the Asklepieion at Lebena
on Crete. Most if not all of the incubation sites of Asklepios contain some chthonic
structure nearby, whether a round *tholos* or a natural cave. The exact function of the
tholos is debated; Kavvadias thinks that the sacrifices and other rituals were conducted
there, in Hamilton, *Incubation*, 11; see also Tomlinson, *Epidauros*, 60–67; LiDonnici,
Epidaurian Miracle Inscriptions, 11–12; Meier, *Antike Incubation*, 69–83.

[189] The extant fragments of these inscriptions are accessible in Herzog, *Die Wunderheilungen* and LiDonnici, *Epidaurian Miracle Inscriptions*. For their location in the *abaton* and
their ritual role in incubation preparation see LiDonnici, *Epidaurian Miracle Inscriptions*,
18, n. 16.

Some *iamata* simply report that a dream of Asklepios occurred and the incubant was cured. However, when dreams are described, they follow the standard pattern of the message dream as indicated in the following inscription:

> A man from Torone, leeches.
>
> I. INTRODUCTION: When he was sleeping, he saw a dream.
>
> II. DREAM: It seemed to him that the god ripped open his chest with a knife, took out the leeches and gave them to him in his hands, and sewed his breast together.
>
> III. CONCLUSION: When day came he left having the animals in his hands, and had become well ... [A13][190]

The message dream contains a token, the leeches, which are meant to prove the veracity of the dream. The stelae functioned to dispel unbelief by the incubants and establish the authority of the dream cult. Two of the inscriptions even describe the subjects as walking around the sanctuary and ridiculing the *iamata* prior to their miraculous recoveries and the dedication of these two *iamata*.[191] Thus, the pre-incubatory reading of the *iamata* created expectations for a miraculous dream and provided strong suggestions for the content of dreams.

Within the *abaton*, the incubant probably slept at the feet of the statue of the god. In fact, Oppenheim theorizes that the ancient Near Eastern pattern of the message dream, in which a person sees a beautiful god of towering size, reflects actual dreams incubated in this fashion.[192] If the incubant was fortunate, he or she was granted a dream of Asklepios, either an ἐνύπνιον or an ὄψις.[193] He appeared in various forms including: a handsome young boy or a bearded old man; the god's companion animals, yellow snakes, dogs, or geese; alone or accompanied by his daughters Hygieia, Panakeia, or Iaso.[194] As in ancient Near Eastern

---

[190] Inscriptions follow the numbering in LiDonnici, *Epidaurian Miracle Inscriptions*, with the letter corresponding to the stela and the numeral indicating line number.

[191] A 3 and A 4.

[192] Oppenheim, *Interpretation*, 190; idem, 'Mantic Dreams,' 348.

[193] LiDonnici argues that ὄψις belongs to an early group of tales, while ἐνύπνιον belongs to a later group, *Epidaurian Miracle Cures*, 80. For discussion on ἐνύπνιον see LiDonnici, *Epidaurian Miracle Inscriptions*, 23, 28, 32–5, 37, 68, 80; for ὄψις see p 23, 25–7, 30, 32, 34–5, 39, 68, 80. For occurrances of ἐνύπνιον see texts A 36, 98, 104, 120; B 2, 5, 6, 11, 23, 28, 39, 51, 61, 83, 111, 117, 120, 124, 130; G 109. For occurrances of ὄψις see A11, 16, 25, 37, 49, 57, 76, 118; B16, 30, 47, 58, 66, 69, 88, 103; G11, 116, 119, 126, 136.

[194] Meier, 'Dream in Ancient Greece,' 315; Hamilton, *Incubation*, 6, 30–31.

dream theophanies, the size and beauty of the god are stressed.[195] He speaks with a harmonious voice and sometimes laughs and jests with the dreamers.[196] In several cases, the god and the dreamer converse at length.[197] The *iamata* state that it 'seemed' (ἐδόκει) that the god was 'standing' (ἐπιστάς) and that he touches or speaks to the dreamer.[198] The iconography of votive sculptural reliefs at Athens and Piraeus also show the god standing by the head of the reclining dreamer and reaching out to touching the dreamer.[199]

According to the *iamata* and the writings of Aelius Aristides, a long-time devotee of the god,[200] Asklepios uses a number of methods to heal the patient in dreams. The god sometimes prescribed medical advice or performed 'divine surgery' as in the example above,[201] but usually he healed through touch, which appears in standard iconography on votive reliefs from Athens and Piraeus.[202] Snakes, dogs and geese, the sacred animals of the god, may have also touched or licked the incubants, as they did in dreams.[203]

After the dream, the priests had a role in interpreting the dreams and possibly in practicing medicine.[204] After the cure, steps were taken to thank the god with sacrifices or money (μισθός).[205] The payment of fees is stipulated in several of the *iamata*. In some cases the failure to pay resulted in the cure reversing itself,[206] but the god once adjusted

---

[195] Hamilton, *Incubation*, 6.

[196] Edelstein, *Asclepius*, 1:240–241; see cure A 8 in LiDonnici, *Epidaurian Miracle Inscriptions*.

[197] Aristides converses at length with Asklepios, according to his *Orations*. For examples of similar conversations in the *iamata* of Epidauros see A 2, 3, 7, 8; B 9?, 14.

[198] In stelae A37, 58, 69; G12, 31. LiDonnici translates ἐπιστὰς φρου ἐφίστημι, as 'came,' but the verb may mean 'stand by or near' as well as 'approach, appear'; see *Epidaurian Miracle Inscriptions*, 80. The phrase ἐδόκει παραστὰ appears in G116.

[199] For instance, see the numerous votive reliefs of Asklepios from Athens and Piraeus in the National Archaeological Museum, Athens. In print, see the relief from the Piraeus Museum of Asklepios and Hygieia standing by head of the reclining dreamer while Asklepios touches the dreamer's head in Hausmann, *Kunst und Heiltum*, plate 1; also in Kerényi, *Asklepios*, 35 (plate 18); cf. the votive relief dedicated to Amphiaraos at Oropos, Kerényi, *Asklepios*, 36, plate 19.

[200] Hamilton, *Incubation*, 3.

[201] Edelstein, *Asclepius*, 2:152–154.

[202] E.g. A 3, A 18; B 11.

[203] See A 17, A 20?, B 6, B 17?, B 19, B 23, C 2?; Hamilton, *Incubation*, 30–31.

[204] Kavvadias does not think medicine was practiced in the first centuries of the cult at Epidauros, against the view of Thrämer, in Hamilton, *Incubation*, 36.

[205] Hamilton, *Incubation*, 31–36. See A 4, 5, 8; B 5; C 3; D 2, 3.

[206] B 2; cf. C 4.

the fees according to one's ability to pay.[207] Votive offerings were also dedicated and sometimes specifically stipulated in the *iamata*. Regional preferences favored different votive styles: Epidauros favored narrative inscriptions, Corinth terra-cotta preferred body-part votives, and Athens and Piraeus used stone votive reliefs.[208]

Clearly, the most common function of incubated dreams is healing, but some incubants also sought knowledge. This information was varied, including being taught a wrestling move, being told the location of buried treasure, and being guided in oratory.[209] In another case, a father who sought his shipwrecked son came to Epidauros for help. According to the inscription, he 'slept here before Asklepios in the Abaton concerning his son and saw a dream,' in which the god led him to his son's location; the man really found his son there afterwards.[210] Some scholars have thus referred to Asklepios' power of 'prophecy' or oracular guidance.[211] In his *Eulogy to Asklepios*, Aristides says, 'To some people the god even foretells times and season. And this we ourselves know' (*Eul. to Askl.*, par. 38).[212]

CONCLUSION: WHAT IS A DREAM?

The broad investigation in Chapters One and Two of the forms, features, and functions of dreams in antiquity confirms a remarkable degree of standardization among both literary and cultic expressions of dreams from the ancient Babylonians to the Romans. Thus, the authors of early Jewish dreams had at their disposal a well-established repertoire of patterns and motifs from which to draw. These traditions differ sharply from modern conceptions and shape the particular definition of 'dream' for this project.

---

[207] A young boy who made Asklepios laugh paid only with ten dice! (A 8).

[208] LiDonnici, *Epidaurian Miracle Inscriptions*, 42; F.T. Van Straten, 'Gifts for the Gods,' in *Faith, Hope and Worship: Aspects of Religious Mentality in the Ancient World* (Leiden: Brill, 1981), 65–151; S.B. Aleshire, *The Athenian Asklepieion: The People, their Dedications, and the Inventories* (Amsterdam: J.C. Gieben, 1989).

[209] For the pankration thrust see B 9, for buried treasure see C 3. Aristides repeatedly gives credit to the god for giving him skill in oratory (281, 283, 309, 324, 327, 328, 332, 333, 354, 360, 361); see Hamilton, *Incubation*, 57–58.

[210] B 4.

[211] Hamilton, *Incubation*, 30, 49–53.

[212] Ibid., 49.

In the ancient mind, message dreams and symbolic dreams are genuine communications originating from the divine world that typically
concern the future. In the case of message dreams, this communication is an epiphany and/or message from an independently existing
divine being, whether the god, a deceased person, or *oneiroi*. The being
is 'real' and can touch the dreamer, leave tokens, perform surgery,
or even kill. Often the figure appears merely in order to wake the
dreamer and impart a message. The typical conclusion to both types of
dreams describes the profound emotional, psychological and/or physical impact that this contact with the divine makes on the dreamer, further emphasizing the genuineness of the contact. Extraordinary knowledge, healing, divine sanction, or their opposites result from contact
with the divine in a dream.

Such well engrained cultural associations may function as political
propaganda, as in the cases of Caesar, Augustus, Tiberius, Vespasian,
Domitian and others. They also translate into social power, and we
have seen an overarching pattern that relegates the clearest, most direct
dreams to males.

Although the real dreams of ordinary people are beyond our reach,
we can know much about the widespread practices of dream interpreters, of incubation and of cultural expectations about dreams that
may have suggested the content of actual dreaming by influencing
dream recall and articulation. Such would appear to be the function
of the *iamata* cure tablets that supplicants read in the cult of Asklepios
at Epidauros prior to incubation.[213]

In addition, we have learned much about the experience of 'dreaming' as a receptive visionary state that may involve sleep or something
between sleeping and waking. Aristides describes an actual dream experience in the incubation cult of Asklepios in this fashion:

> For I seemed almost to touch [Asklepios] and to perceive that he himself
> was coming, and *to be halfway between sleep and waking* (καὶ μέσως ἔχειν
> ὕπνου καὶ ἐγρηγόρσεως) and to want to get the power of vision and to be
> anxious lest he depart beforehand, and to have turned my ears to listen,
> sometimes *as in a dream* (ὡς ὄναρ) sometimes as in a *waking vision* (ὡς ὕπαρ),
> and my hair was standing on end and tears of joy (came forth), and the
> weight of knowledge was no burden—what man could even set these
> things forth in words? But if he is one of the initiates, then he knows and

---

[213] L. LiDonnici, *Epidaurian Miracle Inscriptions*, 18, n. 16.

understands. Having seen these things, when morning dawned, I call the physician Theodotus; and as he comes, I describe to him my *dreams* (τὰ ὀνείρατα).[214]

This passage aptly illustrates the fact that ancient cultures understood a myriad of hypnagogic visionary states in terms of the shared nightly experience of dreaming. In turn they articulated their dreams in terms of the stylized literary conventions for psychological status dreams, message dreams, and symbolic dreams.[215]

As I turn to the Jewish dreams that are the focus of this study, I try to avoid imposing modern notions on ancient dreams, unlike scholars who distinguish between visions and dreams by saying the former are experienced when awake, while the latter are seen while asleep,[216] or who maintain that dreams are 'internal' or imaginary whereas visions are 'external' and 'real.'[217] Therefore, in the chapters that follow, I take 'visions' to be dream episodes if they possess the typical formal elements and features of episodes clearly defined as 'dreams' in the ancient Near Eastern, biblical, Greek and Latin materials. I omit from consideration those visionary episodes that show no form-critical elements that link them to dreams.[218] Although such visions still exist along the vision-dream spectrum, they obviously lie to one extreme end of that spectrum.

Interestingly, modern science confirms the ancient view that dreams and visions exist along a continuum, by establishing that physiological dream states may occur in hypnagogic waking states, at the onset of sleep, in non-R.E.M. sleep or in R.E.M. sleep.[219] Even in deep R.E.M. dreaming, the brain is at least as active or more active than in waking life, only the nerve impulses for large movements are blocked in the spinal cord. This leads sleep research pioneer W. Dement to conclude:

---

[214] Aristides, *Orat.* XLVIII, 31–35; in Edelstein, *Asclepius*, 1:210–211.

[215] See Gnuse, *Samuel*, 140.

[216] J. Pedersen, *Israel: Its Life and Culture* (2 vols.; London, 1926), I:134–140, as cited in Ehrlich, *Der Traum*, 8. Even A. Caquot maintains that one may only speak of an event as a dream if the text specifically mentions sleep, 'Canaan et Israel,' 111.

[217] A. Guillaume, *Prophecy and Divination Among the Hebrews and Other Semites* (London: Hodder and Stoughton, 1938) 217; Ehrlich, *Der Traum*, 8; Hundt, *Der Traumglaube*, 11, 43.

[218] G. Stroumsa has recently declared that 'any study that focuses on dreams while ignoring visions is bound to remain deeply flawed,' 'Dreams and Visions in Early Christian Discourse' in *Dream Cultures*, 189. Although I bracket out patently waking visions for the sake of manageability, I hope that the attention that I pay to visions that possess form-critical elements of dreams fulfills the spirit of his comment.

[219] Sleep Research Society, *Basics of Sleep Behavior*, 21–32.

To certain parts of the brain, there is no difference between waking life and dreaming life. When we are dreaming of eating or fighting or thinking, the brain is sending out the same signals it would if we were awake and eating or fighting or thinking. In a way, all perception is dreaming.[220]

---

[220] Dement, *The Promise of Sleep*, 301.

PART TWO

CHAPTER THREE

DREAMS IN HELLENISTIC JUDAISM:
FORM, VOCABULARY AND FUNCTIONS

> And behold, dreams came upon me,
> and visions fell upon me.
>
> —— 1 Enoch 13:8

The Hellenistic era brought positive change as well as challenge to Mediterranean and Near Eastern communities of antiquity. As both cultural horizons and the perceived limits of the cosmos broadened considerably, Hellenistic peoples reacted to the dissonance by practicing various methods of gaining intimacy with remote gods who suddenly seemed more transcendent.[1] Mystery cults, oracles and divinatory arts soared in popularity, and some practitioners used recipes and rituals from the 'magical papyri' to contact daimons who inhabited the sphere under the moon.[2] Similarly, the practice of dream incubation rapidly expanded, providing close contact with gods and intermediary *oneiroi*. Literary fascination with the theme of divinely-sent dreams mirrored these trends; in both poetry and prose, numerous tales relate how dreamers receive extraordinary knowledge, healing and divine sanction or favor through dreams. Indeed, claiming to be the recipient of a divinely-sent dream could confer tangible blessings in the form of social power, as in the case of Diodorus Siculus' description of Eunus. This former slave led a revolt and made the successful transition to king based in part on social authority that accrued to him due to his own accounts that a goddess imparted her divine sanction to him in his dreams.[3]

For Jews, the Hellenistic age was a particularly dynamic and difficult time. Hellenistic Jews[4] writing sacred literature from the fourth

---

[1] Martin, *Hellenistic Religions*, 3–15.
[2] Ibid., 40–53; Ed. Hans Dieter Betz, *The Greek Magical Papyri in Translation: Including the Demotic Spells* (2nd ed.; Chicago: University of Chicago Press, 1996).
[3] Diodorus Siculus, Books XXXIV/XXXV.
[4] Following M. Hengel, I use the term 'Hellenistic Judaism' to describe all Judaism between the Persian period and late Roman empire. Hellenism profoundly shaped

century B.C.E. through the second century C.E. testify to a plethora
of socio-cultural, religious and political crises, including but not limited to: the Diadochoi wars that wreaked havoc across Palestine; the
threat of Hellenistic syncretism and changing lifestyles; Antiochus IV
Epiphanes' proscription of the Torah in 168 B.C.E.; rule by Macedonian Greeks, Ptolemies, Seleucids and Romans; numerous desecrations
of the Temple by Gentiles and illegitimate Jewish priests; competing
interpretations of Torah and Temple within Judaism; the destruction of
the Second Temple by Titus in 70 C.E.; and the Jewish-Roman Wars of
68–72 and 132–135 C.E.

Like their neighbors, Jews reacted in part to the cultural changes
brought about by Hellenism with a desire for contact with the divine,
reflected in part in a burgeoning interest in dreams sent by the God
of Israel. The apocrypha, pseudepigrapha, Qumran scrolls and Josephus' writings, as well as certain texts in the New Testament, contain
detailed and striking dream reports that draw on the formal patterns,
vocabulary and typical functions of dreams familiar from the Bible,
ancient Near East, Greece and Rome. However, Jewish authors were
not passive inheritors, but rather creative transformers of dream traditions, which were modified to speak to their particular concerns.

In the texts of Hellenistic Judaism, the God of Israel sends dreams to
the pseudepigraphic heroes of Jewish sacred history. The typical benefits conferred by dreams—extraordinary knowledge, healing and divine
sanction—thereby find expression in the form of providential care that
extends not only to biblical characters such as the patriarchs, Enoch,
Levi, and Ezra, but also to their descendants, who constitute the Jewish readership of Hellenistic antiquity. Despite the social realities they
might encounter, audiences were assured of divine blessings and an
exalted future that God had promised their ancestors in dreams. In
many texts, this centering of Jewish concerns operates in tandem with
a symbolic ordering of the universe that views heaven as a Palace-

---

the character of Judaism through the late Roman period, including in cases where
Jews actively resisted certain aspects of Hellenism. See Hengel, *Judaism and Hellenism*
and idem, 'Judaism and Hellenism Revisited,' in *Hellenism in the Land of Israel*, 6–37.
Moreover, I use the terms 'Hellenistic Judaism' and 'early Judaism' as synonymous
epithets, since Hellenistic culture prevailed well after the last Hellenistic kingdom fell in
31 B.C.E. This nomenclature is simply more convenient than 'Judaism of the Hellenistic
and/or Roman Eras' and is more correct than 'Second Temple Judaism,' since I extend
consideration to some Jewish texts composed after 70 C.E. The term 'intertestamental
literature' is likewise false as well as inappropriately Christian-centric.

Temple from which the God of Israel rules over all and in which angels perform various duties, particularly in scribal and priestly capacities. Whether belief in the archetypal Palace-Temple informs socio-religious and political visions for Israel, or whether the stratification of Hellenistic Jewish society informs this conception of heaven, many early Jewish texts interweave priestly and scribal themes throughout their narratives.

In addition to these new accents, several authors transform traditional dream functions further by fully exploiting the motif that dreams suspend the normal constraints of space and time. With the erasure of *spatial limits*, dreamers tour the edges of earth as well as heaven, while angels mix freely on earth. Thus, extraordinary knowledge for the dreamer can include remote earthly as well as heavenly geography, physical healing can occur directly between heavenly angel and earthly dreamer, and divine sanction may entail priestly investiture of dreamers on earth and in the heavenly Temple. With the erasure of *temporal limits*, dreamers are able to see past, present and future. Therefore, dream knowledge may span from the primordial period to the imminent eschaton, psychological healing and consolation can result from witnessing God's impending judgment, and divine sanction may include eschatological exaltation for the dreamer and/or Israel. In addition, according to some authors, dreams can supercede *ontological limits*. Hence, humans as well as angels dream, and some humans are transformed into angels through their dreams.

Part Two, which comprises Chapters Three and Four, examines dreams in the apocrypha, pseudepigrapha, Qumran scrolls, Josephus' writings and the New Testament.[5] Chapter Three establishes continuities between early Judaism and the other traditions examined previously in terms of formal classifications of dreams, vocabulary, and functions. I also show how typical dream functions are permeated with scribal and priestly concerns specific to an early Jewish context.

Moreover, my cross-cultural, form-critical approach not only allows me to establish similarities amongst myriad dream texts, but also enables the identification of several innovations in Hellenistic Jewish texts. In Chapter Four I examine some transformations that Jewish authors make to standard dream motifs, including the soul journey, the role

---

[5] I omit from consideration the philosophical treatment of dreams in Philo, since it represents such a different treatment of dreams. See Berchman, 'Arcana Mundi,' 403–428; and Hay, 'Politics and Exegesis,' 429–438.

of the *oneiroi*, and the character of the dreamer. In addition, since I
am interested in establishing the unique contours of Hellenistic Jewish
dreams, I also investigate the interconnections between dreams and
death, both of which are cast as methods of accessing otherworldly
realms.

Finally, after having examined the literary evidence of dreams in
early Judaism, Part Three, Chapter Five includes my tentative reconstruction of the social milieus of some of the authors of early Jewish
dream texts, including the apocalypses. I also sketch some implications
of my project for numerous topics of study, including the rise of apocalypticism, the rise of early Jewish mysticism, and the social history of
Hellenistic Judaism, particularly as it pertains to priests, scribes, and
dream interpreters.

Form Criticism

Thus far, Oppenheim's formal patterns for dreams have proven especially useful in illustrating the continuity of certain smaller units of
form—the message dream, symbolic dream and their subtypes –across
several cultures for millennia. In earlier chapters I have proceeded in
my application of form criticism mostly by way of example rather than
by discussion. However, since the term 'form criticism' is subject to
so much terminological confusion and variation in its application that
E. Blum has recently wondered if the label should be retained,[6] it is
time for greater precision.

Gunkel's enduring contribution was the introduction of form criticism (although he did not call it that), which isolated literary forms in
texts.[7] Implicit to his method was the idea that investigations of these
forms illuminated pre-literary oral stages of biblical stories, and perhaps even an original social *Sitz im Leben* for each form, which clumsily
preserved vestiges of real history.[8] Gunkel and others such as Gress-
mann seem to have been concerned above all with recovering a lost
history for the events recorded in the Bible, which could be seen in

---

[6] E. Blum, '*Formgeschichte*—A Misleading Category? Some Critical Remarks,' in
Changing Face of Form Criticism, 32–45.

[7] Gunkel, *Genesis*; idem, *Die Psalmen*; idem, *Einleitung in die Psalmen*.

[8] Gunkel, *Genesis*, xlviii–lxix.

their current formulations 'only as though through a mist.'[9] However, the canonization and 'history' of texts in the Hebrew Bible (e.g. of the Tetra/Penta/Hexateuch) have been shown to be much more complex than Gunkel and others had thought, and some have even blamed this type of 'focus away from the present text into a surmised past accessible [only] to a sensitive few' for the overall decline in interest in form criticism in recent decades.[10] Nevertheless, this period has also seen several thoughtful attempts to steer the method in more fruitful directions.[11]

This project does not employ 'form criticism' strictly in the same manner as Gunkel, since his approach is out of place in studies of early Jewish texts, which may or may not involve an oral transmission history. In fact, many Hellenistic Jewish authors create pseudepigraphic fictions within pre-exilic and exilic settings without necessarily drawing on written or oral texts from those eras.[12] Of course, this does not preclude a rich intertextuality with themes in earlier texts. As I will show, early Jewish texts draw on and transform well established patterns of divinely-sent dreams known in the ancient Near East, Bible, Greece and Rome, without necessarily depending on specific texts. By circumscribing my investigation of the formal units of dreams in early Jewish texts within comparisons to similar *literary* forms in antecedent and contemporary texts, I have sought to avoid the pitfalls of Gunkel's necessarily speculative *pre-literary* explorations of forms in terms of their recon-

---

[9] Gunkel, *Genesis*, xvi. A. Campbell censures Gunkel and Gressman for their 'disturbing focus on history as the primary value within their texts,' which ironically leads them 'to devalue the historical aspect [i.e. accuracy] of early story traditions,' A.F. Campbell, S.J., 'Form Criticism's Future,' in *The Changing Face*, 19–20.

[10] So Campbell, 'Form Criticism's Future,' 19.

[11] Several efforts deserve special mention. The difficult distinction between form and genre was greatly clarified by W. Richter in *Exegese als Literaturwissenschaft: Entwurf einer alttestamentlichen Literaturtheorie und Methodologie* (Göttingen: Vandenhoeck & Ruprecht, 1971), esp. 46. R. Knierim summed up the currents in form criticism up to 1985, 'Criticism of Literary Features, Form, Tradition, and Redaction,' in *HBMI* (eds. D.A. Knight and G.M. Tucker; Atlanta, GA: Scholars Press, 1985), 123–165. The boldly conceived *Forms of the Old Testament Literature* series was intended to provide a definitive form critical classification of every pericope in the Hebrew Bible, although progress was slower and the series less uniform than anticipated. See the review by D.L. Petersen of seven volumes through 1992 in *RSR* 18, 1 (Jan 1992): 29–33. Finally, by far the most successful injection of vitality into form criticism is the recent collection of essays stemming from a special session at the 2000 National Meeting of the SBL and collected in *The Changing Face of Form Criticism*.

[12] Even *1 Enoch*, with its long transmission history and *Sagenkränze*, sets the plot in antediluvian times, well before the period of its oral history.

structed oral histories.[13] That is, I hope to show that 'uncertain surmises about a distant past' should certainly be avoided in form critical studies,[14] yet attention to typical forms along diachronic lines allows continuities as well as nuances, transformations, and particular aesthetic-formal structures to emerge more clearly for modern interpreters.

In turn, a better grasp of the concerns and expectations of individual authors might shed light on the thorny issue of authorial social location. While not precisely the same as Gunkel's *Sitz im Leben* of forms, my approach is grounded in the recognition that authors frequently choose literary forms and motifs for their relevance to the authors' social settings.[15] For instance, the authors of 4 Ezra and 2 Baruch set their stories during the fall of the First Temple since this resonates with the destruction of the Second Temple in their recent memory. Throughout Part One I argued that in both literature and cult in ancient Near Eastern and Mediterranean antiquity, certain dream forms signal contact with the divine and afford knowledge, healing and sanction, which could translate into enhanced social authority for the dreamers. When early Jewish authors avidly utilize the same forms, they are able to transmit new theologies to their audiences under the mantle of divine revelation. That is, the literary investigation of dream texts impinges on an examination of the ways in which texts confer or maintain social power. Careful recognition of the unique contours of dream forms and functions in early Jewish literature can lend insight into the social contexts in which certain kinds of divine knowledge, healing and sanction were desirable and valuable for either author or audience.

In my application of form criticism to early Jewish literature, I am guided by the following definition by M. Sweeney: 'a method of linguistic textual analysis … [focusing] especially on the patterns of language that appear within the overall linguistic configuration or form of a text and the role that these patterns play in giving shape and expression to the text.'[16] Part of the value of isolating smaller, typical formal pat-

---

[13] Consider this statement by Gunkel: 'The legends were already very ancient and had already undergone a long history when they were committed to writing. This is the nature of the matter: the origin of legend is always remote from the perspective of the inquirer and *goes back into prehistoric times*. So it is in this case, too.' Gunkel, *Genesis*, xlviii.

[14] Campbell, 'Form Criticism's Future,' 24.

[15] J. Barton also considers the search for social setting to be basic to the method, 'Form Criticism: Old Testament,' in *ABD* 2:838–841, 838.

[16] M.A. Sweeney, 'Form Criticism,' in *To Each Its Own Meaning: Biblical Criticisms and Their Application* (eds. S.L. McKenzie and S.R. Haynes; Louisville, KY: Westminster John Knox, 1999), 58–89.

terns is that it expands our understandings of authorial constructions of meaning and aids us in better approximating the expectations of the original readership. Our cultural history of the phrase 'Once upon a time' communicates expectations to readers and profoundly shapes their interpretations of what follows. Similarly, familiarity with the conventional ancient Near Eastern and Mediterranean dream frame that begins 'And I lay down' both allows one to recognize episodes in Hellenistic Jewish literature as dreams and creates greater sensitivity to permutations on the theme.

My ultimate concern is to illuminate overarching patterns of continuities and discontinuities between the dream traditions of Hellenistic Judaism and other dream traditions and thereby to recognize the unique contours of early Jewish dreams. However, I am mindful of James Muilenberg's call that form criticism attend to rhetorical criticism, which considers the nuancing of language and structure within particular texts.[17] Since my discussion of early Jewish texts comprises over one hundred individual dream episodes, such a mandate is impossible on the wide-scale of this study. However, in the next chapter I explicate in greater detail certain complex dream texts such as *1 Enoch* 13–36, Daniel 7–12 and 4 Ezra; these discussions, I hope, will serve to illustrate the profound artistry and skill of the authors of the texts and to provoke further study.

Two further presuppositions deserve mention before we turn to the early Jewish dream texts themselves. First, as I have stated, although dreams exist on a continuum with visions, the following discussion concerns the dream end of the spectrum. I limit consideration of texts to those hypnagogic episodes which are articulated by their setting or description in terms of the nightly occurrence of dreaming, and/or which follow the formal patterns of other episodes that are clearly labeled as dreams. For the purposes of this project, visionary experiences such as those in the Book of Revelation and ascent texts such as *3 Enoch* therefore fall outside my purview, despite many similarities to some texts under consideration. Certainly, visions in early Judaism and early Christianity are close in form to dreams and deserving of further consideration elsewhere in terms of synchronic aesthetic-formal patterns.[18]

---

[17] J. Muilenberg, 'Form Criticism and Beyond,' *JBL* 88 (1969): 1–18.

[18] M. Fishbane has shown consistency in terminology and structure for biblical

Second, I apply Oppenheim's form-critical patterns of dreams to visionary episodes in the apocrypha, pseudepigrapha, Qumran Scrolls, the writings of Josephus and the New Testament. I also include the two texts in the New Testament that contain dreams. Although obviously Christian, both the Gospel of Matthew and Acts of the Apostles are relatively early (before the end of the first century),[19] and are in obvious conversation with Hellenistic Judaism. Also, it should be restated that I have chosen to include several works that others may prefer to label as texts from early Christianity (e.g. *2 Enoch*,[20] *Testaments of the Twelve Patriarchs*[21] and *Ladder of Jacob*[22]). The Jewish originals of

---

dreams and visions in 'The Mantological Exegesis of Dreams, Visions, and Omens,' in *Biblical Interpretation in Ancient Israel* (Oxford: Clarendon, 1985, 1988), 447–457.

[19] P.C. Miller has investigated Christian dreams in *Dreams in Late Antiquity: Studies in the Imagination of a Culture* (Princeton: Princeton University Press, 1994).

[20] The date, original language and provenance of *2 Enoch* are a matter of debate. The text is extant only in Slavonic and no manuscripts earlier than the fourteenth century survive. Opinions range from that of R.H. Charles, who concludes it was written by a Hellenized Alexandrian Jew in the first century B.C.E., to that of J.T. Milik, who maintains it was written by a Byzantine Christian monk in the ninth century C.E. Moreover, as Andersen notes in his introduction to his translation, scholars have not decided conclusively whether the text stems from Jewish or Christian circles. Based partly on the congruence of the dreams in *2 Enoch* with other dream texts from Second Temple Judaism, I favor the views of F.I. Andersen and C. Böttrich, who incline towards the theory of an original Jewish stratum of an early date, perhaps in the 1st c. C.E. See the introduction by Andersen, *2 (Slavonic Apocalypse of) Enoch*, *OTP* 1:91–100 and Böttrich, *Das slavische Henochbuch*, 812–813; idem, *Weltweisheit*, esp. 108.

[21] The dating and provenance of the *Testaments of the Twelve Patriarchs* have also been a matter of great debate, with M. de Jonge leading the charge in challenging R.H. Charles' classic theory that the testaments are Jewish with Christian redactions, arguing instead for Christian authorship in the late second or early third century. M. de Jonge, *Testaments of the Twelve Patriarchs* and particularly R.A. Kugler, *From Patriarch to Priest*, which argues that *Aram. Levi* is used by an original *T. Levi* to become *Greek T. Levi*. However, Kugler later concludes the *Urtext* is unattainable, but even then maintains a Christian author drew on Jewish themes and directed *T. Twelve* at a Jewish audience. Kugler, *The Testaments of the Twelve Patriarchs*, 31–38. It is probably best to conclude that *T. Twelve* appears to be 'a broad and free tradition' of the twelve sons, at least portions of which originate in Jewish circles, see H.C. Kee, *Testaments of the Twelve Patriarchs*, *OTP* 1:776–781.

[22] The inclusion of the *Ladder of Jacob* necessitates a defense. Its date and provenance are uncertain, since the text survives only in parts of the Slavonic *Tolkovaja paleja*, the component parts of which stem at their earliest from ninth century C.E. Old Church Slavonic. In the introduction to his recent translation, H.G. Lunt ultimately rests in favor of an originally Jewish work in Greek, intended for a Palestinian audience; the superscription to the translation places it in the first century C.E. See H.G. Lunt, *Ladder of Jacob*, *OTP* 2:401–406. I am in favor of Jewish composition in the first several centuries C.E. based on the congruence of the dream and interpretation with other

these texts are uncertain, although I am inclined to posit Jewish authorship with Christian redaction, based in large part on the continuity of
the particular concerns of the dreams in these texts with other Jewish
dream texts.[23] According to the reader's preferences, then, the chapter
may be thought of as including dream texts from early Judaism and
early Christianity.

Classifications of Dreams in Hellenistic Judaism

Using Oppenheim's formal patterns in conjunction with early Jewish
texts makes possible the identification of narrative episodes as 'dreams'
on the basis of ancient expectations, even when the vocabulary for
'dream' is absent. The result is that the dream texts of Hellenistic
Judaism may be situated as part and parcel of the larger diachronic
and synchronic dream traditions in literature and cult of the ancient
Near East, Hebrew Bible, Greece and Rome. All types of divinely-
sent dreams recognizable in those cultures—including the symbolic
dream, message dream, auditory message dream and *Wecktraum*—are
also present in numerous texts of varying genres of Hellenistic Judaism.
The apocalypses *1 Enoch*, Daniel 7–12, *2 Baruch*, *4 Ezra*, *2 Enoch*, *Greek Testament of Levi*, and *Testament of Abraham* contain some of the most complex dreams. However, biblical *midrashim* such as *Liber Antiquitatum Biblicarum (Pseudo-Philo)*, *Jubilees*, Additions to Esther, *Testament of Job*, *Ezekiel
the Tragedian* and *Ladder of Jacob* also display a lively interest in dreams.
These texts not only retell biblical dreams, they modify the dreams
and interweave new ones. Divinely-sent dreams also occur in other
genres, including: the *Testaments of Naphtali* and *Joseph*; the history of
2 Maccabees; Josephus' histories, *Jewish Antiquities* and *Jewish War*; as
well as Josephus' apologetic *Against Apion* and autobiographical *Life*. Reports or commentary on dreams are also present in apocalypses, targu-
mim, hymns and other fragmentary texts in the Qumran scrolls, including: *11QTargum of Job*, *1QGenesis Apocryphon*, *4QEnoch*, *4QBook of Giants*,
4QApocryphon of Jacob, *4QAramaic Levi*, *4QVisions of Amram*, *4QPrayer of*

Jewish dreams, as well as on similarities between the hymn in chapter two and *Hekhalot*
hymns; chapter seven would seem to be a later (Gnostic?) addition.

[23] There are other factors as well which would take me away from the main thrust
of my investigation, e.g. the similarity of the hymn in *Ladder of Jacob* with Jewish *Hekhalot*
hymns.

Nabonidus, 4QVisions of Samuel, 4QPsalms, 11QPsalms, and perhaps *4QElect of God*. Finally, the Gospel of Matthew and the Acts of the Apostles, which I consider here alongside other Hellenistic Jewish literature containing dreams, might be classified respectively in terms of genre as a Graeco-Roman biography and ancient history with travel narratives.[24]

Part One clarified that dream classifications can occur along lines of gender. Ancient Near Eastern and Greek sources tend to relegate symbolic dreams to women and message dreams to men, while the Hebrew Bible contains no female dreamers. Similarly, practically all examples of dreams in early Judaism are those of male dreamers. Out of approximately one hundred dreams in Hellenistic Jewish literature, only five are those of female dreamers (Miriam in *L.A.B.* 9:10; Rebecca in *Jub.* 35:6; Glaphyra in *J.W.* 2.114–116 and the same dream in *Ant.* 17.349–353; Stratonica in *Ap.* 1.206–207; and Pilate's wife in Matt 27:19), and three of these cases are terribly unflattering portraits. Glaphyra and Stratonica are killed by their dreams as punishment for being unfaithful to their deceased husbands, and Pilate's wife apparently suffers from an 'evil dream' for her husband's impending murder of Jesus. Rebecca's dream of her imminent death can hardly be construed as positive, although it does signify divine favor that she was privileged with this knowledge. However, Jacob disbelieves her and laughs when she tells him about it (*Jub.* 35:7).

Similarly, Miriam's parents do not believe her when she relates the story of her annunciation dream of Moses (*L.A.B.* 9:10). Miriam and Rebecca's stories, then, both assume the ridiculousness of a woman receiving a divinely-sent dream, since men's dreams are not mocked in Hellenistic Jewish texts. Moreover, Miriam's dream relates intertextually to the biblical tradition that she is a prophet (Deut 34:10) in a way that diminishes her status in relation to Moses. In *Liber Antiquitatum Biblicarum*, Miriam's dream predicts the future birth and greatness of her brother Moses the prophet, who in biblical memory is a male whose prophetic status is aggrandized directly in relation to those who receive prophetic dreams (Num 12:1–9). In other words, the very content of her dream in *L.A.B.* has the effect of lessening the status of Miriam's revelation in relation to the future prophecies of a male, and the point

---

[24] B. Ehrman, *The New Testament: A Historical Introduction to the Early Christian Writings* (2nd ed.; New York: Oxford University Press, 2000), 122.

is underscored when her parents do not believe her. It should also be noted that the content of Rebecca's dream concerning her own fate is not narrated, while the other four women have dreams solely for the sake of the men to whom they are attached, husbands and brother.[25] As we shall see, since most other dreams in Hellenistic Judaism function to increase the status of the dreamer, the eclipsing of women in the dream tradition once again suggests a larger social reality that privileges males over females.

Part One also illustrated that particular cultures tend to favor certain dream types and motifs. Few psychological status dreams occur in ancient Near Eastern sources, and none in the Bible; however, this dream type is clearly present in Greek and Roman sources. Hittite materials favor auditory message dreams, which are also well known in the Bible and in Latin sources. By contrast, Greek sources revel in depicting the visible dream messenger, whether a deceased person, an *oneiros* or a god in disguise. Latin authors seem to dislike the murky symbolic dreams common to Greek poetry, preferring clear message dreams instead.

Early Jewish texts, like the Bible, are also notably devoid of psychological status dreams, thus locating their interest in dreams squarely in the context of communication from the divine. This lack of concern for ordinary dreaming and the mechanisms of dreaming forms a striking contrast to Graeco-Roman dream traditions such as the investigations of the philosophers and physicians. In the Jewish corpus, the only candidate for a psychological status dream is the episode in Josephus' *Jewish Antiquities* in which the High Priest Matthias has a sex dream (*Ant.* 17.166). Even here, the dream impinges on divine matters, since it renders him ritually impure to perform his priestly services.[26] In contrast to this paucity of psychological status dreams, Oppenheim's other categories—the message dream, *Wecktraum*, auditory message dream and symbolic dream—are each amply attested for male dreamers, who are typically rulers, priests and/or pseudepigraphic heroes from Israel's past.

---

[25] The same is possibly true of Rebecca in *Jub.* 35, since the story focuses on her telling the dream to Jacob and on his reaction.

[26] Gnuse also categorizes the episode as a psychological status dream, *Josephus*, 192, 202.

Message Dreams and Subtypes

The Lord serves as the messenger within numerous dreams in the literature of Hellenistic Judaism. Many of these are retellings of biblical message dreams: *Jub.* 27:19–26 and *Ant.* 1.278–284 relate Jacob's dream at Bethel; *Ant.* 2.171–176 narrates Jacob's dream at Beersheba; and *Ant.* 8.22–25 elaborates on Solomon's dream at Gibeon. Other texts in Josephus' *Antiquities* recast episodes in the Hebrew Bible anew as dreams: *Ant.* 5.215–216 transforms Judges 7–8 into a dream by Gideon; 6.37–40 relocates the theophany from 1 Samuel 18:1–9 in a message dream; and Nathan's prophecy in 2 Samuel 7:4 and 17 is set into a message dream in *Ant.* 7.92–93.

Several other texts utilize the formal pattern of the message dream to create entirely new episodes of revelation in which the Lord is messenger. In *Jubilees* 32:16–26, Jacob has a second dream at Bethel in which the Lord gives him a message. *2 Enoch* records two message dreams apiece for Methuselah (69:4–6 and 70:3–11) and for Nir (71:27–37, 72:3–10), and the Lord is the speaker in both. In *L.A.B.* Phineas relates his father Eleazar's testamentary message dream in which 'the Lord appeared' (28:4–5). Josephus gives Jacob a message dream at Shechem (*Ant.* 1:341–342) and Amram dreams a message by the Lord in *Ant.* 2.212–217. Also, in *1 Enoch* 15:1–16:4 the Lord delivers a message to Enoch during his otherworldly tour of the divine Temple, constituting a component of an auditory message dream within a larger, more complex dream form.

It is important to note that the phrase 'the Lord appeared' does not necessarily imply that the messenger of a dream is the angel of the Lord. Rather, this phrase should be viewed against the Hellenistic Jewish background of theophanic ascent literature in which a pseudepigraphic hero actually sees God as the pinnacle of revelation:

> For you gaze into (my) eyes, a human being created just like yourselves; but I have gazed into the eyes of the LORD, like the rays of the shining sun and terrifying the eyes of a human being … You, you see the extent of my body, the same as your own; but I, I have seen the extent of the LORD, without measure and without analogy, who has no end.
>
> (*2 En.* A 39:4–6; cf. *1 En.* 15:19–20)

Since some early Jewish authors depict the privileged few as seeing the Lord in waking revelation, we might take at face value the literary theme that the Lord appears in dreams to certain pseudepigraphic heroes. For instance, Josephus elaborates on the biblical account of

Jacob's dream at Bethel, clearly casting the episode as a message dream in which God appears: 'plainly visible (ἐναϱγῶς) to him was God' (*Ant.* 1.278–284). Thus in this period, the God of Israel apparently appears in dreams in the same way as do gods of other cultures.[27]

Hence, it is often difficult to know whether the phrase 'the Lord appeared' indicates a visible theophany, and the demarcation of message dreams versus auditory message dreams is subjective. At times the latter category may simply result from omission due to a conscious attempt to avoid the blasphemy of depicting the Lord's material manifestation. In other cases, the voice or word of the Lord is prominent, more clearly marking an episode as an auditory message dream. Tentatively, I identify the following episodes as auditory message dreams of the Lord that are also retellings of biblical episodes: *Jub.* 14:1–17 relates Abram's sacrifice and dream at Mamre; *L.A.B.* 18:4–7 narrates Balaam's dreams; *Ant.* 1.313–314 relates Laban's dream; *L.A.B.* 53:1–13 and *Ant.* 5.348–350 retell young Samuel's dreams at Shiloh, which are also *Weckträumen*; and *Ant.* 1.208–209 may be an auditory message dream of Abimelech. Other auditory message dreams develop biblical traditions; for instance *L.A.B.* 23:3–14 recasts Joshua's covenantal renewal ceremony in what seems to be an auditory message dream and *Ant.* 8.125–129 gives Solomon a second dream at Gibeon. Still others are altogether new accounts, such as Josephus' description of the High Priest Jaddus dreaming after a mass sacrifice in the Jerusalem Temple (*Ant.* 11.326–328) and King Monobazus dreaming of a protective divine voice that spoke to him about the child in his wife's womb (*Ant.* 20.18–19).[28] The Qumran scrolls are an unclear case: Abram's dreams are either message or auditory message dreams in *1QGen. Ap.* (*1Q20*[*1QapGen ar*]) col. XXI–XXII. *Jubilees* 41:24 is a unique auditory message dream in which Judah is forgiven, although it is not clear who does the forgiving (perhaps the Lord and the Angel of the Presence who narrates the bulk of *Jubilees*).

---

[27] Another example is the case of Isis' appearance in a dream, as related by Josephus (*Ag. Ap.* 1.289).

[28] Gnuse's list of auditory dreams is close to mine: *Ant.* 1.208–209, 1.278–284, 1.313–314, 2.171–176, 2.212–217, 5.215–216, 5.348–350, 6.37–40, 7.92–93, 7.147, 8.22–25, 8.125–129, 11.326–328, and perhaps *Ant.* 12.112, 20.18–19, and *Ap.* 1.289. Gnuse, *Josephus*, 201. Most of our discrepancies occur in marginal cases in which determination of category is difficult. However, I do strongly disagree with classifying Jacob's dream at Bethel in *Ant.* 1.278–284 as an auditory message dream.

In addition to message dreams of the Lord Himself, angels also function as messengers in early Jewish dreams. Angelic message dreams include the following: *L.A.B.* 9:10; 4 Ezra 3:1–5:20, 5:21–6:13, 6:35–7:2; *2 En.* 1:3–10; Matt 1:20–25, 2:13–23; Acts 16:9–10; *4QVisions of Amram*^b (*4Q544[4Q'Amram*^b*ar]*) fragment 1; *Life* 208–210; and possibly in *4QApocryphon of Jacob* (*4Q537[4QA Ja ar]*) fragment 1. The actions and messages of the angels are varied. They announce the impending birth of Moses (*L.A.B.* 9:10) and the imminent ascent of Enoch to heaven (*2 En.* 1:3–10). Acting in a protective capacity, they warn Josephus and guide him, as they do with Joseph and Paul in the New Testament (*Life* 208–210; Matt 1:20–25, 2:13–15, 2:19–23; Acts 16:9–10). In a unique case reflecting a particular theology of Qumran, two angels bicker over control of Amram in *4QVisions of Amram*^b (*4Q544[4Q'Amram*^b*ar]*) fragment 1. Finally, Uriel imparts eschatological revelations to Ezra repeatedly in his dreams and discusses theodicy at some length (4 Ezra 3:1–5:20, 5:21–6:13, 6:35–7:2).

The motif of the angelic dream messenger who relays the main revelation marks a clear departure from biblical tradition, in which angels do not typically function in this capacity. However, as I will explore further below, most of the time in Hellenistic Judaism angels appear during or after dreams not in order to relay the main message of revelation, but rather to interpret revelation imparted by God or witnessed by the dreamer (e.g. *1 En.* 16–36; Dan 7:16–28, 8:15–26; *Jub.* 32:22; 4 Ezra 10:29; *Ladd. Jac.* 3:4–7:35; *2 Bar.* 55:3–76:5).

While Hellenistic Jewish texts of course do not depict the Lord materially, they do describe oneiric messenger angels in various ways. Angels appear in fire and solar imagery (*2 En.* 1:5; cf. *1 En.* 14:8, 22), as a bright light that accompanies an auditory message dream (*T. Job* 3:1–4), as humanoid figures, (*1 En.* 17:1; *2 En.* 1:4; *T. Abr.* 3; cf. Dan 7:13, *T. Levi* 5:4 and 4 Ezra 13:3), as winged creatures who fly (*2 En.* A 1:5, 3:1, 4:2, cf. A and J ch. 12; Dan 9:21), and in zoomorphic forms (*T. Abr.* A 17; B 14; cf. *2 En.* J 12). The names of dream messengers suggest their roles and functions but may also suggest their appearance in terms of natural phenomena, as in 'Uriel,' 'light of God' (*1 En.* 29:2, 4 Ezra).[29]

---

[29] This is clearest in the names of the Watchers, who are not dream messengers but are angels: Kokabel, 'star of God'; Ramel, 'thunder of God'; Ziqel, 'shooting star of God'; Baraqel, 'lightning of God'; Matarel, 'rain of God'; Anuel, 'cloud of God'; Setawel, 'winter of God'; Samshiel, 'sun of God'; Sahriel, 'moon of God'; Turiel, 'mountain of God'; and Yamiel, 'sea of God' (*1 En.* 6:7). See G. Nickelsburg, *1 Enoch*, 178–181 for etymological discussions of angelic names. Interestingly, many of the 'bad'

Overall, then, Jewish texts retain and expand the ancient Near Eastern and Graeco-Roman depictions of *oneiroi* in anthropomorphic and naturalistic terms. However, the typical portrayal of dream messengers as wind—implicit in the word *ᵈZaqīqu* and explicit in Greek texts such as *Odyssey* IV.890–895[30]—is lacking. This striking omission warrants further investigation, and may stem from traditions surrounding the Hebrew *ruach* and its relation to God.

Several of the message dreams listed above are *Weckträumen*, including: 4 Ezra 5:21–6:13, 6:35–7:2, *2 En.* 1:3–10, *L.A.B.* 53:1–13, *T. Job* 3:1–4, and Acts 12:6–7. As in other cultures, the logic of this motif appears to be that the dream eases the dreamer into the onset of the waking theophany, which is a terrifying encounter with the divine. The Hebrew Bible contains a few *Weckträumen*: God wakes Samuel three times in order to speak to him (1 Samuel 3:2–15) and an angel wakes Elijah to give him food (1 Kings 19:5–7). Similarly, *Liber Antiquitatum Biblicarum* portrays the episode from 1 Samuel 3 explicitly as auditory *Weckträumen* of the Lord Himself, and not of an angel (*L.A.B.* 53:6–7). In the New Testament, an angel wakes Peter to rescue him from prison (Acts 12:6–7), and in *2 Enoch* two angels wake Enoch in order to tell him of his impending otherworldly journey (*2 En.* 1:3–10). Uriel repeatedly wakes Ezra in order to relay revelations, but his arrival in Ezra's sleep cushions the shock of the angelophany (4 Ezra 5:21–6:13, 6:35–7:2).

In addition to the Lord and angels, humans also sometimes function as messengers in dreams of early Judaism, a concept that would be anathema to biblical authors. In true Graeco-Roman fashion, the dead appear as *oneiroi* in several dreams, including 2 Macc 15:11–16; *J.W.* 2.114–116; and *Ant.* 17.349–353. In one rare case, Alexander the Great sees in his dream the likeness of a living person, the High Priest Jaddus (*Ant.* 11.333–335), who imparts a message to him.[31]

The formal framing and setting of message dreams in early Jewish texts closely follow the formal patterns of message dreams in the

---

angels in *1 Enoch* have names evoking natural phenomena, while the names of 'good' angels speak more to qualities and characteristics of God, such as Raphael, Reuel, Michael, Sariel and Gabriel (*1 En.* 20:1–8).

[30] Oppenheim, *Interpretation*, 234.

[31] Gnuse's list of εἴδωλον dreams is close, as follows: *War* 2.114–116, *Life* 208–210, *Ant.* 11.333–335, 17.349–353. He states that the following contain aspects of this type of dream: *Ant.* 1.278–284, 1.313–314, 2.171–176, 5.213. *Josephus*, 201–202.

ancient Near East, Bible, Greece and Rome. The following example
from Josephus would not be out of place in texts from any of these
cultures:

> I. INTRODUCTION: 'That night I beheld a marvelous vision in my
> dreams. I had retired to my couch, grieved and distraught ...' (*Life* 208)
> Διὰ δὲ τῆς νυκτὸς ἐκείνης θαυμάσιον οἷον ὄνειρον ἐθεασάμην. ἐπεὶ γὰρ
> κοίτην ἐτραπόμην ...
>
> II. DREAM: 'I thought that there stood by me one who said ...' (208)
> ἔδοξά τινα λέγειν ἐπιστάντα μοι ...
>
> III. CONCLUSION: 'Cheered by this dream-vision I arose ...' (210)
> τοῦτον δὴ τὸν ὄνειρον θεασάμενος διανίσταμαι ...

The familiar elements of night, lying on a bed, and grieving establish
the dream setting. The dream itself is a typical message dream of an
oneiros who 'stood by me,' ἐπιστάντα μοι, while the common Greek
ἔδοξά introduces the main portion of the dream theophany. The angel's
message is one of comfort—'let go all fear'—and the main function of
the dream is divine sanction: 'Not in these present trials only, but in
many besides, will fortune attend thee. Fret not thyself then. Remember
that thou must even battle with the Romans' (*Life* 209–210). The usual
conclusion marks Josephus' mood and notes that he arose.

A message dream from *2 Enoch*, which some consider to be a late first
to second century C.E. Jewish text with later Christian redactions,[32]
provides us with another example of a message dream that is also a
Wecktraum:

> I. INTRODUCTION: 'I was in my house alone, weeping and grieving
> with my eyes. When I had lain down on my bed, I fell asleep' (*2 En.* A
> 1:2–3).
>
> II. DREAM: 'And two huge men appeared to me ... and they called me
> by name' (*2 En.* A 1:4–5).
>
> III. CONCLUSION: 'I got up from my sleep, and the men were stand-
> ing with me in actuality ... I stood up and bowed down to them ... and
> the men said to me ... "Be brave, Enoch! Do not fear! ..."' (*2 En.* A
> 1:6–7)

The dream messengers appear in order to wake Enoch; they remain
nearby after he awakens and proceed to relate their message. The
formal pattern of the *Wecktraum* is what we would expect in every
way, including preparatory rituals (weeping and grieving), a setting of

---

[32] See the introduction and translation by Andersen, *2 Enoch*.

lying in bed and sleeping, and the appearance of two large, beautiful humanoid dream messengers. In the 'J' recension, an even more exact parallel with non-Jewish dreams occurs: 'And they stood at the head of my bed' (2 En. J 1:5).[33] The content of the message, namely, that Enoch is bound to travel to heaven today, marks the episode as a Hellenistic Jewish ascent text, a feature I investigate later.

Symbolic Dreams

Early Jewish literature shows none of the Roman dislike for symbolic dreams, which abound in the Jewish texts, e.g.: *1 En.* 83:3–10, 85:3–90:42; Dan 7:1–28, 8:1–27; *Jub.* 39:16–40:12; Add Esth 11:2–12:5; *2 Bar.* 35:1–36:11, 52:7–53:12; *4 Ezra* 11:1–12:3, 13:1–14; *T. Abr.* 5:6–7:15 B; *T. Naph.* 5:1–8, 6:1–10; and *T. Jos.* 19:1–12. In Josephus they occur in *J.W.* 2.112–113, 3.351–354; *Ant.* 1.341–342, 2.10–17, 2.63–73, 2.75–86, 5.218–222, 10.194–211, 10.216–217, 17.345–348 and probably 13.322 and 14.451.[34] Symbolic dreams are well attested in the Qumran scrolls, e.g.: *1 QGenesis Apocryphon* (*1 QApGen ar*) col. XIX; *4 QEnoch^a ar* (*4Q204–4Q207[4QEn^a ar]*); *4 QBook of Giants^b* (*4Q530[4QEn Giants^b ar]*) col. I. In the latter text the dreamers are Watchers; 'Ohyah probably refers to this dream or one like it in *4 QBook of Giants^c* (*4Q531[4QEnGiants]^c*).

Symbolic dreams in Hellenistic Judaism adhere to the widely established patterns of message and symbolic dreams detailed in Part One. A passage in *2 Baruch* in which Baruch dreams while sleeping on the ruins of the Temple serves to demonstrate this well:[35]

> I. INTRODUCTION: 'I fell asleep at that place and saw a vision in the night.' ܟܘ ܫ ܐܠܠܐ ܕ ܠ ܐ ܘܐ ܘ ܐ ܗ ܐ ܕ ܗ 'And behold' ܟܗܐ (36:1–2, 3); 'And I looked, and behold' ܟܗܐ ܕ ܐ ܘ (36:7)
>
> II. DREAM: Symbolic dream of the forest, vine, water and cedar
>
> III. CONCLUSION: 'And I awoke and arose' ܕ ܐܗ ܘ ܐ ܕ ܐ ܐ ܐܪ ܕ ܐ ܐ ܐ ܘ (37:1)

---

[33] For the widespread attestation of this trope see Oppenheim, *Interpretation*, 189.

[34] Gnuse's list is as follows: *J.W.* 1.328, 2.112–113, 3.351–354; *Ant.* 2.10–17, 2.63–73, 2.75–86, 5.218–222, 10.194–211, 10.216–217, 14.451, 17.345–348 and probably 13.322, *Josephus*, 202.

[35] The English translation follows A.F.J. Klijn, *2 (Syriac Apocalypse of) Baruch*, OTP 1:615–652. The Syriac is taken from 'Apocalypse of Baruch,' in *The Old Testament in Syriac According to the Peshitta Version* (ed. S. Dedering; Part IV, fasc. 3.; Leiden: Brill, 1973).

IV. INTERPRETATION: Baruch asks the Lord for 'the explanation of this vision' ܪܐ ܠܘ ܪܐ ܡܢ ܡܢܬܩܐ (38:4, 39:2).

As is the norm, the INTRODUCTION depicts the dreamer asleep, in bed or lying down, with a symbolic dream following. The two main components of temple incubation are present: 1) Baruch has purposefully gone to the ruins of the Holy of Holies to seek revelation from God (34:1) and 2) he sleeps in the sacred space of the Temple (36:1). In addition, 3) his grieving and prayer are typical incubatory rituals practiced from the ancient Near Eastern period onward, as we have seen. The visionary episode that ensues is explicitly a dream, given that Baruch falls asleep and later awakens, despite the fact that only the term ܪܐ ܠܘ describes his hypnagogic state. In this symbolic DREAM, Baruch sees visual objects acting in odd ways, with repeated stress on seeing, e.g.: 'And I looked, and behold' ܪܡܐ ܐܠܘ ܠܝܢܐ. A typical CONCLUSION consists of the dreamer awakening with great emotion or physical symptoms, and in this case Baruch prays fervently for an INTERPRETATION: 'Now, show me the explanation ܡܢܬܩܐ of this vision' (*2 Bar.* 28:3), which the Lord Himself later provides.

Symbolic dreams must be interpreted, and accordingly, an interpretation follows nearly every symbolic dream in Hellenistic Judaism.[36] When the content of the dreams concerns fairly straightforward matters of the future, as in the midrashic retellings of the Joseph cycle's dreams of the butler, baker and Pharaoh, pseudepigraphic heroes such as Joseph interpret dreams (*Jub.* 39:16–40:12). Mordecai interprets his own dream (Add Esth 10:4–8) and Josephus does as well (*J.W.* 3.351–354); yet since this motif is so unusual, these passages may be intended to accent the exceptional insights of Mordecai and Josephus.[37]

However, much of the time in Hellenistic Judaism, the referents of symbolic dreams are cosmological and eschatological. In these cases, symbolic dreams are generally interpreted by angels, often as a result of a petitionary prayer by the dreamer. For instance, Baruch dreams of alternating dark and bright waters (*2 Bar.* 53) and after awakening prays: 'You showed this vision to your servant; open to me its exposition also' (54:7). Shortly thereafter Ramael, 'the angel who is set over true visions,' is sent to Baruch to explain at length the symbolic dream, which concerns the periodization of all of cosmic history, concluding

---

[36] Two exceptions occur in *1 Enoch* 83–90.
[37] Gnuse makes this case for Josephus, *Josephus*, 155.

with an imminent eschaton (55:1–76:5). That is, in this text, the interpretation, which spans over twenty-one chapters, provides the audience with much more information than does the symbolic dream itself,
which is narrated in a single chapter. The character of the interpreting
angel is pervasive, occurring in the following texts: Zech 1–6; Dan 7–12;
1 En. 17–36; 4 Ezra 3–14; *2 Bar.* 55; *T. Levi* 2–5; *T. Abr.* A and B 7; *Jub.* 32;
Ladd. Jac. 4–6; and probably in the fragmentary *4QApocryphon of Jacob*
(*4Q537* [*4QAJa ar*]).

Typical Vocabulary of Dreams in Texts of Hellenistic Judaism

Since it would be an unnecessarily lengthy process to recount the
state of discussions concerning the dating of various extant manuscripts
for each early Jewish text that I include, my examination of typical
vocabulary proceeds with various languages in turn without implying
any chronological sequence of manuscripts. The interested scholar will
find each manuscript I use listed in the footnotes.

As is the case in the ancient Near Eastern, biblical, Greek and
Latin sources, terms for visions and dreams are used interchangeably
in Hellenistic Jewish texts. In Syriac, ܚܠܡ is usually used in its nominal
form of 'a dream' (Dan 7:1) rather than the verbal form 'to dream,'
with related adjectival meanings associated with healing: well, healthy,
whole, sound.[38] Much more often, however, the term for 'dream' is
ܚܙܘܐ in the sense not only of 'a vision,' but also 'appearance, form,
figure'; this typically appears with ܚܙܐ, 'to look' or 'perceive, consider,
notice.'[39] ܚܙܘܐ appears in the sense of 'a dream' in Dan 8:1, 15, 17, 26;
Jub. 4:19, 41:24; *2 Bar.* 36:1, 38:4, 39:1, 40:4, 53:1, 54:6, 55:3, 56:1, 71:2;
4 Ezra 10:37, 10:59, 11:1, 12:10, 13:1, 19, 21.[40] ܚܙܐ appears in Dan 7:1, 2,
7, 9; 8:2; *2 Bar.* 53:1; 4 Ezra 11:1, 2, 12:10, 13:1, frequently with ܚܙܘܐ, as

---

[38] R. Payne Smith, 'ܚܠܡ,' *A Compendious Syriac Dictionary* (ed. J. Payne Smith; Winona
Lake, IN: Eisenbrauns, 1998), 144. The ethpeel carries the meanings of 'to be refreshed
with sleep,' as well as 'to recover health, be healed, cured, made whole.'

[39] 'ܚܙܐ' and 'ܚܙܘܐ,' *A Compendious Syriac Dictionary*, 136.

[40] 'Dodekapropheten, Daniel-Bel-Draco' in *The Old Testament in Syriac According to
the Peshitta Version* (ed. A. Gelston; Part III, fasc. 4; Leiden: Brill, 1980); E. Tisserant,
'Fragments syriaques du Livre des Jubilés,' *RB* 30 (1921), 55–86, 206–232; Dedering,
'Apocalypse of Baruch'; and '4 Esdras' in *The Old Testament in Syriac According to the Peshitta
Version* (ed. R.J. Bidawid; Part IV, Fasc. 3; Leiden: Brill, 1973).

in 'I saw a vision,' ܢܐ ܚܙܐ ܘ ܗܐ (4 Ezra 11:1; cf. 12:10, 13:1; *2 Bar.* 53:1). This seems to stress the visual aspect of dreams, which is particularly the case when both terms appear with ܚܠܡ, for example 'he saw in a vision of his dream,' ܘܚܙܐ ܒܚܙܘܐ ܕܚܠܡܗ (*Jub.* 4:19) or 'Daniel saw a dream and a vision of his head while on his bed': ܕܢܝܐܠ ܚܠܡܐ ܚܙܐ ܘܚܙܘܐ ܕܪܫܗ ܥܠ ܡܫܟܒܗ (7:1).

Aramaic and Hebrew manuscripts use the traditional חלם but also חזה and occasionally מראה for 'dream.' For instance, 'Daniel saw a dream and visions of his head,' דניאל חלם חזה וחזוי ראשה (*BHS* Dan 7:1).[41] 'Dream' appears in the nominal form in the Aramaic of Daniel 7 (חלמא; Dan 7:1) and throughout the chapter we also find the common phrase חזה הוית 'as I looked on' (7:4, 6, 7, 9, 11, 13, 21). Daniel 8, in Hebrew, conveys the idea of seeing a dream by using ראה with חזון, as in the phrase ואראה בחזון (8:2 twice). The Hebrew fragments of *L.A.B.* 9:10 use the standard noun חלום.[42]

The Qumran Scrolls[43] use חלם and חזה interchangeably and in combination with one another in the Hebrew and Aramaic manuscripts. חלם appears most frequently, especially in Aramaic texts (חלמא), in both verbal and nominal forms: *1QapGen ar* col. XIX.14, 18 (4x), col. XX.22; *4QBook of Giants^b ar* (4Q530) col. II.3, 4, 5, 6, 12, 16, 20, 23; *4QBook of Giants^e ar* (4Q531) frag. 17.14; *4QVisions of Amram^b ar* (4Q544) frag. 1.10; *4QPsalms^f* (4Q88) col. VIII.13; *4Q Prayer of Nabonidus ar* (4Q242) frag. 4; *11QPsalms^a* (11Q5) col. XXII.14, XXIV.17; and *11QTargum of Job* (11Q10) col. XXII.9. Sometimes the usage involves both noun and verb: וחלמת אנה אברם חלם בלילה (*1QapGen ar* col. XIX.14). חזה is less than half as frequent, appearing as both verb and noun in the following texts: *1QapGen ar* col. XX.22, XXI.8, XXII.27; *4QBook of Giants^b ar* (4Q530) col. II.6, 16, col. III, frag 6.7; *4QBook of Giants^e ar* (4Q531) frag. 17.10; *4QAramaic Levi^b* (4Q213b) reconstructed in v. 3 (=CTL Bodleian col. a); *4QAramaic Levi^b* (4Q213a) frag. 1, col.II.15–16. Many of these occurrences are in combination with חלם, for instance: בחזוי חזוה די חלמא 'in my vision, the vision of my dream' (*Visions of Amram^b ar* [4Q544] frag. 1.10). *1QHymn^a* (1QH^a) col. VI.7 deserves mention for its unusual formulation

---

[41] All Hebrew quotations from Daniel are from *BHS*.

[42] *The Hebrew Fragments of Pseudo-Philo's Liber Antiquitatum Biblicarum: Preserved in the Chronicles of Jerahmeel* (trans. D.J. Harrington; Missoula, MT: SBL, 1974).

[43] All Hebrew quotations from *The Dead Sea Scrolls Study Edition* (2 vols.; eds. F.G. Martínez and E.J.C. Tigchelaar; Leiden: Brill, 1997–1998).

of 'men of your {God's} vision': אנשי חזונכה, the exact meaning of which is unclear. Finally, a few texts use מראה in the sense of 'dream': *4QVision of Samuel* (4Q160) frag. 1.3 and *4QPseudo-Ezekiel*ᵃ (4Q385) frag. 4.5.

In Ethiopic (Ge'ez) ḥelm is the term for dream or vision[44] in *1 Ethiopic Enoch* 13:8 (ḥelm maṣ 'ani) and *Jubilees* 14:1 (ba-ḥelm), 27:21 (wa-ḥalama), 40:1 (ḥalama … ḥelma … ḥelm) and 41:24 (ba-ḥelm).[45] In addition, re'ya or the plural rā'yāt appear in the context of 'dream,' often with re'iku, thereby emphasizing further the element of sight: *1 En.* 13:8 (re'iku rā'eyāta), 14:1 (ra'ey), 83:2 (ra'iku rā'eya ṣenu'a), 83:3 (re'iku ba-rā'ey), 85:3 (re'iku ba-rā'ey), 85:9 (wa-ra'iku ba-newāmeya); *Jub.* 4:19 (re'ya ba-rā'eya), 32:26 (wa-za-re'ya twice).

Greek manuscripts employ a wider variety of terms for 'a dream' than do Semitic texts. These terms include: ὄνειρος (*T. Abr.* A 5:6, 5:14, B 14:25; LXX 2 Macc 15:11);[46] ἐνύπνιων (*T. Jos.* 19:1);[47] ἐνύπνιον (LXX Add Esther 1:1a,d,l; 10:3); ἐνύπνια (*T. Naph.* 7:1); ὁράματι (*T. Levi* 11:3); ὄραμα (NA²⁷ Acts 16:9); ὕπαρ once, in parallelism with ὀνείρον (LXX 2 Macc 15:11); and the phrase κατ' ὄναρ (*T. Abr.* B 4:14; NA²⁷ Matt 1:20, 2:12, 13, 19, 27:19). In general, ἐνύπνιον and similar terms stress the aspect of sleep, ὄραμα, ὁράματι, and ὕπαρ emphasize that something is seen, and ὄναρ, ὄνειρος have the plainest meaning of 'a dream.'[48] As in all other texts in antiquity, one *sees* a dream, e.g.: ὄνειρον ἐθεάσατο (*T. Abr.* A 5:14).

Gnuse has carefully analyzed Josephus' use of terms in dream reports and I see no need to revise his findings. ὄναρ and ὄνειρος are the best attested, appearing sixty-seven times, and they have the clearest usage of all terms as 'dream' or 'dreamlike.' ὄναρ appears in *J.W.* 2.112, 2.114, 2.116; *Ant.* 1.208, 1.313, 1.314, 2.12, 2.63, 2.70, 2.72 (2x), 2.82, 5.192, 5.219, 5.222, 8.125, 9.85, 10.195(3x), 10.196, 10.200, 10.203 (2x), 10.205, 10.208, 10.211, 10.216, 12.112, 17.238, 17.345, 17.351 (see also 9.85, 17.238

[44] T.O. Lambdin, *Introduction to Classical Ethiopic (Ge'ez)* (HSS 24; Atlanta: Scholars Press, 1978), 405.

[45] *The Ethiopic Version of the Book of Enoch: Edited from Twenty-Three Mss. together with the Fragmentary Greek and Latin Versions* (ed. R.H. Charles; Oxford: Clarendon Press, 1906); *The Book of Jubilees: A Critical Text* (ed. J.C. VanderKam; Lovanii: Peeters, 1989).

[46] *The Testament of Abraham: The Greek Recensions* (trans. M.E. Stone; Texts and Translations 2; Pseudepigrapha Series 2; Missoula, MN: SBL, 1972).

[47] Translations of *T. Levi, T. Naph.* and *T. Jos.* in *The Testaments of the Twelve Patriarchs: A Critical Edition of the Greek Text* (trans. M. De Jonge; Pseudepigrapha Verteris Testamenti Graeca 1; Leiden: Brill, 1978).

[48] 'ἐνύπνιον,' *LSJ*, 579; 'ὄραμα' *LSJ*, 1244; 'ὄναρ,' *LSJ*, 1230; 'ὄνειρος,' *LSJ*, 1231; 'ὕπαρ' *LSJ*, 1853.

for metaphorical use).[49] ὄνειρος, ὄνειρον appear in *J.W.* 1.328, 3.351, 3.352, 3.353, 6.371; *Ant.* 1.341, 1.342, 2.10, 2.11, 2.15, 2.17, 2.63, 2.69, 2.75 (2x), 2.76, 2.77, 2.78, 2.80, 2.84, 2.89, 2.93, 2.176, 2.217, 5.193, 6.334, 10.194, 10.234, 14.451, 17.166, 17.345, 17.348; *Life* 208, 210; *Ap.* 1.177; cf. *J.W.* 6.371, *Ant.* 6.334, *Ap.* 1.177.[50] Josephus also uses ἐνύπνιον eleven times as 'dream' or 'vision': *Ant.* 2.75, 10.196, 10.198(2x), 10.202, 10.217; *Ap.* 1.207, 1.211, 1.294, 1.298, 1.312.[51] Also, Gnuse estimates that ὄψις or 'vision' is used 174 times altogether, thirty-six times indicating an otherworldly phenomenon and twenty-nine times meaning 'dream': *Ant.* 1.279 (2x), 1.341, 2.10, 2.11, 2.12, 2.13, 2.14, 2.17, 2.65, 2.70, 2.75, 2.77, 2.79, 2.80, 2.82, 2.217, 5.220, 10.196, 10.199, 10.216, 11.335, 14.451, 17.345, 17.346, 17.348; *Ap.* 2.54.[52] φάντασμα or 'phantasm' occurs a total of eleven times, four of which refer to dreams: *J.W.* 3.353, 5.381; *Ant.* 1.325, 2.282.[53]

The Latin texts almost always use *somnium* or *somnia* (*L.A.B.* 8:10, 9:10, 28:4;[54] 4 Ezra 11:1, 12:35, 13:15, 16)[55] for 'dream, vision,' or else they employ the verbal form *somniat* (4 Ezra 10:36), 'to dream.'[56] Some texts stress the visual element by using *visionis* or *visiones somniorum* (4 Ezra 10:40, 59; 12:10; 13:21, 25). Again, one does not 'have' a dream but rather one 'sees a dream': '*et vidi somnium*,' (4 Ezra 11:1; *L.A.B.* 8:10, 9:10). In certain passages, such as the symbolic dreams in 4 Ezra 11–13, the phrases '*et vidi*,' '*et ecce*,' and '*et vidi, et ecce*' occur with notable frequency: 4 Ezra 11:1, 2, 3, 7, 10, 12, 15, 20, 22, 24, 25, 26, 28, 33, 35, 37; 12:1, 2, 3, 4, 5, 10, 18, 20, 23, 35; 13:2, 3, 5, 6, 8, 9.

Thus, Syriac, Hebrew, Aramaic, Ethiopic, Greek, and Latin manuscripts of early Jewish texts commonly use words we translate 'dream' and 'vision' interchangeably, often in conjunction with words meaning 'see.' Many other times, however, no noun or verb for 'dream' or 'vision' appears, and it is the setting that clarifies the episode is a dream. A short list will demonstrate that several texts emphasize elements that

[49] Gnuse, *Josephus*, 17.
[50] Ibid., 17–18.
[51] Ibid., 18.
[52] Ibid., 19
[53] Ibid., 20.
[54] G. Kisch, *Pseudo-Philo's Liber Antiquitatum Biblicarum* (Notre Dame, IN: University of Notre Dame, 1949); D.J. Harrington, *Pseudo-Philon Les Antiquités Bibliques* (trans. J. Cazeaux; 2 vols.; Paris: Les Éditions du Cerf, 1976).
[55] *Der Lateinische Text der Apokalypse des Esra* (trans. A.F.J. Klijn; Berlin: Akademie-Verlag, 1983).
[56] '*somniō*' and '*somnium*,' *OLD*, 1790–1791.

are present for most of us during ordinary dreaming, including lying down, a bed, night and/or sleeping:

> *1 En.* 14:2; cf. 85:9, 86:1 'ana re 'iku ba-newāmeya or ἐγὼ εἶδον κατὰ τοὺς ὕπνους μου 'I saw in my sleep'
>
> *1 En.* 83:3 sekub konku ba-bēta Malāl'ēl 'emḥoweya re'iku ba-rä'ey 'I was lying down in the house of Mala'el, my grandfather; I saw in a vision'
>
> *1 En.* 85:3 re'iku ba-rā'eya meskābeya wa-nāhu 'I saw in my vision in my bed and behold'
>
> *T. Levi* 2:5 τότε ἐπέπεσεν ἐπ' ἐμὲ ὕπνος 'And sleep fell upon me'
>
> *2 Bar.* 36:1 ܐܘܗ ܐܠܠܒ ܗܠ ܬܝܘ ܡܕܗ ܗܕܚܬܗܕ 'I fell asleep at that place and saw in the night a vision'
>
> *2 Bar.* 52:7 ܬܟܕ ܗܕܚܬܗܕ 'I fell asleep'
>
> *T. Abr.* A 5:7 Ἰσαὰκ ἀνέστη ἀπὸ τῆς κλίνης αὐτοῦ 'Isaac lay upon his bed'
>
> *L.A.B.* 53:2 *Et Samuel erat dormiens in templo Domini* 'And Samuel was sleeping in the Temple of the Lord'
>
> *T. Job* 3:1, 4[57] καί ἐν τῇ νυκτὶ κοιμωμένου μου ... κατέπεσα ἐπί τὴν κλίνην 'And in the night, I was resting myself ... I turned and fell on my bed'
>
> *4Q Vision of Samuel* (4Q160) frag.1.3 שוכב שמואל 'Samuel was lying down'
>
> *4 Ezra* 3:1 *cubili meo recumbens*; ܬܝܡܐ ܕܠ ܒܡܣ ܐܢܐ 'I was lying on my bed'
>
> *4 Ezra* 9:27 *et ego discumbebam supra foenum*; ܐܘ ܐ ܐܢܐ ܒܡܣ ܠܒ ܐܒܬܕܒ 'and I lay on the grass'

Similarly, Josephus frequently uses κατὰ τοὺς ὕπνους or 'in sleep' to indicate a dream setting: *Ant.* 1.279, 2.10, 2.11, 2.64, 2.67, 2.80, 2.212, 5.215, 7.147, 8.22, 8.125, 8.129, 8.196, 10.195, 10.199, 10.216, 11.327, 11.328, 11.334, 11.335, 13.322; *Ap.* 1.289.[58] The noun ὕπνος appears by itself in Josephus with the meaning 'dream' six times: *J.W.* 7.349; *Ant.* 2.82 (2x), 2.171, 6.37, 11.328.[59] *1 Enoch* 13:7 is a little unusual since the seer sits: (Greek) ἐκάθισα ... ἀναγίνωσκον ... ἕως ἐκοιμήθην and (Ethiopic) nabarku ... 'enza wa-'anabeb ... 'eska daqqasku 'I sat down ... I was reading or reciting ... until I slept'.[60]

Sometimes a dream setting is established by mentioning 'night.' In fact, 'dream of the night' or 'vision of the night' is as common as seeing 'dream' or 'vision' alone. For example: ܐܝܠܝܠܒ ܐܘ ܬ ܬܝܙܚ 'I saw a vision of the night' (4 Ezra 13:1); ܬܝ ܐܘܗ ܬܟܕ ܗܕܚܬܗܕ

---

[57] *Testamentum Iobi* (ed. S.P. Brock; *Pseudepigrapha Veteris Testamenti Graece* 2; Leiden: Brill, 1967).

[58] Gnuse, *Josephus*, 19.

[59] Ibid., 18–19.

[60] 'daqqasa' in Lambdin, *Introduction to Classical Ethiopic (Ge'ez)*, 396, cf. 418.

ܢܦܠܬ ܬܡܢ ܘܚܙܝܬ ܒܠܠܝܐ ܚܙܘܐ 'I fell asleep at that place and saw in the night a vision' (2 Bar. 36:1); in somnis noctu 'in a vision of the night' (L.A.B. 28:4; cf. 53:3); בחלום הלילה 'in a dream at night' (L.A.B. 9:10); καὶ ὅραμα διὰ τῆς νυκτὸς 'and a dream during the night' (Acts 16:9); וחלמת אנה אברם חלם בליליא 'And I, Abram, dreamt a dream in the night' and בחזון די ליליא 'in a vision of the night' (1QapGen ar col. XIX.14, XXI.8); and בחזוי עם־ליליא 'in visions in the night' (Dan 7:2). Daniel also refers to 'the vision of evening and of morning,' which is interesting given the view of some ancient Near Eastern texts and the Greek tradition that the most veridical dreams happen at twilight or just before sunrise:[61] ומראה הערב והבקר or ܪܡܫܐ ܘܚܙܘܐ ܗ̇ܘ ܕܨܦܪܐ (Dan 8:26). Similarly, *Jubilees* 27:19–20 also notes that Jacob's dream of the gate to heaven occurred 'when the sun had set' 'esma ('eska) 'araba ḍaḥāy or *deciderat enim sol* (cf. *Jub.* 14:13 'erbata ḍaḥāy).[62] A different tradition is apparently in view in *L.A.B.*, which states that Samuel's auditory dreams came 'in media nocte' (*L.A.B.* 53:3).

It is important to note the vocabulary used for concluding dream passages, especially since this can establish a setting permitting the identification of certain episodes as dreams. Typical phrases include 'I awoke (from sleep),' 'I arose,' or 'I got up / stood up': καὶ ἔξυπνος γενόμενος or wa naqiheya 'I awoke' (1 En. 13:9); wa-naqha 'em-newăm wa-tanše'a or 'And he woke from sleep, and he got up' (*Jub.* 14:17); wa-naqha 'em-newāmu 'he awoke from his sleep' (*Jub.* 32:26; 40:1); ܣܡܬܟܠ or ואקום 'I got up' (Dan 8:27); ܐܬܬܥܝܪ ܡܢ ܫܢܬܝ 'he woke up' (from ܥܝܪ, to wake up; *L.A.B.* 53:12); ἐξανίσταμ' ἐξ ὕπνου 'I awakened from sleep' (*Ezek. Trag.* 82);[63] καὶ ἐξυπνισθεὶς or ἔξυπνος, 'and I awoke' (*T. Levi* 8:18, 5:7); Et expergetactus Samuel … Et surrexit, 'And Samuel awoke … and he stood up' (*L.A.B.* 53:3, 12; cf. 4 Ezra 13:13); Et evigilavi or ܘܐܬܬܥܝܪܬ, 'And I awoke' (4 Ezra 5:14, 13:13); ויקום, 'and he got up' (*4QVision of Samuel* [4Q160] frag. 1.3) and ואתעירת בליליא מן שנתי, 'I awoke in the night from my sleep' (*1QGenesis Apocryphon ar* [1Qap Gen ar] col. XIX.17).

We have seen that a range of ancient Near Eastern terms for 'interpret a dream' carry meanings related to 'solve,' 'dissolve' and the

---

[61] Oppenheim, *Interpretation*, 187, 240–241.

[62] From the variants edited by J.C. VanderKam, *Textual and Historical Studies in the Book of Jubilees* (HSM; Missoula, MT: Scholars Press, 1977), 79.

[63] B. Snell, *Ezek. Trag.* in *Tragicorum Graecorum fragmenta* (Göttingen: Vandenhoeck & Ruprecht, 1971–1985), 288–301.

like. Similarly, an angel provides Daniel with an interpretation, וּפְשַׁר (*BHS* Dan 7:16) and the Qumran scrolls use פשר for the interpretation of dreams and Scripture (*4QBook of Giants*[b] [4Q530] col. II.15). Latin texts use 'solvit (exsolvit) ei somnia' (*L.A.B.* 8:10). Syriac manuscripts use ܦܫܪ in the sense of 'to explain, to translate, to expound,' e.g.: ܦܘܫܪܗ ܕܚܙܘܐ (*2 Bar.* 39:1, 40:4, 56:1, 71:2; cf. 4 Ezra 12:10, 16, 13:21). Interestingly enough given the usage of פשר in the Qumran scrolls, ܦܫܪ can also mean 'to write commentaries'.[64] To convey the idea of interpretation, 4 Ezra also uses variations of 'This therefore is the interpretation of your vision': in Latin, 'Hic ergo intellectus visionis' (4 Ezra 10:40) and 'Haec est interpretatio visionis' (12:10, cf. 12:18, 20, 23, 35, 13:21, 25, 28); and in Syriac, 'this is the word' ܗܢܐ ܗܘ, ܕܝܢ ܦܬܓܡܐ (4 Ezra 12:23).

Finally, a few unique uses of vocabulary that liken dreaming to death deserve comment. A remarkably poetic passage in *Testament of Abraham* B makes this association clear: ἐπέστρεψεν δὲ ὁ θεὸς καὶ ἐξέτεινεν τὴν ψυχὴν τοῦ Ἀβραὰμ ὡς ἐν ὀνείροις, καὶ ὁ ἀρχιστρατηγὸς Μιχαὴλ ᾖρεν αὐτὴν εἰς τοὺς οὐρανούς, 'And God turned and *drew out the soul (psyche) of Abraham as in a dream*, and Michael the Archistratagos took her into the heavens' (*T. Abr. B* 14:25). The link between death and dreaming is also implicit in some vocabulary used to conclude a dream. The Syriac ܩܘܡ is typically used both in the sense 'to stand; to rise from sleep' and 'to rise from death,'[65] as is the Ethiopic tanše'a, from the verb meaning 'arise, get up' as well as 'to rise from the dead' (*Jub.* 14:17).[66]

Thus far we have seen that early Jewish authors appropriate the formal patterns and kinds of vocabulary that are standard for divinely-sent dreams throughout ancient Near Eastern and Mediterranean antiquity. While certain Jewish texts exhibit a preference for types of dreams, e.g. *2 Enoch* contains only message dreams and *2 Baruch* only symbolic dreams, there are no clear trends of dream types along lines of date, language or provenance. The two most complex dream texts in the group, 4 Ezra and *1 Enoch* 1–36, each contain components of both message dreams and symbolic dreams although 4 Ezra is among the latest

---

[64] 'ܦܫܪ' in *A Compendious Syriac Dictionary*, 468.
[65] 'ܩܘܡ' in *A Compendious Syriac Dictionary*, 494.
[66] Lambdin, *Introduction to Classical Ethiopic (Ge'ez)*, 421.

of the texts and *1 Enoch* 1–36 is the earliest. Also, some dream texts were probably composed in Greek by Egyptian Jews, such as *2 Enoch* and *Testament of Abraham*,[67] whereas others appear to have been composed in Hebrew or Aramaic with a Palestinian provenance.[68]

Typical Functions of Dreams in Hellenistic Judaism

In Part One I demonstrated that divinely-sent dreams in antiquity consistently confer divine knowledge, healing, and/or sanction on the dreamers. Given these shared cultural assumptions regarding dreams, early Jewish authors' utilization of the same formal patterns and vocabulary for dreams suggests a similar set of expectations regarding the functions of dreams.[69] Indeed, we do find that dreams in Hellenistic Judaism impart knowledge, healing, and sanction to the dreamers, but these functions are shaped to address specifically Jewish concerns.

Dream Knowledge

In early Jewish texts, dreamers gain *extraordinary knowledge* of many kinds, including: knowledge of one's own future, knowledge of the future of one's family members or descendants, knowledge of events occurring elsewhere geographically, cosmic knowledge of universal history and the eschaton, knowledge of far-flung regions of the earth and the heavenly Temple, and knowledge of the divine plan for the cosmos. Thus, the scale of revelation ranges from personal to cosmic, and knowledge of the future may or may not entail eschatology.

Most of the dreamers in Hellenistic Jewish literature are pseudepigraphic heroes from the biblical and Jewish traditions; thus, dream

---

[67] E.P. Sanders, '*Testament of Abraham*,' in *OTP* 1:875; Nicolae Roddy, *The Romanian Version of the Testament of Abraham: Text, Translation, and Cultural Context* (Early Judaism and Its Literature 19; Atlanta, GA: SBL, 2001), 1. For the debate surrounding language, date and provenance of *2 Enoch* see F.I. Andersen, '2 (Slavonic Apocalypse of) Enoch,' in *OTP* 1:91–100.

[68] E.g. Daniel 7–12 and *1 Enoch*; see John J. Collins, *Daniel*, 24, 61; G.W.E. Nickelsburg, *1 Enoch*, 1, 4, 9.

[69] I have been guided by the attention paid to Structure, Genre, Setting and Intention as laid out in the commentaries in the FOTL series. By 'functions' I mean literary functions, which is a more modest way of getting at the category of 'Intention.' See for example E. Ben Zvi, *Micah* (FOTL XXIB; Grand Rapids, MI: Eerdmans, 2000).

knowledge of their own and their descendants' future has implications for the shape of the sacred history of Israel, especially when the dream intertwines this knowledge with *divine sanction*. Since even today Jews speak of 'Avraham Avinu and Sarah Imoteinu,' it is reasonable to assume that Hellenistic Jewish audience members reading these dreams felt as if they were reading a family history that assured blessings and providential care for their ancestors as well as for themselves, the descendants of these dreamers.

For example, in *Jubilees* Jacob has a message dream in which the Lord appears in order to bless him with a name change to 'Israel' (*Jub.* 32). In this variation on Jacob's receipt of the covenant, divine sanction is bestowed on him and his descendants, as the Lord states: 'I shall give to your seed all of the land under heaven and they will rule in all nations as they have desired. And after this all of the earth will be gathered together and they will inherit it forever' (*Jub.* 32:19). The messenger then changes; while the LORD goes up to heaven, an angel flies down from heaven and gives Jacob seven tablets from which he learns his own fate as well as the fates of his descendants 'during all the ages' (*Jub.* 32:21–26; cf. *4QApoc. Jac.*). Although the details of these fates are not stated, descendants of Jacob are assured future exaltation and rule over the whole earth. Thus, the typical functions of conveying knowledge and sanction of the dreamer are present, but they are nuanced to relate to the Hellenistic Jewish reader, who feels him/herself to share in these blessings.

The emphasis on gaining extraordinary knowledge through dreams for the benefit of family is pervasive in the early Jewish dream texts. For instance, Miriam learns of her brother Moses' future birth (*L.A.B.* 9:10); Naphtali finds out the fates of his brothers, the ancestors of the twelve tribes (*T. Naph.* 6); Isaac foresees his parents' deaths in (*T. Abr.*); Methusaleh and Nir learn of their son's ordination as priests (*2 En.* 1–2, 70–71, see also *4QVisions of Amram*); Mordecai foresees and understands in retrospect the happy outcome of Esther and the Jewish people (Add Esth 10–11); and Moses learns of the future of his sons (*Ezek. Trag.* vv. 68–82). Rebecca foresees her own death, but the apparent reason for her foreknowledge seems to be so that she can prepare her son Jacob for her demise and take steps to ensure his future success (*Jub.* 35:6). Similarly, Enoch's message dream in *2 Enoch*, in which two large angels tell him of his imminent ascent to heaven, occurs precisely so that his sons may be prepared to take care of his house during his trip and so they will not worry (*2 En.* 1:9–10). Isaac's dreams of the deaths of

Abraham and Sarah are meant to reveal the news to Abraham (*T. Abr.* A 7:11), but they also help prepare Isaac for the bad news. In one of the tenderest scenes in the pseudepigrapha, Isaac cries so hard over the dream that Abraham, Sarah and even the archangel Michael all eventually break down in tears (*T. Abr.* A 5:10–12; B 6:3–4).

In other dreams that are retellings of biblical episodes, non-Israelites gain extraordinary knowledge that also ultimately functions to demonstrate God's providential care for Israelites. For instance, *Jubilees* narrates the episodes of the dreams of the butler and baker and the double-dreams of Pharaoh. Both in Genesis and in this text the dreams allow Joseph to display his divinely-given powers of dream interpretation, occasioning his movement from oppression to exaltation, just as the Pharaoh says: 'We will not find a man wise and knowledgeable as this man because the spirit of the LORD is with him' (*Jub.* 40:5). A comparison of these passages with the dreams in Genesis 41 shows that the author of *Jubilees* omits the actual content of all four dreams, which further demonstrates that the author's interest lies solely in how the dreams enact God's care for Joseph. Similarly, other Hellenistic Jewish authors seem to enjoy retelling biblical episodes in which the dreams of non-Israelites work to the advantage of Israel, including: Balaam's dreams in *L.A.B.* 18, the dream of Hirqanos the servant of the Pharaoh in the sister-wife story with Abraham and Sarah (*1QGenesis Apocryphon*) and, in Josephus' histories, the dreams of Pharaoh Nechaoh (*J.W.* 5.381), Abimelech (*Ant.* 1.208–209), the butler and baker and Pharaoh in the Joseph cycle (*Ant.* 2.63–73, 2.75–86), and the Midianite's dream as overheard by Gideon (*Ant.* 5.218–222).

Josephus' own dreams, which also combine the functions of foreknowledge and divine sanction, should be placed against this background of dream texts featuring God's providential concern for the families of Israel. Whereas the exaltation of pseudepigraphic dreamers implies blessing for their descendants as well, Josephus' dreams concern only his own future exaltation, as the dream messenger states: 'That which grieves thee now will promote thee to greatness and felicity in all things ...' (*Life* 208–210). Moreover, in light of God's constant concern for Israel in other Hellenistic Jewish dream texts, Josephus' appropriation of dream traditions is especially noteworthy in that his dreams predict the success of the Roman sovereigns *over and against Israel* (*J.W.* 3.351–354). The political function of Josephus recording these dreams has not been overlooked by scholars, with Gnuse calling it 'a plaintive self-justification of his actions after his failure as commander and the death of so many comrades.'[70] This self-justification is most evident in Josephus' prayer that follows his interpretations of his dreams and of Scripture:

> Since it pleases thee, who didst create the Jewish nation, to break thy work, since fortune has wholly passed to the Romans, and since thou hast made choice of my spirit to announce the things that are to come, I willingly surrender to the Romans and consent to live; but I take thee to witness that I go, not as a traitor, but as thy minister.
>
> (*J.W.* 3.351–354)

Whether or not Josephus 'actually' dreamt of such things, he uses the literary conventions of dreams to cast his actions as divinely sanctioned, almost against his will, in favor of his and Rome's exaltation.

Although I have been discussing dreams in which characters gain knowledge of the future, most of these accounts lack an eschatological orientation. However, many of the dreams in Hellenistic Jewish texts do reveal information about the eschaton to the dreamers, and this focus is not limited to the apocalypses.[71] Jacob's revelation concerning 'what would befall him and his sons in every age' (*Jub.* 32:21–26) as well as Enoch's dream revealing '[what] will happen among the children of men in their generations until the day of judgment' (*Jub.* 4:19) both have an eschatological flavor. In the poetic tragic drama *Exagōgē*, Moses learns of 'past, present and future' in a slogan suggesting knowledge of the sweep of cosmic history (*Ezek. Trag.* v. 89).[72] Moreover, Nickelsburg has rightly noted that Mordecai's symbolic dream of earthquakes, warring dragons and national calamity in Greek Additions to Esther has a cosmic dimension,[73] even though Mordecai's interpretation of it does not.

Dream Knowledge and the Scribal Domain

To a surprising degree, much of the extraordinary knowledge conferred by dreams in Hellenistic Judaism appears to relate to scribes and their main activities, reading and writing. The scholarly analysis of scribal roles has had a complex history that bears some preliminary discussion.

---

[70] Gnuse, *Josephus*, 196–197.

[71] In Chapter Five I address some distinct differences in the transmission of knowledge in apocalypses and non-apocalypses.

[72] All references to *Exagōgē* are from the translation by R.G. Robertson, *Ezekiel the Tragedian*, *OTP* 2: 803–820.

[73] Nickelsburg, *Jewish Literature*, 173.

E. Schürer established the major contours of the early, standard view
of scribes in Hellenistic Judaism.[74] Schürer, influenced strongly by the
New Testament, Josephus and rabbinic sources, envisioned scribes as
legal experts in the Torah who emerged as a well-defined class by
way of a pious response to negligent priests enamored of Hellenism.
These '*Schriftgelehrten*' became the undisputed spiritual leaders of the
people; although a few joined the Sadducees, most sided with the
Pharisees, who were the predecessors of the rabbis.[75] This portrait
was echoed in the work of J. Jeremias, who maintained that scribes
were aristocratic masters of the written tradition, including Torah and
apocalyptic texts. Like Schürer, he assumed they vied for authority
against priests and lay aristocracy and were continuous with the rabbis.[76] With minor alterations, this view has been recapitulated in the
main by others, such as M. Hengel and J. Neusner.[77] These studies
assume scribes are proto-rabbis whose specialty lay in the legal traditions. In the words of one recent critic, 'the main weakness of this
strand of scholarship … is that all scribes were understood to be Torah
scholars and all those with expertise in the Scriptures taken to be
scribes.'[78]

In recent decades, several important studies have come to different
conclusions, but with no clear consensus. E. Bickerman distinguishes
somewhat between the spheres of knowledge of scribes and sages, ultimately positing that scribes worked in a variety of settings that included
the Jerusalem Temple, royal courts and administrative positions.[79] He
also notes that in the Hellenistic period in both Egypt and Babylonia
'*the priest* was now *the scribe*, the judge and the sole teacher of the people, and *the temples* were the only centers of native learning [i.e. learning
in the native language].'[80] This conflation of roles was so great that

---

[74] Much of the ensuing evaluation of past scholarship on the role of scribes is
indebted to the analysis by C. Schams, *Jewish Scribes*, 15–35.

[75] E. Schürer, *The History of the Jewish People in the Age of Jesus Christ* (eds. G. Vermes.
F. Millar, M. Black and M. Goodman; 3 vols.; Edinburgh: T&T Clark, 1979; 1st English
trans. of German, 1885–1891): II, 322–324.

[76] J. Jeremias, *Jerusalem in the Time of Jesus* (London: SCM Press, 1969; English trans.
of 3rd rev. German ed. 1967; 1st German ed. 1923–1937): IIB, 101–112.

[77] Hengel, *Judaism and Hellenism*, 78–83; 174–247; J. Neusner, *Judaism: The Evidence of
the Mishna* (Chicago: University of Chicago Press, 1981), 232–234.

[78] Schams, *Jewish Scribes*, 24.

[79] E. Bickerman, *The Jews in the Greek Age* (Cambridge, MA: Harvard University
Press, 1988).

[80] E. Bickerman, 'The Historical Foundations of Postbiblical Judaism,' in *Emerging*

Egyptian cuneiform texts of the Hellenistic period use the ideogram 'priest' for notaries.[81] E.P. Sanders identifies Palestinian scribes even more closely with priests than does Bickerman, basically coming to the conclusion that most scribes were non-aristocratic priests and Levites.[82]

By contrast, a recent monograph by D. Orton assumes that the portrait of 'the model scribe' in Ben Sira was the normative view of Jewish scribes in Palestine.[83] Moreover, he argues that apocalyptic texts, Qumran scrolls and Gospel of Matthew extend the domain of the wise scribe from insights concerning Torah to celestial revelations. In other words, Orton maintains that: 'in the literary apocalyptic context the scribe epithet is always related to the eminent, spiritual and charismatic role of the figure, as the *recipient and mediator of divine revelations*.'[84] Elsewhere he argues even more bluntly that the epithet 'scribe' can be equivalent to the modern term 'apocalypticist.'[85] While Orton's conflation of the ideal scribe and apocalypticists certainly cannot be taken as universal in Hellenistic Judaism, his description of the importance of scribes in apocalyptic literature bears further investigation.

A very different conclusion is reached by C. Schams, who maintains that a variety of roles and functions may have been associated with scribes in Second Temple Judaism, in part due to geographical differences in the role in Palestine and the Diaspora and in part due to the multilingual, multicultural milieu of Palestine.[86] In her estimation, a few Jewish scribes may have functioned as officials in courts and armies, and some—but not all—might have been 'scholars, intellectuals, sages, and expert interpreters of the Scriptures and the law.'[87] In identifying the roles of Jewish scribes, Schams repeatedly makes the simple but important observation that reading and writing are emphasized as

---

Judaism: Studies on the Fourth and Third Centuries B.C.E. (eds. M.E. Stone and D. Satran; Minneapolis: Fortress Press, 1989), 9–48, 43.

[81] Bickerman, 'Historical Foundations,' 43.

[82] Sanders, *Judaism: Practice and Belief*, 170–182.

[83] D. Orton, *The Understanding Scribe: Matthew and the Apocalyptic Ideal* (JSNT Supp. 25; Sheffield: Sheffield Academic Press, 1989), 65–75.

[84] Orton, *Understanding Scribe*, especially 78, 82, 94, 99, 102, 103, 107, 111–120, 130–133.

[85] Ibid., 82.

[86] Schams, *Jewish Scribes*, 309–327.

[87] Ibid., 327.

their characteristic activity.[88] Although she notes some overlap between priests and scribes in the sources she examines,[89] the two roles are not to be conflated.

Finally, Anthony Saldarini's expert sociological analysis in *Pharisees, Scribes and Sadducees* produces many solid conclusions.[90] He maintains that scribes were not 'a unified political and religious force,'[91] despite portraits in the New Testament. Scribes were readers and writers and used these skills in a variety of roles.[92] Sociologically, most were retainers or people who left the peasantry and who derived their status from their employers, but scribes could come from a variety of classes.[93] Of the minority of scribes from the governing class, Saldarini states: 'Many of th[is minority group] were probably drawn from the priests or leading families ...'[94] That is, scribes could be laity, priests or Levites and they 'overlapped circles which had priestly, apocalyptic, and wisdom orientations.'[95] Overall, then, scribes functioned in a variety of roles requiring reading and writing: some were experts in the Torah, some were judges, and some were in service to kings, wealthy land-owners, or the Jerusalem Temple.[96]

Since a thorough analysis of the role and functions of scribes is not the central concern of my work, I rely on the cautious findings of Saldarini and Schams and assume that professional scribes were *at least engaged in writing and reading*. Like Saldarini, and with Sanders also in mind, I recognize that *some scribes may have also been priests*, although the two roles are by no means identical. I am not able to identify them with Pharisees, Sadducees, Essenes or other parties, nor can I link them to a social class. With these preliminary definitions out of the way, I wish simply to demonstrate how several early Jewish texts interweave reading, writing and/or the title 'scribe' with dreams.

First, some dreamers gain knowledge from reading heavenly books in dreams. Jacob reads his and/or his sons' futures on seven tablets

---

[88] Schams notes this finding for several texts under investigation in this study, *Jewish Scribes*, 87 (*T. Levi* and *Aram. Levi*); 97 (*1 En.* and *4QEn.*); 121–124 (2 Macc); 134–143 (*J. W., Ant.*); 204 (4 Ezra); 205–208 (*T. Abr.*).

[89] See Schams, *Jewish Scribes*, 58, 65, 68, 71, 89–90, 108, 140–143, 193, 246, 249, 298.

[90] Saldarini, *Pharisees, Scribes and Sadducees*, 241–276.

[91] Ibid., 276.

[92] E.g. Saldarini, *Pharisees, Scribes and Sadducees*, 258, 261, 274.

[93] Saldarini, *Pharisees, Scribes and Sadducees*, 263, 274–275.

[94] Ibid., 275.

[95] Ibid., 273.

[96] Ibid., 273–274.

given to him by an angel (*Jub.* 32; *4QApocryphon of Jacob*). Similarly, Naphtali explains how, in a dream, he and possibly Joseph, Levi and Judah all 'went up … into the heights,' which I take to be heavenly ascent, where they read sacred writing that foretold the future of the nations (*T. Naph.* 5:8).

Second, several dreamers are themselves scribes who write, including Enoch (*1 En.* 14–15; *2 En.* 22–23), Ezra (*4 Ezra* 14), Daniel (Dan 7), Baruch (*2 Bar.* 77–87) and Amram in *4QVisions* of Amram^c (*4Q547 4QcAmram^e ar*]) frag. 1. Enoch is the most famous scribe amongst our dreamers, and he is called 'the Scribe of Righteousness' by the Lord Himself (*1 En.* 15:1). Moreover, Enoch wrote down his *dream revelations*:

> And he saw what was and what will be *in a vision of his sleep* as it will happen among the children of men in their generations until the day of judgment. He saw and knew everything and wrote his testimony and deposited the testimony upon the earth against all the children of men and their generations. (*Jub.* 4:19; cf. *1 En.* 14:1–4)

The author of this passage in *Jubilees* links in rapid succession the activities of seeing in a dream, knowing, writing, and depositing a written document. Similarly, in *1 Enoch* 13–36 and Daniel 7–8, the very texts the audiences read are in fact the scribes' written records of their dreams. Furthermore, since Ezra and Baruch are also famous scribes in the Jewish tradition and *4 Ezra* and *2 Baruch* are composed in the first person, their dream accounts also function as fictional, scribal, dream autobiographies.

Third, it is important to note that some texts containing dreams suggest that writing is a divine or heavenly activity. For instance, in *1 Enoch*, Uriel acts as a scribe for Enoch when he writes down for him all the sights Enoch sees during his dream journey around the heavens and the earth (*1 En.* 33). Similarly, Enoch sees angelic scribes in his symbolic dream of the 'Animal Apocalypse' (*1 En.* 89:70, 76, 90:14, 22). While not in a dream, in *Testament of Abraham* the patriarch ascends and sees heavenly recording angels, pen and papyrus in hand, who write each soul's righteous and wicked deeds so that it may be judged (*T. Abr.* A 12:6–12, 13:9).[97]

Furthermore, divine inspiration seems necessary for certain scribal transmissions. Ezra imbibes a cup of something like fire, symbol of divinity, whereupon he pours forth the Torah and seventy esoteric

---

[97] In another recension Abraham sees 'the scribe of righteousness, Enoch' in heaven writing the sins of repentant souls (*T. Abr.* B 11:3–10).

books, which five scribes record day and night (4 Ezra 14:37–48). It is precisely Ezra's dreams that have prepared him for this moment, which culminates in his ascension to the heavenly realm, as the Lord explains: 'Lay up in your heart the signs that I have shown you, *the dreams that you have seen, and the interpretations that you have heard*; for you shall be taken up from among men …' (4 Ezra 14:9). Finally, according to *Jubilees* Enoch was 'the first who learned writing and knowledge and wisdom, from among the sons of men, from among those who were born upon the earth' (*Jub.* 4:17). That is, Enoch's distinction is that he is the first *human* who learns to write, but this does not mean that he is the first scribe. Rather, there seems to be a larger tradition of scribal angels in the background.

An important passage in *2 Enoch* 22–23 sheds further light on the associations between scribal activity, heavenly ascent and ontological status. Several scholars have commented on a striking scene in which Enoch is clothed in vestments that clearly and progressively transform him into an angel: 'And I gazed at all of myself, and I had become like one of the glorious ones, and there was no observable difference' (22:10).[98] M. Himmelfarb in particular has convincingly argued that priestly investiture occurs through Enoch's being clothed in priestly vestments and his anointing.[99] While she and others are correct in seeing an angelo-priestly transformation in the passage, I suggest this is but a penultimate stage. The culmination of Enoch's angelic transformation actually occurs in scribal activity. Immediately after Enoch's transformation the LORD declares to the archangel Vereveil, 'Bring out the books from the storehouses, and give a pen to Enoch and read him the books' (22:11). At this point, the scribal archangel Vereveil, 'who is wise, records all the LORD's deeds,' and transfers his scribal role to Enoch *by giving him the pen from his hand* and dictating 360 books to him, of which Enoch states 'I wrote accurately' (22:11; cf. 33:5–9).

---

[98] For instance, Himmelfarb, *Ascent to Heaven*, 40–41; and C. Fletcher-Louis, *All the Glory of Adam: Liturgical Anthropology in the Dead Sea Scrolls* (Leiden: Brill, 2002), 23, 49. Also, J. Charlesworth discusses *2 Enoch A* 30:8–11 and concludes that 'There is no reason to assume that the author of *2 Enoch* is simply speaking metaphorically about Adam being an angel. Adam's original state was perceived as glorious, even divine, by some Jews,' 'The Portrayal of the Righteous as an Angel,' in *Ideal Figures in Ancient Judaism* (eds. G.W.E. Nickelsburg and J.J. Collins; Ann Arbor, MI: Scholars, 1980), 135–152, 138.

[99] Himmelfarb, 40–41.

Fourth, according to the work of Saldarini, Schams and Sanders discussed above, scribal and priestly roles were not exclusive of one another in Judaism of the Hellenistic and Roman eras.[100] If it is axiomatic that social organization is reflected to some degree in the symbolic orderings of the universe posited by various religions,[101] we may have literary confirmation that the roles of scribe and priest were sometimes combined in Hellenistic Judaism. Enoch is commissioned as a heavenly scribe only *after* his transformative investiture into an angelic priest in the preceding passage (*2 En.* 22:10–23:6). That is, once he has attained the status of *angelic priest*, he is able to function as *scribe* in the *heavenly Palace-Temple* in place of the scribal archangel Vereveil.

Fifth, scribal status is linked to dream interpretation in several texts. In *4QBook of the Giants*, the semi-divine Giants seek out Enoch the scribe so that he can interpret their dreams:

> Then two of them dreamed dreams … The Giants could [not] find (someone) to explain to the[m] [the dream … to Enoch,] the scribe of distinction, and he will interpret the dream for us. *Vacat* Then ['] Ohyah, his brother, acknowledged and said in front of the Giants: I also saw something amazing in my dream this night … the Giants, and they sent him to Enoch, [the scribe of distinction;] and they said to him: Go […] after him, and death for you if you do [not] listen to his voice. And tell him to expl[ain and in]terpret the dreams …
>
> *4QBook of Giants (4Q530) Col. II*[102]

Although the text is reconstructed, it is clear enough that the semi-angelic Giants experience symbolic 'double dreams,' a common motif from the ancient Near East onward suggesting that the content of the dreams is doubly important and God-sent.[103] In searching for the proper interpretations of their highly significant symbolic dreams, the Giants assume that Enoch 'the scribe of distinction' will provide true interpretations; indeed, they urge that his interpretation must be acted upon at all costs.

A variation of this theme of the scribal dream interpreter may also be evident when the book of Daniel is taken as a whole, redacted

---

[100] Saldarini, *Pharisees, Scribes and Sadducees*, 241–276; Schams, *Jewish Scribes*, 58, 65, 68, 71, 89–90, 108, 140–143, 193, 246, 249, 298; Sanders, *Judaism: Practice and Belief*, 170–182.

[101] For instance, see M. Douglas, *Purity and Danger*; idem, 'Preface,' *Leviticus as Literature*, v–viii; C. Geertz, *The Interpretation of Cultures*.

[102] All citations and quotations from the Qumran Scrolls use *The Dead Sea Scrolls Study Edition* (eds. F. García Martínez and E.J.C. Tigchelaar).

[103] Oppenheim, *Interpretation of Dreams*, 209; A. Wikenhauser, 'Doppelträume,' 100–111.

work from the Antiochan period.[104] Daniel, the scribe who records
his own dreams in chapters 7–8, is dream interpreter in chapters 2
and 4 and also interpreter of the message written by the ghostly hand
in chapter 5. That is, Daniel's gift is that he is able to 'read' dream
symbols as well as words.[105] An earlier passage states this differently:
'To these four young men God gave knowledge and skill in every aspect
of literature and wisdom; Daniel also had insight into all visions and
dreams' (Dan 1:17). Similarly, Josephus repeatedly speaks of 'sacred
scribes' or ἱερογραμματεῖς who can interpret signs and omens, including
a bright light seen in the Temple and the opening of the gates of the
Temple (*J.W.* 6.291, 6.295).[106] Interestingly, in both Josephus' account of
the exodus from Egypt and in his quoting of the Egyptian Chaeremon,
the epithet ἱερογραμματεῖς describes both Egyptian and Israelite scribes,
like Moses and Joseph, who are skilled in the interpretation of dreams
as well as of signs predicting the future (*Ag. Ap.* 1.289–292; *Ant.* 2.205,
209, 234, 243, 255).[107]

Overall, then, images of reading and writing and the epithet 'scribe'
are not tangential themes in dreams in Hellenistic Judaism, but are
integral to numerous dreams through a variety of formulas. Scribes
dream (*1 En.*, *2 En.*, *4 Ezra*, *2 Bar.*, Dan); writing occurs within dreams
on earth and in heaven (*1 En.*, *2 En.*; cf. *T. Abr.*); scribes are credited
with recording the completed dream accounts which the audience
possesses (*1 En.* 14–36, Dan 7–8); dreamers gain dream knowledge by
reading tablets brought to them by angels in dreams (*Jub.* 32, *4QApoc.
Jac.*, *T. Naph.*); an angelic scribe records elements of Enoch's dream
revelations (*1 En.* 33); some dreamers undergo divine transformations
that enable them to act as scribes (*2 En.* 22) or as those who transmit
revelations to scribes (*4 Ezra* 14); and 'scribe' as well as 'sacred scribe'
are roles connected with dream interpretation as well as with the
interpretation of future omens and written words (*4QBook of Giants*,
Ag. Ap. 1, *J.W.* 6, *Ant.* 2). Recalling that the Qumran scrolls use פשר

---

[104] This standard view is explained by J.J. Collins, *The Apocalyptic Imagination: An
Introduction to Jewish Apocalyptic Literature*, (2nd ed.; Grand Rapids, MI: Eerdmans, 1998, 1st
ed. 1984), 87–90.

[105] M. Himmelfarb, 'The Wisdom of the Scribe, the Wisdom of the Priest, and the
Wisdom of the King,' in *For a Later Generation: The Transformation of Tradition in Israel, Early
Judaism and Early Christianity* (eds. R.A. Argall, B.A. Bow, R.A. Werline; Harrisburg, PA:
Trinity Press International, 2000), 89–99, 91–92.

[106] Schams, *Jewish Scribes*, 140–143.

[107] Ibid., 141.

both for dream interpretation as well as for interpreting Scripture, the presence of scribal imagery throughout early Jewish dreams appears to constitute a well-established tradition, probably reflective of social practices, linking scribes to dreams through the activities of writing and interpretation.

Dream Knowledge and the Priestly Domain

In my discussion of scribal themes I have already unavoidably touched upon priestly themes as well. Like 'scribe,' 'priest' is another complicated term that often elicits misconceptions, in part due to their representations in the Gospels. For this reason, some preliminary comments are necessary.

Priests are often assumed to be aristocratic Sadducees, but in fact 'priests' and 'Levites' constituted a number of kinship groups not solely affiliated with any particular sects or parties.[108] Josephus maintains that 20,000 Jews were priests or Levites (*Ag. Ap.* 2.108), which is a significant number in comparison with his estimates of 6,000 Pharisees and 4,000 Essenes (*J.W.* 17.42, 18.21), far from the tiny, unified elite frequently imagined.[109] Although these figures are unreliable, the sheer disparity in proportion suggests priests were more commonplace that we might generally perceive, and as Saldarini has argued, priests could come from any economic class.[110] It seems particularly wise to dispense of the presupposition that the majority of priests were aristocrats given that sociologists such as Weber, Lenski and Turner have shown that locating any group's position in a stratified society is a highly complex endeavor, class being contingent on status, power, prestige and many other variables.[111] To complicate matters more, several priestly lines

---

[108] L. Grabbe's descriptions of the priesthood and the Jewish 'theocracy' are fairly typical, giving the impression that priests were a unified aristocracy until the destruction of the Second Temple. See the sections on 'Temple and Torah,' and 'The Jewish Theocracy from Cyrus to Hadrian,' in *Judaism from Cyrus to Hadrian* (2 vols.; Minneapolis: Fortress Press, 1992), 537–541, 607–616. By contrast, Saldarini strongly makes the point that priests came from all classes and that Josephus, who is our best source for social roles in first century Palestine, nowhere says that all or most priests are Sadducees, see *Pharisees, Scribes and Sadducees*, 121, 300.

[109] P. Fredriksen gives a total population figure of half a million to two and a half million Jews in Palestine in the first century C.E., in *Jesus of Nazareth: King of the Jews* (New York: Vintage, 1999), 64.

[110] Saldarini, *Pharisees, Scribes and Sadducees*, 23–25.

[111] M. Weber distinguished between class, status, and power, and more specifically,

vied for legitimacy during the biblical and post-biblical periods and not all priests worked in the Jerusalem Temple.[112]

For these reasons, it is beyond the scope of this study to identify the social class(es) of priests or to sort out competing lines of Jewish priestly authority in the Hellenistic and Roman periods.[113] Rather, I am interested in general cultural expectations associated with priests. Overall, priests could function in a number of capacities in the biblical and post-biblical periods up to the destruction of the temple, probably including: sacrificing and performing other duties related to maintaining the cult, acting in a mantic role, healing (through the treatment of impurity, purification and apotropaic rites), judging (Deut 17:8–13; 21:5; Ezek 44:24),[114] and as we have seen, acting as scribes. Simply speaking, the identification of 'priests' and 'Levites' involves membership in kinship groups, the self-conceptions of which are grounded in a variety of

---

between power, party, material wealth and prestige, Weber, *Economy and Society* (New York: Bedminster Press, 1968). G.E. Lenski, on whom Saldarini bases his study, provides an evolutionary model of society that separates power, privilege, and prestige, which operate along with a network of other complex variables, such as economic surplus relative to population size, level of available nature resources, and the degree of legitimacy attributed to those holding power. See Lenski, *Power and Privilege: A Theory of Social Stratification* (New York: McGraw, 1966), esp. 45. Finally, J. Turner's formal theory of social stratification seeks to reconceptualize 'social class' as $SC=W_1(DF_{HO})+W_2(RA_{HO})$ where $W_1 \rangle W_2$. In this formula, SC=social class, W_1 and W_2=weighted variables; DF_{HO}=the degree and extent to which subsets of members in a society reveal common behavioral tendencies and similar attitudes so that they can be distinguished from other subsets of members in a society; and RA_{HO}=the degree to which homogeneous subsets of members in a society are differentially evaluated and lineally rank-ordered. That is, assigning a social role to priests is contingent on the relative role of all other subsets of members in society as well as other variables. Turner, *Societal Stratification*, 146–148.

[112] For discussion of priestly dynasties that served in the temples of Dan, Bethel, Shiloh and Nob in the biblical period, as well as of the various functions of priests in later periods, see the excellent articles by M. Haran and M. Stern, 'Priests and Priesthood,' in *EncJud* 13 (16 vols.; Jerusalem: Keter and Macmillan, 1971–1972):1069–1090.

[113] In other words, whether a text stems from priestly circles that are Zadokite, Levite, Mushite, Aaronide, Hasmonean, Enochic, Qumranite, Essene or somehow 'of Melchizedek' is beyond my consideration, as is whether particular priests functioned at the Jerusalem Temple or at other temples. Moreover, many priestly families jockeyed for political power during the Herodian period, including but not limited to: the Boethus, Phiabi and Anan families (*Pes.* 57a; *Tosef. Men.* 13:211); see M. Stern, 'Priests and Priesthood: From the Beginning of the Hellenistic Era until the Destruction of the Temple,' *EncJud* 13:1086–1088. By contrast, see the description by L. Grabbe, 'Temple and Torah,' in *Judaism from Cyrus to Hadrian* 2:537–541, also 2:607–616.

[114] See the description of the priesthood in M. Haran, 'Priests and Priesthood,' *EncJud* 13:1076–1079.

activities associated with temples, whether or not individual members of these clans ever actually functioned in such positions.

With this minimalist definition in mind, it is evident that priestly themes are interwoven with the transmission of knowledge through dreams in early Judaism. First, in early Judaism, many dreamers who receive revelation are priests, including: Josephus in *J.W.*; Amram, Samuel, Jaddus, Hyrcanus, and Matthias in *Ant.*; Josephus in *Life*; Ezra in 4 Ezra; Samuel in *L.A.B.*; Levi in *T. Levi* and in *Jub.*; Methuselah and Nir in *2 En.* Even Miriam is from a priestly family of the Levitical line (*L.A.B.* 9).

Second, some of the knowledge transmitted in dreams is priestly knowledge. For instance, in *L.A.B.* Samuel is able to identify an auditory message dream as being from the Lord through a priestly tradition handed down from Phinehas the priest to Eli to Samuel (*L.A.B.* 53:6). Although fragmentary, *4QAramaic Levi* concerns the transmission of detailed sacrificial rituals as well as Levi's dream visions in which he becomes a priest (*4Q213–214*). Also, before the institution of the priesthood, Abram is instructed to sacrifice in his dream (*Jub.* 14) while Jacob, who does sacrifice after his dream at Bethel, is told in a subsequent dream not to build a temple there as he was planning to do (*Jub.* 32). In addition, foreknowledge of the building of the Jerusalem Temple is suggested to Jacob, and made explicit to Nathan in dreams (*Ant.* 7.92–93).

Third, Hellenistic Judaism departs significantly from the Bible in portraying living and dead *humans* as dream messengers, and it is noteworthy that in two cases the messengers are *priests* who appear to rulers. The deceased Jeremiah and Ananias appear to Judas in 2 Maccabees 15 and the living High Priest Jaddus appears to Alexander the Great in *Ant.* 11:333–335. Although Josephus twice mentions one other departed shade who appears in a dream (*J.W.* 2.114–116; *Ant.* 17.349–353), the appearance of the living in a dream is exceedingly rare in all traditions.

Fourth, many dream texts that are also apocalypses show a marked concern for relating to dreamer and reader detailed descriptions of the heavenly Temple. The dream texts in this study that are commonly recognized as apocalypses include: *1 Enoch* 1–36 and 83–90, Daniel, *2 Baruch*, 4 Ezra, *2 Enoch*, *Testament of Levi* and *Testament of Abraham*.[115] *4QEnoch^a* (*4Q201* [*4QEn^aar*]), and *QAramaic Levi^a* (*4Q213*[*4QTLevi^aar*]) frag.

---

[115] J.J. Collins, 'Jewish Apocalypses,' *Semeia* 14, 21–59.

1, col. II probably fall into this category as well. Himmelfarb has already argued that *1 Enoch* 1–36, *2 Enoch*, and *Testament of Levi* are ascent texts that understand 'heaven as a Temple,'[116] containing episodes in which a seer journeys to the heavenly Temple and sees sights therein, including the Glory of God on his throne and angelic priests serving in various roles (e.g. *1 En.* 14–15, *2 En.* 3 24, *T. Levi* 2–5, 8–10).[117] Also, Daniel's dream in Daniel 7 appears to be a vision of the interior of the heavenly *hekhal*,[118] although that does not necessarily imply ascent (e.g., cf. Isa 6).

2 Baruch, while not an ascent text, it is another example of an apocalypse that contains dreams that are significantly structured around temples and priests. Baruch's first symbolic dream is incubated directly on the ruins of the Holy of Holies (*2 Bar.* 34–36). Incubation presupposes the spot itself is imbued with sacrality and divine presence, and Baruch sleeps on the most sacred spot on earth in Jewish tradition. Regardless of the condition of the earthly building, Baruch's presence at the location of the Holy of Holies would be remarkable if he were not considered to have priestly status.

Perhaps more telling of a priestly emphasis are Ramael's interpretations of Baruch's second dream, permeated by pervasive concerns over temple and priesthood. This dream periodizes cosmic history into 'black' and 'bright' waters, and the content of these periods is alternately deemed to be wicked or righteous. Significantly, several 'black' periods are marked by disrespect to the temple and priesthood. In the ninth black waters, Manasseh abolishes the altars and scatters the legitimate priests, causing the glory of God to withdraw from the earthly sanctuary (64:2–7). Similarly, the current crisis of the eleventh black waters is described in sacrificial imagery: 'the flavor of the smoke of the incense of the righteousness of the Law has been extinguished' (67:6–7). Conversely, several 'bright' periods are characterized by the correct functioning of the legitimate priests and Temple, including: the showing of the sanctuary to Moses (59:4); the dedication and offerings in the Jerusalem Temple (61:2); Josiah's rededication of the Temple cult ('he brought the priests back to their ministry,' 66:2); and the rebuilding of

---

[116] Himmelfarb, *Ascent to Heaven*, 4.

[117] Ibid., vii, 9–44. M. Dean-Otting adds *T. Abr.* A 10–13, B 10–11 and parts of 4 Ezra, *Heavenly Journeys: A Study of the Motif in Hellenistic Jewish Literature* (Judentum und Umwelt; Frankfurt: Peter Lang, 1984).

[118] Himmelfarb rightly implies it is the Holy of Holies of the divine throne-room/Temple, *Ascent to Heaven*, 17–18.

the Second Temple: 'Zion will be rebuilt again, the offerings will be restored, and the priests will again return to their ministry ... But not as fully as before' (68:5). Thus, in the interpretation given for Baruch's dream, the character of much of world history is marked by either the legitimate or illegitimate functioning of the temple cult, demonstrating a clear orientation around priestly concerns. Overall then, it can be stated fairly that numerous dream texts, particularly the apocalypses, reflect priestly concerns.

Finally, since knowledge gained from symbolic dreams is obtained through interpretation, the role of priests in dream interpretation should not be overlooked. Several scholars have maintained that in the Hellenistic and Roman periods Jewish priests acted as dream interpreters.[119] In part, this conclusion is based on the views of Josephus, who seems to connect his priestly background with his ability to interpret dreams and to understand prophecies in Scripture:

> [Josephus] was an interpreter of dreams and skilled in divining the meaning of ambiguous utterances of the Deity; a priest himself and of priestly descent, he was not ignorant of the prophecies in the sacred books. At that hour he was inspired to read their meaning, and recalling the dreadful images of his recent dreams, he offered up a silent prayer to God. (*J.W.* 3.351–353)

The meaning of this important passage is not altogether clear. T. Rajak maintains that here Josephus is casting himself in prophetic and priestly garb to appeal to his Graeco-Roman audience, since using sacred texts to confirm dream interpretation typified the activity of pagan priests rather than Jewish priests, who did not routinely interpret the Scriptures.[120]

To me, in this instance Rajak seems too certain about the activities of Jewish priests based on an argument of silence, which does not necessarily hold up under scrutiny. In fact, S. Mason has convincingly shown that throughout Josephus's writings he consistently avers that priests are the proper guardians of the law (e.g. *Ag. Ap.* 2.21, 1.6–7, 1.10; *Life* 1–

---

[119] S. Schwartz, *Josephus and Judaean Politics* (Leiden: Brill, 1990), 70; S. Mason, *Flavius Josephus on the Pharisees: A Composition-Critical Study* (Leiden: Brill, 1991), 269; idem, 'Priesthood in Josephus and the "Pharisaic Revolution,"' *JBL* 107, 4 (1988): 657–661, esp. 659; H. Lindner, *Die Geschichtsauffassung des Flavius Josephus im Bellum Judaicum* (Leiden: Brill, 1972), 52–53.

[120] T. Rajak, *Josephus: The Historian and His Society* (Philadelphia: Fortress Press, 1983), 19; see also P. Bilde, *Flavius Josephus between Jerusalem and Rome: His Life, his Works and their Importance* (JSOT Suppl. 2; Sheffield: JSOT Press, 1988), 190.

2; *J.W.* 2.17.4), a view that is also found in Ben Sira (45:17; early 2nd c. B.C.E.) and 4 Maccabees (5:4, 29, 7:6; 1st c. C.E.).[121] It seems reasonable, then, to believe that priests were sometimes involved in the interpretation of Scripture. For our purposes, what is most important in the passage cited above is that Josephus equates revelation obtained through dreams with prophecies in Scripture. Thus, Josephus apparently understands priests as skilled interpreters, whatever the medium. Although this does not mean that all priests functioned as dream interpreters, some such as Josephus clearly did.

Summary of Dream Knowledge

Knowledge relayed in dreams in Hellenistic Judaism is varied and ranges from an individual to a cosmic scale. With the exception of some of Josephus' own dreams, early Jewish dreams that employ the theme of foreknowledge generally also convey providential care for and protection of the pseudepigraphic ancestors in Israel's sacred history, which in turn promises blessings for the Jewish readership. A strong concern for family is evident, thus tying the readers even closer to their biblical ancestors. Some dreams of various genres relate eschatological knowledge and revelation of otherworldly realms to their dreamers; yet we will see that only the apocalypses share the details of this temporal and spatial information with the readers.

Much of the content and transmission of extraordinary knowledge in dreams is structured around scribal and priestly themes. Scribal activities of reading and writing are integral to the characters, plots and context of dreams, and priestly themes centered on temples constitute a significant portion of the content of early Jewish dreams. In several cases, such as with Ezra in *4 Ezra* and Enoch in *2 Enoch*, the categories of priest and scribe seem to overlap; this appears to relate to motifs of scribal and priestly angels functioning within the heavenly *hekhal*. Indeed, in some dream texts the peak of revelation is access to the heavenly Palace-Temple, either in a dream (Dan, *1 En.*, *T. Levi*, *T. Naph.*), or announced in a dream (*2 En.*, *T. Abr.*). Significantly, living and deceased priests even appear as dream messengers, a stark departure from biblical dream traditions. Finally, several traditions tie both scribes and priests to the activity of dream interpretation; since these roles could

---

[121] Mason, 'Priesthood in Josephus,' 657–661.

overlap, some persons might have functioned in all three capacities. Overall, it seems fair to say that the transmission of dream knowledge is oriented to a significant degree around both scribal and priestly concerns.

Healing and Dream Incubation

After the transmission of extraordinary knowledge, the second major function of dreams in antiquity is healing, which takes on a different form in early Jewish dreams than it does in ancient Near Eastern or Graeco-Roman sources. Absent is the theme of an ill person who incubates a dream and is subsequently healed by the appearance of a god. Nevertheless, several Hellenistic Jewish dream texts seem to be familiar with rituals and motifs from Graeco-Roman incubation cults.

As we have seen, in the ancient Near East, kings or priests were the major practitioners of incubation, which in its simplest form consisted of sleeping in temples or at other sacred sites.[122] In addition to sleeping at a sacred site, other ancient rituals of incubation include prayer, mourning, crying, self-abasement, fasting, sexual abstinence, wearing special clothes, abstaining from certain foods and/or wine, and making sacrificial offerings or libations.[123] The Hebrew Bible contains only the simplest form of incubation, sleeping at a temple or sacred place. The best candidate for purposeful place incubation occurs in the episode of King Solomon in Gibeon, where Solomon sacrifices at the altar, sleeps near the Tent of Meeting and the altar, and has a divine dream (1 Kings 3:5; 2 Chron 1:5).[124] Other biblical dreams appear to be examples of 'accidental incubation' in a holy place, such as Samuel's dream in the temple at Shiloh (1 Sam 3:2–15) and especially Jacob's dream at Bethel (Gen 28:16–17).[125] Although undeveloped, these texts share the view that divinity resides in certain places with such immanence that one is bound to have a dream if one sleeps there.

---

[122] The Latin word *incubare* encompasses the idea of temple incubation and means 'to sleep in the sanctuary.'

[123] Oppenheim, *Interpretation*, 188. For examples of prayer and mourning in dream incubation see the dreams of Assurbanipal and Sethos, 249, par. 8, no. 10; 252, par. 8, no. 22. See also Ehrlich, *Der Traum*, 14–15; Ackerman, 'Deception of Isaac,' 92–120.

[124] Seow, 'Syro-Palestinian Context,' 141–152.

[125] R. Gnuse has convincingly demonstrated this episode is a dream, although not purposefully incubated., *Samuel*. See also Seybold, 'Der Traum,' 42–43.

The Hellenistic period witnessed an explosion in the practice of incubation,[126] with dream cults springing up all over the Mediterranean
world, including those of: Trophonios, Zeus, Sarapis and Isis, Pluto,
Dionysios, Amphiaraos, heroes such as the Dioscourioi and Achilles,
and above all, Asklepios.[127] Asklepios alone possessed over *four hundred* temple sites throughout the Hellenistic and Roman empires,[128]
including in Palestine at Dor and Shuni.[129] P. Xella has also called
Eschmun, highest god of the pantheon of Sidon, the 'Phoenician Asklepios.'[130]

Since incubation cults permeated the atmosphere of the Hellenistic
world, and since there is biblical precedent for the practice of dream
incubation in the form of temple incubation, it should not be too surprising to find evidence of incubation motifs and rituals in Hellenistic
Jewish dream texts. In fact, this influence is patent in several ways.

To begin, the appearance of angels as messengers in dreams is rare
or absent in the Bible,[131] but prevalent in Hellenistic Judaism. The
depictions of angels in Jewish dream texts owes much to the Graeco-
Roman tradition of dream *oneiroi*, intermediary beings who bring messages in dreams, but also seems to draw on literary and iconographic

---

[126] Prior to the Hellenistic period, Greek references to dream incubation occur but
with less frequency and detail: *Iliad* 16.234; Aristophanes' *Plutus;* Herodotus II.141, I.46,
49, 52, 92, IV.172, VIII.133–134.

[127] For example, dream oracles include the Plutonion near Nysa, a Dionysian dream
shrine at Amphikleia, the cult of the Dioscourioi at Byzantium, the oracle of Trophonios at Lebadeia in Boeotia, the oracle of Amphiaros at Oropos, the hero Achilles'
dream shrine at Leuce, and the many scattered temples of Sarapis and Isis. E. Thrämer,
'Health and Gods of Healing,' 540–556; Jayne, *Healing Gods*, 201–502; and R.J. Clark,
'Trophonius,' 63–75. In the early third century C.E. Tertullian also names, in addition
to the Amphiaraos and Trophonios, the following: Amphilochos near Mallus, Sarpedon
in the Troad, Mopsus in Cilicia, Hermione in Macedonia and Pasiphae in Laconia.
H. Cancik, '*Idolum and Imago*: Roman Dreams and Dream Theories,' in *Dream Cultures*,
169–188.

[128] Strabo xiv.650; Plato *Symp.* viii.10; Hamilton, *Incubation*, 85, 89–90; Meier, *Antike*,
87–111.

[129] C. Dauphin, 'From Apollo to Asclepius to Christ: Pilgrimage and Healing at the
Temple and Episcopal Basilica of Dor,' *Studium Biblicum Franciscanum Liber Annus XLIX*
(1999): 397–430; cf. idem, 'Dora-Dor: A Station for Pilgrims,' 95; E. Shenhav, 'Shuni'
(1988/89), 168; idem, 'Shuni,' 4:1383.

[130] P. Xella, 'Eschmun von Sidon,' 481–498.

[131] The only possible exceptions are two auditory message dreams of an angel in Gen
31:10–13 and possibly Job 4:12–21, and a *Wecktraum* in which an angel feeds Elijah in
1 Kings 19:5–7. Nowhere does an angel appear, stand by the dreamer and deliver a
message; rather 'the Lord' or 'God' acts in this role.

depictions of Asklepios and other dream gods.[132] In both contexts, a beautiful divine being, such as an angel or Asklepios, appears and 'stands' by a dreamer.[133] Usually, the dream figures speak with the dreamer, sometimes touching him or her.[134]

Moreover, there are several instances in early Jewish and early Christian literature in which angels heal dreamers through touch. A common motif is that a dreamer or visionary is overcome by the experience of the numinous, whereupon an angel touches him or holds him during or after his dream, which restores the dreamer's strength, usually making possible further receipt of revelation. For instance, after his first dream Ezra states: 'Then I awoke, and my body shuddered violently, and my soul was so troubled that it fainted. But the angel who had come and talked with me held me and strengthened me and set me on my feet' (4 Ezra 5:14–15; cf. other angels in dreams: Zech 4:1; Dan 8:18; 4 Ezra 5:14–15, 10:30; and in visions: Dan 10:10, 16 and 18; *1 En.* 60:4; *2 En.* 22:6; Rev 1:17, *Ap. Abr.* 10:2–5). Such passages bear a marked similarity to literary and iconographic depictions of Asklepios and Amphiaraos which show the gods standing by the head of the reclining dreamer and reaching out and touching him/her.[135] In the extant *iamata* or healing tales of Asklepios, this divine touch is the primary means by which the deity heals dreamers.[136] In two entries on *iamata*, Asklepios even helps the dreamers stand up (γυμνὸν καταστάσας ὀρωὸν) before receiving healing and instruction, which closely parallels the way in which the angels strengthen dreamers in the early Jewish texts.[137]

There is, of course, a difference between these texts and descriptions of Asklepios' actions, since the Jewish dreamers do not incubate dreams on account of physical illness and the dream experience itself leads to the dreamer's weakness. Nevertheless, the pervasive literary and

---

[132] For extant fragments of the *iamata* see in Herzog, *Die Wunderheilungen*; Edelstein, *Asclepius;* and LiDonnici, *Epidaurian Miracle Inscriptions.*

[133] Meier, 'The Dream in Ancient Greece,' 315; Hamilton, *Incubation,* 6, 30–31.

[134] E.g. cures A 2, 3, 4, 5, 6, 7, 8 in LiDonnici, *Epidaurian Miracle Inscriptions.*

[135] See for example the votive relief of Asklepios from the Piraeus Museum in Hausmann, *Kunst und Heiltum,* plate 1; also Kerényi, *Asklepios,* 35 (plate 18) and 36, plate 19 for the votive relief dedicated to Amphiaraos at Oropos.

[136] An example of divine touch from the Epidaurian *iamata*: 'Andromache from Epirus was barren, and was healed in a dream when a handsome young boy uncovered her and the god touched her with his hand,' B 11.

[137] B 8 and B 9; LiDonnici, *Epidaurian Miracle Inscriptions,* 62, 107.

iconographic depiction of Asklepios' method of healing seems either to
have influenced or to share the depiction in Hellenistic Jewish dream
texts of the angelic dream figure touching, holding, and strengthening
the dreamer, while helping him to stand up.

In addition to similarities between depictions of angels and dream
gods of the incubation cults, numerous early Jewish texts exhibit familiarity with incubation practices. Several texts retell or develop incubation accounts from the Hebrew Bible. Jacob's dream at Bethel is highly
influential and appears in several texts, including: *Ladder of Jacob*; *Jub.*
28; *T. Levi* 9; *1QJubilees*ᵃ (1Q17[1QJubᵃ]); and *Ant.* 1.278–284. These texts
add rituals not present in Genesis, such as Jacob constructing an altar
at Bethel (*Ant.* 1.278–284). *Jubilees* provides a wonderful example of a
Hellenistic elaboration on the biblical account, by adding a subsequent
dream by Levi at Bethel: 'And {Jacob and his two sons} stayed that
night at Bethel. And Levi dreamed that he had been appointed and
ordained priest of the Most High God, he and his sons forever. And he
woke up from his sleep and blessed the Lord' (*Jub.* 32:1–2). Since Jacob
has earlier had a sacred dream at Bethel that caused him to recognize
it as 'the house of God' and 'the gate of heaven' (*Jub.* 27:25), this is a
clear case of place incubation resulting in a dream of divine sanction,
after which Levi 'served as priest in Bethel' (*Jub.* 32:9, 16). Just as in the
cult of Asklepios or other dream cults, Jacob gives God thanks for Levi's
positive dream by offering thanksgiving sacrifices at Bethel (*Jub.* 32:4–9,
22), and he would have built a permanent Temple there had another
angel not appeared to him in a dream to explain 'this is not the place'
(*Jub.* 32:22). Regardless of this frail attempt to minimize Bethel's status, the passage nevertheless clearly preserves a tradition of Bethel as a
site of dream incubation that contains an altar or other demarcation of
sacred space, and it clearly demonstrates the author's familiarity with
conventions of dream incubation.

1QGenesis Apocryphon testifies to a similar tradition, suggesting Abram
lived at Bethel for some time and built an altar there:

> … until I reached Bethel, the place where I had built an altar, and I built
> it once again. Upon it I offered holocausts and an offering to the God
> Most High, and invoked the name of the Lord of the Universe there;
> I praised God's name and blessed God … I lived in the mountain of
> Bethel … God appeared to me in a night vision and said to me …
>   (*1QGenesis Apocryphon* (*1Q20* [*1QapGen ar*]) col. XXI).

Clearly, Bethel is a site associated with sacrifice, dream incubation, and
sacred rituals.

Another case of dream incubation in the Bible that attracts the attention of early Jewish authors is Samuel's dreams at Shiloh. Since even in the biblical version Samuel dreams while sleeping by the ark at Shiloh, the passage contains the primary image of incubated dreams, sleeping in a temple or sacred place (1 Sam 3). *L.A.B.* elaborates on the account, making the association with the temple and priesthood is even stronger. After Samuel twice mistakes the voice of the Lord for Eli's, the old priest instructs the boy to go back to sleep to await a dream, providing him with a priestly tradition from Phinehas for distinguishing the messenger: 'For Phinehas the priest has commanded us, saying, "The right ear hears the LORD by night, but the left an angel"' (*L.A.B.* 53:6). Since Samuel is sleeping in a temple, awaiting a dream, with a priestly tradition in mind to test it, this episode fulfills the definition of an incubated dream (cf. *Ant.* 5.348–350).[138]

Other early Jewish texts transform biblical stories into examples of dream incubation. For instance, whereas Balaam's dreams arguably entail incubation in the biblical version (Num 22), there is no mistaking otherwise in the retellings in *L.A.B.* (*L.A.B.* 18:2–9). *L.A.B.* 18:2–9 explicitly calls Balaam 'the interpreter of dreams' (18:2–9)[139] and portrays him as receiving two dreams that are not only revelations given by God, but also *divination compelled from God* (18:2). The Moabite King Balak summons Balaam from Mesopotamia, renowned for its dream diviners, in order to have him curse the Israelites in exchange for honor and gifts. Balaam replies, saying: 'now wait here, and I will see what the Lord may say to me this night' (18:3). At this point, Balaam is functioning as a dream oracle for Balak. Although the precise method of incubation is not described, a dream is *expected* to come from God, which indeed it does.[140] When Balak rejects the message of the dream, namely that God favors the Israelites, Balaam functions as a dream oracle for a second time, saying again: 'And now wait here this night, and I will see what God may say to me' (*L.A.B.* 18:8; cf. 2 *Bar.* 34:1). Indeed, another dream revelation follows. According to the author of *L.A.B.*, divine revelation not only occurs via dreams, but such dreams can also be reliably induced.

---

[138] Gnuse considers 1 Sam 3 and Josephus' version to be auditory message dreams, but he does not mention incubation, *Josephus*, 169–170.

[139] Harrington renders the river 'Pethor,' mentioned in Num 22:5 and *L.A.B.*, as 'interpreter' because of the root *ptr/pšr*, *Pseudo-Philo, OTP* 2:325, n. 18.

[140] If Numbers 22:7–13 is a dream, the biblical Balaam also compels a dream; cf. 2 *Baruch* 34:1.

Other early Jewish authors create incubation accounts entirely lacking in the Bible. The author of *1 Enoch* 1–36 sketches a precise context
for the onset of Enoch's elaborate dream journey:

> I went and sat by the waters of Dan in the land of Dan, which is south of
> Hermon, to the west. I recited the memorandum of their petition until
> I fell asleep. And behold, dreams came upon me, and visions fell upon
> me…   (*1 Enoch* 13:7)

Anyone familiar with either ancient or contemporary visionary episodes will note several striking features in this brief passage. Wilson
notes that numerous anthropological accounts[141] relate that the repetition of words produces a rhythmic stimulus inducing visionary states;
this is obviously also characteristic of later *Merkabah* mysticism.[142] A setting by a river is associated with trance induction in numerous cultures
as well as in *Merkabah* mysticism because of the rhythmic sound of the
waters;[143] this particular passage also recalls Ezekiel's ecstatic vision next
to the river Chebar (Ezek 1:1).

In addition, *1 En.* 13:7–9, *T. Levi* 2–5, and *4QAramaic Levi^a* (*4Q213*
[*4QTLevi^a ar*]) frag. 1, col. II all mention Abel-Main, near Dan, Mt.
Hermon, Lebanon and Sĕnir. Nickelsburg has shown that this region
of Upper Galilee was known as sacred space to Canaanites, Israelites,
non-Israelites of the Graeco-Roman period, and Christians.[144] D. Suter
maintains that an Israelite incubation cult was active at Dan,[145] and
we at least know that the cult of Pan, which often practiced incubation, operated in a nearby cave at Banias. The place, the river and
the recitation all work together to produce a dream journey in which
Enoch is present in the heavenly temple. River and temple are conflated, and incubation by one is effectively incubation in the other—a
mystical twist on ancient temple incubation.

The *Testament of Levi* furnishes several more examples of incubatory
rituals. Levi grieves over the plight of humankind, prays, falls asleep

---

[141] Wilson, *Prophecy and Society*, 40.

[142] For trance-inducing recitations in Jewish mysticism see G. Scholem, *Major Trends
in Jewish Mysticism* (New York: Schocken, 1995), 57–63. Note also that sitting is the
characteristic posture of *Merkabah* mystics; see P. Schäfer, *Hidden and Manifest God: Some
Major Themes in Early Jewish Mysticism* (trans. A. Pomerance; New York: SUNY Press,
1992), 154; *Hekh. Zut.* section 424.

[143] As M. Idel, I. Gruenwald and D. Halperin note, there is a close tie between water
divination and *Merkabah* mysticism; in Halperin, *Faces of the Chariot*, 231–232.

[144] Nickelsburg, *1 Enoch*, 239.

[145] D. Suter, 'Mapping the First Book of Enoch: Geographical Issues in George
Nickelsburg's Commentary,' in *George W.E. Nickelsburg in Perspective*, 2:387–394.

and dreams, traveling in the dream to the heavenly temple in the highest heaven (*T. Levi* 2:5–5:7). Levi's second dream, in which he undergoes priestly ordination and transformation into an angel, is also a heavenly ascent in a dream that occurs at the famous incubatory site of Bethel (*T. Levi* 8:1–19). This dream occurs after a period of seventy days, which may also indicate a ritual period of preparation (cf. forty days in *2 En.* 72:1). After Levi's dream, Jacob sleeps at Bethel and has a confirmatory dream telling him that Levi should be anointed as a priest (9:1–8), the earthly fulfillment of Levi's heavenly investiture.

4QAramaic Levi (*4Q213*) shares some kind of close relationship with *Greek T. Levi*, although determining the exact nature has proven difficult.[146] Whatever their relationship, *4QAramaic Levi* supplies us with other incubation rituals, depicting Levi undergoing purification through washing and praying before a dream ensues. Interestingly enough, *4QAramaic Levi* (*4Q213–214*) also clearly stipulates that washing is a preparation for approaching the altar. In this context, Levi's washing rituals that precede his dream may specifically anticipate a dream of ascent to the heavenly Temple.

4 Ezra contains the most complex incubation rituals of any early Jewish text. Ezra has six dreams in which particular rituals are correlated with specific dream types, as follows:

1. mourning, prayer (3:2–36)—results in a message dream of Uriel
2. prayer, weeping, fasting for 7 days (5:13)—results in a message dream of Uriel
3. prayer, weeping, fasting for 7 days (6:31–37)—results in a message dream of Uriel
4. staying in a special field of flowers, eating only flowers for 7 days, abstaining from meat and wine, prayer (9:23–37)—results in a combination message / symbolic dream of a woman who turns into the heavenly Jerusalem, which remains after Ezra awakens (i.e. a token dream)

---

[146] R. Kugler suggests that an early Jewish *Aram. Levi* from the 3rd c. B.C.E. furnished a source for an original (*Greek*) *T. Levi* that was Christian, later edited into its extant Christian form, *From Patriarch to Priest*, 171–220. While admiring much in that work, M. de Jonge offers a critique of Kugler's reconstructed 'original *T. Levi*' and concludes it is unrecoverable. De Jonge, 'Levi in Aramaic Levi and in the Testament of Levi' in *Pseudepigrapha Perspectives: The Apocrypha and Pseudepigrapha in Light of the Dead Sea Scrolls: Proceedings of the International Symposium of the Orion Center for the Study of the Dead Sea Scrolls and Associated Literature, 12–14 January, 1997* (STDJ XXXI; eds. E.G. Chazon and M.E. Stone; Leiden: Brill, 1999), 71–90.

5. residing and sleeping in the field of flowers (10:58, 12:51)—results
   in a vivid symbolic eschatological dream
6. residing and sleeping in the field of flowers, eating only the flowers
   for seven days (12:50–13:1)—results in a vivid symbolic eschatological dream

In each case, the type of incubation ritual corresponds to a certain
dream type. In the first three instances, the text links weeping, grieving,
prayer and fasting—all well-established methods of incubation—with
message dreams.

The last three instances of incubation in 4 Ezra involve abstaining
from meat and wine and sleeping in a certain field and eating nothing but certain flowers, which apparently induces vivid *symbolic* dreams.
Special diets are common incubation rituals, and the consumption of
flowers to induce dreams or visions is well known in antiquity. In fact,
narcotic poppies were so well associated with dreaming that iconography sometimes depicts Somnus, Nyx and Hypnos holding poppies
in their hand.[147] Thus, not only is the author of 4 Ezra familiar with
fairly complex incubation rituals, but particular practices are consistently linked to certain *types of dreams*.

---

[147] An association between certain types of narcotic flowers, especially opium poppies, and sleep and dreams was well known in antiquity. In the 3rd c. B.C.E., Theophrastus notes that poppy heads crushed in wine or honey and water brings sleep.
Dioscorides, writing in 77 C.E. also notes that 'the leaves and head [of the poppy]
when boiled in water bring sleep ... drunk to remedy insomnia.' In the *Aeneid* and
in *Georgics*, Virgil speaks of the *soperiferumque paparva* (soporific poppy) and *Lethaeo per-
fusa papavera somno* (poppies soaked with the sleep of Letho). In Ovid's *Metamorphoses*
11, the entrance to the cavern of Somnus, the god of sleep, is garlanded with poppies;
inside lies Somnus, surrounded by his children, 'The empty dream-shapes.' In Roman
iconography, Somnus is typically portrayed as a young boy carrying a bunch of poppies
and an opium horn. From this association comes the Latin name for the opium poppy,
Papaver somniferum. Similarly, Nyx and Hypnos are sometimes depicted on sarcophagi
as holding poppies. C. Robert, *Die antiken Sarkophagenreliefs III 1*(1897) nos. 50, 58, 65,
83; D. Kleiner, *Roman Imperial Funerary Altars with Portraits* (Rome: Giorgio Bretschnei-
der Editore, 1987), plate XI, no. 4. In *Acts of Thecla*, women throw an abundance of
flower petals upon raging animals to put them to sleep. Poppies were used to induce
sleep as well as altered states. Sometimes this occurred in religious contexts, e.g. in the
Eleusinian mysteries, poppy juice may have been taken to bring on a hypnagogic state
between sleeping and waking that symbolized passing from winter to spring and death
to life. The aetiological myth for this practice appears in the *Homeric Hymn to Demeter*,
in which Demeter put Triptolemos to sleep with poppy juice. Moreover, Booth suggests
that priests at Asklepios' sanctuary at Epidauros may have given opium to those who
sought healing at the temple, thereby inducing sleep and dreams. M. Booth, *Opium: A
History* (London: Simon & Schuster, 1996), 15–17.

In a peculiarly Jewish twist on incubation, several texts describe an otherwise rare phenomenon in which the nation as a whole incubates a dream. In *L.A.B.*, Joshua gathers 'all the people along with the women and children' and instructs them to stay all night next to the Ark of the Covenant in Shiloh, apparently to sleep (23:2–3). In the exact language Balaam uses while provoking his oracular dreams, Joshua instructs the Israelites to 'wait here this night and see what God will say to me on your behalf,' after which he subsequently has a testamentary dream that renews the covenant (*L.A.B.* 23:2–3; cf. 18:3, 8). Thus, this appears to be a mass incubation in a sacred space, in which Joshua is the receiver of revelation.

Although surprising, this pattern occurs in at least two other early Jewish texts. In *2 Enoch*, a festival is held at 'Azukhan, whence Enoch had been taken up,' and an altar is built and animals are brought to be sacrificed. The elders implore Methuselah (with variant spellings) to act as their priest. Methuselah instructs them to wait for an answer from the LORD, proceeding to incubate a dream: 'And the people waited all that night at the place Azukhan. And Mathusalom ... remained near the altar and prayed to the LORD ... and Mekhusalom fell asleep, and the LORD appeared to him in a night vision ...' (*2 En.* A and J 69:3–5). Again, this repeats the pattern of the people as a whole sleeping in a sacred space (next to the altar at Azukhan) and expecting an oracular dream, which comes that night to Methuselah, telling him of his priestly investiture. However, it is unclear whether in this passage the reference to 'the people' is meant to include women.

The clearest example of mass incubation occurs in Josephus. Jaddus the High Priest was in agony over the imminent arrival and conquest of Alexander the Great and the Macedonian army:

> He [Jaddus] therefore ordered the people to make supplication, and, offering sacrifice to God together with them, besought Him to shield the nation and deliver them from the dangers that were hanging over them. But, when he had gone to sleep after the sacrifice, God spoke oracularly to him in his sleep (κατακομηθέντι δὲ μετὰ τὴν θυσίαν ἐχρημάτισεν αὐτῷ κατὰ τοὺς ὕπνους ὁ θεὸς θαρρεῖν. Thereupon he rose from his sleep, greatly rejoicing to himself, and announced to all the revelation that had been made to him ...   (*Ant.* 11.326–327)

Structurally speaking, the following steps occur: 1) Jaddus is on the Temple Mount together with the people, 2) they sacrifice, 3) he prays, 4) he falls asleep and hears God in an auditory message dream, 5) he awakens with joy, and 6) he tells the people.[148] We know the sacrifice takes place in the Temple since the High Priest is cultically bound there and since the context of the larger passage is Alexander's approach to Jerusalem (*Ant.* 11.325). Since the people are there with Jaddus before and immediately after his dream, this appears to be another mass incubation, this time at the Temple itself.[149] The rapidity and conciseness of the Greek do not suggest the insertion of a scene suggesting that after the sacrifice on the Temple mount, Jaddus and the people all went home, went to bed and slept.[150]

If this claim of incubation in the Jerusalem Temple seems remarkable, it is not unique. Another striking example of purposeful place incubation in the sacred space of the Jerusalem Temple occurs in *2 Baruch* 34–36, which has been discussed above.[151] Like Balaam and Joshua in *L.A.B.*, Baruch intentionally engages in dream incubation and *expects* divine guidance as a result, telling the Israelites: 'I shall go to the Holy of Holies to ask from the Mighty One on behalf of you and Zion so that I may receive in some ways more light' (*2 Bar.* 34:1). He sits on the ruins, weeps, laments and prays. He then falls asleep and sees a symbolic dream concerning God's impending judgment of Rome (*2 Bar.* 36:1). Again, all of these preparations—praying, weeping, mourning and sleeping in a temple are well-established techniques of incubation (cf. *2 Bar.* 47:1).[152]

Finally, besides the presence of incubation rituals preceding dreams and the depictions of angels within dreams, several early Jewish texts seem to know the rituals that follow incubated dreams. In the Asklepios cult, for instance, one thanked the god after a dream with prayer, sacrifices, monetary payments, and votive offerings to be displayed to others, particularly inscriptions that describe the contents of the dream.[153]

---

[148] In this case, 'the people' are probably men, given that they are clothed in white, reminiscent of the priests who lead them (*Ant.* 11.331).

[149] Gnuse agrees this is an incubation, *Josephus*, 185–186.

[150] Moreover, the scene as a whole, with Alexander's army approaching against Jaddus and a host of priests and people in white clothing, is reminiscent of the assaults of foreign armies on the Temple Mount during the Maccabean wars; this may further suggest the location is the Temple Mount itself. See for instance 1 Macc 6:18, 51–54; 7:33–38; 2 Macc 10:24–31.

[151] The translation used is by A.F.J. Klijn, *2 Baruch*, *OTP* 1:615–652.

[152] Oppenheim, *Interpretation*, 188.

[153] Hamilton, *Incubation*, 31–36. In LiDonnici, *Epidaurian Miracle Inscriptions*, see cures A4, 5, 8; B 5; C 3; D 2, 3. Regional preferences resulted in different votive styles: Epidauros favored narrative inscriptions, Corinth terra-cotta body-part votives, Athens and

Similarly, after dreaming Ezra and Baruch both offer prayers of thanks-giving (4 Ezra 13:57–58; *2 Bar.* 38 and 54) while Enoch raises a prayer of supplication (*1 En.* 84). We might also reconsider the context of the scribal activity of Daniel and Enoch in terms of the conventional Hel-lenistic practice of providing cultic and public testimony of a divinely-sent dream (Dan 7:1; *1 En.* 14:1, cf. 83:10).

· In addition, numerous pseudepigraphic dreamers in early Jewish texts also thank God by means of sacrifices, but in a variation on the Graeco-Roman incubation cults, they themselves function as the sacrificers, i.e. in a priestly capacity. For instance, *Jubilees* adds the detail that after Abram's dream of the covenant between the pieces, Abram really offers a sacrifice (*Jub.* 14:19), as he does in *1QGenesis Apocryphon* [1Q20] col. XXI. Similarly, Jacob offers a sacrificial tithe as a thank offering for his son Levi's dream of priestly investiture (*Jub.* 32:3–9) and according to Josephus, he promises to do so after the Bethel dream only if it comes true (*Ant.* 1.278–284). Again, in *2 Enoch* Methuselah incubates a dream by sleeping by the altar, receives priestly investiture in a dream, awakens and is clothed in priestly garb, whereupon he begins sacrificing in a miraculous manner: 'while Methusalom (var.) was praying, the altar was shaken, and the knife rose up from the altar, and leaped into Methusalom's hands in front of the face of all the people' (*2 En.* 69:16; cf. 59; 70:4).

Despite these similarities to Graeco-Roman incubation rituals before, during and after dreams in early Jewish dream texts, an important difference arises in that Jewish dreamers do not practice incubation because of physical illness. Rather, almost without exception dreamers are motivated by concern over the future of Israel, which is faced with some sort of present crisis. The crisis could be a change in leadership, as when Joshua instructs the people, saying 'Gather before the ark of the covenant of the LORD in Shiloh, and I will establish a covenant with you before I die' (*L.A.B.* 23:1), or when Methuselah incubates a dream by the altar at 'Azukhan' while the people await the nomination of a priest by God (*2 En.* 69:3). The crisis could also concern destruction of the Temple and Gentile occupation, which are the cause of distress for Ezra and Baruch, and a catalyst for their incubations (e.g. 4 Ezra 3:9; *2 Bar.* 35–36). Conversely, the scope of a dreamer's distress might extend farther, as in the case of Levi's grief over the entire sinful human

---

Piraeus stone votive reliefs. LiDonnici, *Epidaurian Miracle Inscriptions*, 42; Van Straten, 'Gifts for the Gods,' 65–151; Aleshire, *Athenian Asklepieion*.

race (*T. Levi* 2:4). Then again, in one account, Enoch simply 'weeps and grieves' on his bed, for no apparent reason (*2 En.* 1:3–10).[154]

In sum, the authors of early Jewish dream texts feel no compunction about appropriating incubation rituals that were well-known in pagan dream cults.[155] The presence of incubation rituals in the literature of Hellenistic Judaism is diffuse, including: *1 Enoch* 12–36; *Jubilees* 27:19–26, 32:1–2; *1QJubilees* (1Q17[1QJub[a]]), *L.A.B.* 18:3–9, 23:3–14, 53:1–13; *2 Baruch* 34–36; *4 Ezra* 3:1–5:15, 5:21–6:13, 6:35–7:2, 9:27–10:33, 10:60–12:5, 13:1–13; *Testament of Levi* 2:5–5:7, 8:1–19; *4QAramaic Levi*; *2 Enoch* 1:3–10, 69:1–71:1; *Antiquities* 1.278–284, 8:22–25, 11.326–328; *1QGenesis Apocryphon* (1Q20 [*1QapGen ar*]) col. XIX, XXI and probably *4QVision of Samuel* (*4Q160* [*4QVisSam*]) frag. 1. Not only is interest in incubation much more pervasive than in the Hebrew Bible, the rituals go far beyond the simple place incubation of biblical traditions. Moreover, depictions of healing angels in early Jewish dreams either draw directly on, or else resonate intertextually with, iconographic and literary descriptions of dream gods such as Asklepios. Whether or not early Jewish authors themselves practiced incubation remains conjecture, but their marked literary interest in modifying biblical accounts of incubation and creating altogether new ones, along with their familiarity with some detailed incubatory practices, suggests to me that some of them did.

In either case, their articulation of incubation is decidedly Jewish, a constellation of images including pseudepigraphic heroes of Israel's sacred history, the priesthood, sacred sites particular to Israel, incubation in the Jerusalem Temple, and incubation that results in ascent to the heavenly Temple.

Divine Sanction

By now it should come as no surprise that the vast majority of early Jewish dreams imply the divine sanction of their dreamers, almost always males from Israelite sacred tradition, or of the Jewish people as a whole. The granting of covenants through dreams to Abraham

---

[154] Oppenheim, *Interpretation*, 188, 249, par. 8, no. 10; 252, par. 8, no. 22; Ehrlich, *Der Traum*, 14–5; S. Ackerman, 'Deception of Isaac,' 92–120.

[155] Gnuse argues that Josephus was reluctant and cautious in his portrayal of Jewish incubation, since 'The plethora of [dream] cults ... presumably would have overwhelmed the pious sensitivities of a monotheistic Jew from Palestine with his priestly

and Jacob has implications for the Jewish readership, who share in
these blessings (*Jub.* 14, 27, 32; *Ladd. Jac.*; *4QJacob*; *1QGen. Apoc.*). Warning dreams that come to the patriarchs and others also function to
enact divine protection for the patriarchs and their future descendants
(Abram in *1QGen. Apoc.*; Abimelech, Laban and Pharaoh in *Ant.* 1.208–
209, 1.313–314, 2.75–86; Isaac in *T. Abr.* 7). It is in a similar context
that we should view the dreams of Joseph that provide divine protection for Jesus in the New Testament (Matt 2). Moreover, dreams often
promise that the dreamer will be exalted to a special reward, such as
when Moses is enthroned over all (*Ezek. Trag.* vv. 68–72) or when angels
explain to Enoch that he will ascend to heaven (*2 En.* 1).

From the ancient Near East onward, dreams have also functioned
in the opposite manner, announcing the withdrawal of divine favor or
the imposition of divine punishment. The most obvious case in early
Judaism must be the punishment of the Watchers and rejection of their
petition in *1 En.* 15 and 88 (cf. *2 En.* 7). This is probably how we should
understand the Giants' own dreams, which 'depress' them (*4QBook of
Giants*). These do not appear to be simple anxiety or 'psychological
status dreams,' since the Giants are so desperate to find a reliable
interpreter in Enoch. Similar descriptions appear in the *Assyrian Dream-
Book*, in which the protasis reads: 'If a man has had an evil/bad/wrong
dream and it depresses him.' This is followed by an apodosis offering an
apotropaic ritual, including supplication to a god.[156] By analogy we can
surmise that the Giants' dreams are symbolic dreams that signify they
have incurred divine wrath, which squares perfectly with the traditions
preserved in *1 Enoch* 1–36.

Furthermore, several texts articulate the dream function of the granting and withdrawal of divine sanction in relation to the priestly cult.
As I have already noted, several dreamers in Hellenistic Judaism gain
priestly status through their dreams (Methusaleh and Nir in *2 En.* 69–70
and Levi in *T. Levi* 8, *4QAram. Levi*, *Jub.* 32 and *4QJub.*). On the other
hand, Samuel dreams of the demise of Eli's priestly line (*4QVisions of
Samuel*; *Ant.* 6; *L.A.B.* 53), signifying the withdrawal of divine favor and
priestly legitimacy. Finally, in *Jubilees* 4:24, Judah receives forgiveness

---

training,' *Josephus*, 230. I come to a different conclusion not only with respect to other
Jewish authors of this period but also with Josephus, who explicitly portrays Jacob,
Solomon and the High Priest Jaddus as incubating dreams connected to sacrifice, *Ant.*
1.278–284; 8.22–25, 11.326–328.

[156] Oppenheim, *Interpretation*, 303–304.

in a dream. If the plural subject of the dream who does the forgiving includes the LORD and the Angel of the Presence from the heavenly Temple who narrates the *Book of Jubilees* to Moses, this forgiveness proceeds through a divine intermediary from the heavenly *hekhal*, perhaps an angelic priest.[157]

Summary of Functions of Dreams in Hellenistic Judaism

Overall, we have seen that the early Jewish texts uphold traditional functions of dreams from the ancient Near East, Hebrew Bible, Greece and Rome, but with some changes that give each function a uniquely Jewish emphasis. Receipt of extraordinary knowledge intertwines with divine sanction, portraying providential care for pseudepigraphic Israelite heroes, their families, and their descendants (the Jewish readership of the Hellenistic and Roman periods). Cosmic and eschatological dream revelations center on a portrait of the universe in which God rules from the heavenly Palace-Temple. This orienting tier of reality is pictured as breaking into the earthly plane (whether gradually or suddenly on the Day of Judgment), usually also implying the future exaltation of Israel. Especially in apocalypses, dream knowledge may be interconnected to the divine sanction of dreamers who become angelic priests and/or scribes and ascend to the heavenly *hekhal*. The function of healing the sick through dreams, a Graeco-Roman obsession, takes on new contours in the Hellenistic Jewish literature. Although dreams are not sought for physical healing, seers who experience turmoil on behalf of the nation or people freely implement known rituals from incubation cults and expect a dream to come from God. During moments of national crisis, the entire people might even gather to incubate a dream, which would be received by a special intermediary such as the High Priest.

The many dreams I have examined testify to the remarkable innovation and artistry of early Jewish authors who use standardized, cross-cultural dream forms, vocabulary and functions, while enlivening these dream traditions in creative ways that speak more directly to a context in Hellenistic Judaism. In the next chapter I turn to further variations

---

[157] Oppenheim, *Interpretation*, 293. Forgiveness through dreams also has ancient Near Eastern precedents in dreams of cult images, the interpretations of which state 'they have removed the sin of the man [i.e., the dreamer] …'

and transformations that early Jewish dreams make to certain motifs, including: the soul journey that occurs in dreams, the role of the *oneiros* or dream messenger, the character and activities of the dreamer himself, and the relationship between dreams and death.

.

CHAPTER FOUR

DREAMS IN HELLENISTIC JUDAISM: CREATIVE
TRANSFORMATIONS AND ELABORATIONS

> 'I got up from my sleep, and the men
> were standing with me in actuality.'
>
> —2 Enoch 1:6

As we have seen, Jewish dreams of the Hellenistic and Roman eras
are remarkably continuous with pagan dreams of the ancient world. In
addition to sharing common vocabulary and dream functions, divinely-
sent dreams found throughout the literary and cultic sources of antiquity are articulated within a standard formal frame. This fairly ubiqui-
tous *dream pattern* consists of: 1) an INTRODUCTION that establishes
a setting of sleep, night, or lying down, 2) a DREAM in which a divine
or semi-divine being delivers a message or symbols that convey a coded
message, and 3) a CONCLUSION that notes the mood of the dreamer
and states that he or she has awakened.[1] Yet even while exhibiting these
well-established patterns, early Jewish texts display profound creativity and flexibility in their individual formulations of dreams. Within
the controlling formal frame of dreams is space for the content of the
dream itself, and given the cultural presuppositions that dreams transcend the normal limits of reality, this interior space of the dream
proves to be especially open and fluid. Thus, the dream form itself is
at once limiting and liberating.

In this chapter, I investigate in greater depth certain creative developments in the dreams of Hellenistic Judaism, including variations on
otherworldly journeys, transformed roles for dream messengers, and
new characteristics and activities of dreamers. I also explore the many
ways in which dreams are connected with death, a theme we have seen
in other cultures as well. These discussions illuminate in greater depth
the worldviews of particular dream texts, which I find are permeated
by scribal and priestly concerns.

---

[1] Oppenheim, *Interpretation*, 186–190.

Soul Journeys or Access to Otherworldly Realms in Dreams

The motif of the soul traveling to other regions is familiar in the ancient Near East, Greece and Rome, but it cannot said to be a prevalent theme.[2] This is even truer in the case of the Bible, being absent from biblical dream texts other than possibly being implied in Daniel's throne vision (Dan 7). By contrast, soul journeys are much more plentiful in Hellenistic Jewish dream texts than in any other ancient culture. The earliest example of a Jewish dream journey occurs in *1 En.* 13:7–36:4, when the scribe Enoch dreams and travels to the heavenly Temple and around the earth. The same ascent tradition is apparently recounted in *4QEnoch*[a] (*4Q201* [*4QEn*[a]*ar*]). Similarly, Levi also ascends in a dream to the heavenly Temple in *Greek T. Levi* 2:5–5:7 and 8:1–19, as well as in *4QAramaic Levi*[a] (*4Q213* [*4QTLevi*[a]*ar*]) frag. 1, col. II. *2 Enoch* does not describe an ascent within Enoch's dream, but his dream accurately announces his later ascent to the heavenly Temple, and thus dream and ascent are closely connected (*2 En.* 1–2). Similarly, Isaac's dream in *Testament of Abraham* predicts his father's imminent ascent to heaven in death, which is preceded by a literal ascent to heaven during Abraham's lifetime. Several scholars have studied the phenomenon of ascent in antiquity, and I do not wish to duplicate their findings here.[3] Instead, my goal is to investigate the ascents that take place within dream texts as they relate to other dreams in early Judaism that also provide access to otherworldly realms.

Within the context of dream research, ascents as a category can actually be limiting, since ascents are only one articulation of how dreamers reach otherworldly realms. The common phrase 'otherworldly journey' is also misleading since it has come into usage with reference to a spe-

---

[2] See for example *The Story of Sinuhe*, trans. J.A. Wilson (*ANET*, 18); Enkidu's dream in *Epic of Gilgamesh*, trans. S. Kramer, *ASOR Bulletin* 94:6, n. 11; *Somnium Scipionis* in Cicero, *Resp.* VI.x.10-xxvi.29; and Plato, *Resp.* X:613–620, although not in a dream.

[3] See Bousset, *Die Himmelreise der Seele*; C.R.A. Morray-Jones, 'Paradise Revisited (2 Cor 12:1–12): The Jewish Mystical Background of Paul's Apostolate, Part 1: The Jewish Sources' and 'Part 2: Paul's Heavenly Ascent and Its Significance,' *HTR* 86 (1993): 177–217, 265–292; Dean-Otting, *Heavenly Journey*; Himmelfarb, *Ascent to Heaven* and 'Apocalyptic Ascent and the Heavenly Temple,' *SBL Seminar Papers 1987* (Atlanta: Scholars, 1987), 210–217; J.J. Collins, 'Journeys to the world beyond in ancient Judaism,' in *Apocalyptic and Eschatological Heritage: The Middle East and Celtic Realms* (ed. M. McNamara; Dublin: Four Courts, 2001), 20–36; see also A.Y. Collins, *Cosmology and Eschatology*, 21–54.

cific group of apocalypses[4] and gives the impression that a dreamer must travel to another place in order to enter a different dimension. Instead, there are many formulas by which *dreams provide a dreamer with access to an otherworldly realm*, and not all of these occur in apocalypses or involve spatial journeys. Alongside the heavenly ascents in *1 En.* 14–36 and *T. Levi* 2–5 and 8, we should also consider 4 Ezra 9:38–10:37, since Ezra transcends the mundane realm when he tours the heavenly Jerusalem which has descended to earth in his dream. Similarly, in Dan 7, the dreamer appears to see the interior of the divine throne-room in the eschatological future, although no location is specified.[5] Furthermore, the biblical dream of Jacob's ladder on the mountain of Bethel (Gen 28) and the early Jewish retellings it inspires (*Ladd. Jac.*; *Jub.* 32; *Ant.* 1.278–284) are likewise dreams that provide access to an otherworldly realm, since Jacob finds himself at 'the gate of heaven,' sees angels ascending and descending, and converses with the Lord who stands in heaven at the top of the structure. In addition, some dreamers are able to perceive an otherwise hidden divine realm nestled at the tops of other sacred mountains, such as Sinai, Horeb and Zion. For instance, in the drama by Ezekiel the Tragedian, Moses dreams and sees a divine throne on Sinai (*Ezek. Trag.* vv. 68–82), which in many ways resembles the heavenly throne-room in Isa 6 and Dan 7.

The earliest dream journeys in Hellenistic Judaism occur in 'The Book of the Watchers' and are so influential they are worth examining rather closely. After establishing some aspects of this example the contours of these paradigmatic journeys, I turn to an investigation of how other early Jewish texts articulate the formula of access to otherworldly realms through dreams.

The Book of the Watchers

The collection of writings known as *1 Enoch* revolves around the receipt and transmission of wisdom to such an extent that G.W.E. Nickelsburg has recently referred to it as a 'sapiential-apocalyptic tradition.'[6] It is significant that the major mechanism for Enoch's receipt of eschato-

---

[4] The phrase applies to types 'IIb and IIc' apocalypses, according to the definitive study on 'apocalypse' as a genre in *Semeia* 14. See Collins, 'Introduction: Towards the Morphology of a Genre,' 1–19.

[5] See Collins, *Daniel*, 300–303.

[6] All citations and English quotations are from Nickelsburg's recent translation. Nickelsburg, *1 Enoch*, 50.

logical and cosmological wisdom is a series of soul journeys that takes place within a dream,[7] one which merits our full attention. The 'Book of the Watchers' (*1 En.* 1–36) was most likely composed by the middle of the third century B.C.E.,[8] and Himmelfarb notes it is the first Jewish text to depict ascent.[9] Enoch's dream journeys in 'The Book of the Watchers' are more complex than any dream in the earlier ancient Near Eastern or Greek materials[10] and have no exact biblical parallel, combining aspects of Isaiah 6 and Ezekiel's earthly tours, which do not occur in dreams. Although Enoch's dream does somewhat resemble Latin dream journeys such as Cicero's 'Dream of Scipio,' it predates them by centuries, and is distinctly Jewish in that heaven is conceived of as a temple.[11] *4QEnoch* also knows the tradition of Enoch's otherworldly journeys and places these in visions (ובחזיה לי [את]חזית), which are probably also dreams.

The precise parameters of the dream in the extant text of 'The Book of the Watchers' are somewhat unclear, since the dream frame is detached from the recitation of the content of the dream.[12] The formal pattern of the *dream frame* is standard:

> I. INTRODUCTION (*1 Enoch* 13:7): ' *... so I fell asleep.* ('eska daqqasku; ἕως ἐκοιμήθην) And, behold, *dreams came upon me, and visions fell upon me.*' (wa nāhu ḥelm maṣ'ani wa rā'eyāt dibēya wadqu; ὄνειροι ἐπ' ἐμε ἦλθον καὶ ὁράσεις ἐπ' ἐμὲ ἐπέπιπτον)

> II. DREAM report (*1 Enoch* 13:8): '*And I saw visions of wrath*, (wa re'iku rā'eyāta maqšaft) and there came a voice, saying, "Speak to the sons of heaven to reprimand them."'

---

[7] Nickelsburg, *1 Enoch*, 32.

[8] Ibid., 1 Enoch, 7.

[9] Himmelfarb, *Ascent to Heaven*, 7, 29. She identifies the following as ascent texts: *Book of the Watchers, T. Levi, 2 En., Sim. En., Apoc. Zeph., Apoc. Abr., Asc. Is.* and *3 Bar.*

[10] A. Segal summarizes and discusses the breadth of the ascent and descent motifs in antiquity, almost of none of which occur in a dream. Segal's valuable article critiques Bousset's work on the Persian materials and discusses further *XXII Yasht* or *Hadokht Nask* and the journey of Arda Viraf; he also reviews Widengren's investigations on Mesopotamian materials and comments further on Greek materials, including Parmenides of Elea's *On Nature*, Plato's *Myth of Er* (*Republic* Book 10.614ff.), Plutarch's 'On Those Who Are Punished by the Deity Late,' as well as Roman materials, including Cicero's *Somnium Scipiones* and Ovid's and Livy's accounts of the ascension of Romulus. A. Segal, 'Heavenly Ascent in Hellenistic Judaism, Early Christianity and their Environment,' in *ANRW* II.23.2 (1980), 1333–1394.

[11] Himmelfarb accurately speaks of the Jewish understanding of 'heaven as temple' rather than of heaven *containing* a temple, 14–16.

[12] Greek and Ethiopic excerpts from *1 Enoch* are taken from R.H. Charles, ed. *The Ethiopic Version of the Book of Enoch*, 34–35, 40–41.

III. CONCLUSION (*1 Enoch* 13:9) '*And when I had awakened* (wa naqiheya; καὶ ἔξυπνος γενόμενος), I went to them.'

The typical INTRODUCTION states that Enoch fell asleep. The linking particle 'And, behold,' standard in biblical dreams, introduces the DREAM report (13:7). 'Dreams' and 'visions' are used in parallelism with unspecified form and content. An element of an auditory message dream occurs in 13:8 when a voice commands Enoch to reprimand the sons of heaven or Watchers. In the typical CONCLUSION for message and symbolic dreams, Enoch awakens (13:9). The recitation of the dream itself follows, which is an important element of symbolic dreams in the ancient Near East.[13] Thus, the dream frame combines elements of auditory message dreams and symbolic dreams.

The content of the dream that Enoch subsequently narrates includes at least Enoch's heavenly ascent and commissioning (13:7–16:4) and may include one or more of his tours across the earth as well (chapters 17–36).[14] Two points support identifying the rest of the 'Book of the Watchers' as occurring within Enoch's dream. First, the locations that Enoch witnesses on his earthly tours testify to God's ultimate judgment and corresond well to the 'visions of wrath' cited in the earlier dream report (13:8). As Nickelsburg has beautifully stated, 'Cosmology undergirds eschatology,'[15] since Enoch sees the eventual places of reward for the righteous and of punishment for the wicked stars, angels and people. Second, no narrative clues in the earthly journeys suggest that Enoch's recitation of his dream has ended. I regard Enoch's otherworldly and earthly journeys as parts of Enoch's dream, the narration of which thus extends from chapter 14 to chapter 36.

If I am correct, the structure of the dream is quite complex and may be outlined as follows:

IV. DREAM (*1 Enoch* 14:1–36:4)
  a. Introductory dream formula: 'And I recited in [the Watchers'] presence all the visions which I had seen in the dream, and I began

---

[13] Liebovici, 'Babylone,' 67; Oppenheim, *Interpretation*, 205–206, 219.

[14] Nickelsburg believes that chapters 17–19 are a duplication of a tradition about Enoch's journey to the divine throne, secondarily attached to 12–16, *1Enoch*, 278.

[15] Nickelsburg, 'The Apocalyptic Construction of Reality in *1 Enoch*' in *Mysteries and Revelations: Apocalyptic Studies since the Uppsala Colloquium* (JSPM9; Sheffield: JSOT Press, 1991): 50–64. For example, on his tour Enoch sees the places where the souls of the dead are separated and awaiting judgment, and the future mountain throne of God where the righteous will dwell in Eden.

to speak the words of truth and the vision and to reprimand the
watchers of heaven.

b. Title of dream account: 'THE BOOK OF THE WORDS OF
TRUTH AND THE REPRIMAND OF THE WATCHERS
WHO WERE FROM ETERNITY, according to the command of
the Great Holy One in the dream that I dreamt' (14:1).

c. Otherworldly journey account (14:8–17:1).

d. Auditory message dream within the dream journey: 'And the Lord
called me with his mouth and said ...' (14:24–16:4; cf. 13:8).

e. Dream journeys around earth (17:1–36:4).

f. Request for interpretation of the visions (18:14; 21:4; 22:6, 8; 24:6–
25:2; 27:1).

g. Angelic INTERPRETATION of the visions (Uriel: 19:1–2; 18:14–
16; 21:5, 9–10); (Raphael: 22:3–4, 7, 9–13); (Raguel: 23:4); (Michael:
24:6–25:6); (Sariel: 27:2–4); (Gabriel: 32:6).

h. Visionary swoon, angelic touch, Enoch is helped to stand up
(14:25).

Several elements from different dream types combine in a new formulation. The visions Enoch sees on the tours require explanation, much
like *symbolic dreams*. The appearance of an angel who converses with
the dreamer is evocative of Greek *message dreams* and the *oneiros* figure.
Here, however, the angel's primary function is not to impart a divine
message, which is delivered by the voice of the Lord in the fashion of
biblical texts. Rather, the angel serves as a sort of psychopomp or tour
guide and as *angelus interpres* for the sights that Enoch sees in heaven
and the remote parts of the earth. This latter image almost certainly
derives from the angelic-human discussions in Zechariah's night-visions
(Zech 1–6) and perhaps from the psychopomp/interpreter who appears
in Ezekiel's visions, which are closely related to dreams but lack their
formal characteristics (Ezek 8–11, 40–48). Thus, *1Enoch* 14–36 apparently draws on pre-existing biblical depictions of angels as visionary
tour guides / interpreters in order to craft a new role for angelic dream
messengers, a portrait that is quite influential in subsequent dreams in
early Judaism.[16] Finally, the divine voice mentioned in 13:8 as well as the
divine voice that speaks in 14:24–16:4 are suggestive of an *auditory message dream* that relays revelation through the voice of the Lord, accord-

---

[16] For instance, angels act as otherworldly guides in dreams, often also interpreting
or explaining sites, in *1En.* 19:1–33:4; *T. Levi* 2:7–5:6, *2En.* 72:3–10; *T. Naph.* 5:7; *4QEnoch^c*
(*4Q206[4QEn^ar]*) frag. 3. In other formulas of access to otherworldly realms, angels also
explain and interpret dream information (whether they themselves appear in or after
dreams) in Dan 7:16–28, 8:15–26; *Jub.* 32:22; 4Ezra 4:1, 5:31, 7:1, 10:29; *Ladd. Jac.* 3:4–
7:35; and *2Bar.* 55:3.

ing to the style of many biblical dreams. This earliest Jewish ascent text is therefore an innovative pastiche of antecedent and contemporary dream motifs, resulting in a new dream figure, the *angelus interpres /* tour guide, as well as a new dream type.

Ever since the definitive *Semeia* 14, the title 'Otherworldly Journey' has been applied to *1 Enoch* 1–36 to indicate a sub-type of the genre apocalypse.[17] However useful in that context, this phrase may lead us to miss what is important about Enoch's dreams, since it implies *journeying* to an otherworldly *place*. In the larger context of dreams in antiquity, *1 Enoch* 14–36 operates according to 'dream logic,' namely, the idea that dreams suspend the normal constraints of reality, although Enoch's dream is a new, bold articulation of that logic in terms of a Hellenistic Jewish worldview. Hence, for my purposes I redefine *1 Enoch* 14–36 as *a dream that provides the dreamer with access to otherworldly realms.* These otherworldly realms include spatial, temporal and ontological dimensions, which are not discrete, but rather overlapping states of reality. Spatially, Enoch sees heaven (14–18), remote regions of the earth (23–36), and underworld regions (19, 21, 22). Temporally, Enoch learns of the eschatological future through spoken revelation as well as the cosmological sites he witnesses. Ontologically, Enoch, a living human being, is able to enter the heavenly *hekhal* (14–15), which is holy space inhabited by divine beings, and he is also able to see the realm of the dead without dying (22).

Enoch's dream journeys operate towards similar ends as do other dreams in antiquity, but the traditional functions are pressed into a new context. On the simplest narrative level, the dream journey in chapters 14–16 allows Enoch to take the Watchers' petition to heaven and to interact with the awesome Great Glory on the throne in the ultimate Palace-Temple (14:20–16:3). This is no small feat, given that not even the angels can 'come near' the figure (14:22) and that no one of flesh can see the Great Glory and live (14:21). Enoch is able, through his dream, to come up to the door of the Holy of Holies and perhaps to enter it (15:1),[18] whereupon he receives God's response to the Watchers, with which Enoch returns to earth. The utter rejection of the Watchers' petition and decree of their punishment fulfills one tra-

---

[17] *1 Enoch* 1–36 is classified as type IIb: 'Otherworldly Journey with Cosmic and/or Political Eschatology.' See Collins, 'Introduction: Towards the Morphology of a Genre,' 15.

[18] Nickelsburg, *1 Enoch*, 270.

ditional function of dreams, the *withdrawal of divine favor*, which is conveyed through Enoch's dream ascent to and descent from the heavenly Palace-Temple.[19]

Perhaps the more important dream function in the text is the *bestowal of extraordinary knowledge*. As Nickelsburg has asserted, Enoch's revealed wisdom lies at the heart of the theology of the entire corpus.[20] His dream journeys allow him to witness the inner workings of the heavenly *hekhal* and the entire cosmos, including heaven, earth and the nether regions. Each site he sees, from the treasuries of the winds to the mountain of the dead, underscores the orderliness of the universe and points to God's majesty and ultimate control.[21] Moreover, in his dream Enoch receives eschatological and cosmological revelations concerning a coming judgment, which would restore order to the earth as well as to heaven.[22]

Intertwined with Enoch's receipt of knowledge of the universe and its future is the bestowal of *divine sanction* on Enoch. As the one who writes and recites the Watchers' petition and God's response, Enoch acts as a heavenly scribe (12:4, 13:4–7). Nickelsburg has argued further that one form of the journey is a prophetic commissioning that resembles biblical call narratives such as 1 Kings 22:19–22, Isaiah 6 and Ezekiel 1–2.[23] Additionally, in his dream journey to heaven in chapters 12–16, Enoch may act in a priestly capacity, entering the heavenly Temple and performing intercession there on behalf of the Watchers, who failed in their former role as priests of the divine sanctuary.[24] If Enoch does actually enter the Holy of Holies, which Nickelsburg has suggested may be the case,[25] his status as a heavenly priest seems to be implied, although this does not necessarily mean that he was thought to occupy the same role in the Jerusalem Temple on earth (particularly given the harsh criticism of the Jerusalem Temple and its priests in *1 En.* 85–90). Himmelfarb comes to this conclusion: 'For our author the three roles of prophet, priest, and scribe coexisted as ideals, and only by bringing them together could he define the role of the most exalted

---

[19] E.g. 1 Sam 3, Num 22:9–13, Gen 31:10–13
[20] Nickelsburg, *1 Enoch*, 50–53.
[21] Ibid., 51.
[22] Ibid., 55, 64.
[23] Ibid., 254.
[24] Ibid., 67, 269–271.
[25] Since 14:25 brings Enoch to the door, Nickelsburg indicates the second invitation in 15:1 may bring him inside, *1 Enoch*, 270.

of men.'[26] Furthermore, although 'no angel could enter into this house and behold his face' (14:21), the Lord tells Enoch to approach him as he sits on the throne in the Holy of Holies (14:24, 15:1). Thus, Enoch appears to be exalted above the angels.[27]

Overall then, Enoch's dream facilitates his transcendence of humanity's regular spatial, temporal and ontological realms, resulting in Enoch, a living human, gaining unparalleled access: to the heavenly *hekhal*, (domain of angels and God); to remote regions of the earth; to the netherworld (domain of the dead and wicked angels); and to the primordial past and eschatological future.

Intertextuality and Dreams of Access to Otherworldly Realms in *1 Enoch* 1–36

Since Enoch's dream in the 'Book of the Watchers' is the earliest of many early Jewish dream journeys, it is worthwhile to investigate intertextual resonances this text shares with other traditions. Numerous scholars have sought the roots of the Jewish ascent traditions and have come to varying conclusions: Anz suggests Mithraism and Gnosticism, Bousset argues for Persian influence, Widengren documents the Mesopotamian background of ascent and Culianu explores the parameters of Babylonian influence.[28]

In the most thorough exploration to date of the roots of the dream ascent in *1 En.* 13–36, H. Kvanvig suggests the influence of three conflated traditions: 1) Mesopotamian *ascent* texts of Mesopotamian sages and kings, (including Enmeduranki in *Enmeduranki and the Diviners* and UtuabbaAdada in *Bīt Mēseri*);[29] 2) flood narratives, in which heroes of Mesopotamian flood literature (including Ziusudra in *Atrahasis* and Berossos and Kabtiilani-Marduk in the *Poem of Erra*) receive foreknowl-

[26] Himmelfarb, *Ascent to Heaven*, 25.

[27] VanderKam notes that Enoch can enter heaven, unlike the Watchers, and can enter God's immediate presence, unlike the celestial angels. J. VanderKam, *Enoch: A Man for All Generations* (Columbia, SC: University of South Carolina, 1995), 48.

[28] W. Anz, *Zur Frage nach dem Ursprung des Gnostizismus: Ein religionsgeschichtlicher Versuch* (TU 15.4; Leipzig: Heinrichs, 1897); Bousset, *Die Himmelreise*; G. Widengren, *The Ascension of the Apostle and the Heavenly Book*, (Uppsala: Uppsala Universitets Årsskrift, 1950); I.P. Culianu, *Expériences de l'extase: Extase, ascension et récit visionnaire de l'Hellénisme au moyen âge* (Paris: Payot, 1984); see also A.Y. Collins, *Cosmology and Eschatology*, 21–23.

[29] Helge S. Kvanvig, *Roots of Apocalyptic: The Mesopotamian Background of the Enoch Figure and of the Son of Man* (Wissenschaftliche Monographien zum Alten und Neuen Testament; vol. 61; Neukirchen-Vluyn: Neukirchener, 1988), 319–338.

edge of the impending catastrophe *in dreams* (cf. *1 En.* 83–84);[30] and 3)
Ezekiel's traditions about the *merkabah*. Of these texts, only the flood
narratives contain dreams. Kvanzig postulates that these various traditions coalesce in the 'Book of the Watchers' to produce a *dream* journey
that is an *ascent* to the heavenly temple and the *merkabah*.

Of course, the clearest influences on Enoch's dream are biblical traditions concerning temples and the throne of God, including the temple traditions in Ezek 40–48 and Isaiah 6 and the Ezekiel *merkabah*
traditions in 1–2, 8–10.[31] The description of the heavenly temple in
1 Enoch contains several elements from Ezekiel's traditions of the *ḥayyot*
and *merkabah*, including fire, lightning, and a shining ceiling (*1 En.* 14:9–
12).[32] Ezekiel 10:20 identifies the *ḥayyot* of the *merkabah* with the *cherubim*,
who are present in the temple in Ezekiel 10. Similarly, *1 Enoch* 14 identifies cherubim as part of the divine throne present in the temple. The
throne in *1 Enoch* is clearly the moveable *merkabah* of Ezekiel 1 since it
has shining wheels (*1 En.* 14:11, 18; Ezek 1:15–21). Nevertheless, although
Ezekiel's *merkabah* descends to earth, the *merkabah* of *1 Enoch* is firmly
fixed in heaven; hence, Enoch must ascend to present the Watchers'
petition.[33]

This array of possible influences is daunting, and more recently
A. Segal has rightly argued that the search for any one source for the
Jewish ascents is fruitless. Rather, he suggests there is a vast corpus of
traditions throughout the ancient Near East, Egypt, Greece and Rome
that share deeply held mythic structures in which the various planes of
existence (heaven, earth and underworld) are bridged through ascent
and descent.[34] According to him, 'the journey up and the journey
down are structurally equivalent,' since both movements bridge parts
of the cosmos.[35] Segal's insights into this aspect of ancient worldviews

---

[30] Kvanzig, *Roots of Apocalyptic*, 173–178, 181–186, 211–217, 288–295, 335–340.

[31] For more on *1 Enoch* 12–16 and the development of the Ezekiel traditions, see Nickelsburg, *1 Enoch*, 234–275, esp. 255–256, 261. See also Kvanzig, *Roots of Apocalyptic*, 319–
338; H.L. Jansen, *Die Henochgestalt* (Oslo: Dybwed, 1939), 114–117, cited in Nickelsburg,
'Enoch, Levi and Peter: Recipients of Revelation in Upper Galilee,' *JBL* 100 (1981):
575–600, 576–577.

[32] The crystal dome in Ezek 1:22 may have inspired the idea of water and ice in
1 Enoch 13–14.

[33] Nickelsburg, 'Enoch, Levi and Peter,' 581; *ibid.*, *1 Enoch*, 259; Scholem, *Major Trends*,
40–79.

[34] A. Segal, 'Heavenly Ascent in Hellenistic Judaism,' 1338–1351.

[35] See Segal's structural chart on ascents and descents, 'Heavenly Ascent,' 1339–
1340. His insights about the vectors between heaven, earth and the underworld also

reorient us as interpreters by redefining and widening what texts may be relevant to Enoch's ascent and ascents in general.

In fact, by employing Segal's paradigm and exploring descent traditions, important elements of Enoch's ascent *as a dream* are rendered intelligible. The Mesopotamian *descent* traditions, many of which occur *in dreams*, greatly clarify the structure and cosmology of Enoch's dreams and bring together in one type of text many of the features of temple, throne, flood and hero texts named earlier. Although I am not suggesting that specific descent texts serve as textual sources for *1 Enoch*, it is clear that several themes in the descent traditions relate intertextually[36] to the dream ascent in *1 Enoch* 14–36 and illuminate the worldview in the Enochic corpus.

Following Glasson, Nickelsburg has already recognized that certain features of Enoch's journeys in *1 En.* 17–19 take their cue from Greek *nekyia* traditions, such as *Od.* 11, Plato's 'Myth of Er' (*Resp.* 10.614–621), *Phaedo* 113D–114C, and Plutarch's *Mor.* 563–568.[37] Similarly, the descent in *A Vision of the Nether World* (Akkadian, early 7th c. B.C.E) bears closely on certain aspects Enoch's dream in *1 En.* 14–16, particularly since the vision is a 'night vision' or dream. Kvanvig actually examines *A Vision of the Nether World* in relation to Daniel, but Collins correctly notes that it is unconvincing as a specific referent, and 'is more relevant to the otherworldly journeys of Enoch than to the symbolic vision of Daniel.'[38] A brief summary of the Akkadian account and the discussion following are meant to expand this observation.

In *A Vision of the Nether World*, a king named Kummaya finds himself in the netherworld, where he sees several human-animal hybrid gods[39] and a throne upon which sits Nergal, god of that realm. An attendant

---

illuminate Mesopotamian texts that portray the gods of the Nether World ascending to heaven, including Zu and Namtar, both of whom appear in *A Vision of the Nether World*. *The Myth of Zu*, trans. E.A. Speiser (*ANET*, 111–113); *Nergal and Ereshkigal*, trans. E.A. Speiser (*ANET*, 103–104). Similarly, Collins consistently refers to 'round-trip[s] to heaven' as well as to ascent, 'Journeys to the world beyond,' 23.

[36] S.J. Huskey provides a helpful distinction of 'allusion' and 'intertext' in his review of these terms in recent classical scholarship: 'Allusions, then, involve authorial control over the imitations of one text by another. In contrast, intertextuality applies to the involuntary resemblances that arise between texts because they exist in a shared universe of discourse.' Huskey, 'Ovid's Tristia,' 13–19.

[37] T.F. Glasson, *Greek Influence in Jewish Eschatology* (London: SPCK, 1961), 8–11; also in Nickelsburg, *1 Enoch*, 280.

[38] Kvanvig, *Roots of Apocalyptic*, 389–441; Collins, *Daniel*, 285.

[39] Kvanvig argues this figure is transformed into the Son of Man in Daniel, *1 Enoch* and 4 Ezra 13; Kvanvig, *Roots of Apocalyptic*, 491–502, 514–535, 558–564.

brings Kummaya to the throne; he trembles, kisses Nergal's feet, whereupon he stands up.[40] For some reason the god decides to put him to
death, but a divine counselor intercedes and spares him. The description of Nergal shows him surrounded by the Annunaki, the great gods,
as lightning flashes from his arms. Nergal then imparts a message to the
dreamer concerning his sins[41] and decrees his punishment: future rebel-
lion in his royal line and the annihilation of two of those rulers. Finally,
Nergal banishes the dreamer back to the upper regions. The dream
concludes in typical ancient Near Eastern fashion, with Kummaya stating, 'As he spoke to me, I awoke,' and noting the tremendous impact
of the dream: 'while his heart pounded … he emitted a lamentation,
saying "Woe, my heart!"' (*A Vision of the Nether World*).[42]

Formally, there are several similarities to *1 Enoch* 13:7–16:4. Both accounts are dreams that provide the dreamer with access to otherworldly
realms. The dreams combine pronounced visual imagery befitting symbolic dreams, as well as messages from various divine dream figures,
in the manner of message dreams. Furthermore, both accounts contain
similar themes:

– a terrified dreamer who finds himself in an otherworldly realm
– a vision of a throne, upon which is seated a god (cf. *1 Enoch* 14:18–
23)
– divine attendants, who appear as part humanoid and part animal
(cf. the cherubim in *1 Enoch* 14:11, 18; Ezekiel 1:4, 10:20)
– a trembling dreamer who is brought to the throne, who bows low
and then stands up before the throne (cf. *1 Enoch* 14:24)
– lightning (cf. *1 Enoch* 14:8, 11, 22)
– mention of a counselor (cf. *1 Enoch* 14:22)
– an atmosphere of danger
– a divine message given by the one seated on the throne which is
a recitation of past sins against the divine realm, and a decree of
future punishment (cf. *1 Enoch* 15:1–16:4)

In both cases the 'otherworldly realms' attainable through dreams are
multifaceted. On one axis, the realm is spatial, since Enoch ascends
to a heavenly throne-room and Kummaya descends to a throne-room

---

[40] This is noteworthy as a rare instance in an ancient Near Eastern dream in which
the verb 'to stand' is applied to the dreamer rather than to deities or dream messengers.
[41] See Kvanvig, *Roots of Apocalyptic*, 403.
[42] Ibid., 405.

in the netherworld. On another axis, the realm is temporal, since the figure on the throne reminds Enoch of the Watchers' past sins and tells him of the day of eschatological judgment, while the figure on the throne in Kummaya's dream reminds him of his own past sins and proclaims his future punishment. On yet another axis, the otherworldly realm is ontological. Were it not for his dream, Enoch could not, as a human being of flesh, enter the heavenly *hekhal* filled with divine beings (*1 En.* 14:21); likewise, Kummaya should not be able to enter the realm of divine beings and the dead in his state as a living human being. Furthermore, in Enoch's dream journeys in *1 Enoch* 19 and 22, he is also able to see the underworld realms of divine beings and of deceased humans, much like Kummaya.

Of course, the parallels between the two accounts are not exact. In *1 Enoch*, Enoch ascends because of the sins of the Watchers, whereas in *A Vision of the Netherworld* the dreamer descends in order to receive his own divine punishment. But the direction of their journeys should not distract us from the overall function of both dreams. Without suggesting the 'Book of the Watchers' depends directly on *A Vision of the Nether World*, I propose that their structural and thematic parallels are sufficient to illustrate a shared mythic background of *dream* traditions in which the focus is the collapsing of planes of reality (spatial, temporal, and ontological) through various kinds of ascent and descent, centered around access to a divine throne-room.[43]

Having thus sketched some features of the earliest Jewish dream of access to otherworldly realms, I turn to other articulations of this concept in Hellenistic Jewish literature. This overarching category is so pervasive that I do not attempt an exhaustive treatment in the following discussion. Rather, I intend to demonstrate the range of creative ways in which dreams can provide dreamers access to otherworldly realms. My examination includes the following texts: *Greek Testament of Levi*, *4QAramaic Levi*, *Ezekiel the Tragedian*, *2 Enoch*, *4 Ezra*, and *Ladder of Jacob*.

---

[43] In the 'Book of the Watchers,' Enoch's *ascent* to heaven is actually necessitated by the *descent* of the heavenly Watchers to earth, who are placed in pits of punishment and banned from ascending: 'from now on you will not ascend into heaven for all the ages ...' (*1 Enoch* 14:5). That is, mixing of the realms of heaven and earth in an improper manner can only be rectified through Enoch's mixing in both realms in his dream.

Greek Testament of Levi

The *Testaments of the Twelve Patriarchs* include three testaments that contain dreams, namely, the *(Greek) Testament of Levi, Testament of Naphtali* and
Testament of Joseph. The date and provenance of this collection of texts
is widely debated, but I am most convinced by those arguments that
favor an early Christian reworking of Jewish sources still evident in the
texts,[44] in part because of the close coherence between thematic content
of dreams in the *Testaments of the Twelve Patriarchs* and the other Jewish
dream texts I examine. Despite the variety of opinion on the matter,[45]
most agree that the testaments are familiar with many Hellenistic Jewish traditions and the intended audience of the extant texts probably
comprised Jews as well as Christians.[46]

Two complex dream journeys drive much of the plot of *(Greek) Testament of Levi.* In fact, Levi's receipt of revelation and priestly investiture
via dreaming constitute significant portions of the plot.

---

[44] R.H. Charles, *Greek Versions of the Testaments of the Twelve Patriarchs* (Oxford: Oxford
University Press, 1908); idem, *Apocrypha and Pseudepigrapha of the Old Testament* (2 vols.;
Oxford: Clarendon, 1913); Hultgård, *L'eschatologie*; Becker, *Untersuchungen*; and Kee, 'Testaments of the Twelve Patriarchs,' *OTP* 1:776–828. By contrast, De Jonge, with Kugler
following, maintains that the testaments are Christian compositions, stating that there
was no Jewish *Grundschrift* or if there ever was, it is unrecoverable at present. De Jonge,
Testaments of the Twelve Patriarchs; idem, *Jewish Eschatology, Early Christian Christology and the
Testaments of the Twelve Patriarchs: Collected Essays of Marinus de Jonge* (Leiden: Brill, 1991);
and idem, 'Levi in Aramaic Levi,' 71–90. For summaries of the state of scholarship see
also John J. Collins, 'Testaments,' in *Jewish Writings of the Second Temple Period*, 325–355;
and Slingerland, *Testaments of the Twelve Patriarchs*; Kugler, *From Patriarch to Priest*; idem,
Testaments of the Twelve Patriarchs. M. Philonenko, following Dupont-Sommer, hold the
minority view that the testaments have an Essene origin in the Qumran sect sometime
in the first century B.C.E. Philonenko, *Les interpolations chrétiennes.*

[45] See a fuller summary of scholarship in Collins, 'The Testamentary Literature in
Recent Scholarship,' in *EJMI*, 268–286.

[46] Even de Jonge states 'The Testaments must be studies as a Christian composition
which makes use of a suprising number of Jewish traditions ...,' in 'Levi in Aramaic Levi,'
71. Elsewhere he states: 'it remains important to show how various traditions in the
Testaments were used, especially in what form and with what contents and within
which groups, in Jewish and Christian circles.' M. de Jonge, ed. *Studies on the Testaments
of the Twelve Patriarchs: Text and Interpretation* (SVTP 3; Leiden: Brill, 1975), 189–190.
Similarly, Kugler argues for a Jewish and Christian audience, *Testaments of the Twelve,*
38–39.

Levi's First Dream: Testament of Levi 2:5–5:7

The form of this dream is standard for message and symbolic dreams throughout antiquity:[47]

> I. INTRODUCTION: 'I kept grieving ... and I prayed ... *then sleep fell upon me and I dreamed.*' (2:4–5) (τότε ἐπέπεσεν ἐπ' ἐμὲ ὕπνος καὶ ἐθεασάμην ὄρος ὀψηλόν)
>
> II. DREAM: A journey through heaven. (2:7–5:7)
>
> III. CONCLUSION: 'After this I awoke and blessed the Most High.' (5:7)

Like Enoch's dream journey that is also an ascent to the heavenly temple, this dream combines different dream types.[48] The presence of an angel who speaks throughout is suggestive of a message dream, but since Levi sees sites that require explanations, the episode also resembles aspects of symbolic dreams (3:1).

Levi's dreams first 'take him' to a high mountain (2:5), often considered to be numinous in Israelite and Jewish tradition.[49] From thence he sees the heavens open and hears an angel saying 'Levi, Levi, enter!' (2:6). These heavens either contain or constitute a temple.[50] In Himmelfarb's reading, the extant Greek version contains seven heavens, the uppermost four of which make up the heavenly temple.[51] In earlier versions of *T. Levi* 2–5 there are three heavens,[52] which seem to match up well with each part of the Jerusalem Temple, a correspondence that is probably also evident in the three heavenly buildings in *1 Enoch* 13–16.[53]

---

[47] The translation of the *Testaments of the Twelve Patriarchs* is that of Kee. The Greek text follows de Jonge, *Testaments of the Twelve Patriarchs*.

[48] In addition to being an otherworldly journey, the dream is also a Greek style token dream. After the angel and Levi return to earth, the angel presents him with a shield and a sword to avenge Dinah against Shechem. The conclusion conventionally states the dreamer awoke. Soon afterwards Levi finds a brass shield that is probably the one presented to him in his dream (6:1).

[49] See Jon D. Levenson, *Sinai and Zion: An Entry into the Jewish Bible* (San Francisco: HarperSanFrancisco, 1985).

[50] Himmelfarb, *Ascent to Heaven*, 33.

[51] Ibid., 33.

[52] See note 2.d in Kee, 'Testaments of the Twelve Patriarchs,' *OTP* 1:788. For three or seven heavens in *T. Levi* and other Jewish texts, see A.Y. Collins, 'The Seven Heavens in Jewish and Christian Apocalypses,' in *Death, Ecstasy*, 57–92; idem, *Cosmology and Eschatology*, 21–54.

[53] Himmelfarb notes that the three heavenly buildings in *1 Enoch* 13:7ff. correspond nicely to the tripartite temple. In the Ethiopic, Enoch passes through a wall (14:9), an outer house (14:10–14) and an inner house (14:15–17) whereas in the Greek he passes

If the first heaven in *T. Levi* is mirrored by the outer court or portico ('*ulam*) of the tripartite Jerusalem Temple, the 'much water suspended'[54] (2:7) may refer to the outer marble façade of the temple, which several ancient writers likened to water due to the reflection of sunlight on its highly polished surface.[55] The second heaven sounds like the main hall or *hekhal* of the Temple itself, in which 'there was a measureless height' (2:8). The third heaven 'beyond compare' (2:9) then correlates to the Holy of Holies or *debir* in which Levi later sees the 'Holy Most High sitting on the throne' (5:1).[56] However, in the ancient Jewish mind this is all putting the matter backwards: the heavenly Temple is a macrocosm of the world that the world, including the Jerusalem Temple, reflects (Ps 11:4; cf. Exod 25:9, 40).[57]

Levi's ascent to the heavenly Temple fulfills many of the traditional functions of divinely-sent dreams. Levi receives *unusual cosmological knowledge* of the structure and contents of the heavens and heavenly sanctuary (3:1–10) as well as *eschatological knowledge* about the coming judgment (4:1–6). The *divine sanction* of Levi is likewise clear. If Enoch's priestly status is debatable in the 'Book of the Watchers,' Levi's status as priest is obviously conferred through his dream ascent: 'And when you have mounted there, you shall stand (στήσῃ) near the Lord. You shall be his priest ...' (2:10).

---

through three houses. Himmelfarb, 'Apocalyptic Ascent,' 210–217. Nickelsburg's critical notes illustrate the difficulties of this passage, *1 Enoch*, 257–259.

[54] The correspondence between the heavenly and earthly temples, along with the fact that several ancient commentators viewed the Jerusalem Temple as a microcosm of sea, earth and heaven (*Ant.* 3.181; *Numbers Rabbah* 13:19), may further explain the water in the first heaven in *T. Levi 2*. See Fletcher-Louis, *All the Glory of Adam*, 62; see also Richard J. Clifford, *The Cosmic Mountain in Canaan and the Old Testament*, (HSM 4; Cambridge, MA: Harvard University Press, 1972), 177–181.

[55] For the mystical tradition of those who cry out 'Water! Water!' upon first seeing the heavenly *hekhal*, see: *Hekh. Rabb.* section 259; *Hekh. Zut.* sections 345, 407–410; Schäfer, *The Hidden and Manifest God*, 38; idem, *Hekhalot-Studien* (Tübingen: Mohr Siebeck, 1988), 244–249; Scholem, *Major Trends*, 53, n. 48; idem, *Jewish Gnosticism, Merkabah Mysticism, and Talmudic Traditions* (New York: Jewish Theological Seminary of America, 1960), 14–20; I. Gruenwald, *Apocalyptic and Merkabah Mysticism* (Leiden: Brill, 1980), 87–90.

[56] For a simple comparison of tripartite long-room temples in Syria-Palestine, see J. Monson, 'The Ain Dara Temple: Closest Solomonic Parallel,' *BAR* (May-June 2000): 22–35.

[57] Levenson explores this correlation and relates Rabbi Shimeon bar Yohai's explanation of the name for the Temple mount, Mt. Moriah '*Môrîyâ*', which is that it was located 'appropriately' (*rā'ûy*) over and against the heavenly Temple, *Sinai and Zion*, 140–141.

It may be that Levi not only becomes a priest, but an angel as well: 'καὶ μυστήρια αὐτοῦ ἐξαγγελεῖς τοῖς ἀνθρώποις' (2:10). An implied contrast is set up between the intermediary who announces (ἐξαγγελεῖς) God's mysteries to human beings (ἀνθρώποις) (*T. Levi* 2:10), a structure that sets 'ἄγγελος' over and against 'ἄνθρωπος' and locates Levi in the former camp. Perhaps it is as a future angelic priest that Levi is allowed, like Enoch, to see into the Holy of Holies of the heavenly Temple (5:1).[58]

Levi's Second Dream: Testament of Levi 8:1–19

Whether or not *T. Levi* had a *Vorlage* and whatever its contents,[59] in the extant text Levi's second dream fulfills the promises made in the first dream that Levi would become a priest. Although the normal INTRODUCTION of dreams is absent, the episode is likened to the first episode, patently a dream (8:1), and the typical CONCLUSION of dreams is present: 'I awoke' (8:18). The setting of the dream is at Bethel, the mountain site of Jacob's ladder dream and a famous incubatory site throughout early Judaism.[60]

In this remarkable dream, Levi is ordained as a heavenly priest. Seven angels anoint him, wash him and successively clothe him in priestly vestments, complete with a 'priestly diadem' (8:10) and 'the apron for prophetic power' (8:2).[61] These are not only priestly garments, but garments reserved for the high priest. The diadem (מצנפת) is the high priest's 'crown' or the mitered turban (Exod 28:39–40; 39:28–31; Ezek 24:17; Isa 62:3; cf. *1QM* col. VII) with its gold נזר plate, typically inscribed with 'קדש ליהוה' (Exod 28:36–38; *Ant.* 3.178; *J.W.* 5.235; Philo *II Mos.* 115, 132; *Arist.* 98). The apron sounds like the priestly ephod (האפוד), a tool of divination (Exod 28:6–12; 39:2–7; Judg 8:27; 17:5; Hos 3:4).[62] Thus, divine sanction is clearly conferred through the dream and Levi becomes a high priest who also possesses oracular powers.

---

[58] Himmelfarb notes that many other apocalypses reverse the illogical order of steps laid out by Levi's dreams, namely that he gains access to the heavenly Temple (2–5) and *then* becomes a priest (8), *Ascent to Heaven*, 37.

[59] Kugler, *From Patriarch to Priest*, 175–176, 186; cf. de Jonge, 'Levi in Aramaic Levi,' 84–88.

[60] Gen 28:10–17; *Jub.* 27:19ff., 32:1–2; and *Ladd. Jac.*

[61] Himmelfarb, *Ascent to Heaven*, 37; Collins, 'A Throne in the Heavens,' in *Death, Ecstasy*, 41–56, 52.

[62] M. Haran, 'Priestly Vestments,' *EncyJud* 13:1063–1069; see also Fletcher-Louis, *All the Glory of Adam*, (crown: 24, 30, 50, 129, 158, 198, 199, 231, 247, 288, 351, 353–355; ephod: 230, 231, 235, 300, 356, 358, 362, 372, 376). The extant, Christianized form may

Moreover, since the clothing of the seven angels is also mentioned
(8:2), the act of angels progressively clothing Levi resonates with angelic
overtones and suggests he becomes like one of them.

The passage closely resembles Enoch's transformation in *2 Enoch*
22:8–10, in which he is explicitly likened to an angel, after likewise having been anointed and having received angelic changes of clothing.[63]
Enoch's investiture clearly takes place in the heavenly Temple, which
is probably also the location of Levi's investiture, although the exact
location of the dream events is not mentioned in *T. Levi*.

Both passages evidently draw on biblical prescriptions for priestly
changes of clothing throughout various steps of the sacrificial rituals
and in certain areas of the tabernacle and temple (Lev 6:10–11; Ezek
42:14, 44:19). Thus, it is a reasonable assumption that Levi's changes
of clothing may also be linked to issues of purity and access to sacred
space on earth and/or in heaven. The scene in Zechariah of Joshua's
investiture as high priest also probably served as a source for Levi's
second dream, since in Zechariah an angel clothes Joshua in priestly
vestments, including a ritually pure diadem or miter (הצניף הטהור; Zech
3:5). However as in *T. Levi* 8, no location is specified. In addition,
some Mesopotamian ascent/descent texts may furnish an even closer
parallel, although this does not necessarily indicate direct dependence.
The *Adapa*[64] myth describes a mortal who *ascends* to heaven and is
clothed with a new garment and even anointed, just as in the scenes
in both *T. Levi* 8 and *2 Enoch* 22. This and other Mesopotamian ascent
/descent texts[65] share a mythic structure of reality that links access to
divine realms with progressive changes, which likely entail ontological
transformation for humans who enter divine sacred space.[66] Similarly,

---

be confused over the many articles of priestly clothing, mentioning 'three offices': a
great office, the priestly office and a 'new' kingly priesthood whose High Priest is Christ
(*T. Levi* 8:12–14).

[63] See Himmelfarb, *Ascent to Heaven*, 3–5, 36–37 and Fletcher-Louis' study of 'angelo-
morphism' in the Dead Sea Scrolls, *All the Glory of Adam*, 1–32. The otherworldly journey in *2 Enoch* does not occur within a dream, but it is closely tied to the *Wecktraum* in
2 Enoch 1:3–10 that announces the imminence of Enoch's ascent to heaven.

[64] *Adapa*, trans. E.A. Speiser (*ANET*, 101–103).

[65] Compare also the Akkadian *Descent of Ishtar to the Nether World*, which describes
the goddess descending through seven gates of the underworld before arriving at the
thrones of Ereshkigal and the Annunaki, whereupon she ascends through the seven
gates past various guardians to reach her former abode, progressively being clothed
and adorned, at last passing through the seventh gate and receiving a great crown.
Descent of Ishtar to the Nether World, trans. E.A. Speiser (*ANET*, 106–108).

[66] Later *Hekhalot* texts apparently also draw a similar worldview, depicting a '*yored*

Levi's dreams provide access to an otherworldly realm, and the new garments in his second dream mark the transformation of the dreamer into a state of greater purity.

Considering the extant Greek version of *T. Levi* as a whole, Levi's dreams and their fulfillment form a significant portion of the narrative and drive much of the plot of the larger story, whereas the story of Levi's revenge against the Shechemites for the rape of Dinah is related only briefly. In fact, the structure of chapters 1–9 could be mapped as follows:

    I. Editor's Introduction (1:1–2)

    II. Levi's first dream at Abel-Maoul (2:1–5:7)
        a. ascends to heaven and is promised priestly investiture (2:10)
        b. is given a shield and instructed to perform vengeance (5:3)

    III. Fulfillment of Levi's first dream
        b¹ (earthly) fulfillment of Levi's dream: he finds a shield and performs vengeance (6:1–7:4)
        a¹ (heavenly) fulfillment of Levi's dream in the form of Levi's second dream at Bethel, in which he receives angelic investiture (8:1–19)
            1. earthly fulfillment of Levi's two dreams (IIa and IIIa¹)
                (a) Isaac blesses him 'in accord with the vision' (9:1–2)
                (b) Jacob has a vision at Bethel confirming Levi's priestly status (9:3)
                (c) Isaac teaches him 'the law of the priesthood' at Hebron (9:5–14)

That is, Levi's two dreams form a chiastic structure a,b:b¹, a¹ where activity shifts between earthly and heavenly planes in terms of dream and fulfillment. The subsequent activity in chapter 9, which includes Isaac and Jacob both recognizing Levi's new status, fulfills on an earthly level the priestly investiture that Levi received in his second dream. Jacob also sees a vision or dream (ὁράματι) at Bethel, which convinces him of Levi's priestly status.

---

merkabah' or 'descender to the *merkabah*' who ascends through numerous gates past angelic guardians until eventually arriving at the throne of God in the seventh heaven and the seventh *hekhal*. As the confusing terminology of 'yored' indicates, the *direction* of the journey becomes nonsensical in the larger context of subjectively collapsing planes of reality, whether the mechanism is mystical practice or a dream.

Levi's Third Dream: Testament of Levi 11:5

Finally, Levi has either a vision or a third dream that could also be construed as fulfillment of his prior dream, which promised that his descendants would be 'priests, judges, and scribes, and by their word the sanctuary would be controlled' (8:17). In this visionary episode, Levi sees 'ἐν ὁράματι' his son Kohath *standing* (ἵστατο) *in the heights, in the midst of the congregation*' (11:5). 'Stand' is a technical term sometimes used for priestly service, which here recalls the angel's earlier promise to Levi: 'when you have mounted [to heaven] you shall *stand* (στήσῃ) near the Lord. You shall be his priest' (2:9–10). Since Kohath is seen 'standing in the heights,' Levi's vision or dream probably implies Kohath's investiture into the priesthood of the heavenly Temple via ascent, in the manner of Levi's second dream. Given that it is Isaac who teaches Levi the 'law of the priesthood' (9:7–9), there is an implied priestly lineage in *T. Levi*, beginning with Isaac and running through Jacob, to Levi, to Kohath, whom Levi most likely sees in a dream acting as a priest in heaven.

Overall, Levi's dreams are structured quite clearly around priestly concerns.[67] The dreams provide him with access to the heavenly Temple and transform him into a priest like the angelic priests who serve there (2:10, 3:5, 8:10), conflating the realms of earth and heaven, human and angel, earthly and heavenly priesthoods.

Moreover, priestly themes saturate the remainder of the text. Levi exhorts his sons to avoid future forms of priestly impiety, which he predicts would spell the doom of both Israel and the nations (14:4–7) and result in the desolation of the sanctuary (15:1). He then imparts revelation that seventy weeks are decreed for the profanation of the priesthood (15:1), before proceeding to give a sweeping overview of cosmic history in which each jubilee period is characterized by a concomitant priesthood (17:1). In other words, each historical epoch, or the nature of each unit of time that demarcates Israel's sacred story, is marked precisely by the character of the priesthood that flourishes at that time (17:1–11).[68] This *priestly temporality* culminates in chapter 18 in the escha-

---

[67] See also Kugler, 'The Levi-Priestly Tradition in *Testament of Levi*,' in *From Patriarch to Priest*, 171–220.

[68] J. Marsh has argued that the Hebrew Bible possesses no word or concept for *chronos* in the sense of successive temporal units, but operates instead by 'realistic time,' or time known by its content. J. Marsh, *The Fulness of Time* (New York: Harper & Brothers, 1952), 20–21, 77, 179.

tological figure of the new priest. Whether the Christian elements stem from composition or redaction,[69] the figure of the ideal priest patently fulfills Levi's second dream (8:14). In both settings a priest receives divine sanctification from the heavenly Temple (8:2–17, 18:6–7) and acts as intermediary between heaven and earth, between divine and human realms. Throughout extant *T. Levi* as a whole, then, an abiding concern has been the heavenly priestly sphere breaking into the earthly one, a scenario made possible by dreams and then by the eschaton.

Finally, it should be noted that the otherworldly realm of the heavenly Temple is accessed while Levi dreams in sacred earthly space: at the famous incubation site of Bethel and in the area of Abel-Maoul/ Main, which is also sacred in *1 Enoch* (*1 En.* 13:9).[70] These mountainous areas appear to form earthly points of correspondence with the heavenly Temple that are akin to Jacob's 'gate to heaven' in Genesis 28.

Aramaic Testament of Levi

Although the relationship to *Greek Testament of Levi* is far from clear, most scholars recognize that *Greek T. Levi* and *Aram. Levi* are intimately connected in some fashion.[71] The general consensus is emerging that *Aram. Levi* or a text very close to it served as a written source for the later (Jewish or Christian) *T. Levi*.[72] *Aramaic Levi* is a Jewish text probably written between the 3rd and 2nd centuries B.C.E.,[73] and as such, it provides an important early witness to Jewish dreams. However, the text must be approached carefully due to its fragmentary state.[74]

A preliminary issue that arises is whether *Aram. Levi* contains one or more dreams. The Qumran fragment *4Q213a* is the most important

---

[69] Kugler, *From Patriarch to Priest*, 189, 215 n. 155; also Becker, *Untersuchungen*, 291–300; Hultgård, *L'eschatologie*, 1: 268–270, 287–290.

[70] See Nickelsburg's excursus on 'Sacred Geography,' *1 Enoch*, 238–247.

[71] Kugler, *From Patriarch to Priest*, 131–134, 221–226; De Jonge, 'Levi in Aramaic Levi,' 84–89.

[72] De Jonge, 'Levi in Aramaic Levi,' 79.

[73] See the concise summary of dating in Kugler, *From Patriarch to Priest*, 131–134. Kugler himself favors a date in the 3rd c. B.C.E., *From Patriarch to Priest*, 134, which agrees with the assessment of M. Stone, 'Enoch, Aramaic Levi, and Sectarian Origins' in *JSJ* 19 (1988): 159–170, 160, n. 2.

[74] For the critical edition of the Aramaic fragments see M.E. Stone and J.C. Greenfield, 'Aramaic Levi Document,' in *DJD XXII: Qumran Cave 4, XVII Parabiblical Texts, Pt. 3* (DJD; ed. E. Tov et al; Oxford: Clarendon, 1996), 1–72. Kugler offers a reconstructed *Aram. Levi* in *From Patriarch to Priest*, 52–59.

witness at hand. For the phrase אדין אחזית חזיון, Kugler prefers 'Then I was shown a *vision*,' while Stone and Greenfield translate 'Then I was shown *visions*.'[75] For our purposes the issue is not crucial, since either way *4Q213a* contains only a short fragment of the vision(s). Though brief, these lines are enough to demonstrate important continuities with other dreams of divine access examined above.

The following partial lines of fragment 2 seem to indicate that Levi lies down (probably at Abel Main) and dreams of heaven, ascent, and an angel:[76]

> 14. I lay down and I remained [
> 15. Then I was shown visions [
> 16. in the vision of vision and I saw the heaven[s
> 17. beneath me, high until it reached to the heaven[s
> 18. to me the gates of heaven, and an angel[

Since lying down is the typical formal introduction to dreams, and since Levi sees heaven or the heavens beneath him in his 'vision(s),' his ascent in a dream seems to be indicated.[77]

Furthermore, several rituals are evident in the fragments from Qumran that may suggest an oneiric setting. In reconstructing *Aramaic Levi*, Kugler and Stone and Greenfield each place the purification ritual and prayer immediately before the dream sequence.[78] In other early Jewish dreams we have seen that prayer triggers a dream (e.g. 4Ezra 3:1–4:1; *2Bar.* 35:1–36:1; cf. Dan 9:3–20). We have also seen that in the ancient Near East and Mediterranean worlds washing is a standard purification ritual for dream incubation and sacrifice is an incubation ritual[79] as well as an apotropaic or thanksgiving ritual conducted after a divinely-sent dream.[80] The presence of sacrificial instructions in much of the rest of

---

[75] Kugler, *From Patriarch to Priest*, 78, see also 52–59 for arguments for one vision; Stone and Greenfield, DJD XXII, 30–31.

[76] Stone and Greenfield, DJD XXII, 30–31, lines 14–18.

[77] Collins discusses the significance of Levi ascending through more than one heaven in 'Journeys to the world beyond,' 32.

[78] Kugler, *From Patriarch to Priest*, 56–57; Stone and Greenfield, DJD XXII, 31–33. If the purification is a dream incubation ritual, as we have repeatedly seen in non-Jewish texts, we need not accept Kugler's hypothesis that the washing sequence necessarily must follow the story of the murder at Shechem. See Kugler, *From Patriarch to Priest*, 57–59.

[79] In 1 Kings, Solomon sacrifices before and after a dream in a sacred space, 1 Kings 3:3–15 (cf. 8:62–9:3).

[80] For washing, sacrifice and prayer as ancient Near Eastern incubation rituals see Ackerman, 'The Deception of Isaac,' 92–120, 108–112; Ehrlich, *Der Traum*, 57;

the Qumran fragments of *Aram. Levi.* is of course explainable by Levi's priestly status. I simply wish to add that washing, praying, dreaming and sacrificing also fit a priestly milieu of dream incubation at a sacred site, particularly when these activities occur in a related sequence. Also, if Stone and Greenfield's reconstruction of *4Q214* is correct, washing is, as in the Torah, presented as a requirement for approaching the altar.[81] Therefore, the fact that in *4Q213a* Levi washes and prays before dreaming signals an enhanced state of purity that might anticipate entry into sacred space, perhaps into the heavenly *hekhal*, although in the extant texts the destination of his ascent is unfortunately missing.

Ezekiel the Tragedian

In Judaism, the prophet par excellence is Moses, yet he is curiously marginal in dream texts, probably due to the influence of the tradition in Numbers 12:6–8 that God spoke 'mouth to mouth' with Moses and not in dreams. Nevertheless, Ezekiel the Tragedian, the author of a thoroughly Hellenistic Jewish work *Exagōgē* (ca. 1st or 2nd c. B.C.E.), employs iambic trimeter to tell a story of Moses' dream on Sinai.[82] Like *Testament of Levi* 2–5 and 8, *Ladder of Jacob*, and *1 Enoch* 24, the dream describes a mountain that appears either to be a divine throne-room or a gateway to the heavenly throne-room. In other words, this is an early Jewish dream providing access to otherworldly realms in yet another creative formulation:

> On Sinai's peak *I saw what seemed* (ἔδοξ' ὄρους) a throne
> so great in size it touched the clouds of heaven.
> Upon it sat a man of noble mien,
> becrowned, and with a scepter in one hand
> while with the other he did beckon me.
> I made approach and stood before the throne.
> He handed o'er the scepter and he bade
> me mount the throne, and gave to me the crown;
> then he himself withdrew from off the throne.

Oppenheim, *Interpretation*, 188, 200; Vieyra, 'Hittites,' 87–98, 90. For washing as a ritual in Graeco-Roman dream cults see Tomlinson, *Epidauros*, 16–17; Hamilton, *Incubation*, 11.

[81] Stone and Greenfield, DJD XXII, 48–49; Exodus 30:17–21, 40:30–32.

[82] English is from the translation by R.G. Robertson, *Ezekiel the Tragedian*, OTP 2:803–806; the Greek is from the edition by Bruno Snell, 'Tragicorum Graecorum fragmenta,' (Göttingen: Vandenhoeck & Ruprecht, 1971–1985), 288–301. The general scholarly consensus is that Ezekiel was a Jewish poet writing in Alexandria. Robertson, *Ezekiel the Tragedian*, OTP 2:803–804.

I gazed upon the whole earth round about;
things under it, and high above the skies.
Then at my feet a multitude of stars
fell down, and I their number reckoned up.
They passed by me like armed ranks of men.
Then I in terror wakened from the dream.
(εἶτ᾽ ἐμφοβηθεὶς ἐξανίσταμ᾽ ἐξ ὕπνου)
(*Ezek. Trag.* vv. 68–82)

Moses' dream collapses various planes of reality in two distinct ways.
First, like Jacob's dream in Genesis 28, the mountain 'touches the
clouds of heaven,' and thus is a gateway to heaven. The mountain
throne is therefore also a heavenly one. Second, from his seat on the
mountain throne, Moses is able to see the whole cosmos, including
things under the earth, all over the earth and above the skies.[83] That
is, his dream provides him with a type of access to the netherworld,
earth and heaven.

Like Enoch and Levi's dreams, this dream is clearly transformative
for the dreamer. It is a prophetic/royal commissioning that goes much
farther than dream commissionings in *1 En.*, *2 En.*, *T. Levi*, *4QEn.* and
4QAram. Levi. In early Jewish texts, the figure that sits on thrones,
especially on numinous thrones, is typically divine (*1 En.* 15; Dan 7;
2 En. 22; cf. 4 Ezra 8:21, *2 Bar.* 21:6), but in this text Moses actually
sits on the throne in the place of the divine figure! Thinly symbolic,
the dream is interpreted by Moses' father-in-law, a priest, as meaning
that 'you yourself shall rule and govern men' and 'things present, past,
and future you shall see' (*Ezek. Trag.* vv. 87–89). However given the
symbolic implications of enthronement, mountains and dreaming in
early Judaism, the deeper connation of the dream may be Moses' future
attainment of angelic or divine status. Similarly, Philo maintains that
Moses is the expression of God's Logos or even in a sense 'God,' given
the entire cosmos for a possession (*Migr. of Abr.* 121; *Life of Moses* I:155–
160).[84] In *Ezek. Trag.*, the dream imparts to Moses some type of divine
sanction and exaltation, along with extraordinary knowledge of the
spatial and temporal cosmos.

---

[83] Cf. *1 En.* 13:7–36:4; *L.A.B.* 18:5; 4 Ezra 3:14; *2 Bar.* 4:2.

[84] In addition to Prophet, Philo calls Moses King, Lawgiver, and High Priest (*Life of Moses* II.3).

2 Enoch

Like the dreams in *1 Enoch* 13–16, *4QEnoch* and *Testament of Levi* 2–5 (and probably 8), *2 Enoch* links dreams, temples and angelic/priestly investiture with an ascent motif, but it does so in a distinct way. The text opens as Enoch has a message dream of two large angels who announce his imminent heavenly ascent (1:3–8). The dream is a classic *Wecktraum*, since the angels arrive in Enoch's dream and wake him in order to impart further revelation (1:3–8). The ascent itself results in Enoch receiving priestly clothing changes and anointing in terms quite reminiscent of Levi's transformation in *T. Levi* 8 (*2 En.* 22:8–10), only here Enoch's new status as an angel is made strikingly clear: 'And I gazed at all of myself, and I had become like one of the glorious ones, and there was no observable difference' (*2 En.* 22:10). Thus, I include this text as an example of a dream that provides access to otherworldly realms, in that the dream initiates a storyline in which various planes of spatial, perceptual and ontological reality collapse for Enoch.

In structural terms, Enoch's dream appears as follows:[85]

I. INTRODUCTION: 'When I had lain down on my bed, I fell asleep' (1:3).

II. DREAM: *Wecktraum*
a. Enoch meets two angels while he is *asleep*: '... two huge men appeared to me, the like of which I had never seen on earth ...' (1:4).
b. Enoch meets the two angels after he *awakens*: 'And they stood at the head of my bed and called me by my name ...' (1:5).

III. CONCLUSION: 'I got up from my sleep, and the men were standing with me in actuality ...' (1:6). They announce Enoch's ascent.

IV. FULFILLMENT:
a. Enoch leaves *earth* and ascends to *heaven* accompanied by the two angels (3:1–22:6).
b. Enoch becomes like an *angelic priest* (22:6–10) and then acts as a heavenly, *angelic scribe* (22:11–67:1)
c. Enoch permanently ascends the highest heaven with angels (67:1–3)

The dream first collapses planes of the *perceptual realm* by facilitating Enoch's meeting with angels in a sleeping state, which transitions into a waking reality in which the angels remain in Enoch's earthly envi-

---

[85] English translation and citations follow F.I. Andersen, *2 (Slavonic Apocalypse of) Enoch, OTP* 1:91–100.

ronment (IIa–IIb). The angels reveal that Enoch will ascend, awake, into heaven, thereby transcending the dichotomy of heaven and earth on the *spatial plane of reality* (III). Since during that ascent (IVa) Enoch is subsequently transformed into angelic priest and scribe (IVb), the fulfillment of the dream also collapses the *ontological realms* of human/ angel. Finally, Enoch permanently ascends to heaven (IVc), transcending the limitations of earthly existence in the ultimate fulfillment of his initial dream.

Subsequent dreams in *2 Enoch* are a logical extension of Enoch's heavenly transformation as a heavenly priest, since they secure a priestly line through dream investiture. Again, the dreams are associated with access to heaven, either through dream ascent or through death that is announced in the dream. First, Mathusalom (var. spelling of Methuselah) receives priestly investiture in a dream (69:1–70:1).[86] Later, he has a dream that invests his son Nir into the priesthood (70:3–13) and after that dream Mathusalom dies as 'he stretched out his hands to heaven … and … his spirit went out' (*2 Enoch* 70:16). In other words, this is a testamentary dream of priestly investiture followed by the ascent of Mathusalom's spirit to heaven after death. Next, Nir dreams of his adopted son Melchizedek's priestly investiture and is told that Gabriel 'will take the child and put him in the paradise of Edem' (71:27– 72:11). Edem or 'Eden' is probably in heaven (71:28; 72:5), thus this dream of priestly investiture also implies permanent ascent. In sum, this unusual text uses dreams and access to otherworldly realms to establish a priestly lineage from Enoch, to Methuselah, to Nir, to Melchizedek.

4 Ezra

4 Ezra 9:26–10:59 is another creative articulation of a dream that provides access to the otherworldly realm of the heavenly Jerusalem, although the dreamer does not journey there through ascent. Rather, the 'there' becomes 'here,' as the heavenly Jerusalem appears in Ezra's dream and remains after he has awakened.

Several formal elements enable this visionary episode to be identified as a dream. A fairly typical INTRODUCTION states: 'I lay on the grass, my heart was troubled again as it was before' (9:27).[87] Moreover,

---

[86] Cf. Levi's priestly investiture dream in *Jub.* 32:1.

[87] Michael Stone's main reason for classifying visions one through four in 4 Ezra as waking visions and not as dreams is that they are preceded by psychological 'excite-

extensive parallels with the episodes beginning in 11:1 and 13:1, each of which is explicitly called a dream (*somnium*), secures this interpretation:[88]

I. INTRODUCTION
   a. completion of prescribed incubation (vision four: 9:26) (vision five: 10:60) (vision six: 12:51, 13:1).
   b. mention of lying down, sleeping or night (vision four: 9:27) (vision five: 10:60) (vision six: 13:1)

II. DREAM:
   a. message dream that transforms into a symbolic vision (vision four only: 9:27–10:24)
   b. introductory dream formula: 'And I looked, and behold' or variant (vision four: 10:27, 29, 32) (vision five: 11:1, 2, 5, 7, 10, 12, 20, 22, 24, 28, 33, 37;12:1, 3) (vision six: 13:2, 3a, 3b, 5, 8, 12)
   c. symbolic visions (vision four: 10:25–27) (vision five: 11:1–12:3a) (vision six: 13:2–13a)

III. CONCLUSION
   a. awakening with great emotion and/or physical effects (vision four: 10:29–37) (vision five: 12:3b, 5) (vision six: 13:14)

IV. INTERPRETATION
   a. interpretation by Uriel (vision four: 10:37–57) (vision five: 12:10–36) (vision six: 13:20b–55)
   b. INCUBATION instructions (vision four: 10:58) (vision five: 12:39)

These clear structural parallels suggest that the vision that ensues in 9:38 is a dream. The episode begins as a message dream, in which a dream figure appears as a mourning woman, recalling the Graeco-Roman motif of the disguise of the divine and semi-divine *oneiroi* (9:38). Ezra and the woman engage in a dialogue,[89] and the woman is subsequently transformed into a vast city, Zion (10:44). The dream proceeds as a symbolic dream in which revelation is given in visual symbols,[90] introduced by the formula 'And I looked … and behold,' (*Et vidi … et*

---

ment' he feels precludes dreaming, *Fourth Ezra*, 57. However, as I show in Part One, such grief and distress is typical in the introductions of dreams in Greek, Latin, and early Jewish literature, e.g.: *Od.* 4.840, *Hist.* 2.141, *Metam.* VII.634–664, *T. Levi* 2:5, *2 En.* [A] 1:3–4.

   [88] The Latin text follows A.F.J. Klijn, *Der Lateinische Text der Apokalypse des Esra* (Berlin: Akademie Verlag, 1983); the English translation is from 'The Fourth Book of Ezra,' trans. B.M. Metzger, *OTP* 1:517–559.

   [89] Stone has astutely noted that Ezra functions in relation to the woman in his vision as the angel did to Ezra in the first three visions. Stone, *Fourth Ezra*, 312–316.

   [90] Oppenheim considers the symbolic dream to be a subtype of the message dream, *Interpretation*, 206–208.

ecce), which occurs with notable frequency in the dreams that follow: 10:27, 29, 32; 11:1, 2, 5, 7, 10, 12, 20, 22, 24, 28, 33, 37;12:1, 3; 13:2, 3a, 3b, 5, 8, 12.

This dream experience is striking in its profound liminality, in that the borderline between dream and waking reality shifts for the dreamer. Ezra cries out: 'behold! I saw, and still see, what I am unable to explain … Or is my mind deceived, and my soul dreaming?' (10:32, 36). His exclamation implies that the city that Ezra saw in his dream remains in his waking reality, causing him to question whether or not he is still dreaming.[91] Although it occurs on a large scale, this scene fits the pattern of the Graeco-Roman token dream, in which an object that appears in a dream actually exists upon awakening.[92]

The motif of a dream token is also known in more subtle variations in other Jewish dream texts, including *T. Levi* 5:3, 6:1 and 2 Macc 15:12–16. In the former dream, an angel hands Levi a shield in the dream that he finds just after awakening, and in the latter dream Jeremiah hands Judas Maccabee a sword that he evidently uses to defeat his enemies. Also closely related are Jacob's dreams in *Jub.* 32 and *4QApoc. Jacob* in which an angel descends from heaven and hands Jacob seven tablets which he reads. In the former text, the tablets imparted in a dream persist in a sense after Jacob awakens, since Jacob writes down or reproduces all the contents of the tablets, which he is able to memorize perfectly with the help of the angel. The city that Ezra still sees upon awakening is thus an extreme representative of this wider tradition of dream objects that cross the liminal threshold of waking reality.

The woman/city that appears in Ezra's dream is the heavenly Zion, evident from the hierophanic language of lightning and earthquakes that accompany the woman's transformation (10:25–6). Uriel the angel tells Ezra to 'go in and see the splendor and vastness of the *building*, as far as it is possible for your eyes to see it, and afterward you will hear as much as your ears can hear' (10:56).[93] The building without compare is most likely the heavenly Temple,[94] a thesis strengthened by surrounding

---

[91] See Stone, *Fourth Ezra*, 335.

[92] E.g. Pindar, *Olympian* XIII, 61–80; Suetonius VII.4; Virgil, *Aeneid* VIII.27–68. As van Lieshout has noted regarding this phenomenon, 'the token left mark [*sic!*] the experience as a [*sic!*] enstatic *dream* rather than as a *waking vision*,' van Lieshout, *Greeks on Dreams*, 22.

[93] Stone, *Fourth Ezra*, 340–341.

[94] *2 Baruch* 4:2–3 also interchanges 'city' and 'building' when discussing the heavenly Temple.

discussion of the Jerusalem Temple (10:46) and by the fact that the woman herself laments the destruction of the Temple shortly before her transformation (10:21–23).[95] It is Ezra's righteous conduct in lamenting the destruction of earthly Zion (10:39) and probably also his canonical status as Zadokite priest (Ezra 7:1–5, 21; 4 Ezra 1:1–3) that qualifies him for the exceptional privilege of touring the heavenly Temple. In other words, in 4 Ezra a priest has a dream which enables him to tour the heavenly Temple through its manifestation on earth. As Earl Breech and others have noted, this episode marks a turning point for Ezra, who progresses from a depressed to a joyous state.[96] As I argue later, it is his *dream that provides him with access to otherworldly realms* that occasions this emotional transformation, since he actually *experiences* future and heavenly dimensions of reality in a way that his former dialogue with Uriel was not able to accomplish.

Ladder of Jacob

H.G. Lunt has provided a textual reconstruction and English translation of *Ladder of Jacob* that allows a wider range of commentators to work, with caution, with what had hitherto only been preserved in various traditions in the heavily edited Slavic *Tolkovaja paleja*.[97] Although the reconstruction of the text is far from secure and date and provenance are still a matter of debate, I provisionally accept the argument of H.G. Lunt that *Ladd. Jac.* stems from an early Jewish composition (1st-2nd c. C.E.).[98] If this conclusion is correct, *Ladd. Jac.* adds an important articulation of dreams that provide access to otherworldly realms.

Ladder of Jacob is a retelling of Jacob's dream at Bethel in Genesis 28. In *Ladder of Jacob*, however, Jacob sees a staircase reaching from earth to heaven that is lined with statues on either side. In his notes on the text H.G. Lunt remarks, 'surely *prosōpon* [is used] in the sense of "bust" or "portrait." We retain the traditional "ladder," although surely this

---

[95] Also, the canonical Ezra's commissioning takes place in conjunction with the rebuilding of the Jerusalem temple, Ezra 6–7.

[96] E. Breech, 'These Fragments I Have Shored Against My Ruins: The Form and Function of 4 Ezra,' *JBL* 92 (1973): 267–274; E. Brandenburger, *Die Verborgenheit Gottes im Weltgeschehen* (ATANT 68; Zurich: Theologischer Verlag, 1981), 87; Stone, *Fourth Ezra*, 31.

[97] Lunt, *Ladder of Jacob*, OTP 2: 401–411.

[98] Lunt suspects the original composition was in Greek and presumed some knowledge of Hebrew, *Ladder of Jacob*, 401–404.

is rather a solid staircase, lined with statues, as on a ziqqurat.'[99] Several scholars have already suggested that in the original source text of Genesis 28, Jacob's 'ladder,' the 'house of God and the gate of Heaven,' is actually a ziqqurat.[100] The names of several ziqqurats support such an identification, for example, Babylon's *E-temen-anki*, 'The House, Foundation Platform of Heaven and Earth,' Assur's 'House, the Mountain of the Universe,' and Larsa's 'House, Link of Heaven and Earth.'[101]

Evidence from Herodotus's 5th c. B.C.E. *Histories* further illuminates the concept of the ziqqurat as the 'house of God.' While discussing Babylonian ziqqurats, Herodotus explains that the god was thought to descend to the upper temple and rest there on a great κλίνης (*Hist.* I.181; cf. *1En.* 25:3). He also notes the rituals of ascending and descending ziqqurats and describes a special kind of dream incubation that takes place there: a Chaldean woman, chosen by the god, slept in the shrine at night, as did an Egyptian woman who slept in the temple of Theban Zeus and a Lycian prophetess at Patara who is similarly shut up in the temple at night for purposes of divination and prophecy (*Hist.* I.181–182).[102] This testimony from Herodotus links ziqqurats and ritual ascents and descents with dream incubation, which sheds light on several images in the dream in Genesis 28, including: Jacob's accidental *dream incubation* on the mountain of Bethel, his dream of a *ziqqurat-like structure* reaching from earth to heaven, and a staircase on which angels are *ascending and descending*.[103] Also, if *Ladder of Jacob* is in fact a Hellenistic

---

[99] Lunt, *Ladder of Jacob*, 407, n.1b.

[100] See Kuntz, *Self-Revelation of God*, 125; Seybold, 'Der Traum,' 43; E.A. Speiser, *Genesis* (The Anchor Bible; Garden City, N.Y.: Doubleday, 1964), 218–220; Gerhard von Rad, *Genesis* (trans. J.F. Marks; Philadelphia: Westminster, 1961), 279.

[101] Clifford, *Cosmic Mountain*, 15. Note Clifford also sees a Canaanite mountain tradition behind Genesis 28, *ibid.*, 105; H. Gunkel also sees parallels between ziqqurats and Jacob's structure but is unconvinced of Babylonian influence in Genesis 28, H. Gunkel, *Genesis* (6th ed.; Göttingen: Vandenhoeck & Ruprecht, 1964), 318.

[102] While Herodotus does not explicitly state the woman in the ziqqurat temple incubates dreams, her sleeping in the temple is clearly connected in the following passage to divination and prophecy, *Hist.* I.182.

[103] The 7th-6th c. B.C.E. ziqqurat E-temen-anki, probably the inspiration for the Tower of Babel story, had seven levels and a temple on top (thus, eight stages) and was probably the inspiration for the Tower of Babel story. For a reconstruction see A. Parrot, *The Arts of Assyria* (New York: Golden Press, 1961), 227–228 and Figure 283. Descriptions of E-temen-anki survive in Herodotus, *Histories* I.181 and the Esagil Tablet in the Louvre (AO 6555).

Jewish composition, it demonstrates that such an association amongst ziqqurats, dream incubation, and ascent/descent was preserved in early Judaism.

Furthermore, since ziqqurats are stepped, mountain-like structures with a temple at the top that probably functioned as the throne-room / resting chamber of the deity,[104] concepts associated with ziqqurats may also shed light on the motif of mountain-thrones[105] *associated with dreaming* that appear in early Judaism. In *Ezek. Trag.* Moses dreams of a mountain-throne that reaches heaven (*Ezek. Trag.* vv. 68–69) and in *1 En.* 24–25 Enoch dreams of a mountain 'whose peak is like the throne of God,' on which God will sit when he descends to earth (*1 En.* 25:3). I am not implying that the symbol of a mountain-throne draws directly on the idea of ziqqurats; in fact, ziqqurats may be a cultural expression of beliefs associated with cosmic mountains.[106] However, I am suggesting that a mythic background that layers symbols of mountains with ziqqurats helps explain the association of mountain-thrones with dreaming. It also sheds light on the repeated motif in early Judaism of dreamers having dreams, on mountain tops, that provide them with varying levels of access to the heavenly Temple. This thickly intertwined constellation of images is evident in numerous passages, including: Enoch's dream in the shadow of Mt. Hermon (*1 En.* 13:7; cf. *Jub.* 4:26), Levi's dream on a mountain in Abel-Maoul (*T. Levi* 2–5) and again at the mountain at Bethel (*T. Levi* 8), Jacob's dream at Bethel (*Jub.* 27, *Ant.* 1.278–284) and Jacob's dream at Bethel in which an angel brings tablets down from heaven (*Jub.* 32; cf. *4QApoc. Jac.*; Levi's dream at Bethel in *Jub.* 32).

Whether or not Jacob sees a ziqqurat, his dream provides access to otherworldly beings in several ways. Not only does Jacob see God in heaven in a dream, after awakening he is able to meet the angel Sariel, who is in charge of dreams. As in *2 Enoch*, the text makes it clear that the earlier dream prepares the dreamer for a subsequent angelic-human meeting made in a waking state:

---

[104] Clifford reviews four theories for the meaning of ziqqurats and accepts only the first three as valid: they are the throne /altar of the god, the habitation of the god, a structure with cosmic significance, or the tomb of the gods or kings, *Cosmic Mountain*, 21–22. See also A. Parrot, *Ziqqurats et Tour de Babel* (Paris: Michel, 1949), 202–217.

[105] For discussion of the cosmic mountain in Ugaritic texts see Clifford, *Cosmic Mountain*, esp. 3; Levenson, *Sinai and Zion*; and Himmelfarb, *Ascent to Heaven*, 11.

[106] Clifford, *Cosmic Mountain*, 15–25.

> And Sariel the archangel came to me and I saw (him), and his appear-
> ance was very beautiful and awesome. But I was not astonished by his
> appearance, for *the vision which I had seen in my dream* was more terrible
> than he. And I did not fear the vision of the angel.
>
> (Ladd. Jac. 3:4–5)

As we saw was the case for Enoch (*1 En.*, *2 En.*, *4QEn.*), Methuselah
(*2 En.*), Nir (*2 En.*), Levi (*T. Levi*), Ezra (*4 Ezra*), and Moses (*Ezek. Trag.*),
the dream is transformative for Jacob: it is this dream and not the
biblical event of wrestling with an angel that occasions his name change
to Israel (4:2). Finally, in true oneiric fashion, the dream conflates
spatial and temporal dimensions of reality, in that Sariel's interpretation
reveals that each of the twelve steps of the staircase represents an age in
Israel's history (5:1–17).

Summary

My discussion has shown a number of creative formulas by which early
Jewish dreams provide dreamers with access to otherworldly realms,
i.e., realms beyond normal human existence on earth in the present.
Too often, the category of 'otherworldly journey' occludes discussion of
the breadth of this motif, especially in non-apocalypses. Also, 'journey'
language can limit our thinking to spatial movements, i.e. ascents or
descents. In the case of dreams, we need a new lens, since spatial
constraints as well as other boundaries mean little in oneiric settings. I
suggest that many Jewish dream texts are actually better understood as
entailing *a merging of alternate planes and dimensions of reality*, whether spatial
(heaven, earth and the underworld), perceptual (sleeping and waking),
ontological (humans and angels) or temporal (past, present and future).
I chose to examine some outstanding examples that combine several
of these dimensions, but there are certainly other dream texts in early
Judaism that articulate this concept.

We have also seen that authors of some Hellenistic Jewish dreams
syncretistically draw on a host of other traditions to arrive at their
new formulations of dreams. These include Ezekiel's descriptions of
the merkabah (Ezek 1–3, 8–10) and biblical depictions of the heavenly
Palace-Temple (Isa 6, cf. Ezek 40–48), as well as motifs that are also
evident in Mesopotamian ascents and dream descents, Greek *nekyia*
texts, and traditions surrounding ziqqurats. The resulting worldview
pictures God sitting on his throne in the heavenly Palace-Temple,
surrounded by priestly angels, accessible through dreaming. Sometimes

an earthly mountain or mountain-throne mirrors this heavenly tier of architectural reality.

The dreamers of such remarkable dreams are pseudepigraphic heroes woven into the sacred history of Israel. Their dreams of access to otherworldly realms usually result in personal transformation of some kind, sometimes indicating an enhanced state of purity or fitness for entering sacred space. Often, this dream transformation is associated with entering the priesthood, whether heavenly and/or earthly (e.g. Enoch in *1 En.* and *4QEnoch*; Enoch, Methuselah, and Nir in *2 En.*; Levi in *Jub.*, *Greek T. Levi* and *4QAramaic Levi*). Since Ezra is already a priest, he needs no new ordination in order to tour a manifestation of the heavenly Temple; however, he still undergoes a profound spiritual transformation through the experience. Finally, despite the ubiquity of priestly motifs, since different priestly lineages are attested in the various dream texts (e.g. Isaac-Jacob-Levi-Kohath in *T. Levi*, but Enoch-Methuselah-Nir-Melchizedek in *2 En.*), it is very likely that the texts do not all stem from the same social group.

Transformed Oneiroi: *Angels, the Dead and High Priests*

Early Jewish dream texts display remarkable openness in transforming the standard biblical depiction of the LORD as the messenger of message dreams. Suddenly, a syncretic range of dream messengers appears, including angels, dead personages and one rare example of a living figure.

As I have already mentioned, the appearance of angels in dreams in pre-exilic biblical texts are limited to an auditory dream of an angel's voice (Gen 31:10–13), Job's dream vision of a murky phantom that speaks cryptically (Job 4:12–21), and the angel who wakes Elijah and feeds him but imparts no message (1 Kings 19:5–7). In none of these cases does a clearly visible angel appear as a dream messenger. By contrast, some post-exilic biblical texts, such as Daniel 7–8 and Zechariah 1–6, contain angelic interpreters who appear in dreams and explain what the dreamer sees.[107] Non-canonical Hellenistic Jewish texts develop earlier biblical traditions about angels even further, giving them

---

[107] The ghostly hand that writes a message in Daniel 5:5 might belong to an intermediary angelic being but does not appear in a dream.

personal names and specific duties, and describing their appearance and personalities.[108] Much has been written on angels in this period and I will confine my discussion to angels who appear as dream figures.

Early Jewish dream texts describe angels as beings of light (*T. Job* 3:1, *T. Abr.* 7:5, *2 En.* 1a:4, 5) and fire (*1 En.* 15:22, 17:1, *2 En.* 1a:4, 5, *Ladd. Jac.* 1:6, cf. Dan 7:9), making them fitting messengers of the God of Israel, who appears in similar ways in biblical theophanies (e.g. Ex 19:18, Isa 6:4 and many more). Conversely, some angels resemble ice or snow (*2 En.* 37:1; Dan 7:9). Like ancient Near Eastern dream messengers, they are large (*T. Abr.* 7:5, *2 En.* 1:3) and beautiful (*Ladd. Jac.* 3:4).[109] Some are cherubim (*1 En.* 14:12, 14; cf. Ezek 1, 2, 10), but others look more like men (Dan 7:13, 8:15; *2 En.* 1:3). They descend from heaven (*Jub.* 32:21, *T. Abr.* 7:5) and fly on wings (*2 En.* 1:5, 3:1, 4:2, Dan 9:21). Sometimes attention is drawn to their distinctive clothing, whether white (*T. Levi* 8:1), linen (*L.A.B.* 9:10; cf. *Ap. Abr.* 11:2; Dan 10:5, 12:6–7; Ezek 9:2–3, 11; 10:2; Ex 39:27–28) or 'singing' (*2 En.* 1:5). The descriptions of their clothing grow out of a wider tradition that angels are priestly attendants of the heavenly temple (e.g. *Jub* 30:18, 31:14; *T. Levi* 3:5–6; *4Q and 11QSongs of the Sabbath Sacrifice*; Isa 6).

The sudden ubiquity of angelic dream messengers in early Judaism can be explained in part by the influence of the Greek and Latin *oneiros*, who resembles the angel in several respects. Both the angel and the *oneiros* are intermediary figures sent by god(s) to deliver a message to humans in dreams. Like the angel, the *oneiros* stands by the dreamer and speaks a readily understandable message to the dreamer on behalf of the god.[110] This message may require clarification or elaboration, which sometimes sparks a question and answer dialogue between the dreamer and the *oneiros*. Such conversations can be extensive, as when Penelope speaks at length with the dream figure disguised as Iphthime (*Od.* 4.795ff.; cf. Ezra and Uriel in 4Ezra). Both angels and *oneiroi* occupy a liminal place between the materiality of humans and the immateriality of gods, but *1Enoch* 17:21 makes it clear that angels are similar to *oneiroi* in that they can either disguise themselves in human form or appear in their supernatural state.[111] For the *oneiros* this is as

---

[108] C. Newsom, 'Angels,' *ABD* 1:248–253, 252.

[109] Oppenheim, *Interpretation*, 189.

[110] Kessels, *Studies*, 199; Van Lieshout, *Greeks on Dreams*, 20.

[111] In Tobit, Raphael assumes a disguised identity and pretends to eat, Tobit 5:13, 12:19; cf. *Ap. Abr.* 13.4; *T. Abr.* 4:9–10; *Ant.* 1.11.2.

amorphous wind, whereas for angels it is fire.[112] However, both *oneiroi* in Greek tragedy and angels in early Judaism sometimes appear as winged creatures who fly.[113]

In addition, many dream angels in Judaism, like *oneiroi*, impart messages including: annunciations (*L.A.B.* 9:10), encouragement and directions for a specific action to be taken (*T. Job* 4:11; *Life* 208–210; Matt 2:13, 19; Acts 16:9 and probably 23:11), and foreknowledge of one's future (*2 Enoch* 1:3–10). A unique instance of angelic dream figures appears in *4QVisions of Amram^b* (*4Q544* [*4QcAmram^b ar*]), in which two angels fight over Amram and ask him to choose between them. This is an evident allusion to the Qumranic belief in two spirits, two ways, or the portions of light and dark in human souls.[114]

However, even when angels appear in a dream, most Jewish dream texts follow the biblical model, wherein God is the main deliverer of revelation. Often this occurs in an auditory message dream in which only the voice of God is heard (e.g. *1 En.* 14:24–16:4; *L.A.B.* 18:4–7, 23:3–14, 53:1–13; *Jub.* 14:1–17; 41:24; *Ant.* 11:326–328, 20:18–19). The voice is most often God's and *not* that of the angel of the Lord; e.g. *Liber Antiquitatum Biblicarum* goes so far as to explain that the priest-prophet Samuel heard God and not an angel, since he heard Him with his right ear and not his left (*L.A.B.* 53:6). Several dreams use the phrase 'the Lord appeared' or 'God appeared' and thus intend to denote a message dream of God (*Jub.* 27:19–26, 32:16–26; *2 En.* 69:1–70:1, 70:3–13, 71:27–72:11; Isis appears in *Ag. Ap.* 1.289; *Ant.* 2.171–176, 2.212–217, 5.215–216, 7.92–93, 8.22–25; *L.A.B.* 28:4–5; cf. *Ezek. Trag.* vv. 68–82; also *Ant.* 1.278–284). Since several early Jewish texts maintain that seeing God is the pinnacle of revelation, as when the seer in *2 Enoch* declares 'I saw the Lord' (*2 En.* 22:1–11), we cannot assume that the phrase 'the Lord appeared' either precludes the visible presence of God in dreams or necessarily implies that it was the angel of the Lord who appeared.[115] For example, Josephus emends Genesis 28 to state that above Jacob's ladder 'plainly visible to him was God' (τὸν θεὸν ἐναργῶς αὐτῷ φαινόμενον) (*Ant.* 1:279). Such texts appear

---

[112] Where winds appear in Second Temple texts they are not angels. See *1 En.* 14 and Nickelsburg, *1 Enoch*, 262.

[113] E.g. *2 En.* 1:5, 3:1, 4:2; Dan 9:21; Euripides, *Phoen.* 1540–1546; *Hec.* 31–32, 702–704.

[114] See 4Q473; 1QRule of the Community (1QS) col. III, lines 20–26.

[115] Gnuse, *Josephus*, 15–17.

to consider a message dream or an auditory message dream of the Lord Himself to be a greater level of revelation than an angelic message dream.

In these early Jewish texts in which the Lord is still the main dream messenger, angels appear in transformed dream roles. Most frequently their new role in dreams is as *angelus interpres* and tour guide. As we have already seen, angels explain, interpret and answer questions in dreams in numerous texts, including: Dan 7:16–28, 8:15–26; *Jub.* 32:22; 4 Ezra 4:1, 5:31, 7:1, 10:29; *Ladd. Jac.* 3:4–7:35; *2 Bar.* 55:3; *T. Levi* 2:7–5:6; *1 En.* 19:1, 21:5, 9, 27:2, 33:4, 22:3, 5, 32:5, 23:4, 24:6–25:6, 27:2–4, 32:6. In this interpretive role, Sariel is specifically named the angel 'in charge of dreams' (*Ladd. Jac.* 3:3) and Ramael is set over true dream visions (*2 Bar.* 55:3). Many angels provide interpretations while also acting as tour guides to otherworldly places.[116] For example, an angel who is probably Michael guides Levi through heaven and explains what he sees in *T. Levi* 2:7–5:6, and numerous angels escort Enoch on his journeys (*1 En.* 17–36). The horde of angels that clusters around Enoch is surely intended to augment his status vis-à-vis other visionary traditions (*1 En.* 19:3): Uriel and Raphael appear as his dream guides in *4QEnoch* (*4Q206* [*4QEn^ar*]) frag. 3; Semeila and Rasuila appear in a dream and later escort him through heaven in *2 Enoch* (33:6); and in *1 Enoch* he is guided by Uriel (19:1, 21:5, 21:9, 27:2, 33:4), Raphael (22:3, 6; 32:5), Reuel (23:4), Michael (24:6–25:6), Sariel (27:2–4), and Gabriel (32:6), each of whom take turns explaining various sites on his earthly dream journeys. The figure of the *angelus interpres* draws on the angelic-human conversations in Zechariah 1–6,[117] which occur in the prophet's night-visions (Zech 1:8) and in a what is most likely a *Wecktraum* in Zechariah 4:1.[118]

At other times angels seem to function as otherworldly transport in dreams, such as when Gabriel carries Melchizedek away to Eden

---

[116] In *Testament of Abraham*, Michael guides Abraham through heaven, but it is not a dream.

[117] Stone, *Fourth Ezra*, 50, 115.

[118] Zechariah 4:1 states the angel 'woke me as a man is wakened from sleep' ויעירני כאיש אשר־יעור משנתו. Whereas the prefix 'כ' could mark this episode as a waking vision by use of a dream simile, the passage may also mean that the prophet awakens from sleep into a visionary state resembling the liminal reality of a *Wecktraum*. That is, the angel who figured prominently in earlier night-visions or dreams (1:8) arrives now while the prophet is asleep and wakens him in a classic *Wecktraum* in order to continue his revelation in a waking state. Cf. C.A. and E.M. Meyers, *Haggai, Zechariah 1–8*, 229.

in Nir's dream in *2 Enoch* 72:3–10, or when Joseph grasps a cherub and ascends into the heights in a symbolic dream in *T. Naphtali* 5:7. The early Jewish portrayal of angel as transportation or tour guide recalls Ezekiel's tours via the 'spirit of the Lord' and his conversations with the 'word of the Lord' in Ezekiel 8–10. However, in Ezekiel the accent is frequently on the awesome appearance of the angels of the *merkabah*, whereas in Hellenistic Jewish dream texts the focus is not on the angelophany, but rather on the revelatory visions that the angel helps interpret.

An important motif in the depiction of angels in early Judaism involves the mode of their manifestation to the dreamer. Frequently, angels appear first inside dreams and then transition to the waking reality of the dreamer (e.g. 4 Ezra 5:15, Dan 9:21, *Ladd. Jac.* 3:2–3, *2 En.* 1:6). A French translation of *2 Enoch* captures the idea well: 'Moi, je me levai de mon sommeil, et les hommes se tenaient près de moi en réalité.'[119] Similarly, after his first message dream of Uriel, Ezra is shaken and startled upon awakening, yet states: 'But the angel who had come and talked with me [in the dream] held me and strengthened me and set me on my feet' (4 Ezra 5:15). Although the angel's revelations within the dream were upsetting to Ezra, the fact that the dream messenger remains in his waking reality is obviously comforting, particularly in later scenes in which Uriel helps interpret Ezra's dreams.

The motif of divine dream interpreters has precedent in antiquity. Gilgamesh's mother in the *Epic of Gilgamesh* and Tammuz' divine sister both interpret dreams.[120] However, liminal beings such as *oneiroi* do not typically interpret dreams in antecedent traditions in the ancient Near East and Greece, and closer Latin parallels such as Cicero's *Somnium Scipiones* are much later than the earliest Jewish examples of angels who are dream interpreters or tour guides.

A possible influence on the early Jewish traditions of angels who interpret dreams may stem from the pervasive Jewish tradition of angels serving as priests in the heavenly Temple. Priestly intermediaries of various kinds functioned as dream interpreters in the ancient Near East

---

[119] The French translation of the Slavonic by A. Vaillant, *Le Livre des Secrets d'Hénoch* (Paris: Institut d'Études Slaves, 1952), 5.

[120] Frymer-Kensky, *In the Wake of the Goddesses*, 38–39, 41, 115; Oppenheim, *Interpretation*, 246–247, nos. 2–4.

and classical world,[121] and recognition of this role may appear in *Ezekiel the Tragedian* when Jethro, priest of Midian, interprets Moses' dream.[122] Although the evidence for priestly dream interpreters is less definitive in ancient Israel and early Judaism than in the pagan world, we do know that Israelite priests were responsible for divination through various kinds of oracles, lots and the Urim and Thummim.[123] Several scholars maintain that dream interpretation was in fact a priestly activity in early Judaism, but the argument mainly hinges on one passage in Josephus.[124] Josephus connects his priestly lineage with his ability to interpret dreams and Scripture, stating of himself: 'He was an interpreter of dreams and skilled in diving the meaning of ambiguous utterances of the Deity; a priest himself and of priestly descent, he was not ignorant of the prophecies in the sacred books' (*J.W.* 3.8.3).[125] Thus, I may only conclude that *if* Jewish priests in the Persian, Hellenistic and/or Roman periods were associated with dream interpretation, then given that angels were thought of as priests in the heavenly *hekhal*, the combination of these concepts could easily give rise to the motif of the *angelus interpres*. Hence, when Daniel is puzzled by scenes in his throne-room dream, he has only to turn to one of the divine attendants in the *hekhal* to ask for an interpretation (Dan 7:16, 19). Perhaps we see a vestige of this tradition in the widespread idea that the priestly blessing (Num 6:24–26), which was incorporated into the *Amidah* benediction of the synagogue service, had the power to neutralize bad dreams.[126] Of course, the interpreter *par excellence* in Jewish dreams is the Lord himself, who appears in this role in *2 Baruch* 39 (cf. *2 Enoch* 25:2 and *4 Ezra* 12:10, 13:21).

The image of angels serving as priests probably informs another prominent motif in early Jewish dreams. Throughout the First and

---

[121] Oppenheim, *Interpretation*, 222–225.

[122] Cf. *4QVision of Samuel*, where Eli seems to interpret Samuel's dreaming.

[123] E.g. for the Urim and Thummim see Num 27:21, Ex 28:30, Lev 8:8, Ezra 2:63, Neh 7:65; for lots see Isa 34:17, Ezek 24:6, Micah 2:5, Ps 22:19; Prov 1:14, 16:33; Lev 16:7–10; and for an oracle see Num 5:11–31.

[124] Schwartz, *Josephus*, 70; Mason, *Flavius Josephus*, 269; idem, 'Priesthood in Josephus,' 659; Lindner, *Die Geschichtsauffassung*, 52–53. Bilde and Rajak are less certain; Bilde, *Flavius Josephus*, 190; Rajak, *Josephus*, 19.

[125] Interestingly, his rereading of prophecies in Scripture allows him subsequently to interpret prior dreams he has had (*J.W.* 3.8.3). Thus Mason argues that priests in early Judaism were both guardians of the law and dream interpreters, 'Priesthood in Josephus,' 659; Mason, *Flavius Josephus*, 269.

[126] 'Priestly Blessing,' *EncyJud* 13:1061.

Second Temple periods, priests are responsible for certain kinds of healing in cultic settings since illness is associated with purity and impurity.[127] Hence, one would expect by analogy that angels, who are heavenly priests, would excel at healing. In fact, several early Jewish dream accounts depict angels as imparting healing touches to dreamers or visionaries who have been overcome by their experiences. Angels touch, hold, strengthen or help lift up dreamers or visionaries in Daniel 8:18, 10:10, 16 and 18; *2 Enoch* 22:6 (in the heavenly *hekhal*); and *4 Ezra* 5:14–15, 10:30 (in the vicinity of the heavenly *hekhal*) (cf. *1 En.* 60:4; Rev 1:17; *Ap. Abr.* 10:2–5; Acts 13:7; cf. 1 Kings 19:5–7).[128] As we have seen, the image has close parallels in pagan descriptions of healing, specifically, the iconography and descriptions of divine beings in Graeco-Roman dream cults. In the *iamata* at Epidauros, Asklepios' primary method of healing is reaching out and touching the reclining dreamer.[129] This scene is standard in iconography of Asklepios in votive reliefs at Athens and Piraeus and appears in depictions of Amphiaros as well.[130] In other words, the Hellenistic world was thoroughly familiar with the image of divine beings healing dreamers through touch within cultic settings, which some early Jewish texts seem to evoke.

Angels are not the only intermediary dream messengers in early Judaism. In 2 Macc 15, Josephus' *J.W.* 2:114–116, and *Ant.* 17:349–353, dead people also appear in dreams. Rare in the ancient Near East and taboo in the Hebrew Bible, the patent influence for this Hellenistic Jewish motif is the Graeco-Roman obsession with shades who frequently appear in dreams.[131] Notably for our purposes, in 2 Maccabees 15 the two deceased dream messengers who appear to Judas are also two priests—Onias and Jeremiah.

Finally, in a startling passage in *Ant.* 11:333–335, a living person appears in a Jewish dream, and it is the High Priest.[132] The theme of a living human appearing as a dream messenger is rare throughout all of

---

[127] In ancient Israel disease was often related to impurity, which fell under the domain of priests. See Deut 24:8, Lev 13–15.

[128] See Collins, *Daniel*, 338; Stone, *Fourth Ezra*, 115.

[129] LiDonnici, *Epidaurian Miracle Cures*, see for example nos. A3, A 18, B 11.

[130] See Hausmann, *Kunst und Heiltum*, plate 1; Kerényi, *Asklepios*, 35 (plate 18), see also 36, plate 19.

[131] See the earlier discussions on death and dreams in Chapter Two.

[132] In *1QGenesis Apocryphon* col. XX, Hirqanos might see Abram in a dream, but the meaning is unclear and the text restored: [בני לם[חז ח] ב. *Dead Sea Scrolls Study Edition* (2 vols.; eds. F.G. Martínez and E.J.C. Tigchelaar; Leiden: Brill, 1997–1998, repr. 2000), 1: 43.

ancient Near Eastern and Mediterranean antiquity, the governing logic being that a dream is a sort of otherworldly reality which only divine beings (such as angels) and the dead are able to inhabit. However, according to Josephus, Alexander the Great recognizes the high priest Jaddus and does obeisance to him precisely because he has seen him in these vestments previously in a message dream. What are we to make of this claim, shocking at it is in its ancient context?

The key to this puzzle may lie in Jaddus' clothing. We know from other texts in early Judaism that the vestments of the high priest were thought to mirror the appearance of divine beings described in Ezekiel (*Letter of Aristeas* 97–99) and the likeness of angelic high priests (*4QSongs of the Sabbath Sacrifice* [*4Q405*] *4QShir Shab*[*j*] 23, frag. 2).[133] As Josephus has Alexander the Great explain: 'It was not before him that I prostrated myself but the God of whom he has the honour to be High Priest' (XI.333). Thus, it is likely the case that Jaddus's vestments are an earthly copy of those of the angelic high priest, whom Alexander has seen in a dream. In this case the episode is another case of an angelic *oneiros* appearing in a message dream. The other possibility is that the idea that the high priest as an intermediary between humans and the divine is pressed here to the point that Jaddus was actually thought to be capable of transcending normal constraints of reality such that he could appear in dreams, in the fashion of divine beings and the dead.

Summary

Unlike pre-exilic biblical texts, many early Jewish dream texts contain angels who sometimes impart messages in the typical fashion of Greek and Latin *oneiroi*. More often, however, angels act as interpreters and guides for the main revelation, which occurs in the form of symbolic visions, otherworldly journeys, or messages from the LORD. The motif of the *angelus interpres* draws on Zechariah 1–6 but probably also on the traditions associated with the idea that angels serve as priests in the heavenly Temple, since priests were associated with dream interpretation throughout antiquity. The influence of iconography and therapeutic tales from Graeco-Roman dream cults, in which gods touch reclining dreamers and thereby strengthen and heal them, also seems

---

[133] Himmelfarb, *Ascent to Heaven*, 19–20. See also Philo's *On Moses* 2:109–135; *Special Laws* 1:84–97; *Ant.* 3.184–187 for speculation on the high priest's vestments.

to influence the motif of angels who strengthen prostrate dreamers and visionaries with a healing touch. Angels who appear in dreams frequently transition to the waking reality of dreamers, further blurring the boundary between the dream-world and waking-world.

In addition to angels, the dead also appear on rare occasion as dream figures in early Judaism, as they do throughout Greek and Roman dream texts. Two of the cases in Jewish texts are by Josephus and describe the same event, in which the deceased husband of Glaphyra appears in a dream in order to punish her (*J. W.* 2:114–116, *Ant.* 17:349–353). The other case involves the appearance of two deceased priests, Jeremiah and Onias, to Judas the Maccabee, in order to urge him to defend Israel (2 Macc 15). Finally, in one unique passage, either the living high priest Jaddus or the angelic high priest who looks like him appears to Alexander the Great and thereby saves Israel from destruction. Thus, the appearance of human priests in dreams may derive from associations of priests with angels.

All of these dream messengers, including angels in new roles, deceased priests and possibly a living high priest, are evidence of the flexibility and ingenuity of early Jewish authors who appropriate and transform existing dream traditions while fitting them for a uniquely Jewish context.

Transformed Dreamers: An Oneiric Priesthood

The portrayal of dreamers in Hellenistic Judaism is also distinctive in several ways vis-à-vis traditions from other cultures. First, as we have seen, the dreamers are typically pseudepigraphic heroes of Israel's past sacred history. In the case of Josephus we have do an actual person who reports his dreams, but Gnuse points out that Josephus engages in no small amount of personal propaganda when he places his own dreams alongside those of Joseph, Jeremiah and Daniel.[134]

Second, many of the dreamers in early Judaism are connected to priestly activities. A quick survey of pseudepigraphic dreamers reveals several members of the priestly line, including Ezra (4 Ezra), Baruch (*2 Baruch* 6, 34–35), and Samuel (*L.A.B.* 53). While not typically viewed as a priest, Isaac teaches Levi the laws of the priesthood (*T. Levi* 9:5–

---

[134] Gnuse, *Josephus*, 28–31.

14). Also, one of the few female dreamers, Miriam, is also of Levitical descent (*L.A.B.* 9). In addition, the *Book of Jubilees* may preserve priestly traditions associated with other characters not typically thought of as priests, depicting Enoch, Abram, and Jacob sacrificing in juxtaposition with dreams (*Jub.* 4, 14, 32), and noting that Joseph marries the daughter of the priest of Heliopolis (*Jub.* 40). In other texts, several dreamers receive priestly investiture via their dreams, such as Levi in *T. Levi* 8 and Enoch, Methusaleh, Nir, and Melchizedek in *2 Enoch* (22, 70, 71, 72). Furthermore, numerous dreamers in Josephus are priests, including:[135] Josephus in *Jewish War* 3.351–354 and in *Life* 208–210; Amram in *Antiquities* 2.212–217; Samuel in *Ant.* 5.348–350, 6.37–40, 6.332; Jaddus in *Ant.* 11.326–328; Hyrcanus in *Ant.* 13.322; Matthias in *Ant.* 17.166. Finally, some texts establish priestly lineages through dreams (*2 En.*, *T. Levi*), and *L.A.B.* 53 relates a priestly tradition, handed down from Phineas to Eli to Samuel, regarding how to recognize the voice of God in a dream (53:6).

Third, several dreamers are scribes, an important role in Judaism given the emphasis on written Scripture. Enoch is the scribe without parallel (*1 En.*, *2 En.* *4QEn.*), but Baruch (*2 Bar.*) and Ezra (*4 Ezra*) are also scribes who are shown recording Scripture, the latter in an inspired state. Also, other dreamers who are not necessarily scribes are depicted as being able to read, including Naphtali (*T. of Naph.*) and Jacob (*4QApoc. Jac.*, *Jub.* 32).[136]

Fourth, early Jewish dream texts, unlike other texts, depict dreamers as 'standing.' Throughout dream texts in antiquity, whether in cult or literature of the ancient Near East, Bible, Greece or Rome, 'standing' is the typical verb that describes the actions of dream messengers.[137] Hence it is the prototypical action of gods, semi-divine *oneiroi* or deceased persons who appear in dreams. Whenever a human dreamer stands up in dream texts from these traditions, it typically means the revelations are over. For example, the Sumerian *Dream of Tammuz* ends with: 'He arose—it was a dream, he arose …'[138] By contrast, in sev-

---

[135] Of the fifty or so dreams in Josephus' writings, nearly all are dreamt by priests, rulers or in a few cases the wives of rulers.

[136] Schams identifies reading and writing as quintessentially scribal activities, *Jewish Scribes*, 87, 97, 121–124, 134–143, 204–208.

[137] Oppenheim, *Interpretation*, 189.

[138] *Ibid.*, 246, par. 8, no. 2. See also par. 8, nos. 3, 4, 5; cf. Pindar, *Olympian XIII*, in which Bellerophon 'sprang upright on his feet' at the conclusion of his dream of Athena.

eral Jewish texts the dreamer stands, signifying he has awakened, yet the revelation continues in a waking state,[139] as when Uriel says to Ezra after his dream, 'Stand up like a man (*Sta ut vir*) and I will instruct you' (4 Ezra 10:33; cf. 4 Ezra see also 7:2; Dan 8:17–18; *1 En.* 14:24).

In reading this image, a range of semantic meanings should be considered. In part, the motif of the standing dreamer stems from biblical motifs that one 'stands' (in Hebrew, typically עמד but sometimes קום) in order to receive revelation (e.g. Ezek 2:1, Num 23:18, Judg 3:20, Dan 10:11, *2 Bar.* 13:2 and 2). Another connotation of the verb in early Judaism is that it can function as a technical term for acting in priestly service before God (e.g. *2 En.* 69:1, 5; 70:1, 4; *T. Levi* 2:11). Hence, the angel in *Testament of Levi* describes Levi's priestly investiture by stating: 'And when you have mounted [to the third heaven], you shall stand (στήσῃ) near the Lord. You shall be his priest ...' (*T. Levi* 2:11). Accordingly, 'standing' is precisely what angels do in the heavenly Temple,[140] since they are also priests before God, e.g.: 'a great fire stood (παρειστήκει) by him ... and ten thousand times ten thousand stood before him' (*1 En.* 14:22). Finally, divine beings such as angels and the LORD 'stand' in dreams, with no indication of priestly activity, in accordance with ancient Near Eastern and ancient Mediterranean conventions for divine dream figures (Dan. 7:9; *L.A.B.* 9:10; *Jub.* 27:21; *Ladd. Jac.* 1:8; *2 En.* 1:5–6).[141]

Given these exalted associations with the verb 'stand,' it is particularly noteworthy that Jewish texts are virtually the only dream texts in all of antiquity that make use of the motif of the dreamer standing.[142] When the range of meanings of the verb 'stand' is considered,

---

[139] Scholem notes that standing 'without hands and feet' in bottomless space is a characteristic ecstatic experience mentioned in the *Greater Hekhalot*, Scholem, *Major Trends*, 52; Ms. Oxford 1531f. 45a (bottom).

[140] 'παρίστημι,' Georg Bertram, *TDNT* 5 (1967), 838–839.

[141] Furthermore, Fletcher-Louis has argued that Qumran texts such as *4Q377* and the *Twelfth Sabbath Song* draw on a theme of 'the-immutability-of-the-righteous-who-stand.' He further finds the theme in *On Dreams*, in which Philo explains that passages such as Exodus 24:10 in which God stood (εἱστήκει) refer to God's immutability. Fletcher-Louis, *All the Glory of Adam*, 146–148, 352. Fossum has similarly noted that in Samaritan texts Moses is called 'the (immutable) Standing One' (*Memar Marqah* 4:12). Jarl Fossum, *The Name of God and the Angel of the Lord: Samaritan and Jewish Concepts of Intermediation and the Origin of Gnosticism* (WUNT 35; Tübingen: Mohr Siebeck, 1985), 56–58, 120–121; Fletcher-Louis, *All the Glory of Adam*, 146.

[142] I know of only four exceptions in the rest of antiquity. Kummaya stands before the throne of Nergal in a dream in *A Vision of the Netherworld*, and in a dream of the *Epic of Gilgamesh*, a beautiful dream figure appears who '*set [Gilgamesh's] feet (again) on*

the image appears to suggest that the dreamer has attained a certain
level of intimacy with and/or likeness to divine beings such as angels,
such that ensuing revelation from a divine being can proceed in a waking state without harm to the recipient.

Progression of Dreamers

4 Ezra and Daniel are two texts in particular that carefully organize
dream types and the motif of the dreamer standing, thereby charting
an overarching schema in which seers steadily progress in their capacity
for receiving divine revelation. A detailed examination of these literary
patterns can increase our appreciation of the complexity and artistry of
the texts and shed light on their overall structures and meanings.[143]

4 Ezra

The dream in 4 Ezra (3:1) ends with the standard phrase 'Then I awoke
… and my soul was so troubled that it fainted' (5:14). Next comes this
scene: 'But the angel who had come and talked with me held me and
strengthened me and set me on my feet (*statuit me super pedes;* Syriac
ܐܘ ܟܐ ‬ܩܡ ܚܠܝ ܐܙܝܦ ܠܟ)' (5:15). Here, as in dream texts from other
cultures, standing up is synonymous with awakening. In this instance,
the angel helps Ezra stand up while he recovers from the shock of
his dream (5:14). The passage marks the transition of the angel who
appeared within Ezra's dream to the waking reality outside of Ezra's
dream, holding him, strengthening him, and finally, helping him to his
feet.

The typical CONCLUSION to Ezra's first visionary episode, 'And
I awoke,' marks it as a dream. Extensive parallels in both form and
content amongst Ezra's next two visionary episodes (5:21–6:34; 6:35–
9:25) suggest they are also dreams:

> I. INTRODUCTION
>   a. lying in bed in an anxious emotional state
>   – episode one: I was troubled as I lay on my bed, and my thoughts
>   welled up in my heart … My spirit was greatly agitated … (3:3,
>   4)

---

the ground'; in Oppenheim, *Interpretation*, 248, par. 8, no. 5. Also, two inscriptions on the
Epidaurian *iamata* state that Asklepios stood up the dreamer; LiDonnici, *Epidaurian
Miracle Inscriptions*, B 8, 9, 106–107.

[143] R.F. Melugin and A. Campbell in particular have recently called for increasing

– episode two: ... after seven days the thoughts of my heart were very grievous to me again ... (5:21)
– episode three: ... on the eighth night my heart was trouble within me again ... For my spirit was greatly aroused, and my soul was in distress. (6:35–37)
   b. Introductory dream formula
– episode one: I began to speak anxious words to the Most High ... (3:3)
– episode two: ... I began once more to speak words in the presence of the Most High. (5:22)
– episode three: ... I began to speak in the presence of the Most High. (6:36)

II. DREAM
   a. Address (episode one 3:4–36, episode two 5:23–30, episode three 6:38–59)
   b. Message DREAM
– episode one: ... the angel that had been sent to me ... answered and said to me ... (4:1)
– episode two: ... the angel who had come to me on a previous night was sent to me, and he said to me (5:31)
– episode three: ... the angel who had been sent to me on the former nights was sent to me, and he said to me ... (7:1–2)

III. DREAM INCUBATION INSTRUCTIONS
– episode one: ... pray again, and weep as you do now, and fast for seven days, you shall hear yet greater things than these. (5:13)
– episode two: ... pray again and fast again for seven days, I will again declare to you greater things than these ... (6:31)
– episode three: But if you will let seven days more pass—do not fast during them however; but go into a field of flowers ... and eat only flowers, and pray to the Most High continually—then I will come and talk with you. (9:24–25)

Several elements of the episodes are typical of dreams. Each of the first three episodes begins with Ezra in a similar emotional state of mourning/grieving, and episodes two and three add that Ezra has completed the prescribed dream incubation of fasting and mourning (5:20, 6:35). A technical formula introduces the DREAM (5:22; 6:36), which continues with Ezra's lengthy address to God (5:23–30, 6:38–59), followed by the sending of Uriel the angel (4:1, 5:31, 7:1). Moreover, all three episodes occur at night (5:31, 6:30, 6:36). Finally, incubation instructions are given at the end of each episode, with the promise

---

attention to literary artistry in form-critical studies. See Campbell, 'Form Criticism's Future,' 23; Melugin, 'Recent Form Criticism Revisited,' 46–64.

that the next vision would be greater (6:31, 9:23–24). These pervasive
structural similarities in the three visionary episodes suggest that all
three begin as dreams.

However, there is one significant structural difference in the CON-
CLUSION of each dream, namely, the placing of the scene of Ezra's
awakening and rising to his feet and the manner in which he does so.
In the first dream the angel comes, holds Ezra, strengthens him and
sets him on his feet just after he has awakened from the dream in a
frightened state (5:15), enabling him to transition to waking reality. This
action concludes the dream for Ezra and there is no further contact
between Ezra and the angel in the first dream. To put it in terms of
the structure outlined by Michael Stone, the first DREAM includes the
Address, Dispute, Prediction 1 and *Prediction 2*, and concludes with the angel
setting Ezra on his feet (see Table 2).

This scene plays out differently in the second dream. After the
Address, Dispute, and *Prediction 1* in Ezra's second dream, the angel says to
Ezra 'Rise to your feet' (6:13; see Table 1). This is a classic *Wecktraum*,[144]
and this time, Ezra wakes up much more easily, with the angel simply
telling him to get up. Most importantly, his awakening does not mark
the end of revelation. After Ezra stands up, the angel continues to
impart information and Ezra then hears an auditory message dream
of the voice of God (6:17, 29). In terms of Stone's schema, *Prediction 2*, a
revelation involving signs and the voice of God, occurs after Ezra arises
(Table 2).[145]

The placement of Ezra standing up occurs earlier still in the third
dream. Although this dream begins with the same *Traumeröffnungsformel*
as episodes one and two, Uriel arrives immediately after Ezra's *Address*
and wakes him by saying, 'Rise, Ezra, and listen …' (7:2; see Table
2). Next follows the longest revelation and description of eschatological
events thus far, which Stone labels as follows: *Dispute* (7:3–25), *Prediction
2* (7:26–44), *Dispute* (7:45–74), *Prediction 1* (7:75–115), *Dispute* (7:116–8:3),
Dispute (8:37–62), and *Prediction 2* (9:1–22) (Table 2).[146]

What are we to make of the varied placement in the three episodes
of the scene where Ezra stands up, if the second and third episodes

---

[144] Oppenheim, *Interpretation*, 189, 248, par. 8, no. 5; 1Sam 3:2–14, *Il.* 24:683, *Od.*
20:32.
[145] Stone, *Fourth Ezra*, 169. Also in Prediction 2, note the allusion in 4Ezra 6:26 to
Joel 2:28, which speaks of revelation by dreams.
[146] Stone, *Fourth Ezra*, 51.

both begin as dreams, as the pervasive parallels with the first dream suggest? We have seen that from the ancient Near East onward the act of standing is associated with waking up from sleep and/or a dream. Thus, the fact that this scene is successively moved up in the second and third dreams indicates that the period in which Ezra is asleep is shorter in his second dream and shortest in his third dream.

Table 2: Form-critical elements in 4 Ezra 3:1–9:25

	episode one	episode 2	episode 3
Introduction	3:1–3	5:21–22	6:35–37
Address	3:4–36	5:23–30	6:38–59
Dispute	4:1–25	5:31–40	7:1–25 *Ezra rises to his feet 7:2*
Prediction 1	4:26–52	5:41–6:10	7:26–44 Prediction 2
Dispute			7:45–74
Prediction 1			7:75–115
Dispute			7:116–8:3
Monologue			8:4–19
Prayer			8:20–36
Dispute			8:37–62
Prediction 2/ Revelation	5:1–13	6:11–29 *Ezra rises to his feet 6:13*	9:1–22
Conclusion/ Injunctions	5:14–20 *Ezra is set on his feet by Uriel 5:15*	6:30–34	9:23–25

Adapted from M. Stone, *4 Ezra*, 51; my additions in italics.

The overall effect is that Ezra progresses in his capacity to receive revelation. In his first dream, Ezra receives revelation from Uriel wholly within his dream and is so overwhelmed by the dream revelation that he needs the angel to comfort him, strengthen him, and physically stand him on his feet (5:14–15). In his second dream, Ezra is able to stand or awaken from his dream on his own (at the angel's behest) and to listen to the voice of God giving him a revelation about the eschatological endtime (6:2–29). He is, however, unable to respond, and the angel still needs to comfort Ezra at the conclusion of the episode, say-

ing 'Believe and do not be afraid!' (6:33). By the third dream, Uriel
awakens Ezra immediately upon arriving and imparts to him extensive revelation, even engaging in a lively interchange concerning the
endtime and the fate of humans in the judgment (7:3–9:25). However,
even in this instance the arrival of the angel still must take place in a
dream, since a dream cushions the transition to waking revelation,[147] as
an example from *Ladder of Jacob* makes clear: 'But I was not afraid of
[the angel's] glance, for the face *I had seen in my dream was more terrifying
than this;* and I was not afraid of the angel's glance' (*Ladd. Jac.* 3:2–3).[148]

As Stone has already demonstrated, the repeated shifts from *Dispute*
to *Prediction* in Ezra's third revelatory episode indicate the seer's progressive acceptance of the revelation he is receiving, which prepares
him for the change he experiences in his fourth dream, the dream of
the descent of the heavenly Zion.[149] My analysis has shown additional
structural evidence that charts Ezra's progression throughout episodes
one through three, in that the revelation he receives is increasingly
mediated in a waking state.[150] Ezra has transformed from trembling
dream-seer to someone who, awake, speaks 'mouth to mouth' with
God's angel, able to make inquiries that elicit revelations, thereby progressing to greater levels of understanding. He has been transformed
from *active dream participant* in the first dream, to a *passive recipient of waking revelation* in the second dream, to an *active participant of waking revelation*
in the third dream. This progress continues in his subsequent dreams.

Formal parallels with the first three dreams suggest the fourth visionary episode also begins as a dream. The INTRODUCTION again
stresses that Ezra lies down while in a troubled emotional state: 'I lay
on the grass, my heart was troubled again as it was before' (9:27). Also,
the incubation instructions have been fulfilled in the same fashion as in
episodes two and three (9:26) and the technical formula that leads to
the DREAM and *Address* reappears here, '… I began to speak before
the Most High …' (9:26; 29–37). After Ezra repeats the phrase, 'I said

---

[147] Oppenheim calls it a '(dream-) revelation,' in that the dream figure formerly inside
the dream gives the revelation to the awakened dreamer. Oppenheim, *Interpretation*, 190.

[148] *Ladder of Jacob*, trans. by A. Pennington in *The Apocryphal Old Testament* (ed. H.F.D.
Sparks; Oxford: Clarendon, 1984, repr. 1990), 453–464.

[149] Stone, *Fourth Ezra*, 24, 51.

[150] The issue of whether the various dream traditions consider waking revelation
to be higher than revelation imparted in dreams is complex, and does not alter the
internal evidence of 4 Ezra, which appears to ranks waking revelation higher. There
is also biblical precedent for this view in Numbers 12:6–8 (see also Diodorus Siculus,
XXXIV/XXXV.2.5).

these things in my heart' (9:38) he begins to experience a dream unlike any Ezra has experienced before.

As many scholars have noted, the fourth episode (9:26–10:59) is a crucial turning point for Ezra,[151] and the dream content reflects this transformation. Instead of Uriel, Ezra sees a mourning woman who transforms into the heavenly Jerusalem, a message dream that becomes a symbolic dream. The CONCLUSION to this dream suggests that Ezra is absolutely overwhelmed. He cries out, 'Where is the angel Uriel, who came to me at first?' (10:28). When Uriel does arrive, he finds Ezra in an even worse state of fear than after his first dream:

> … I lay there like a corpse and I was deprived of my understanding. Then [Uriel] *grasped my right hand and strengthened me and set me on my feet*, and said to me, 'What is the matter with you? And why are you troubled? And why are your understanding and the thoughts of your mind troubled?'   (10:29–31)

Both Ezra's prostrate position and Uriel's questions illustrate Ezra's profound psychological distress, and as was the case after Ezra's first dream, the angel must once again strengthen Ezra and help him to his feet. Yet Ezra has not regressed, he has entered a new and greater level of revelation.

After the pattern that has been established in the story, the attentive reader expects further revelation to ensue when Uriel tells Ezra to stand up (10:33). Yet as Stone has astutely noted, '[Ezra's] resolution is no longer found at the level of discussion and argument … Instead, there is a basic reorientation of the author's perception of the world …'[152] This reorientation is accomplished by a convincing sensorial *experience* of the eschatological reality of the heavenly Zion. The borderline between dream and waking reality shifts for Ezra, causing him to cry out: 'behold! I saw, and still see, what I am unable to explain … Or is my mind deceived, and my soul dreaming?' (10:32, 36). That is, Ezra wonders whether or not he is still dreaming, since he still sees the heavenly Zion after awakening.[153] Just as Uriel appeared in his dream and remained afterwards, so does Zion. Uriel tells him to tour the city and to see it 'as far as it is possible for your eyes to see it, and afterward

---

[151] Brandenburger, *Die Verborgenheit Gottes;* Harnisch, *Verhängnis und Verheißung der Geschichte: Untersuchungen zum Zeit- und Geschichtsverständnis im 4.Buch Esra und in der syr. Baruchapokalypse* (FRLANT 97; Göttingen: Vandenhoeck & Ruprecht, 1969); Breech, 'These Fragments,' and Stone, *Fourth Ezra*, 31.

[152] Stone, *Fourth Ezra*, 308.

[153] See Ibid., 335.

you will hear as much as your ears can hear' (10:56), indicating the
profundity of the experience.

After this visionary experience, Ezra sees two symbolic dreams (11:1,
13:1), which follow the same formal pattern as his earlier message
dreams, except that the message occurs in the form of symbolic visions
which requires interpretation. Although we saw that the ancient Near
East had a general prejudice against symbolic dreams, no such neg-
ativity accompanies them in the Hebrew Bible[154] or in early Judaism.
In fact, in 4 Ezra his symbolic dreams provide Ezra with the most
detailed knowledge of eschatological revelation thus far. When Uriel
predicts these symbolic dream visions earlier, he notes that Ezra has
been favored with the revelation because: '[God] has seen your righteous conduct, that you have sorrowed greatly for your people and
mourned greatly over Zion' (10:39). The eschatological symbols in the
eagle dream are deemed to be 'great secrets' (12:36), a term used only
rarely in 4 Ezra to indicate a pinnacle of revelation given to Abraham
and Moses (3:14, 14:5–6; cf. 10:38).[155]

The change in the form of revelation from message dreams to symbolic dreams mirrors Ezra's progression in his ability to withstand successively greater levels of revelation. Ezra not only receives verbal revelation as in his earlier message dreams, he dramatically *experiences* eschatological revelation in his symbolic dreams. Sensory verbs, such as seeing and hearing, substantially increase in his fifth and sixth dreams, e.g.
the repetition of '*Et vidi … et ecce*' (4 Ezra 11:2, 5, 7, 10, 12, 20, 22, 24,
28, 33, 36, 44; 12:1, 2, 3, 11, 17, 19, 22, 26, 29, 30, 31, 35; 13:3, 5, 8, 10,
12, 20, 25, 27, 32, 39, 47, 51, 53). This marked emphasis on seeing fulfills
Uriel's earlier statement that Ezra might be granted a chance to *see* the
signs of the endtime (4:43, 5:4). That is, Ezra's symbolic dreams allow
him to see endtime events proleptically, whereas the majority of people
must wait for the eschaton.

Other evidence testifies to Ezra's progress. Although earlier Ezra had
counted himself along with the doomed sinners (7:46, 76), after his fifth,
symbolic dream 'all the people … from the least to the greatest' explic-

---

[154] A few scholars have argued that symbolic dreams were understood in antiquity
to constitute a higher level of revelation than message or speech dreams, citing the
view of the 12th c. Eustathius that the Homeric passage about the 'gates of horn and
ivory' refers to the superiority of sight dreams to speech dreams (*Od.* 19:560–567). See
A. Amory, 'The Gates of Horn and Ivory,' 3–57; P. Cox Miller, *Dreams in Late Antiquity*,
15–17; Van Lieshout, *Greeks on Dreams*, 38–39.

[155] Stone, *Fourth Ezra*, 334.

itly refer to Ezra as the last of the prophets (12:42). Ezra himself boldly
requests a divine interpretation of his symbolic dreams, saying 'for you
have judged me worthy to be shown the end of the times and the last
events of the time' (12:9; 13:14–15). Uriel likewise affirms Ezra's transformed status, saying of the fifth dream: 'And you alone were worthy
to learn this secret of the Most High' (12:36). Stone agrees that at this
point 'Ezra's self-consciousness and the way he is presented in the book
have changed,'[156] maintaining that this change is 'the consummation
of a process' evident from vision three onwards.[157] I concur, but trace
this progression from his first dream onward, in that Ezra has steadily
progressed in his capacity for receiving revelation from the beginning.

After his sixth, symbolic dream, Ezra stands in a very different
manner than before. Whereas earlier he needed Uriel's help to stand
up, after the sixth dream Ezra stands up wholly on his own initiative
and in a new frame of mind: 'Then I arose (*et profectus sum*) and walked
in the field, giving great glory and praise to the Most High because of
his wonders' (13:57). Ezra is ready for the culmination of his revelatory
journey.

The final vision that Ezra experiences (14:1–50) is the pinnacle of
a revelatory progression evident throughout the text. The interpreting
angel is gone entirely, and it is none other than God who instructs
Ezra.[158] The vision of the burning bush is clearly *not* a dream, but a *waking revelation* exactly like Moses' call, occurring after a forty day period
of preparation (14:1–26; cf. Exodus 3:2).[159] God calls Ezra's name twice,
and Ezra replies 'Here I am,' whereupon Ezra rises to his feet on his
own initiative, '*et surrexi super pedes meos*,' as he did after the sixth dream
(14:2). The voice of the Most High instructs Ezra to take five scribes and
many writing tablets to the field, after which Ezra has another waking
vision in which he hears the voice of God telling him to drink from a
cup full of fiery water (14:37–39; cf. Isa 6:6–7).[160] After drinking the con-

---

[156] Stone, *Fourth Ezra*, 376.

[157] Ibid., 376.

[158] Ibid., 411.

[159] Stone has shown this calculation as follows: three weeks (6:35), plus seven days
between visions 3 and 4, two days between visions 4 and 5, one week between visions
5 and 6, and 3 days between visions 6 and 7—for a total of 40 days. Stone, *Fourth Ezra*,
35.

[160] In addition to similarities with Isaiah 6:6–7, the scene is strikingly similar to the
Vedic accounts of the sacred Indian soma sacrifice, the *agnishtoma*, named for Agni, god
of fire. Drinking soma brought visions of the gods and sensations of power, and even

tents he is endowed with 'understanding,' 'wisdom,' and 'memory,' and during another forty day period pours forth not only the Torah known to have been given to Moses, but another seventy esoteric books as well (15:47).[161] Finally, like Enoch and Elijah, Ezra is taken up to heaven, and becomes 'the Scribe of the knowledge of the Most High forever' (14:9, 50). His capacity for receiving revelation is at its highest and he is henceforth a heavenly figure—a scribe.

Neither the visions of the burning bush nor of the cup of fiery water exhibit the formal pattern of dream visions established above, nor do they contain any of the typical features of dreams. Ezra does not begin the visions by lying down, but by sitting under an oak tree (14:1; cf. Gen 18:1) and the voice of God simply speaks. Since the burning bush and cup of fiery water are not dream symbols, but are themselves divine realities, no interpretation is provided regarding them. There is no conclusion to the visions describing Ezra awakening and he has no physical or psychological symptoms as a result of the experience. In fact, he is wholly composed, and it is he who suggests that he write down the public and secret Torah before being taken up (14:22). Thus, it is evident in vision seven that Ezra no longer needs the comfort of Uriel, the cushioning of a dream, or the interpretations of Uriel. He is able, like Moses, to speak 'mouth to mouth' with God:

> When there are prophets among you, I the LORD make myself known to them in visions; I speak to them in dreams. Not so with my servant Moses … With him I speak face to face—clearly, not in riddles; and he beholds the form of the LORD. (Numbers 12:6–8)

Thus, in the span of the text as a whole, Ezra has three message dreams followed by increasingly long periods of waking revelation, followed in turn by a dream in which the heavenly Zion is manifested, followed by two symbolic dreams illustrating eschatological events in detail, culminating in a waking vision in which Ezra speaks directly with God. The organization of these dream types and visions charts Ezra's psychological growth as a character in terms of his increasing capacity for receiving revelation. In the end, Ezra completes an odyssey begun by dreaming.

---

identification with the gods. See R. Baird and A. Bloom, *Indian and Far Eastern Religious Traditions* (New York: Harper & Row, 1971), 12, 15.

[161] These seventy esoteric books were apparently also transmitted to Moses; see 4 Ezra 14:6.

Daniel

Like 4 Ezra, Daniel 7–12 also arranges various dream types in an over-arching structure that depicts a main character progressing in his ability to receive revelation. These chapters of the biblical book of Daniel were written by one or more authors around 167–163 B.C.E. in Aramaic (ch. 7) and Hebrew (ch.8–12).[162] In terms of genre, they constitute an historical apocalypse that imparts extraordinary knowledge of temporal and otherworldly realities through the use of *ex eventu* prophecy.[163] Although integrated with earlier material in Daniel 1–6 by a Hellenistic author, one of the many places in which the seam is noticeable is with respect to dreams. In Dan 1–6, Daniel is a divinely gifted dream interpreter, whereas in Dan 7–12 he himself is the dreamer who dreams about future events: the rise of Gentile nations, Antiochus IV's proscription of the Torah and desecration of the Temple, and an eschatological culmination that ends the reign of evil on earth and in heaven.[164]

In the beginning of chapter 7 Daniel 'saw a dream' (חלם חזה), a 'vision of his mind in bed,' (וחזוי ראשה על־משכבה) (Dan 7:1), or night-visions (בחזוי ליליא) (7:2, 7). Daniel writes down the dream, the record of which we are presumably reading, in the style of an ancient Near Eastern literary commissioning dream (Dan 7:1b).[165] The symbolic dream contains two visions, the vision of the four beasts from the sea (Dan 7:2–8) and the throne vision of the Ancient of Days who sits in judgment and hands dominion over to the Son of Man (Dan 7:9–14). The verb 'to see' (חזה) introduces numerous scenes in the dream (7:2, 4, 6, 7, 9, 11, 13, 21; cf. vv. 5, 8), stressing its highly visual nature.

In the ancient Near East and Egypt, symbolic dreams require interpretation by ritual experts, lest the dreams become 'evil dreams.'[166] After the dream had ended, the dreamer would typically go to a priestly expert who would interpret the dream for him/her.[167] Similarly, in the

---

[162] Collins, *Daniel*, 33–35, 37.

[163] Ibid., 54, 60, 61.

[164] For contrasting views on the causes and circumstances of Antiochus IV Epiphanes' banning of the Torah and desecration of the temple, see the following sources: J.A. Goldstein, *1Maccabees* (AB 41; Garden City, NY: Doubleday, 1976), 104–160; D.J. Harrington, *The Maccabean Revolt: Anatomy of a Biblical Revolution* (Wilmington: Glazier, 1988); Hengel, *Judaism and Hellenism*, 1:267–314; Tcherikover, *Hellenistic Civilization*, 191–203.

[165] Cf. Oppenheim, *Interpretation*, 193–194.

[166] Ibid., 349–350.

[167] Egypt had the most renowned priestly dream interpreters, who were summoned to interpret royal dreams in Assyria. Oppenheim, *Interpretation*, 222–225, 238.

Book of Daniel, the 'attendants' of the heavenly *hekhal* are present inside of Daniel's dream episode (7:16) and he asks these angels for an interpretation what he sees (Dan 7:16–18, 23–27). Thus, the interpretation of the symbolic dream actually occurs within the dream and is provided by a divine dream figure, who is perhaps acting in the capacity of an attendant of the *hekhal*. While interpretation within a dream is not completely unknown in the ancient Near East,[168] the motif is exceedingly rare before the Hellenistic era.

In early Jewish texts, symbolic dreams in particular are capable of making a deep impression on dreamers, as they powerfully interweave deeply layered mythic symbols with rich visual images that are evocative and polyvalent. For instance, the image of animals arising from the sea in Daniel 7 resonates with a range of cultural meanings, including associations between 'unclean' animals and Gentile nations,[169] Ugaritic and Canaanite associations of the sea with chaos and monsters, and animals from Babylonian astrology.[170] In addition, the visual nature of symbolic dreams allows audiences to concretize abstract ideas such as evil, thereby enabling the expression and formulation of the apocalyptic worldview so as to 'persuade … readers of the reality of this supernatural dimension.'[171] Indeed, after awakening from the dream, Daniel is greatly disturbed (7:28b). As in 4 Ezra, the pseudonymous Daniel keeps his revelation secret, saying '[I] kept the matter in my heart,' while recording the dream for the 'later' audience of Antiochan times (Dan 7:1, 28; cf. 12:4).[172] However, like Ezra, Daniel's psychological capacity

---

[168] See 'Another Dream of Nabonidus,' trans. Oppenheim, *Interpretation*, 250, no. 13.

[169] Douglas, *Leviticus as Literature*, 134–151.

[170] Several interesting sources have been posited for these animal symbols, including hybrid animals in the Akkadian *A Vision of the Netherworld*, dragons from Ugaritic myths and Babylonian animal astrology. Kvanvig, *Roots of Apocalyptic*, 442–602; F.M. Cross, *Canaanite Myth and Hebrew Epic* (Cambridge, MA: Harvard University, 1973), 112–120; J. Day, *God's Conflict with the Dragon and the Sea: Echoes of a Canaanite Myth in the Old Testament* (Cambridge: Cambridge University, 1985), 151–178; P. Porter, *Metaphors and Monsters: A Literary-critical Study of Daniel 7 and 8* (ConB 20; Lund: Gleerup, 1983). F. Cumont thinks the animal imagery derives from Babylonian animal astrology, *Astrology and Religion*. Others take up Cumont's suggestion, including: A. Bentzen, *Daniel* (HAT 19; 2nd ed.; Tübingen: Mohr, 1952), 69; A. Caquot, 'Sur les quatre Bêtes de Daniel VII,' *Semitica* 5 (1955), 10; Hengel, *Judaism and Hellenism*, 1.184; N.W. Porteous, *Daniel: A Commentary* (Philadelphia: Westminster, 1965), 122; J.C.H. Lebram, *Das Buch Daniel* (Zürich: Theologische Verlag, 1984), 97–98 in Collins, *Daniel*, 330, n. 24.

[171] Collins, *Daniel*, 61.

[172] Ibid., 276.

to receive revelation will increase over the course of the book, and he will grow in both understanding and confidence.

The vision in chapter 8 is likened to the first dream (8:2),[173] and although the Masoretic text of Daniel 8 does not explicitly call the episode a dream, some recensions do, including the Syriac.[174] I understand the visionary episode to be a symbolic dream that includes animal symbols of the type in Daniel 7, as well as a rather transparent symbolic vision of the cessation of the Temple sacrifice. Again, an angel within the dream provides the interpretation, and the dream concludes by mentioning the psychological and physical impact it made on Daniel, who could stand up only after several days (8:27). Finally, Daniel states, 'Then I arose (ואקום)' (8:27b), a typical conclusion for dream episodes.

In Daniel 7:16, the angel's interpretation is initiated by Daniel's request. In chapter 8, Daniel's mere desire for understanding the vision seems to induce the angel's appearance, for as soon as Daniel tries to understand it: 'behold, standing (עמד) before me was one who looked like a man' (8:15). Daniel himself is 'standing' (עמדי) in the dream, but he swoons when the angel approaches. The angel touches him and helps him stand again (עמדי) (Dan 8:18). As we have seen, among the associations of the verb 'stand' is the receipt of revelation, and immediately after Daniel is made to stand up, a 'human voice' commands Gabriel to explain the vision to Daniel (8:16; cf. *1 Enoch* 14:24–16:4 and 4 Ezra 6:13–28). Since the voice commands Gabriel, it apparently belongs to a divine being of a higher rank than the angel, with whom Daniel has probably spoken in his first dream. From all this it is clear that the angel's interpretation constitutes profound dream revelation that Daniel receives while 'standing,' although he had some angelic help in doing so.

Although the seer therefore seems somewhat more resilient than before, the dream experience is still difficult for him. At the conclusion of the interpretation and dream, Daniel first 'was stricken and languished for days' before finally arising (8:27). Moreover, even though Gabriel attempts to explain the vision to him, Daniel cannot comprehend the meaning, saying: 'I was depressed on account of the vision and did not understand' (8:27). One reason for Daniel's difficulty may

---

[173] Collins also concludes it is a symbolic dream, *Daniel*, 342.
[174] Ibid., 329.

be that his dreams are not simple symbolic dreams, but rather dreams that provide access to otherworldly realms. In his first dream, he sees a throne-room, which may indicate a dream transport to heaven (e.g. *1 En.* 14–15, *T. Levi* 2–5, 8), or perhaps a glimpse of some future merging of the heavenly throne-room with earth (4 Ezra 9–10). In his second dream, Daniel finds himself transported to the faraway Ulai river, from the midst of which comes the mysterious voice (8:1–3, 6, 16).[175] The two eschatological dreams reinforce one another and confirm one another's veracity, adding to the overall impact on Daniel as well as on the reader (cf. *1 Enoch* 83–90).[176]

Daniel's next encounter with divinity does not occur in a dream, although it shares some features in common with dreams. In chapter 9, Daniel is frustrated at his lack of understanding regarding a prophecy of Jeremiah, namely that Jerusalem would be desolate for seventy years.[177] Daniel engages in ritual preparations, including prayer, supplication, fasting and donning sackcloth and ashes (9:3), which results in the appearance of an angel who imparts a message:

> … while I was speaking my prayer, the man Gabriel, whom I had seen in the vision, was sent forth flying and approached [touched] me … He made me understand by speaking to me and saying, 'Daniel, I have come now to give you understanding …'   (Daniel 9:21–22)

Although some of the rituals in which Daniel engages are also rituals of dream incubation, no formal elements are present to indicate that Daniel is dreaming. Rather, the angel appears simply to interpret Jeremiah's prophecy (9:22, 25).[178] Whereas after his second sym-

---

[175] Such visionary transport is familiar from Ezekiel 8:3, 11:24 and 40:2, and this particular setting seems to recall Ezekiel's vision by the Chebar canal. In Daniel, the river itself is a richly evocative dream symbol that occurs several times in the vision. The two-horned ram stands between the river and the dreamer (8:3, 6) and the 'human voice' that mysteriously speaks in the vision does so from the midst of the Ulai river (Dan 8:16). Collins, *Daniel*, 329.

[176] Collins, *Apocalyptic Imagination*, 107–108.

[177] For the pseudonymous Daniel, the interpretation is not overly problematic, but it is indeed of great import from the viewpoint of the author of the text, who is contemplating a second desolation of Jerusalem in Antiochan times.

[178] The text is markedly similar to later *Merkabah Sar ha Torah* texts. In the same manner as those mystics, Daniel engages in preparatory rituals of mourning, fasting and prayer that induce an epiphany of the angel Gabriel, who, like the *Sar ha Torah* imparts knowledge of the Torah. Although Daniel does not receive complete mastery of the Torah, it is clear that the angel's epiphany has the purpose of imparting understanding of Jeremiah's prophecy to Daniel, and that this event occurs in response to Daniel's preparatory (and theurgic) actions. Schäfer, *Hidden and Manifest*, 52, 85; idem,

bolic dream Daniel explained 'he did not understand,' here he states Gabriel 'made me understand,' which appears to result from Gabriel's 'approaching' or 'touching' him (נגע).[179] Thus, this episode is a waking epiphany in which Daniel is fully capable of interacting with a divine angel and of understanding his explanations.

Finally, in chapters 10–12, Daniel's capacity to receive revelation increases even more. Whereas he was deeply disturbed after his first two dreams (7:28; 8:27) and had no understanding after his second dream (8:27), the lengthy vision that spans chapter 10–12 begins differently: 'The oracle was true, but it was a great task to understand the prophecy; understanding came to him through the vision' (10:1).[180] Like Gabriel's appearance in chapter 9, the vision in Daniel 10–12 appears to be a waking vision like those of Ezekiel,[181] that is, *not a dream*.[182] None of the typical framing features of dreams are present, and the vision appears to be induced by a three week period of mourning and asceticism, the rituals that formerly induced a waking visit from Gabriel (10:2–4).[183]

The vision in Daniel 10–12 does contain the familiar sequence of the visionary swoon into a trance, followed by a strengthening touch from an angel, and the act of standing up. However, slight but important alterations are made to this formula. Although the angel touches and strengthens Daniel after his visionary swoon, this only helps him onto his knees—Daniel actually stands up on his own initiative (10:10–

Hekhalot-Studien, 281–294; M. Swartz, *Scholastic Magic: Ritual and Revelation in Early Jewish Mysticism* (Princeton, N.J.: Princeton University Press, 1996).

[179] The verb נגע is used to mean 'touch' in Dan 8:18 and 10:16.

[180] Although the text later states that Daniel hears something and does 'not understand,' the referent is the revelation of the exact timing of the *eschaton*, which is sealed and kept secret from all (12:8–9). However, on the level of audience reception, it is clear that the endtime is the time in which the readership is living.

[181] Collins points out numerous parallels between Daniel 10–12 and Ezekiel's visions: Daniel by the Tigris river and Ezekiel by the Chebar canal; the man dressed in linen and Ezek 9:2, 3, 11; 10:2, 6, 7; the man's loins and the description in Ezek 1:27; the man's chrysolite body and Ezek 1:16; the face of lightning and eyes of torches and Ezek 1:13; his feet that glance like burnished bronze and Ezek 1:7; and the sound of his words like a multitude are like the sound of mighty waters that the wings of the *ḥayyot* make in Ezek 1:24. Collins, *Daniel*, 373–374.

[182] Whereas in chapter 8, Daniel's position next to the Ulai River is the setting inside his dream, Daniel is 'actually' present next to the Tigris river in chapter 10, since mention is made of 'The men who were with me' (10:7).

[183] Although Collins notes 'a close affinity' between the vision in Daniel 10–12 and ancient Near Eastern message dreams, the formal elements of dreams are absent. Collins, *Daniel*, 402.

11). Two more times the angel touches Daniel's mouth and gives him strength to speak, but he seems to be standing the whole time (10:16,18).

In a rough way, these variations on the swoon-touch-stand formula seem to parallel Daniel's general stages of understanding. Within the dream vision in Daniel 8, at the conclusion of which Daniel had 'no understanding,' the angel touched the prostrate and sleeping Daniel and set him on his feet. However, in Daniel 10–12, in which Daniel explicitly understands the waking vision and the interpretation, the angel touches him and helps him onto his knees, but Daniel stands up on his own (10:10). As the revelation continues Daniel loses strength and the angel touches Daniel twice more on the lips (10:16, 18), but Daniel is standing all the while. Thus, it is clear that the receipt of revelation takes its toll on a visionary, but overall Daniel is progressing steadily in his capacity to receive revelation.

Also, as Table 3 indicates, the Book of Daniel pairs ritual preparations with certain types of dreams and visions. Daniel engages in no ritual preparations for his dreams (7, 8), both of which trouble him greatly and neither of which he understands. Chapter 9 marks a turning point in both preparation and result. Daniel engages in a ritual of prayer and penitence for an unspecified length of time (9:3–4), whereupon he receives a revelation from Gabriel about a passage in Jeremiah, which he explicitly *does* understand (9:22). By engaging in a preparatory ritual, Daniel has become an active participant in procuring divine revelation. Finally, in chapters 10–12, Daniel performs a three week long preparatory ritual of prayer, penitence and fasting (10:2) and subsequently has a waking epiphany by the Tigris river. Unlike before, he understands the content of the difficult vision (10:1; cf. 8:27). Although he does swoon once and needs the strengthening touch of the angel, he stands up on his own and remains standing throughout the rest of the revelation (10:11). The angel touches him twice more on the mouth to give him additional strength, and perhaps also a prophetic commissioning (10:16, 18; cf. Isa 6:6).[184] Finally, having progressed in his capacity as a seer, Daniel is several times called 'precious' by Gabriel, and is promised a special destiny at the end of time (10:11, 19; 12:13).

[184] Daniel was regarded as a prophet in early Judaism, with Josephus calling him 'one of the greatest prophets,' and Matthew 24:15 and *4QFlor.* 2, 4 both referring to 'Daniel the prophet.' J. Barton, *Oracles of God: Perceptions of Ancient Prophecy in Israel after the Exile* (London: Darton, Longman & Todd, 1986), 35–37; K. Koch, 'Is Daniel Also among the Prophets?' *Interpretation* 39 (1985), 117–130.

Table 3: Dreams in Daniel 7–12.

	chapter 7	*chapter 8*	*chapter 9*	*chapters 10–12*
vision type	symbolic dream vision and a vision of the divine throne-room (visionary transport?)	symbolic dream vision set within a dream transportation to the Ulai River	rituals induce a waking epiphany of an angel who interprets Jeremiah	waking epiphany in which an angel imparts a lengthy endtime prophecy
ritual preparations	None	None	prayer, fasts in sackcloth and ashes(9:3)	three weeks of mourning and fasting
swoon-touch-stand formula	–	Daniel swoons, the angel touches him, the angel helps Daniel stand up	–	Daniel swoons, the angel touches him, Daniel stands; the angel twice touches Daniel's mouth to help him speak while he stands (10:9–11, 16, 18)
references to Daniel's level of understanding	–	does not understand the vision (8:27)	Gabriel gives Daniel under-standing (9:22)	Daniel understands the difficult vision (10:1)
characterization of Daniel after vision and interpretation	disturbed and alarmed, darkened face (7:15, 28)	terrified, stricken for days, dismayed (8:17, 27)	called 'precious' by the angel (9:23)	called 'precious' (10:11, 19); promised a special destiny at the end of times (12:12)

Like Ezra in 4 Ezra, Daniel is transformed by his dream experiences. After receiving two unbidden dreams, Daniel purposefully engages in rituals that induce a divine response (9, 10:2–3), at which point he no longer requires the psychological cushion of a dream-state in order to interact with divine beings.[185] By his last vision he is singled out for a special eschatological reward, probably the astral immortality or exaltation of the wise mentioned in Dan 12:3.[186]

In sum, 4 Ezra and Daniel 7–12 have much in common with respect to dreams and visions. Although some details vary, 4 Ezra and Daniel 7–12 share many themes: both rank waking revelation over dream revelation, signal the difficulty of receiving revelation through the use of a swoon-touch-stand formula, relate certain rituals to particular kinds

---

[185] Oppenheim, *Interpretation*, 190.
[186] Nickelsburg, *Jewish Literature*, 89.

of visionary experiences, and maintain that angels who appear inside
one's dreams can transcend the liminal dream boundary and enter
one's waking world. Furthermore, both authors organize various dream
types, visions, rituals, and the motif of the dreamer standing to create
overarching schemas in which a fear-stricken dream seer becomes a
prophet capable of receiving profound revelation from divine beings
in a waking state. Thus, each of these two texts recounts a visionary
journey that begins with dreams and that ultimately culminates in an
individual ascent that most likely takes place after death (4 Ezra 14:9;
Dan 12:3, 12).

Jewish Dreams and Death

It hardly needs to be said that little unanimity exists amongst portraits
of an afterlife in texts of Hellenistic Judaism. Some texts only address
reward and punishment in terms of what happens to the soul after
it is freed from the body (e.g. *1 En.* 22; *T. Job* 52; *J.W.* VII:349–351;
Jub. 23:31; *T. Abr.* A 20:10–11, B 14:7), while others emphasize the
reconstitution of the body (2 Macc 6:18–7:42). Some conceive of astral
immortality or exaltation to heaven (Dan 12:3; *1 En.* 108; *T. Moses* 9–10),
while other texts envision a return to earthly Eden (*1 En.* 25). Moreover,
some texts seem only to envision a limited resurrection in the eschaton
(Dan 12:3), whereas a text like 4 Ezra tries to offer explanation both
for what occurs in an individual's afterlife (4 Ezra 7:78–101) as well
as in the universal, collective afterlife judgment of the post-messianic
eschatological age (4 Ezra 7:32, 78–101; cf. *1 En.* 22). Finally, some special
individuals apparently never die; these include not just Enoch (*2 En.* 67;
3 En. 4; cf. Gen 6:1–7), but also probably Ezra (4 Ezra 14:9) and Baruch,
e.g.: 'For you will surely depart from this world, nevertheless not to
death but to be kept unto (the end) of times' (*2 Bar.* 76:2).

    Much has been written about death and the afterlife in Hellenis-
tic Judaism, whether directly or indirectly as part of commentaries on
individual texts.[187] Ever since Bousset illuminated the ways in which
ascent accounts prefigure death,[188] a focus on ascents has had a ten-

---

[187] Unfortunately, the publication of Alan Segal's monograph of the topic is too
recent for me to have incorporated his research here. Segal, *Life After Death: A History of
the Afterlife in the Religions of the West* (New York: Doubleday, 2003).

[188] Bousset, *Die Himmelreise*, 136.

dency to dominate the discussion of death in early Judaism.[189] Without diminishing the importance of the ascent motif, I wish to contribute an additional piece to the overall puzzle, by investigating the pervasive associations amongst death and dreams in early Judaism, as well as the nexus of death, dreams and ascent.

In Part One I discussed many thematic connections made between death and dreams in the ancient Near East, Greece and Rome. For instance, some ancient Near Eastern vocabulary underlines the similarity of the disembodied soul in dreams and in death, e.g.: '*abālu*' is used both in the sense of the Dream God 'carrying' a dreamer and for dying, and '*salalu*' signifies both sleep and a peaceful death.[190] Also, from Enkidu's death dream in *Epic of Gilgamesh* onward, examples abound of dreams that foretell an impending death, whether the dreamer's or someone else's.[191] Hesiod dubs Night the mother of Sleep, Death and Dreams (*Theog.* 211–225), making the two siblings. Spatially, death and dreams are also closely interconnected, in that numerous texts picture the underworld as home to both dreams and the dead, (e.g. *Epic of Gilgamesh*; *Od.* 19:562 ff., 4:808 ff., 24:12; Aeschylus' *Pers.* 521–523; Virgil's *Aen.* 6:282–284, and Ovid's *Metam.* XI.565–627).[192] This may be one reason why spirits of the dead frequently appear as dream messengers, especially in Greek and Latin texts.[193] The connections between dreams and death are so intimate that Roman sarcophagi often depict Somnus, the Sleep God, alongside Morpheus, the Dream God.

---

[189] A review of the papers on early Judaism at Culianu's 1991 conference, 'Other Realms: Death, Ecstasy and Otherworldly Journeys in Recent Scholarship' makes this focus on ascent clear: J.J. Collins, 'A Throne in the Heavens,' A.Y. Collins, 'Seven Heavens in Jewish and Christian Apocalypses,' 57–92; Alan F. Segal, 'Paul and the Beginning of Jewish Mysticism,' and M. Himmelfarb, 'The Practice of Ascent in the Ancient Mediterranean World,' in *Death, Ecstasy, and Other Worldly Journeys* (eds. J.J. Collins, M. Fishbane; New York: SUNY, 1995). But more recently Collins concludes that Bousset's argument that ecstatic ascent was 'nothing other than an anticipation of the heavenly journey of the soul after death … is an over-generalization,' in 'Journeys to the world beyond,' 34.

[190] *CAD* A 1, 1: 10–31, 16–17, '*abālu*.' T. Abusch points out that in the Ancient Near East, death and sleep are often equated, and notes this usage of *salalu*, 'to be asleep,' Abusch, 'Ascent to the Stars in a Mesopotamian Ritual,' *Death, Ecstasy*, 15–38, 26.

[191] Leibovici, 'Babylone,' 65–66; Sauneron, 'l'Égypte,' 19–20; Schmidtke, 'Träume, Orakel und Totengeister,' 240–246. See also *Epic of Gilgamesh*; Aeschy. *Pers.* 175–200; Herodotus *Hist.* I.34–45, 209, III.124–125; V.55–6; Suetonius *Lives* I.81, III.74, IV.57.

[192] See also Oppenheim, *Interpretation*, 234–235.

[193] E.g. *Il.* 23:62 ff.; Sophocles *El.* 410–425; Euripides *Hec.* 1–97, *Or.* 618–620, *Alc.* 349–356; Aeschylus *Eum.* 94–104; Ennius *Annals* 2–10; Cicero *Resp.* VI.x.10-VI.xxxvi.29; Virgil *Aen.* I.341–372, II.264–294, IV.326–360, V.705–739; Suetonius *Lives* VII.7.

Early Jewish writings share some of these associations. A valuable passage in Josephus' writings (*J.W.* 7.349) illuminates some of the complex ways in which some Hellenistic Jewish texts intertwine death and dreams. As part of Eleazar's stirring speech urging the Jewish fighters on Masada to commit suicide rather than to submit to Rome, he describes how the soul journeys in both states:

ὕπνος δὲ τεκμήριον ὑμῖν ἔστω τῶν λόγων ἐναργέστατον, ἐν ᾧ ψυχαὶ τοῦ σώματος αὐτὰς μὴ περισπῶντος ἡδίστην μὲν ἔχουσιν ἀνάπαυσιν ἐφ' αὐτῶν γενόμεναι, θεῷ δ' ὁμιλοῦσαι κατὰ συγγένειαν πάντη μὲν ἐπιφοιτῶσι, πολλὰ δὲ τῶν ἐσομένων προθεσπίζουσι. Τί δὴ δεῖ δεδιέναι θάνατον τὴν ἐν ὕπνῳ γινομένην ἀνάπαυσιν ἀγαπῶντας;

Let sleep furnish you with a most convincing proof of what I say—sleep, in which the soul, undistracted by the body, while enjoying in perfect independence the most delightful repose, holds converse with God by right of kinship, ranges the universe and foretells many things that are to come. Why then should we fear death who welcome the repose of sleep? (Josephus, *J.W.* VII.349–351.)

Several portions of this passage are noteworthy. Dreaming and sleep are likened to death in that the soul is freed from the body, providing access to otherworldly realms in both spatial and ontological dimensions.[194] In addition to allowing the soul to travel, dreams enable the soul to have conversations with God and to gain knowledge of the future. That is, both dreams and death can provide a person with access to divine knowledge, including regarding the temporal axis of reality, that the soul cannot apprehend under normal circumstances while in the body. Finally, the soul has 'right of kinship' with God, which I take to mean that the unfettered soul is like a divine being. This passage then also helps explain why Greek *oneiroi*, angels and souls of the dead are all acceptable dream messengers in the Hellenistic and Roman worlds: each is a type of spirit and thus is capable of entering the otherworldly space of people's dreams.

In fact, the themes of death and dreams are enmeshed in a variety of ways in dream texts of early Judaism, six of which I explicate here. First, the dead appear as dream messengers in some texts of early Judaism, which represents a complete departure from the Hebrew Bible, since the motif of receiving messages from the dead could easily smack of Graeco-Roman paganism or even of necromancy (1 Sam 28:8, 15). In

---

[194] This passage and others such as 4 Ezra 7:78, 100 serve as a warning against inferring bodily resurrection in early Jewish texts that do not explicitly posit the involvement of the body in the afterlife of the soul, such as Daniel 12 and *1 En.* 22–23.

contrast to biblical authors, Greek and Roman authors often revel in portraying the dead as dream messengers,[195] to such an extent that Aristophanes is able to mock the motif in a florid passage in *Ran.* 1331–1334:

> What vision of dreaming, Thou fire-hearted Night, Death's minion dark-gleaming, Hast thou sent in thy might? ... Black dead was his robe, and his eyes all blood, and the claws of him great; ... Yea, bring me a cruse of hot water, to wash off this vision of fate.

It is similar traditions from Greek and Roman dream texts, and not biblical traditions of dreaming, that clearly inform Josephus' accounts of the deceased appearing in dreams. In the dream of the 'unfaithful' Glaphyra, her husband appears in order to punish her infidelity and cause her death (*Ant.* 17.349–353, *J.W.* 2.114–116). Josephus likes the story so much he tells it twice, also telling a similar version of the story about a woman named Stratonica (*Ap.* 1.206–207). The dead in these dreams appear in order to punish. Conversely, in 2 Maccabees, the deceased priests Onias and Jeremiah appear to Judas Maccabee in a dream in order to give him confidence in his battles (2 Macc 15:11–27). Since Jeremiah hands him a golden sword, 'a gift from God,' these deceased dream figures are acting as messengers who promise divine sanction and protection of Judas.

Second, as in dreams from the ancient Near East, Greece and Rome,[196] some characters foresee their own death in dreams, as do Rebecca in *Jub.* 35:6 and Methuselah in *2 En.* 70, or else they foresee a family member's death, as in Isaac's dream of his father's and mother's impending deaths in *T. Abr.* 5–7. As I mentioned earlier, in early Judaism these dreams are best understood within a larger context of familial care, in that they seem to function for the benefit of family members. Rebecca's dream allows her to share the news with her son and to give his father proper instructions for Jacob's care. Methuselah's dream announces his imminent demise and also facilitates the conferral of priestly investiture on his son Nir. Isaac's dream helps him prepare for his parents' deaths, while gently introducing the topic to Abraham.

---

[195] E.g. Sophocles *El.* 410–425; Euripides *Hec.* 1–97; *Orestes* 618–620, *Alc.* 349, 356; Aeschylus *Eum.* 94–104, 155; *Pers.* 175–200; Virgil *Aen.* I.341–372, IV. 227–261; IV.326–360; V. 705–739; Suetonius *Lives* VI.46, VII.7.

[196] *Epic of Gilgamesh*; Aeschy. *Pers.* 175–200; Herodotus *Hist.* I.34–45, 209, III.124–125; V.55–6; Suetonius *Lives* I.81, III.74, IV.57.

Third, as in some biblical texts,[197] death itself is sometimes likened to sleep. This motif is especially prominent in *Testaments of the Twelve Patriarchs*, as in the following typical conclusion to one of the testaments: 'When [Zebulon] had said this, he fell into a beautiful sleep, and his sons placed him in a coffin' (*T. Zebulon* 10:6; cf. also *T. Simeon* 8:1; *T. Judah* 26:4; *T. Issachar* 7:9; *T. Dan* 7:1; *T. Gad* 8:4; *T. Asher* 8:1; *T. Joseph* 20:4; also *T. Job* 53:7). *Testament of Levi* equates death and dreaming more subtly, by placing the death scene explicitly in a bed, which as I have shown above is a typical formal introduction to a dream throughout antiquity:[198] 'He stretched out his feet on his bed and was gathered to his fathers' (*T. Levi* 19:4). Similarly, the shorter recension of *Testament of Abraham* directly compares death and dreaming, stating: 'God turned and *drew out the soul of Abraham as in a dream*, and the Commander-in-chief Michael took it into the heavens' (*T. Abr. B* 14:7).

Fourth, in early Judaism, death and dreams are both closely connected to ascent. Death may involve ascent, as is implied in the astral immortality developing in texts such as *1 En.* 108 and Dan 12:3, or as is evident in the image of Michael carrying Abraham's soul into the heavens 'as in a dream' (*T. Abr. B* 14:7, cf. *T. Job* 52:10–12). Similarly, in early Jewish texts such as *1 En.* 14–15 and Greek *T. Levi* 2–5, 8, dreams also entail heavenly ascent; thus both death and dreams are means of accessing heaven. A connection between dreams and ascent is expressed in other ways as well. Enoch's dream announces his impending ascent (*2 En.* 1), and prepares him for his eventual permanent ascent that replaces death[199] (*2 En.* 1:3–10, 70:3–13). Likewise, I argued above that the dreams of Ezra and Daniel lead to progressively greater visions, culminating eventually in ascent in the former case and astral immortality in the latter (*4 Ezra* 11:1–12:51; 13:1–14:26, 14:9; Dan 7–8, 12:3). In a different way, dreams also prefigure the eventual ascent of Baruch (*2 Bar.* 36:1–43:2, 53:1–76:3). After interpreting Baruch's dream of the alternating bright and dark waters as periods of cosmic history, the angel Ramael explains:

> Since the revelation of this vision has been explained to you as you prayed for, hear the word of the Most High that you know that which

---

[197] E.g. see 1 Kings 2:10; 11:43; 14:20; 14:31, and so forth.
[198] Oppenheim, *Interpretation*, 187.
[199] Cf. Bousset, *Die Himmelreise der Seele*, 5.

will happen to you after these things. For you will surely depart from this
world, nevertheless not to death but to be kept unto (the end) of times.

(*2 Bar.* 76:1–2).

The passage clearly connects Baruch's dream revelations with revelations of his imminent ascent; it might even be the case that since he can
understand the former he is rewarded with the latter.

Fifth, several pseudepigraphic figures give testamentary speeches in
which the bulk or an important part of the narrative includes retelling
a dream, including: Levi (*T. Levi*), Naphtali (*T. Naph.*), Joseph (*T. Joseph*),
Joshua (*L.A.B.* 23), and Phineas (*L.A.B.* 28:4) (cf. Enoch in *2 En.* 64–
67). Oddly enough, although testaments are not uncommon in other
cultures and in the Hebrew Bible,[200] it is rare for a dying person
to relate *a dream* in a testamentary speech, unless the dream directly
concerns a prediction of the dreamer's imminent death.[201]

Sixth and finally, dreams can provide knowledge of the realm of the
dead itself. Nickelsburg has already made it clear that when Enoch travels around the cosmos, he not only ascends to heaven, he sees remote
areas of earthly geography that concretize eschatological reward and
punishment, that is, 'cosmology undergirds eschatology.'[202] Enoch is
able, for instance, to see the mountain of the dead in which souls are
already separated (*1 En.* 22) and the trees in Eden of which the righteous will partake after judgment (*1 En.* 29–32). What I would add is
the importance of Enoch's dream state in facilitating this access: while
Enoch could not normally gain access to the realm of the dead as a
living human, like Kummaya of *A Vision of the Netherworld*, he is able to
gain knowledge of the realm of the dead and the afterlife in a dream
journey.

Thus, early Jewish dream texts are quite unlike biblical dreams in
their views of death. In biblical dreams the deceased do not appear as
messengers, dreamers do not gain access to the realm of the dead, and
dreamers do not foresee their own or other's imminent deaths. Dreams
are not narrated as part of biblical testaments, and no biblical dreams
prefigure or predict dreamers' ascents to heaven at death. Rather, with
respect to death and dreams, early Jewish dreams resonate culturally

---

[200] For a broader discussion of testaments see Collins, 'Testaments,' in *Jewish Writings*,
325–356.
[201] The closest example is when Enkidu narrates his dream of the underworld shortly
before he dies. See Oppenheim, *Interpretation*, 248–249, par. 8, nos. 6–7.
[202] Nickelsburg, 'Apocalyptic Construction of Reality,' 50–64

much more with ancient Near Eastern, Greek and Roman dreams than
they do with biblical ones.

However, one important difference remains between Jewish dream
texts on the one hand and pagan dreams on the other. Early Jewish
texts emphatically *do not* understand the underworld to be the source
of dreams; rather, dreams come from God who is in heaven. This
portrait is so familiar to us that we usually miss the uniqueness of
this formulation. H. Bientenhard and more recently M. Himmelfarb
have cogently argued that Hellenistic Judaism pictures the abode of
God as a throne-room/Temple in heaven.[203] It is important to note the
concomitant presupposition that the heavenly Temple is also the locus
of dreams and of angelic dream messengers who appear in people's
dreams. This notion contrasts quite sharply with the chthonic source
of dreams and dream messengers found widely in pagan sources, e.g.:
Epic of Gilgamesh; *Od.* 19:562ff., 4:808ff., 24:12; Aeschylus' *Pers.* 521–523;
Virgil's *Aen.* 6:282–284, and Ovid's *Metam.* XI.565–627.

Having thus sketched the broader portrait of how early Jewish authors relate the themes of death and dreams, I turn now to some
interesting expressions of this idea in three texts, *Testament of Abraham*,
Testament of Naphtali and *Testament of Joseph*.

Testament of Abraham

This text, which is not a true testament since it lacks an exhortatory
speech by Abraham, may reflect an Egyptian Jewish provenance from
about 100 C.E.[204] The main problem addressed by this story is that
Abraham stubbornly refuses to accept his mortality. God proposes to
solve the problem by giving Isaac a premonitory dream in which he
foresees his father's death (and in recension A, his mother's as well) as a
way of introducing the idea to Abraham as well as to Isaac, who cries
hysterically at the thought of losing his father (A 4:8, 5:8–14; B 4:16,
6:2–5).[205] The text interweaves the themes of dreams and death in more
ways than one, and bears careful consideration.

[203] H. Bietenhard, *Die himmlische Welt im Urchristentum und Spätjudentum* (Tübingen:
Mohr Siebeck, 1951), 53–70; Himmelfarb, *Ascent to Heaven*, 29–46.
[204] Sanders dates the testament to about 100 C.E., plus or minus 25 years, and thinks
the text was originally written in Greek in Egypt, *OTP* 1: 875. Roddy agrees, *Romanian
Version of the Testament of Abraham*, 1.
[205] G.W.E. Nickelsburg, 'Stories of Biblical and Early Post-Biblical Times,' in *Jewish
Writings of the Second Temple Period*, 33–88, 63.

As in *1 Enoch* 13:7–10, the introduction and conclusion of Isaac's dream are compressed and the narration of the dream's content follows later:[206]

> I. INTRODUCTION: Isaac is ready to sleep, and goes to his room to rest. (*T. Abr. A* 5:6; *B* 5:6)
>
> II. CONCLUSION: 'around the third hour of the night, Isaac woke up and rose from his couch' (A) '… crying out …' (B) (*T. Abr. A* 5:7; *B* 6:1–3)
>
> III. DREAM: symbolic dream of sun and moon ascending with an angel (*T. Abr. A* 7:1–7; *B* 7:1–15)
>
> IV. INTERPRETATION: provided by both Isaac and Michael (*T. Abr. A* 7:8–12; *B* 7:15–17)

Isaac's dream is a symbolic dream, only parts of which are interpreted, perhaps owing to the history of redaction. Isaac sees the sun, the moon and 'an enormous man,' representing Abraham, Sarah and an angel respectively (A 7:2–12; B 7:1–15).[207]

In both recensions, the dream not only foretells Abraham's (and in A, Sarah's) death, but also the ascent of his soul to heaven. In recension B Isaac says the man (angel) carries the sun from 'lowliness into height' (B 7:14), and in recension A, the man takes the sun from Isaac as 'he went up into the heavens, whence he had come' (A 7:4). Other early Jewish texts associate astral imagery with the transfiguration of the soul of the departed into an incorruptible state. For instance, 4 Ezra describes the souls of the righteous departed thusly: ' … their face is to shine like the sun, and how they are to be made like the light of the stars, being incorruptible from then on' (4 Ezra 7:98; Dan 12:3; *1 En.* 104:2).[208] However, the layering is even richer in *T. Abr.*, since it intertwines astral imagery, death and ascent with dreams. In

---

[206] The English translation of the A and B recensions are from E.P. Sanders, *The Testament of Abraham: A New Translation and Introduction*, in *OTP* 1:871–902.

[207] The moon is only clearly identified as Sarah in recension A. Note that the angel is large, like messengers in ancient Near Eastern dreams. Oppenheim, *Interpretation*, 189–190.

[208] In recension A, Isaac dreams that a light-bearing man takes up to heaven both the sun (representing Abraham) and the moon (representing Sarah) (7:1–9); cf. Gen 37:9. For the transformation of human beings into angels in early Judaism see the following: A. Segal, *Two Powers in Heaven: Early Rabbinic Reports about Christianity and Gnosticism* (Leiden: Brill, 1977), 188; J. Charlesworth, 'Portrayal of the Righteous as an Angel,' 135–151; Himmelfarb, *Ascent to Heaven*; C.R.A. Morray-Jones, 'Transformational Mysticism in the Apocalyptic-Merkabah Tradition,' *JJS* 43 (1992):1–31; and most recently Fletcher-Louis, *All the Glory of Adam*.

recension A, Isaac is illuminated (φωταγωγοῦντα) by the sun. Several scholars, including Dean-Otting, Delcor, and Dupont-Sommer, understand φωταγωγοῦντα as 'mystical language.'[209] Since in this recension other angels are called 'a light-bearing man,' including the angel in this dream (A 7:1–9; cf. 12:5, 9, 14; 13:1–2), the solar imagery applied to Abraham's soul indeed appears to evoke the idea of an angelic or divine nature.[210]

Another stratum of this dream involves the angel who accompanies the sun / Abraham's soul up to heaven. This role of a divine being *in dreams* has a long cultural history, judging from the fact that an Akkadian term for dying (*abālu*) is same as for the Dream God carrying (*abālu*) a dreamer.[211] Angels accompany people to heaven in other scenes in early Judaism (*2 En.* 3ff.; *T. Job* 52:10; *T. Abr. A* 9:8, *B* 8:3), but Isaac's dream in *T. Abr.* contextualizes this angelic transport in a dream. This constellation of ideas is also evident in at least two other texts in early Judaism: Gabriel carries Melchizedek away to Eden in Nir's dream in *2 Enoch* 72:3–10, and Joseph grasps a cherub and ascends into the heights in a symbolic dream in *T. Naphtali* 5:7.

The FULFILLMENT of Isaac's dream of the future ascent of Abraham's soul thus occurs in two ways in the ensuing story. First, Michael's interpretation of the dream is juxtaposed with Abraham's pre-death ascent to heaven, in which Michael the angel does in fact accompany Abraham to heaven (A 9:8; B 8:3), just as predicted in Isaac's dream. In this temporary ascent Abraham sees various scenes in heaven, including Abel portrayed as 'a wondrous man, bright as the sun, like unto a son of God' sitting on a throne[212] 'flashing like fire' (A 12:4–13:2); or in another recension, Adam sitting on 'a throne of great glory,' surrounded by angels (B 8:1–16).[213] Such scenes suggest the exaltation

---

[209] Dean-Otting, *Heavenly Journeys*, 191. A. Dupont-Sommer discusses the word in connection to 4 Macc, *Le quatrième livre des Maccabées, introduction, traduction et notes* (Paris: Bibliothéque des hautes études, 1939), 149; M. Delcor points out its usage in *T. Abr.* and *1QHymns* IV.27, Delcor, *Le Testament d'Abraham* (Leiden: Brill, 1973), 115.

[210] Compare the development of Moses' shining face from Exodus 34:29 in *4Q374* frag. 2 and Philo's *On Dreams*, 221–230.

[211] *CAD* A 1, 1: 10–31, 16–17, '*abālu*.' Also see Abusch, 'Ascent to the Stars in a Mesopotamian Ritual,' *Death, Ecstasy*, 15–38, 26.

[212] E. Wolfson argues that the goal of many ascent experiences is the enthronement of the *yored merkabah* that transforms him into an angelic being, 'Mysticism and the Poetic-Liturgical Compositions from Qumran,' *JQR* 85 (1994):185–202, 193.

[213] Abraham also sees Enoch functioning as the heavenly scribe (11:1–10, B), which I would argue on the basis of other early Jewish texts also involves exaltation (*1 Enoch* 12:3,

and enthronement of humans in heaven in clearly divine terms, both foreshadowing Abraham's final ascent at death and reinforcing the angelic/astral imagery in Isaac's dream.

Second, Isaac's dream is fulfilled at Abraham's death, when God 'turned and drew out the soul of Abraham as in a dream, and the Commander-in-chief Michael took it into the heavens' (B 14:7; cf. A 20:10–12). Thus Isaac's dream of Abraham's ascent to heaven with an angel is twice fulfilled in the story, and death is explicitly likened to dreaming.

Furthermore, the death scene in the longer version of *Testament of Abraham* knows and transposes other dream motifs as well. In recension A, the patriarch asks for a respite from the company of Death, saying: 'Leave me yet a little while, that I may rest on my couch' (*T. Abr. A* 20:4). As we have seen, lying on a bed or couch is the prototypical setting or introduction for dreams in all of ancient Near Eastern and Mediterranean antiquity.[214] However, as we have also seen in *T. Levi* 19:4, death scenes also occur while a person is lying in bed. Thus, given the pervasive associations between dreaming and beds on the one hand and dreaming and death on the other, Abraham lies down to rest, perchance to dream, but the reader is not surprised when he dies instead.

In addition, the manner in which death ensues is a dream trope itself. In this longer recension (A), Death says to Abraham, 'Come, kiss my right hand, and may cheerfulness and life and strength come to you' (A 20:8–9). This entire scene, from Abraham lying on a couch to Death standing nearby and Abraham touching the divine being in order to be strengthened, resonates with other early Jewish scenes of an angel touching a prostrate dreamer or visionary (Daniel 8:18, 10:10, 16 and 18; *2 Enoch* 22:6; and *4 Ezra* 5:14–15, 10:30).[215] The image has even closer parallels in the iconography and testimonials from Graeco-Roman dream cults, which depict divine beings like Asklepios reaching out and healing reclining dreamers by touch.[216] Knowing these intertextual references, the reader is rewarded even more through

---

15:1; *2 Enoch* 23:1–4, 40:13, 53:2, 64:5, 68:2).

[214] Oppenheim, *Interpretation*, 187.

[215] See Collins, *Daniel*, 338; Stone, *Fourth Ezra*, 115.

[216] LiDonnici, *Epidaurian Miracle Cures*, see for example nos. A3, A 18, B 11. See Hausmann, *Kunst und Heiltum*, plate 1; Kerényi, *Asklepios*, 35 (plate 18), see also 36, plate 19.

the clever inversion of the trope, since 'Death deceived Abraham' and Abraham's soul cleaves to Death's hand as a result of this action (A 20:9).[217]

Finally, this longer recension also evokes dream incubation in another scene, which is clearest in the Romanian version.[218] Abraham instructs Isaac to prepare a bedchamber for Michael and himself that is outfitted with several items that resemble the appurtenances of the Temple:

> Go into the room, my beloved son, and set up two beds. Prepare one for me to lie down upon, the other for this stranger, for he is a traveler. Arrange things very nicely, put candles in the candlesticks, set a beautiful table, and dress the beds in finest linen. Burn the best incense and take sweet-smelling herbs from the garden and bring them into the house for their fragrance. Then light seven candles …

> Pasă, fiiul mieu cel drag, în cămara de rădică doâ pâturi,
> și aşternă unul să mă culc eu iară în celalant streinul acesta, că iaste călătoriu.
> Și grijaşti foarte frumos şi pune lumănari în sfeşnice şi masa cea bună
> şi cearşafurile cele frumoase să purpre pături. Și să tămâe de cea cinstită
> şi ia iarbă cea mirositoare din raiu să aduci să pui în casa să mirosească.
> Și şa aprinzi şapte candele … (*Rom. T. Abr.* 10–12).[219]

Not only are representatives of the showbread table, the menorah lampstand, the linen of the priestly garments and incense present (see Exod 25–30), the mock temple[220] also includes beds on which to lie down. This bedchamber thus inventively evokes a temple setting of dream incubation, and the author plays on the trope in several clever ways. If Abraham were to incubate a dream in a real temple, he would likely have a message dream of an angel who would stand beside him. Of course, in the story Michael stands beside Abraham throughout this scene, but in disguise, which helps explain why the bedchamber is set up for them both. Also, as we have seen, the narrative image of a bed is almost always a cue that either a divinely-sent dream or a death will

---

[217] Perhaps we are to think of the scene in the *Aeneid* when the Sleep-God gives Palinurus a dream simply so that he might kill him, *Aen.* V.838–871.

[218] Roddy, *Romanian Version of the Testament of Abraham.*

[219] Ibid., 28–29. Recension A as translated by Sanders contains similar Temple imagery in chapter 4 and adds purple material and oil, but Recension B entirely lacks this emphasis in a similar passage in chapter 5. See *OTP* 1:883, 897.

[220] In *Joseph and Aseneth*, Aseneth's bedchamber is also depicted as a temple. See R.S. Kraemer, *Joseph and Aseneth: A Late Antique Tale of the Biblical Patriarch and his Egyptian Wife, Reconsidered* (New York: Oxford University Press, 1998), 119–120.

follow. Ironically, shortly after this scene Isaac receives a divinely-sent dream that predicts Abraham's death (*Rom. T. Abr.* 17–19).

Moreover, the same bed is the setting for Abraham's eventual death. In the Romanian version the tension builds near the end of the narrative as Abraham repeatedly tries to take his rest on his bed (45, 50, 52). Death (Moartea) follows him like a dog, sitting at his feet at the bed (45), following him to the bed again (50), and following him to the bed a third time as Abraham says: 'Go away from me awhile. I would like to lie down in my bed awhile, for I am worn out …' (*Rom. T. Abr.* 52, cf. 50). Once he lies on the bed,[221] the conventional setting of dreams as well as death, Abraham is tricked into kissing Death's hand, which results in his actual death (54).

Thus, in all of its recensions, *Testament of Abraham* is an inventive pastiche of dream traditions, altogether incorporating the following themes familiar from dream texts: the prediction of death in a dream; the prediction of ascent, both temporary and permanent, in a dream; dream incubation in a temple setting; and the healing role of a dream figure, inverted in the figure of Death.

Testaments of Twelve Patriarchs

The *Testaments of the Twelve Patriarchs* includes three testaments that contain dreams, namely, the *Testament of Levi*, *Testament of Naphtali* and *Testament of Joseph*. I have already discussed in depth Levi's two dreams at Abel-Maoul and Bethel. I simply note here that the narration of the two dreams of heavenly ascent and priestly investiture occur within the larger context of a testamentary speech given by Levi before he dies. Also, Levi's dreams share much with Methuselah's testamentary dream that invests his son Nir into the priesthood in *2 Enoch* 70:3–13, since both texts contain a priestly investiture in a dream, followed soon after by the death of the dreamer.[222] Like other dreamers in *T. Twelve* who 'sleep the eternal sleep,' Levi dies in bed, the same setting as dreams (*T. Levi* 19:4;

---

[221] In fact, in the Romanian version the tension builds as Abraham repeatedly tries to take his rest on his bed. Death follows him, sitting at his feet at the bed (45), following him to the bed again (50), and finally tricking him into kissing his hand as Abraham sits up in bed (52–54).

[222] Mathusalom [Methuselah] dies after his dream when 'he stretched out his hands to heaven … and … his spirit went out' (*2 En.* 70:16). See also Nir's dream, in which he told that Melchizedek will be a priest and that Gabriel 'will take the child and put him in the paradise of Edem [Eden],' which is probably in heaven (*2 En.* 71:28; 72:5).

cf. *T. Judah* 26:4, *T. Issachar* 7:9, *T. Zebulon* 10:6, *T. Dan* 7:1, *T. Gad* 8:4, *T. Asher* 8:2, and *T. Joseph* 20:4).

Testament of Naphtali contains a dream not commonly recognized as a heavenly ascent.[223] In Naphtali's fortieth year, (a number resonating with biblical significance), he has a symbolic dream (5:1–8). The regular formal frame of dreams is missing, but this visionary episode and the next are explicitly called dreams (τὰ δύο ἐνύπνια) (7:1). In this dream, 'the sun and the moon stood still,' and as in the case of *T. Abr.* the solar imagery is evocative of angels or divinity. Isaac tells his sons to run and grab them 'according to his capacity.'[224] Levi grasps the sun and Judah the moon,[225] and each undergoes a transformation, becoming like the sun and the moon (5:1–4; cf. 4Ezra 7:98). These metamorphoses indicate transformation into an angel (cf. *2En.* 22, *T. Levi* 8).[226] The transformed figures of Levi and Judah are associated with symbols of exaltation and rule, (probably priestly and royal), since an angel or 'young man' gives Levi twelve date palms, while a luminous Judah has twelve rays under his feet (5:4–5).

A bull with two great horns and eagle's wings, most likely representing a cherub, also appears in the dream (*T. Naph.* 5:6; cf. Ezek 1–3, *1En.* 85–90, Dan 7). Naphtali sees that neither Levi nor Judah can catch the cherub, but Joseph overtakes them and 'seized [the bull] and went up with him into the heights' (5:7). If the animal is indeed a cherub then ascent is quite clear, and *merkabah* imagery is probable (Ezek 1–3, 8–10; cf. *T. Abr.* A 9:8; *T. Job* 52:11). The thesis that the animal symbol is an angel of some kind is strengthened even more in light of wide-ranging intertextual traditions from Assyrian dream-books that explain the meaning of seizing various animals in symbolic dreams as follows: 'If he seizes a lion/wolf/fox/cat/snake/he-goat/ram/female dog: he will have a protective angel.'[227] Naphtali himself also appears to attain a dream ascent, since he states: 'And I looked, *since I was there*, and

---

[223] This text is not labeled an ascent by Bietenhard, *Die himmlische Welt*, Dean-Otting, *Heavenly Journeys*, or Himmelfarb, *Ascent to Heaven*. Fletcher-Louis has noted the solar imagery and its relation to the priesthood, *All the Glory of Adam*, 46.

[224] Cf. Gen 37:9 and *T. Abr.* 7:4ff.

[225] The discussion of the number, nature and relation of messiahs in the text is subject to the discussions of date and provenance. See the bibliography in Collins, 'Testaments,' 354, and especially Hultgård, *L'eschatologie*, 15–81.

[226] See Segal, *Two Powers*; Himmelfarb, *Ascent to Heaven*; Morray-Jones, 'Transformational Mysticism'; Charlesworth, 'Portrayal of the Righteous'; and Fletcher-Louis, *All the Glory of Adam*.

[227] *Assyrian Dream-Book*, fragment of 'Tablet B,' in Oppenheim, *Interpretation*, 281.

behold a sacred writing appeared to us [to Naphtali and Joseph] …'
(5:8).[228] Thus, the dream not only provides a mechanism for ascent to
the heavenly realm, but also provides Naphtali and his brothers with
esoteric knowledge in the form of heavenly tablets (cf. *Jub.* 32:21–26 and
4QApocryphon Jacob (4Q537 [4QAJa ar]) frag. 1), which they are able to
read.[229] The contextualization of the dream within a testament makes
the dream's content revelation for Naphtali's sons.

Naphtali relates a second symbolic dream in his testament that is an
eschatological dream that again singles out Joseph, Levi and Judah.
Like the first dream, it is left uninterpreted, although the meaning
is understood by Jacob (*T. Naph.* 6:1–10, 7:1). In the larger scheme
of ancient dream traditions, this is unusual and should be considered unpropitious.[230] Yet other examples, such as *1 Enoch* 85–90, do
occur in early Judaism. I suggest that in these exceptional cases, interpretation becomes part of the audience's privileged, esoteric revelation.

Testament of Joseph

Like the *Testament of Levi* and *Testament of Naphtali*, the *Testament of Joseph*
is also concerned with heavenly ascent, but its presentation in the form
of an uninterpreted symbolic dream makes precise identification of the
subjects of the ascent difficult (19:1–12).[231] As in the case of *Testament of
Naphtali*, the referents were surely known by the intended audience.

Joseph's dream, an ἐνυπνίων (19:1), contains animal imagery like
T. Naphtali, *1 Enoch* 85–90 and Daniel 7–8. Most of the referents are
unclear to me, but at one point:

> … twelve bulls were nursing from one cow, who furnished a sea of milk.
> The twelve herds and the innumerable herds drank from it. And the
> *horns of the fourth bull ascended to heaven and became as a rampart for the herds.*
>
> (19:3–7)

---

[228] Oppenheim, *Interpretation*, 250.

[229] For scribal activity (reading or writing) in dreams in other texts, see Dan 7; 4 Ezra
14:40–48; *2 En.* 23:4–6, 36:3; *1 En.* 15:1, 13:10, 33:4; cf. *Jub.* 32:21–26 and *4QApoc. Jac.*
(*4Q537 [4QAJa ar]*) frag. 1.

[230] Oppenheim, 'Mantic Dreams,' 349–350.

[231] Kee includes two recensions of Joseph's dream, a long and a short one that follow
different manuscripts; see *OTP* 1:824–825. This text is also excluded from the studies on
ascent by Bietenhard, Dean-Otting and Himmelfarb, perhaps due to its cryptic nature.

Although any interpretation should remain tentative, in the context
of the collection of testaments the twelve male bulls definitely sound
like the twelve sons of Jacob. In this case, the twelve herds and the
innumerable herds would be the twelve tribes of Israel and the Gentile
nations. If this interpretation holds, the fourth bull would then be
Judah, the fourth son of Jacob and Leah and subject of the fourth
testament. However, although Judah is clearly associated with a special
royal authority inferior to Levi's priestly authority in the testaments, he
is never mentioned in the context of ascent.[232] In fact, in the *Testament
of Judah* he clearly states, 'To me he gave earthly matters and to Levi
heavenly matters' (*T. Judah* 21:3). In Joseph's dream, though, it is not
the fourth bull or Judah that ascends, but rather his two horns. The
referents of the two horns, which also appear in *Testament of Naphtali*,
cannot definitively be determined,[233] but in any case the motif of ascent
is present. Moreover, the ascent seems to pave the way for the later
ascent of 'the herds,' perhaps the Gentile nations, whether the referent
is mystical ascent or ascent of the soul at death (19:6). Finally, Joseph
dies in a manner evocative of a dream: 'he stretched out his feet and
fell into a beautiful sleep' (20:4).

Overall, then, numerous early Jewish texts intertwine death, dreams,
and ascent to heaven in a variety of ways. In *T. Levi*, *T. Naph.* and
T. Jos., dreams of ascent are part of the testamentary speeches that
patriarchs relate to their sons before dying. The *Testament of Abraham*
weaves a dream ascent, a literal ascent during Abraham's lifetime and
his death in myriad ways. Underlying all of these complex associations
seems to be the image of death as sleep: both death and dreams provide
access to heaven, which exists as both a spatial and an ontological zone.
While other cultures share some of these ideas concerning death and
dreams, early Jewish texts contrast sharply with the ancient Near Eastern and Graeco-Roman conception of the underworld as the home of
dreams in depicting heaven is the sole source of dreams and of angelic
dream messengers. Finally, since early Jewish texts do consistently link
the heavenly Temple with dreams, priestly scenes as well as temple settings abound in many dream texts, whether overtly as in Enoch and

---

[232] *T. Naph.* 5:3; *T. Judah* 21:3, 4; Hultgård, *L'eschatologie*, 15–81, 268–381.

[233] Possibilities include Levi and Joseph, both of whom are singled out for special
ascents in the dreams in the testaments, or Joseph and Naphtali, who ascend together
in *T. Naph.* (*T. Levi* 2:5–5:7; *T. Naph.* 5:6); alternatives also include the kingdoms of Israel
and Judah, Ephraim and Manasseh, or a later Christian redaction referring to Jesus
and King David, both of the tribe of Judah.

Levi's ascents to the heavenly Temple in dreams (*1 En.* 14–15; *2 En.* 3ff.; *T. Levi* 2–5), or more subtly, as in the *hekhal*-like bedchamber in *T. Abraham*.

Summary of Dreams in Hellenistic Judaism

Early Jewish authors are profoundly interested in dreams, with over one hundred dreamers appearing in the apocrypha, pseudepigrapha, Qumran scrolls and writings of Josephus. The dreams exhibit the conventional vocabulary, forms and functions of ancient Near Eastern, biblical and Greek and Roman dreams, but a broad synchronic and diachronic approach has illuminated some distinctive contours as well. Many Jewish dream texts creatively elaborate on traditional depictions of the otherworldly dream journey, dream messengers, dreamers, and death, spinning them within an overarching worldview that is distinctively Jewish.

To be more precise, dream narratives in Hellenistic Judaism both construct and deconstruct symbolic orderings of the world. Their contents articulate categories that order cosmological, temporal and ontological reality, revealing a heavenly sphere above earth, a present related to Israel's past, and visible angels who bridge the gap between an invisible divine and the human realm. At the same time however, dreams also allow for the imaginative transcendence of these categories, since dreamers are not bound by space, time, or bodily constraints. Through their dreams, the righteous of Israel may leave earth and ascend to heaven, glimpse the future, mix freely with angels, or even become angels themselves.

PART THREE

CHAPTER FIVE

REFLECTIONS AND IMPLICATIONS

> Form ever follows func-
> tion.
>
> —Louis Henry Sullivan

The dreams examined in this study are social projects[1] as well as the creations of individual authors. Our post-Freudian conceptions of dreaming cannot be applied to ancient literary motifs of divinely-sent dreams, at least not without contorting and missing much of what ancient authors were trying to communicate. To ancient authors, divinely-sent dreams were coded messages about the future from the divine realm, actual visits from deities, or messages imparted by voices or messengers of the deities. No hard boundary existed between the imaginative realm of sleep and the objective realm of waking reality, and one could 'awaken' to find a dream messenger from inside one's dream standing there in one's waking state. Whatever physio-psychological dreams the authors of ancient dream texts may have had, the literary depictions of divinely-sent dreams followed dream patterns that were well-known from Mesopotamia to Rome, and shared by early Jewish authors.

Despite the enormous resonance between non-Jewish and early Jewish dreams, the latter also contain many innovations particular to a Jewish audience. Dreamers are figures from Israel's sacred past who share familial ties with the audiences of the texts; thus, the receipt of divine sanction or knowledge by the pseudepigraphic dreamers entails divine blessings and revelation their Jewish audience. Moreover, Jewish dream texts elaborate on traditional depictions of the otherworldly dream journey, angelic dream interpreters, and dreamers within a *Weltanschauung* in which God sends dreams from the throne in the heavenly *hekhal* and in which earthly and heavenly priests and scribes figure prominently.

---

[1] P. Berger and R. Luckmann, *The Social Construction of Reality* (Garden City, NY: Doubleday-Anchor, 1967).

This wide-ranging project has touched on many related areas of investigation. In this final chapter, I reflect on some of the literary and social implications of my study of dreams for the related topics of form-criticism, priestly and scribal roles in early Judaism, apocalypticism, and early Jewish mysticism.

One: Form-Criticism, Individual Artistry and 'Sitzen'

By definition, form-criticism allows for the identification of what is typical across groups of texts, and we have seen that ancient literary depictions of divinely-sent dreams, including early Jewish dreams, follow rather rigid formal patterns of message dreams, symbolic dreams, and their subtypes. At the same time, form-criticism can also facilitate our recognition of innovations made to typical forms in particular texts,[2] thereby enhancing our appreciation of the sophistication and aesthetics of early Jewish authors.

To take but one example: it is axiomatic in antiquity that symbolic dreams require interpretation. Yet while symbols were typically interpreted by qualified professionals throughout the ancient Near Eastern and Mediterranean worlds, in early Jewish literature dreams are interpreted by a range of human intermediaries, some priestly and some not. What distinguishes them is that they are heroes from Israel's sacred history (Daniel in Dan 2, 4; Enoch in *4Q Book of Giants*, Mahalel in *1En.* 83:8–9; Jethro in *Ezek. Trag.*, Mordecai in *Add. Esth.* 10:4–9; Josephus in *J.W.* 3:351–354 and *Life* 208–210). In addition, dream symbols may also be interpreted during or after the dream by angels (4Ezra 4:50, 10:29–54; *2Bar.* 55:3–74:4; *T. Abr.* A 7:8, B 7:15; *Ladd. Jac.* 3–6) or indeed by the LORD (4Ezra 12:10–39, 13:21–56; *2Bar.* 39:1–40:4), particularly when dream symbols are reconfigured as unusual sights in heaven or in mythic parts of the earth (e.g. *1En.* 14–36, Dan 7–8, *T. Levi* 2–5, 4Ezra 9–10, *Ladd. Jac.* 1–2). At other times dream 'symbols' are words written on heavenly tablets (*T. Napht.* 5); these are also usually interpreted by angels (*Jub.* 32, *4Q Apocr. Jac.*; cf. Dan 5). Finally, at least two texts (Dan 7–12 and 4Ezra) organize elements of symbolic dreams and

---

[2] Some recent authors who have called for increased attention to form criticism's illumination of artistic elements in texts are Campbell, 'Form Criticism's Future,' 23; Blum, '*Formgeschichte*,' 43–44; and particularly Melugin, 'Recent Form Criticism Revisited,' 46–64.

their interpretations, along with other dream types and waking visions, within overarching schema that depict seers steadily progressing in their capacities to receive revelation.

In addition to highlighting creative formulations of traditional patterns, form-criticism is also able to shed some light on how ancient readers interact with texts.[3] For instance, the example of symbolic dreams in apocalypses is a particularly fertile opportunity for attending to how meaning is constructed by ancient readers. I have argued that in the case of 4 Ezra, the success of the 'progress of the seer' schema turns on the formal characteristics of the symbolic dream, which are able to evoke for the reader (both ancient and modern) a sensory rich, emotive response. Rich visual symbols and a thick accumulation of the phrases 'I saw ... and I heard ...',[4] allow readers to picture the eschaton vividly, providing a sort of proleptic experience that contributes to confidence in the veracity of the predictions. Moreover, the nature of symbols is that they are multivalent, so that the symbol is always larger than the interpretation provided in the narrative, allowing a broad range of interpretive possibilities by the readership.[5] Understanding the formal characteristics of symbolic dreams thus sheds some light on the role of the ancient readers in producing meaning.

Finally, this study demonstrates that some forms, such as dreams, allow room for enormous creativity. Dream logic allows for the traversing of spatial, temporal and ontological boundaries such that *within the confining dream frame, almost anything imaginable is logical.* I suggest that the use of this literary form, along with varying degrees of permeability to Graeco-Roman dream motifs, significantly catalyzed the rich variety of early Jewish stories of access to otherworldly realms. More so

---

[3] Most critics understand 'reader-response' as it applies to the modern reader as interpreter. See Boorer, 'Kaleidoscopic Patterns and the Shaping of Experience,' in *Changing Face of Form-Criticism*, 199–216, esp. 213. However, in calling for more attention to reader-response criticism, R. Melugin calls E. Ben Zvi's work on Micah an example of 'reader-response' in the sense that Ben Zvi tries to ascertain how ancient readers construct meaning. E. Ben Zvi, *Micah* (FOTL 21B; Grand Rapids, MI: Eerdmans, 2000), 5–10; Melugin, 'Recent Form Criticism Revisited,' 46–64.

[4] ' *Et vidi ... et ecce*' occurs repeatedly the Ezra's symbolic dreams: 4 Ezra 11:2, 5, 7, 10, 12, 20, 22, 24, 28, 33, 36, 44; 12:1, 2, 3, 11, 17, 19, 22, 26, 29, 30, 31, 35; 13:3, 5, 8, 10, 12, 20, 25, 27, 32, 39, 47, 51, 53.

[5] Both W. Harnisch and M. Stone have noted that Uriel's interpretations of Ezra's symbolic dreams do not address all the elements therein, and in the second symbolic dream (13:1) there are elements in the interpretation that have little basis in the dream. Harnisch, *Verhängnis und Verheißung*, 253–254; Stone, *Fourth Ezra*, 362, 396.

than any other ancient culture, early Judaism explores the theme of
dream access to otherworldly realms in a remarkable array of formulas:
through ascent or travel of dreamers; by means of the descent of angels,
the LORD, Zion, heavenly tablets, or ascended dreamers; through perceptual shifts of dreamers in *Wecktraumen*; or via ontological changes in
dreamers.

Form-Criticism and Settings

The phrase *Sitz im Leben*, which Gunkel coined to indicate the social
setting of a *Gattung* or the 'typical communication situations of genres'[6] rather than of individual texts, is sometimes used rather loosely in
form-critical studies. Several recent critics have pointed to the importance of allowing for multiple 'settings,' for content, author, and especially reader.[7] Clearly, attending to our own social location as post-
Freudian readers is crucially important if we are to avoid imposing
our own conceptions of dreaming (as an interior, subjective, imaginative phenomenon) on dreams in antiquity. Indeed, in the case of early
Jewish dreams, multiple settings of content, author and ancient reader
deserve consideration, which are not limited to Gunkel's sense of a *Sitz
im Leben*.

The controlling formal frame of early Jewish dreams has multiple
settings: literary, individual, and social. The antecedent *literary* settings
have been well established in Part One of this study; the formal patterns
of message dreams and symbolic dreams have an enduring history
in ancient Near Eastern, biblical, Greek and Roman literary as well
as cultic sources. Within Hellenistic Judaism, these inherited dream
forms are in turn 'set' within a wide range of genres (or larger literary
compositions as wholes), including histories, midrashic retellings of the
Bible, apocalypses, autobiography, gospel, and testaments.

By the *individual* setting of the dream frame, I mean to indicate
that every person dreams, including ancient authors and readers. R.
Knierim has argued that the typicality of certain forms may arise

---

[6] This is E. Blum's phrase, '*Formgeschichte* – A Misleading Category?,' 35; see also
M.J. Buss, who notes it pertains in Gunkel to 'the home ... of a genre, not the context
of a particular text.' Buss, *Biblical Form Criticism in Context* (JSOT Sup 274; Sheffield:
Sheffield Academic Press, 1999), 234.

[7] H.C.P. Kim, 'Form Criticism in Dialogue with Other Criticisms,' in *Changing Face
of Form Criticism*, 85–106, 96–97; W. Lee, 'The Exclusion of Moses from the Promised
Land: A Conceptual Approach,' in *Changing Face of Form Criticism*, 217–239, 218–219.

from 'underlying matrices which the human mind generates,' rather than from specific socio-religious settings.[8] The literary fiction of the divinely-sent dream articulates an extraordinary experience in terms of an ordinary experience of dreaming that is both individual and shared on a subjective level. Thus, the frame contains elements from *the real life settings of dreams* most people encounter: someone lies down to sleep, their dream includes visual and auditory elements, the dreamer's ego or notion of self is somehow present in the dream, the dreamer awakens with emotions or reflections, the dreamer stands up in the morning. *I am in no way suggesting that specific dream frames or dreams in Hellenistic Jewish texts are actual dreams that have been recorded.* Even in the Graeco-Roman dream cults, in which actual dreaming purportedly takes place, the articulation of dreams follows well-established, rigid patterns; thus the original dream, if there was ever one, is largely unrecoverable.[9] Rather, I am arguing that although not all of us will pronounce a prophetic oracle or utter a casuistic law, we all do dream. Therefore, the form present in the dream frame reflects to some extent the shared physio-psychological event of ordinary dreaming, and this accounts in part for the shape and constancy of the form across cultures for millennia as well as for its continued resonance with readers.

On another level, there is also a *social Sitz im Leben* of the dream frame in the Gunkelian sense. Oppenheim posited that the literary form of message dreams was ultimately inspired by a cultic setting of incubation, in which the incubant slept at the foot of the god's statue.[10] Moreover, we know from royal records in the ancient Near East that kings and priests did incubate dreams using prescribed rituals, and in the Hellenistic and Roman empires a range of citizens of both genders did the same, although the articulation of dreams is highly stylized. Thus, we are not dealing with a wholly literary phenomenon and the communication situation of the genre as a whole may be cultic. Specifically, we have cultic evidence that incubants sought out divinely-sent dreams for the purposes of receiving knowledge, healing and divine sanction, the very dream functions we find expressed in

---

[8] R.P. Knierim, 'Old Testament Form Criticism Reconsidered,' *Int* 27 (1973):435–468

[9] See the Epidaurian *iamata* from the Asklepios cult in Edelstein, *Asclepius* or LiDonnici, *Epidaurian Miracle Inscriptions*.

[10] Oppenheim does not suggest that all message dreams are incubated, only that the pattern of the incubated dream became 'theologically acceptable' and thus a literary paradigm, *Interpretation*, 190.

literature. The cultic evidence thus provides a context for any move
we might make from literary functions of dreams to social settings and
functions of dreaming.

In addition to these settings of the *dream frame*, the interior *dreams*
also have their own multiple 'settings' in Hellenistic Judaism on literary, individual and social levels. On the *literary* level, each dream functions in particular ways within each larger text as a whole, which I
have explored to an extent in certain cases, such as 4 Ezra, Daniel 7–
12, and *T. Abr.* Although many fine commentaries exist on early Jewish dream texts, additional investigations of the literary relationships
between dream units and whole texts in light of the synchronic worldview evinced by early Jewish dreams would be worthwhile.

Another setting of dreams (as opposed to dream frames) is the *individual* setting of particular dream stories, which raises the question in
many instances of actual practices behind the dreams in early Judaism.
Despite some insights from psychological studies on mysticism and the
induction of dreams,[11] it is my current position that although everyone
dreams, any 'real' instances of authorial dreams lie outside the scope of
historical, social or literary investigation. My position calls for explanation, since J. Lindblom and C. Rowland do think that certain apocalyptic visions or dreams are transmissions of actual visions or dreams
experienced by the authors.[12] In discussing the Book of Revelation,
Lindblom provides eight indicators of genuine visionary experiences,
including: 1) spontaneity; 2) concise visions which are only expanded
later; 3) dreamlike character of the experience: the vision may be clear
in its detail but as a whole has an unreal and fantastic quality; 4) the
vision is entirely fresh and unsophisticated in its form and content; 5)
the vision concerns things on an other-worldly plane; 6) there are difficulties in expressing the experience in words; 7) the experience has

---

[11] For example, D. Merkur has explored the induction of ecstatic states and dream
visions and concludes that the apocalypticists's rituals have a basis in actual practice.
He maintains the act of weeping and mourning may have 'induced an alternate psychic
state by manipulating the bipolar structure of the superego.' D. Merkur, 'The Visionary
Practices of Jewish Apocalyptists,' in *Psychoanalytic Study of Society* (vol. 14; eds. L.B. Boyer
and S.A. Grolnick; Hillsdale, NJ: Analytic Press, 1989), 119–148.

[12] J. Lindblom, *Gesichte und Offenbarungen: Vorstellungen von göttlichen Weisungen und über-
natürlichen Erscheinungen im ältesten Christentum* (Lund: Gleerup, 1968), 218ff., as cited in
Rowland, *Open Heaven*, 214–247, 232–236. Cf. D. Halperin, 'Heavenly Ascension in
Ancient Judaism: The Nature of the Experience,' in *SBL Seminar Papers 1987* (Atlanta:
Scholars Press, 1987): 230.

emotional side-effects and 8) mention is made of the date and place
of the vision. Rowland accepts all these criteria except the first and
the fifth.[13] Unfortunately, the majority of these criteria apply to many
of the dreams we have examined in antiquity, particularly the third—
a 'dreamlike' or 'unreal' quality.[14] Penelope's symbolic dream of the
geese killed by an eagle may serve as an example of a dream that
fulfills all but perhaps the fifth criterion of an otherworldly plane (*Od.*
19.534), but no one suggests 'Homer' or 'Penelope' actually dreamt that
dream.

Even D. Halperin, who rejects most of Lindblom and Rowland's criteria, accepts that some visions are literary records of 'real' visions, by
which he means subjectively perceived psychological hallucinations as
distinguished from 'fantasy' or consciously composed literary visions.[15]
Halperin provides only one criterion for identifying genuine visions preserved in ascent texts: 'Do the images used by the writer have symbolic meanings which, when deciphered, yield a more or less coherent
and convincing interpretation, but which the writer gives no indication he is *consciously* (my italics) aware of?'[16] Clearly, this criterion is
fraught with difficulty and ignores the subjectivities of today's readers
and their interpretive roles in producing meaning.[17] Thus, although it is
certainly possible that specific, physio-psychological dreams lie behind
literary accounts in early Judaism, in most cases they remain inacces-
sible.

The most secure information we possess for the actual dreams of
an individual early Jewish author arises in Josephus' autobiographical
reports of his own dreams, although we should not underestimate
the degree of political propaganda and stylization of the reports. In

---

[13] Rowland, *Open Heaven*, 235–236.

[14] The adjective 'unreal' betrays a modern interpretive stance of dreaming.

[15] Surprisingly, in arguing *against* a background of ecstatic trance for material in
visionary reports, Halperin posits dreams as a possible source, although it is unclear
why dreams should be any more likely a source than trance. Halperin, 'Heavenly
Ascension,' 230.

[16] Halperin, 'Heavenly Ascension,' 218–232, 226.

[17] Halperin's own example of Revelation 12:13–18 aptly illustrates the inherent prob-
lems. Since he finds sexual imagery in the earth opening up to swallow the river that
comes from the dragon's mouth, an interpretation apparently unbeknownst to the biblical author on a conscious level, the passage fulfills his stated criterion and passes as
a real visionary experience. But this is to ignore the role of the reader, and one may
instead ask how Halperin's innate subjectivity as a post-Freudian reader leads him to
construct meanings unknown (consciously or unconsciously) to the author. Halperin,
'Heavenly Ascension,' 226.

Life, Josephus relates a self-aggrandizing message dream that clearly functions to impart divine sanction:

> That night I beheld a marvelous vision in my dreams (ὄνειρον). I had retired to my couch, grieved and distraught by the tidings in the letter, when I thought that there stood by me one who said: 'Cease, man from they sorrow of heart, let go all fear. That which grieves thee now will promote thee to greatness and felicity in all things. Not in these present trials only, but in many besides, will fortune attend thee. Fret not thyself then. Remember that thou must even battle with the Romans.' (*Life* 208–210)

The dream messenger assures Josephus of favor, fortune and protection, traditional functions of divinely-sent dreams in cult as well as literature.

In another text, Josephus also reports he has 'nightly dreams' in which 'God had foretold to him the impending fate of the Jews and the destinies of the Roman sovereigns' (*J.W.* 3.351–352). The point cannot be missed that Josephus was directed by God in one dream to battle the Romans, and in others to surrender, as Gnuse states: 'One becomes suspicious that Josephus uses these dream reports to justify the rather vacillatory direction of his military career.'[18] Again, we must be careful in claiming access to his original dreams even here, but the passage is still illuminating:

> ἦν δὲ καὶ περὶ κρίσεις ὀνείρων ἱκανὸς συμβαλεῖν τὰ ἀμφιβόλως ὑπὸ τοῦ θείου λεγόμενα τῶν γε μὴν ἱερῶν βίβλων οὐκ ἠγνόει τὰς προφητείας ὡς ἂν αὐτός τε ὢν ἱερεύς καὶ ἱερέων ἔγγονος.   (*J.W.* 3.352)

Since the 'nightly dreams' require interpretation, they are most likely symbolic dreams. Several points of this interpretation necessitate a remark. First, Josephus seems to explain his ability to interpret dreams in terms of his priestly lineage. Second, it is extremely rare for someone to interpret one's *own* dream. Given the defensive, propagandistic nature of his autobiographical accounts, Josephus probably includes this element to enhance his own stature as a remarkably gifted interpreter.[19] Third, Josephus apparently identifies interpretation of the sayings of God as a priestly capacity. The activity of interpretation can apply to dreams, in which God communicates with humans, as well as to the prophetic books, through which God also communicates with humans.

---

[18] Gnuse, *Josephus*, 198.
[19] Ibid., 24–27, 137–138.

Even accounting for Josephus' propagandistic leanings, working backwards from literary dream content of dreams throughout his books to the author's *Sitz im Leben* furnishes us with much of the same information that he himself provides us with in his autobiographical writings. Of around forty dreams in his writings, nine are by priests (*J.W.* 3.351–354, *Ant.* 2.212–217, 5.348–350, 6.37–40, 6.332, 11.326–328, 13.322, 17.166; *Life* 208–210) and several more dream accounts display priestly themes, including: non-priests offering sacrifices (*Ant.* 1.183–185, 1.278–284, 1.341–342, 2.63–73, 8.22–25; cf. a priest offering sacrifice in 11.326–328), a prediction of the priesthood of Aaron (*Ant.* 2.212–217), a prediction of the building of the Temple (*Ant.* 7.92–93), the covenant with Solomon regarding the Temple (*Ant.* 8.125–129), Amenophis' dream in which Isis rebukes him for destroying her temple (*Ap.* 1.289), a case of apparent incubation in which the High Priest Jaddus sacrifices and then sleeps (*Ant.* 11.326–328), and the appearance of the High Priest in a dream (*Ant.* 11.333–335). Thus, roughly half of the dreams can be said to concern priestly matters, while practically all the remaining dreams are those of rulers or wives of rulers. If we were extrapolating to a social location we might well conclude Josephus was familiar with priestly and royal settings; and indeed, Josephus tells us he is of priestly lineage (*J.W.* 3.351–354) and an advisor of Vespasian (*J.W.* 3.400–402).

Again, working backwards from dream forms, we might note that an abundance of symbolic dreams abounds, requiring interpretation from a professional intermediary (*J.W.* 1.328, 2.112–113, 3.315–354; *Ant.* 1.341–342, 2.63–73, 2.75–86, 5.218–222, 10.194–211, 10.216–217, 13.322, 14.451, 17.345–348). As I mentioned earlier, several scholars maintain that priests interpreted dreams in early Judaism,[20] although Sanders is probably correct when he cautiously states that both priests and non-priests probably interpreted dreams in this period.[21] Josephus does appear to take pride in his ability to 'read' both interpretations of dreams and Scripture, and he connects this ability to his priestly lineage (*J.W.* 3.351–354).

Finally, these conclusions about Josephus' priestly and scribal *Sitz im Leben* lead us to the final setting to be considered, the wider *social setting of the authors of the dream stories*. We have repeatedly seen that priestly and

[20] Schwartz, *Josephus*, 70; Mason, *Flavius Josephus*, 269; idem, 'Priesthood in Josephus,' 659; Lindner, *Die Geschichtsauffassung*, 52–53. Cf. Bilde, *Flavius Josephus*, 190.
[21] Sanders, *Judaism: Practice and Belief*, 172.

scribal concerns permeate dreams in early Judaism. However, the move from a literary theme to positing a social setting requires amassing a 'thick description' from a variety of angles.[22]

Two: Social Location of Dream Authors, Priestly and Scribal Settings

The literary evidence clearly suggests that most dreams in early Judaism evince priestly concerns. Repeatedly, we have seen priests who dream (Josephus in *J.W.*; Amram, Samuel, Jaddus, Hyrcanus and Matthias in *Ant.*; Josephus in *Life*; Ezra in *4 Ezra*; Baruch in *2 Bar.*; Samuel in *L.A.B.*; Levi in *T. Levi*; Methuselah, Nir and Melchizedek in *2 En.*), dreamers who become priests in their dreams (*2 En.* 22; *T. Levi* 8), dreamers who perform sacrifices in connection with dreams (Abraham in *Jub.* 14 and *1QGenesis Apocryphon* [1Q20] col. XIX, XXI; Levi in *Jub.* 32:9, 16; Jacob in *Ant.* 1.278–284, *Jub.* 32; Methuselah in *2 En.* 69, cf. 59), dreamers who enter the heavenly temple (*1 En.* 13:7–36:4; *4QEnoch^a* (*4Q201* [*4QEn^aar*]); *T. Levi* 2:5–5:7 and 8:1–19; probably *4QAramaic Levi^a* (*4Q213*[*4QTLevi^aar*]) frag. 1, col. II; *4 Ezra* 9:38–10:37; cf. *Ezek. Trag.* vv. 68–82); dreamers who incubate dreams at the past, present or future site of the Jerusalem Temple (*2 Bar.* 34–36; *Ant.* 11.326–328; *2 En.* 69:4); angelic functionaries of the heavenly *hekhal* who interpret dreams or elements within dreams (Dan 7:16–28, 8:15–26; *Jub.* 32:22; *4 Ezra* 4:1, 5:31, 7:1, 10:29; *Ladd. Jac.* 3:4–7:35; *2 Bar.* 55:3; *T. Levi* 2:7–5:6; *1 En.* 19:1, 21:5, 9, 27:2, 33:4, 22:3, 5, 32:5, 23:4, 24:6–25:6, 27:2–4, 32:6) or who impart healing touches to dreamers (Dan 8:18; *2 En.* 22:6; *4 Ezra* 5:14–15, 10:30); and even priests who appear in dreams (*Ant.* 11:333–335, a living high priest; and *2 Macc* 15, two deceased priests, one of whom is a high priest). Although not every motif appears in every dream I have examined, the early Jewish dream corpus as a whole is clearly saturated with priestly concerns.

This overall emphasis on priestly themes takes on particular contours according to dream type. Many message dreams in which the LORD is the messenger are retellings of biblical accounts suggestive of

---

[22] B. Longenecker sums up the dilemma nicely: 'On the one hand, there remains the danger of a simplistic "referential fallacy"—the assumption that literary elements correspond to concrete social realities outside the narrative. On the other hand … narratives frequently betray aspects of their social contexts, so that an author and/or a community are recognizable to one extent or another within the narrative.' Longenecker, 'Locating 4 Ezra: A Consideration of its Social Setting and Functions,' *JSJ* 28 (Aug. 1997): 271–293, 271.

incubation, e.g.: *Jub.* 27:19–26 (Jacob at Bethel); *Ant.* 1.278–284 (Bethel); and *Ant.* 8.22–25 (Solomon's dream at the altar at Gibeon). However, it is even more striking to consider the group of message dreams of the LORD that lack biblical parallels, including: *Jub.* 32:16–26 (Jacob has a second dream at Bethel); *2 En.* 69:4–6, 70:3–11 (Methuselah dreams), 71:27–37, 72:3–10 (Nir dreams); *L.A.B.* 28:4–5 (Phineas dreams); *Ant.* 1:341–342 (Jacob dreams at Shechem), 2.212–217 (Amram dreams) and *1 En.* 15:1–16:4 (the message dream or auditory message dream portion of Enoch's larger dream of his otherworldly journey). Wholly new dreams, created 'whole cloth' with no biblical precedents, arguably provide even more freedom for creating dream content than do retellings of traditional dreams (although some of these instances might rest on older non-canonical traditions), and thus may be even better indicators of an author's concerns. *Thus, it is altogether striking that every example of this group of message dreams addresses priestly concerns.* Methuselah, Nir, Amram and Phineas are all priests who dream (*2 En.* 69:4–6, 70:3–1171:27–37, 72:3–10; *Ant.* 2.212–217; *L.A.B.* 28:4–5. 2) and the dreams of Methuselah, Nir and Amram all function to convey divine sanction for priests and actually to confer priestly ordination on the dreamers and their sons (*2 En.* 69:4–6, 70:3–1171:27–37, 72:3–10; *Ant.* 2.212–217). Jacob's second dream in *Jubilees* deters him from his plan to create a temple at Bethel and suggests another temple is 'the place' (*Jub.* 32:16–26), while in Josephus God commands Jacob in his dream at Shechem to go and perform sacrifices at Bethel, where he had previously dreamt (*Ant.* 1:341). Finally, Enoch's message from the Lord takes place within the Holy of Holies of the heavenly Temple and divine throne-room (*1 En.* 14–15).

Next, considering *auditory message dreams for which the Lord is messenger* (*Jub.* 14:1–17, 41:24; *L.A.B.* 18:4–7, 23:3–14, 53:1–13; Ant. 1.313–314, 5.348–350, 8.125–129, 11.326–328, 20.18–19), we find a similar scenario. Biblical dreams featuring sacrifice and temples garner the attention of early Jewish authors employing this dream form, as for example Abram's dream and sacrifice (*Jub.* 14:10–12) and Samuel's dreams in the Temple of Shiloh (*L.A.B.* 53:1–13; *Ant.* 5.348–350). Priestly themes are also added to existing biblical accounts. In *L.A.B.* 53:1–13, Samuel recognizes his auditory message dreams are from the Lord and not from an angel because of a priestly tradition handed down by the priest Phineas to Eli to Samuel (*L.A.B.* 53:6). Also, in *L.A.B.* 18:10 Balaam performs sacrifices in conjunction with his auditory message dream (cf. *Jub.* 4:25).

Even more striking is that, again, *several of the 'new' auditory message dreams (i.e. those lacking biblical parallels) are centered around activities at sacred temples*: the High Priest Jaddus sacrifices and incubates a dream, apparently on the Temple Mount (*Ant.* 11.326–328); Joshua's covenantal renewal ceremony is recast as the retelling of a dream in front of the ark in Shiloh (*L.A.B.* 23:3–14); and Solomon is given a second dream at Gibeon, which discusses the fate of the Jerusalem Temple (*Ant.* 8.125–129). Overall, out of all the auditory message dreams featuring the Lord as messenger, only the dreams of Laban, Monobazus and Abimelech in Josephus do not exhibit any priestly concerns whatsoever, perhaps because the dreamers worship foreign gods (*Ant.* 1.208–209, 1.313–314, 20.18–19).

By contrast, the accent on priestly themes is less consistent in angelic message dreams, or dreams in which an angel is the primary deliverer of a message. 4 Ezra is one text that employs this dream type in the service of exhibiting a strong concern for priestly matters, since the angel Uriel discusses the destruction of the Temple with Ezra, a priest-scribe (4 Ezra 3:1–5:20, 5:21–6:13, and 6:35–7:2; cf. 10:29). The angelic announcement in *2 En.* 1:3–10 may tangentially address priestly themes, since it heralds the ascent that will occasion Enoch's transformation into an angelic priest (*2 En.* 22). Also, since Josephus is of priestly lineage, his angelic message dreams in *Life* (208–210), which promise him future greatness, might be considered as relating to priestly themes, but only in an indirect way. However, other texts in which angels deliver annunciations (*L.A.B.* 9:10), warnings (Matt 1:20–25, 2:13–23), commissions (Acts 15:9–10), and predictions of divine sanction for the dreamer (*4QApocryphon of Jacob*) do not appear to touch on priestly concerns at all.[23] Overall, then, it cannot be maintained that angelic message dreams as a group feature priestly themes, and most of the time messages concerning the heavenly or earthly Temple are reserved for the LORD.

Symbolic dreams present a generally cohesive but imperfect portrait. Some striking examples of symbolic dreams occur in priestly domains: Baruch incubates a symbolic dream on the ruins of the Holy of Holies (2 Bar 35:1–35:11); Daniel has a symbolic dream of the divine temple/throne-room (Dan 7:1–28), and the priests Ezra (4 Ezra 11:1–12:3, 13:1–14) and Josephus (*J.W.* 3.351–354) have symbolic dreams. If

---

[23] The unusual episode in *4QVisions of Amram^b* (4Q544 [*4Q^cAmram^bar*]) stands without parallel in either Graeco-Roman or early Jewish sources. In this dream, the priest

we add to our list otherworldly dream ascents that contain elements of symbolic dreams, the list grows considerably. *1 Enoch* 14:1–16:1 and *4QEnoch* contains a dream journey to the heavenly Temple, as do *T. Levi* 2–5 and probably 8, and *4QAramaic Levi*. However, some symbolic dreams do not concern temples, sacrifices or priests in any way. Interestingly, these dreams are almost without exception the dreams of non-Israelites[24] (*Jub.* 39:17–18, 40:1; *J.W.* 2.112–113; *Ant.* 2.63–73, 2.75–86, 5.218–222, 10.194–211, 10.216–217, 17.345–348).

To sum up the matter for Hellenistic Jewish dreams: a distinctive thread of priestly concerns runs through divinely sent message dreams featuring the LORD as messenger, while not excluding other types of content. 'New' message or auditory message dreams of the LORD show a marked concern for priestly matters (altars, temples, priests and sacrifice). By contrast, with the exception of Uriel in *4 Ezra*, angels who deliver messages in dreams tend to bypass discussion of priestly issues. Also, several symbolic dreams feature priests, temples or sacrifice, but the symbolic dreams of Gentiles[25] do not. Finally, dream ascents such as in *1 En.*, *4QEn.*, *2 En.* and *Gk. T. Levi* and *Aramaic Levi* clearly envision the cosmic center to be a heavenly Temple with functionaries.

Overall, then it may be said quite fairly that the *Weltanschauung* of the majority of dreams in Hellenistic Judaism entails priestly concerns, but this is particularly the case in message dreams and auditory message dreams in which the LORD is the main dispenser of revelation. Three possible explanations present themselves: 1) if Oppenheim is correct, message dreams gain their format from temple incubation,[26] in which case there may be an association between temple-related matters and this dream form, 2) priestly matters may be so important that they necessitate the LORD functioning as messenger, or 3) angels and human priests may appear to be redundant in dreams, since angels are priests in the heavenly Temple. However, the reasons for the marked emphasis on priestly matters in message dreams of the LORD are not entirely clear and bear further investigation.

Amram has a dream in which two angels battle for control over him; this expresses the distinctive two ways / two Spirits theology of Qumran, and may derive from Zoroastrianism.

[24] Greek Additions to Esther 11:2–12 is an exception.

[25] Josephus includes Archelaus, eldest son of Herod the Great, amongst those who have symbolic dreams that do not concern priestly matters, perhaps because he considers him to be an Idumean, *Ant.* 17.345–348.

[26] Oppenheim, *Interpretation*, 190.

One might object, with some justification, that my portrait of priestly literary themes neglects the role of dreamers as prophets rather than as priests (Moses, Ezra, Baruch, Daniel, Enoch, and Josephus, who believes that he himself has prophetic skills[27]). There are in fact several cases in which two are intertwined. For instance, Josephus, our only identifiable author of dreams, is himself a priest-prophet (*J.W.* 3.351–354), who connects his priestly lineage to his ability to interpret dreams, interpret Scripture, foretell the future and God's ordained will. Moreover, other priests in Josephus also display prophetic ability (Hyrcanus, *Ant.* 13.282–283; Jaddus, *Ant.* 11.327; and perhaps the Essenes, *J.W.* 1.78, 2.113; *Ant.* 13.311–312, 15.371–379, 17.346, 17.345–348).[28] Similarly, Enoch of *1 Enoch* seems to function as a prophet-priest-scribe in his ascent to the heavenly Temple with a written petition.[29] In *2 Enoch* 22, Enoch receives 'the apron of prophetic power,' which is apparently the priestly ephod, a tool of divination. The priest-scribe Ezra is also clearly a prophet, pouring forth the Tanakh as well as secret books of Scripture (4 Ezra 14:37–48). This is certainly not to say that everyone who displays mantic ability is a priest,[30] but that the two are often intertwined. Given the overall concerns of early Jewish dreams and their focus on earthly and heavenly Temples, I locate the accent on the priesthood.

An emphasis on priestly themes and temples casts a new light on another prominent development in early Jewish dreams, namely, a sharp rise in the presence and variety of dream rituals that induce dreams. I argued in Chapter Three that numerous texts display familiarity with rituals of dream incubation, including: *1 Enoch* 12–36; *Jubilees* 27:19–26, 32:1–2; *1QJubilees*ᵃ (1Q17[1QJubᵃ]), *L.A.B.* 18:3–9, 23:3–14, 53:1–13; *2 Baruch* 34–36; *4 Ezra* 3:1–5:15, 5:21–6:13, 6:35–7:2, 9:27–10:33, 10:60–12:5, 13:1–13; *Testament of Levi* 2:5–5:7, 8:1–19; *2 Enoch* 1:3–10, 69:1–71:1; *Ant.* 1.278–284, 8:22–25, 11.326–328; *1QGenesis Apocryphon* (*1Q20* [*1QapGen ar*]) col. XIX, XXI and probably *4QVision of Samuel* (*4Q160*

---

[27] Gnuse, *Josephus*, 24–33.

[28] Ibid., 21–30.

[29] According to Himmelfarb, *Ascent to Heaven*, 23–25.

[30] It might be worth revisiting the conclusions of A.R. Johnson and H.G. Reventlow, who argued partly on the basis of form criticism that the biblical prophets were cultic functionaries. A.R. Johnson, *The Cultic Prophet in Ancient Israel* (Cardiff: University of Wales Press, 1962, 2ⁿᵈ ed.), H.G. Reventlow, *Das Amt des Propheten bei Amos* (Göttingen: Vandenhoeck & Ruprecht, 1962). One might ask, in both biblical and Second Temple texts, to what extent a priestly background correlates with prophets who have dreams and visions versus those prophets who receive an oracular 'word of the Lord.'

[*4QVisSam*]) frag. 1. Incubation appears far more frequently than in the Hebrew Bible and there is more variety in the kinds of rituals that induce dreams.

Early Jewish authors do *not* assume, as do some modern interpreters, that incubation entails compulsion of God, any more than does priestly use of the ephod.[31] Moreover, *2 Baruch* 34–36 explicitly depicts incubation at the ruined site of Holy of Holies, and perhaps even more striking is Josephus' depiction of the High Priest Jaddus calling for public prayer, sacrificing, sleeping and dreaming:[32] κατακοιμηθέντι δὲ μετὰ τὴν θυσίαν ἐχρημάτισεν αὐτῷ κατὰ τοὺς ὕπνους ὁ θεὸς θαρρεῖν (*Ant.* 11.326–327). Since the context of the larger passage is Alexander's approach to Jerusalem (11. 325), the scene is reminiscent of many episodes in which besieged groups sought refuge on the Temple Mount in the Maccabean wars.[33] Thus, this appears to be a case in which the people of Israel incubate a divinely-sent dream in a time of crises, whereupon the High Priest receives a communication from God in a dream. Similarly, in *2 Enoch* the people stay all night at the Temple mount, anachronistically called 'Azuchan,' while Methuselah sleeps by the altar and receives a divinely-sent dream.[34]

Furthermore, myriad early Jewish texts mention incubation rituals in connection with dreams—sacrifice, making prayers or laments, fasting, eating special foods, sleeping in sacred spots (particularly near an altar), washing, preparing for certain prescribed periods (of 7 or 40 days), and recording one's divinely-sent dream—that are the same rituals *actually*

---

[31] Robert Gnuse maintains, '{Incubation} activities would offend the biblical mentality, for they manipulated the deity ... Josephus instinctively would have been reluctant and cautious in his portrayal of a Jewish incubational experience ...' *Josephus*, 230. I disagree, but if Gnuse is correct, then the evidence I have presented has been muted and incubation at the Temple is all the more likely.

[32] Cf. Gnuse, *Josephus*, 228–229.

[33] The Temple Mount was periodically fortified, see 1 Maccabees 4:60–61, 6:18, 6:62; cf. 10:43. Gnuse also notes this dream relates intertextually to Solomon's dream at Gibeon (I Kings 3:4–5), which links sacrifice at an altar with incubation and God's favor. Gnuse, *Josephus*, 230–233.

[34] In *2 En.* 69 the people wait all night at 'the place Azukhan' with Methuselah incubating a dream near the altar. Böttrich cites several scholars who connect 'Azukhan' or 'Achuzan' to the ancient place name of David's altar where the Jerusalem Temple is to be built, i.e. at Araunah/Ornan's threshing floor (cf. 2 Sam 24:16–25; 1 Chr 21:18–28). C. Böttrich, *Das slavische Henochbuch* (Jüdische Schriften aus hellenistisch-römischer Zeit V.7; Gütersloh: Gütersloh Verlaghaus, 1996), 992–993, n. 2b. Böttrich notes that Ginzberg sees a word play on 'ארונה /אחזא.' L. Ginzberg, *Legends of the Jews* (7 vols.; Philadelphia: Jewish Publication Society, 1909–1938), 5:162.

practiced in Graeco-Roman dream cults.[35] These cults are not isolated, but rather reach into the hundreds across the Mediterranean world, including Syria-Palestine.[36] Thus, early Jewish authors existed in a historical landscape dotted with pagan dream cults, and they also record abundant references in which pseudepigraphic figures practice known incubation rituals that are linked literarily in a cause-effect sequence with dreams. I conclude that although we cannot know the identities of most of the dream authors, there are ample grounds for maintaining that dream practices such as incubation and interpretation[37] were a familiar part of the authors' wider social setting, and they themselves may have participated in these activities.

The evidence has mounted for the tricky move from a literary, priestly genre to positing that the socio-historical setting of the real authors is also priestly. First, there are arguments from literature. We have in early Jewish dreams depictions of temples, sacrifice, predictions of the building of temples, ordination of priests, priests who dream, incubation rituals, incubation on the Temple mount, angelic priests who heal and interpret dreams, and dreamers who become angelic priests. Priestly themes are the most focused in dreams in which the LORD is messenger and in dreams in which dreamers ascend and meet the LORD in the heavenly *hekhal*, perhaps indicating the importance of the topic. Whoever the authors are, they are people for whom temple settings and activities such as dream incubation have currency and are the vernacular.

Second, we have cultic arguments from social history. Those Jewish dream authors who are known to us—Josephus and the Qumranites— have a self proclaimed priestly identity (e.g. *J.W.* 3.351–354; *1QM* col.

---

[35] For incubation practices in Greece and Rome see Aristides *Oratio* XLVIII,27; M. Hamilton, *Incubation: or the Cure of Disease in Pagan Temples and Christian Churches* (London: W.C. Henderson & Son, 1906), 11–12; R.A. Tomlinson, *Epidauros* (New York: Granada, 1983), 60–67; LiDonnici, *Epidaurian Miracle Inscriptions*, 11–12; C.A. Meier, *Antike Incubation und Moderne Psychotherapie* (Zürich: Rascher & Cie.AG., 1949), 69–83. For a modern example of dream incubation in Israel see Y. Bilu and H. Abramovitch, 'In search of the saddiq: visitational dreams among Moroccan Jews in Israel,' *Psychiatry* 48 (Feb. 1985): 1.83–92.

[36] C.M. Dauphin, 'Dor, Byzantine Church, 1983,' in *IEJ* 34 (1984): 271–274; E. Shenhav, 'Shuni,' *Excavations and Surveys in Israel* 7–8 (1988/1989): 166–168; also idem, 'Shuni,' *NEAEHL* 4:1382–1384; Xella, 'Eschmun von Sidon,' 481–498.

[37] Schwartz considers dream interpreters to rank amongst the lower priestly echelons, along with 'wandering holy men and assorted charlatans' and below 'legal experts and teachers.' Schwartz, *Josephus*, 70.

VII–IX; *1QS* col. II; *CD-A* col. IV), and at least Josephus links dream interpretation with his priestly lineage. Pagan dream cults abound across the Hellenistic and Roman empires, and dreamers in texts of early Judaism employ the same rituals known to have been utilized in Graeco-Roman incubation cults. Finally, archaeology has uncovered the presence of Asklepieia with purificatory baths even in Syria-Palestine at Dor, Shuni and Sidon.[38] Thus, we know as well as we can that dream incubation and interpretation were practiced in the vicinity.

The overarching picture suggests to me that the authors of most early Jewish dream texts are priests, meaning that they are of priestly lineage and have some familiarity with temples. Since around twenty thousand priests and Levites lived in Israel at the turn of the era,[39] this in no way implies that the authors of early Jewish texts are uniformly priests of the same social location or families.[40] As I have stated earlier, many priests operated in spheres apart from the Temple and there were numerous competing priestly lineages. Rather, the evidence from dreams does suggest that temple activity, whether real or ideal, was important to the self-conception of many priestly authors of early Jewish dream texts. Given that temples were bases of fiduciary, political and religious power in antiquity, it would be odd if this association did not contribute to the social prestige of priests to some degree.[41]

Finally, it must be said that the priestly setting of dream texts that I am positing supports in the main the conclusions of E.P. Sanders,[42]

---

[38] Dauphin has found an archaic Greek to Hellenistic Asklepieion at Dor, 'Dor, Byzantine Church, 1983'; idem, 'Dora-Dor: A Station for Pilgrims in the Byzantine Period on their Way to Jerusalem,' in *Ancient Churches Revealed* (ed. Y. Tsafir; Jerusalem: Israel Exploration Society, 1993), 90–97. Shenhav has found an Asklepieion from the 3rd c. C.E. at Shuni, 'Shuni,' 166–168; also idem, 'Shuni' in *NEAEHL* 4:1382–1384. Cf. Xella for Asklepios at Sidon, 'Eschmun von Sidon,' 481–498.

[39] Sanders accepts Josephus' figure from *Apion* 2.108, *Judaism: Practice and Belief*, 78. Jeremias extrapolates from estimates in the *Letter of Aristeas* and arrives at a figure of 18,000, which is close, but Sanders severely critiques his methods. Sanders, *Judaism: Practice and Belief*, 79, n. 5–6, see also J. Jeremias, *Jerusalem at the Time of Jesus*, 200, 203.

[40] See Sanders, 'Common Judaism and the Temple,' 'The Ordinary Priests and the Levites' and 'The Priests and Levites Outside the Temple' in *Judaism: Practice and Belief*, 72–76, 77–102, 170–189.

[41] Turner, *Societal Stratification*, 59–63, 146–148.

[42] Of course, Sanders' reconstruction has its critics. He does rely mostly on Josephus for his reconstruction of Judaism in the 1st c. C.E., and his final chapter, 'Who Ran What?' tends to cast priests as aristocrats, despite earlier chapters that stress a variety of social locations for priests. Schams criticizes him for identifying 'virtually all scribes as priests or Levites … an over-reaction,' *Jewish Scribes*, 28. For a more extensive critique see M. Goodman, *Scottish Journal of Theology* 47, 1 (1994): 89–119.

who has offered a reworked portrait of Judaism around the turn of the era in *Judaism: Practice and Belief, 63 C.E.-66 C.E.*[43] Sanders argues that a focus on literary categories ('apocalyptic, rabbinic, philosophical, mystical and the like'[44]) as well as on parties—Pharisees, Sadducees and Essenes—is misleading in reconstructing ancient Jewish society. Instead, he avers that 'common Judaism' was oriented around three foci, the Temple, synagogue and home, and maintains that 'isms' such as 'apocalypticism' were not exclusive of worship in the Temple nor particular to certain party affiliations.[45]

A Scribal Sitz im Leben

Since I discussed scribal images in early Jewish dreams earlier in Chapter Three, I have only to recapitulate briefly some of the evidence of the emphasis on scribal themes in early Jewish dreams. As both Sanders and Saldarini have shown, priestly and scribal roles sometimes overlap in Hellenistic Judaism,[46] although latent associations between priests and Sadducees on the one hand and scribes and Pharisees on the other have sometimes distracted us from this fact.[47] Schams has suggested a minimalist description of scribal activity as reading and writing,[48] which in no way precludes priestly lineage or implies party affiliation; it is to this minimalist portrait of scribal activity that I adhere.

Several dreamers are readers of heavenly tablets, including Jacob (*Jub.* 32; *4QApocryphon of Jacob*) and Naphtali (and Joseph, Levi and Judah?) (*T. Naphtali* 5:8). Other dreamers are themselves scribes who write, including Enoch (*1 En.* 14–15; *2 En.* 22–23), Ezra (*4 Ezra* 14), Daniel (Dan 7), Baruch (*2 Bar.* 77–87) and Amram in *4QVisions* of Amram[e] (*4Q547 4QcAmram[e] ar*]) frag. 1. The most famous scribe is Enoch, 'the Scribe of Righteousness,' who records his dream revelations (*Jub.* 4:19; cf. *1 En.* 14:1–4), as do other scribes such as Daniel (Dan 7:1).

Several dream texts portray writing as a divine or heavenly activity. Uriel acts as Enoch's scribe in *1 Enoch* (*1 En.* 33), and Enoch also sees angelic scribes in his symbolic dream of the 'Animal Apocalypse' (*1 En.*

[43] Sanders, *Judaism: Practice and Belief.*
[44] Ibid., 9.
[45] Ibid., 8.
[46] Saldarini, *Pharisees, Scribes, and Pharisees,* 249–250, 263; Sanders, *Judaism: Practice and Belief,* 170–182.
[47] Sanders, *Judaism: Practice and Belief,* 174.
[48] Schams, *Jewish Scribes,* 97, 121–124, 143, 204, 205–208.

89:70, 76, 90:14, 22). Abraham ascends in *Testament of Abraham* and sees heavenly recording angels among other sights, although he does not ascend in a dream (*T. Abr.* A 12:6–12, 13:9).[49] Similarly, Ezra's inspired dictation to five scribes involves a transformation in which he consumes a cup of something like fire (4 Ezra 14:37–48), and the pinnacle of Enoch's metamorphosis into a priestly angel (22:10)[50] appears to be scribal activity like that of the archangel Vereveil.

If scribal and priestly roles were not exclusive of one another in Judaism of the Hellenistic and Roman eras,[51] the interpretation of dreams and Scripture are two areas in which they seem to overlap significantly. The influential passage from Josephus that I discussed above (*J.W.* 3.351–354) links his priestly lineage both with the interpretation of dreams *and with the interpretation of Scripture, which requires literacy.* This and other passages have led S. Mason to argue that despite the Pharisees' acknowledged authority over the law in the centuries around the turn of the era, Josephus, who himself is a priest and not a Pharisee, 'believes that the priests are the real adepts at scriptural exegesis' and that 'priests are the proper guardians of the law.'[52]

Significantly, the Qumranic term for both the interpretation of Scripture and dreams is *pesher.* The Nahum pesher and others exhibit the format of biblical verse followed by 'פשרו' or its interpretation (e.g. *4QNahum Pesher* frag. 3, col. IV [*4QpNah*] 4Q169). Likewise, when the Watchers have puzzling symbolic dreams, one of them suggests they go to Enoch, 'the scribe of distinction, and he will interpret the dream for us ויפשור לנא חלמא' (*4QBook of Giants* [b]*ar* col. II, 14–15 [*4Q530*] *4QEn-Giants*[b]*ar*). Similarly, Daniel possesses both kinds of abilities: '… knowledge and skill in every aspect of literature and wisdom; Daniel also had insight into all visions and dreams' (Dan 1:17). The ἱερογραμμα-

---

[49] In another recension Abraham sees 'the scribe of righteousness, Enoch' in heaven writing the sins of repentant souls (*T. Abr.* B 11:3–10).

[50] For instance, Himmelfarb, *Ascent to Heaven,* 40–41; and Fletcher-Louis, *All the Glory of Adam,* 23, 49. Also, Charlesworth discusses *2 Enoch A* 30:8–11 and concludes that 'There is no reason to assume that the author of *2 Enoch* is simply speaking metaphorically about Adam being an angel. Adam's original state was perceived as glorious, even divine, by some Jews,' 'The Portrayal of the Righteous,' 135–152, 138.

[51] Schams, *Jewish Scribes,* 58, 65, 68, 71, 89–90, 108, 140–143, 193, 246, 249, 298; Sanders, *Judaism: Practice and Belief,* 170–182; Saldarini, *Pharisees, Scribes and Sadducees,* 241–276; Himmelfarb, *Ascent to Heaven,* 24. See also Fishbane, who discerns Temple-based scribal activity in the transmission of cultic and legal material, *Biblical Interpretation,* 78–79.

[52] Mason, 'Priesthood in Josephus,' 657–661.

τεῖς mentioned in Josephus, which Sanders translates as 'priest-scribes'[53] can interpret signs and omens connected with the Temple (*J.W.* 6.291, 6.295).[54] Thus it could be that the 'reading' of both Scripture and dreams was viewed in both cases as interpretation of divine messages, and that some of those with priestly self-identities, such as Josephus and the Qumranites, were familiar with both activities.

Finally, a scribal *Sitz im Leben* for the authors of many dream texts may be gleaned from the fact that they themselves wrote the texts, texts that fictional first-person, dreaming scribes claim to have written, suggesting some authorial self-identification with those characters (*1 En.* 14–36, *2 En.* 22–24, Dan 7–8, *4 Ezra* 14, *2 Bar.* 78–87).[55] If this is so, the fact that writing is portrayed as a heavenly or divine activity takes on a propagandistic meaning on the social level.[56] On the level of literary story, dreamers gain dream knowledge by reading tablets brought to them by angels in dreams (*Jub.* 32, *4QApoc. Jac.*, *T. Naph.*); angels function as scribes (*1 En.* 33; *2 En.* 22; *T. Abr.* A 12; *Rom. T. Abr.* 30); and some dreamers undergo divine metamorphoses that enable them to act as scribes (*2 En.* 22–23) or as the one who dictates divine revelations to scribes (*4 Ezra* 14). If scribes or priest-scribes are composing the dream revelations, these literary motifs function to confer or maintain a level of social authority by adding to their prestige, which Turner has shown is closely linked to social power.[57] If some scribes or priest-scribes are also responsible for interpreting dreams, Scripture and/or omens of the future, as some passages suggest (*4QBook of Giants, Ag. Ap.* 1, *J.W.* 6, *Ant.* 2), the importance attached to dreams in early Judaism likewise functions to secure or maintain some religious authority in society.

---

[53] Sanders, *Judaism: Practice and Belief*, 172.

[54] Schams, *Jewish Scribes*, 140–143.

[55] Nickelsburg argued that the ideal Scribe Enoch has social counterparts in the 'wise' (*phronimoi*) of *1 En.* 98:9, 15, 99:10, who are literate writers of books that are read by enemies. Without positing a unified scribal movement, he also detects social reality behind such figures as the wise interpreters of the law in *2 Bar.* 77, the *maskîlîm* in Daniel 7–12 and 1QS 3, as well as sages (*chkmym*) and persons of perception (*nbwnym*) in CD. Nickelsburg, 'Wisdom and Apocalypticism in Early Judaism: Some Points for Discussion,' in *George W.E. Nickelsburg in Perspective*, 1:279–283.

[56] With respect to pseudepigraphy and any elite authorial status in society, Himmelfarb maintains: 'the prominence of scribes as heroes [in the ascent texts] surely indicates authorial self-consciousness on this point,' *Ascent to Heaven*, 99–102.

[57] Turner, *Societal Stratification*, 60, 203.

Male Authorship, Female Practice

I have hitherto suggested that early Jewish priests and/or scribes may have been responsible for dream interpretation and for facilitating dream incubation in sacred settings. While I have not explicitly said so, this social history implies that the authors of the dream texts were probably males. Although the gender of scribes was not definitively male, it was very likely male, if we are to judge from later rabbinic injunctions on female learning,[58] and the abundance of priestly motifs increases the chance that the authors are male.

However, in a curious passage in *Satires* 6.542 that is only slightly later than most dream texts we have studied, Juvenal mocks a Jewish interpreter who is a woman:

> … a palsied Jewess, leaving her basket and her truss of hay, comes begging to her secret ear; she is an interpreter of the laws of Jerusalem, a high priestess of the trees, a trusty go-between of highest heaven. She, too, fills her palm, but more sparingly, for a Jew will tell you dreams of any kind you please for the minutest of coins.

> … cophino faenoque relicto arcanam Iudaea tremens mendicat in aurem, interpres legume Solymarum et magna sacerdos arboris ac summi fida internuntia caeli. implet et illa manum, set parcius; aere minuto qualiacumque voles Iudaei somnia vendunt.   (*Satires* 6.542)

Several points deserve comment. First, the dream interpreter is a paid professional. Second, she is a female. In a striking departure from practices in the ancient Near East, no biblical texts or early Jewish dream texts suggest that females could function in this capacity. In fact, only five women even receive dreams in early Jewish texts; three of these are punished and the other two are disbelieved.[59]

Third, the Jewess is also called *internuntia caeli*, a fitting term for an intermediary such as a priest, and she is also dubbed *magna sacerdos arboris*. I think it highly unlikely that this is a slur meant to recall an

---

[58] Although somewhat later, the Mishnah may serve as a guide to cultural memory on the topic of women and education. A minority opinion is expressed in the saying, 'A man is obliged to have his daughter taught Torah,' while the majority position is clear in the apodasis, 'Whoever teaches his daughter Torah is as though he taught her obscenity' (Sot. III, 4). One Rabbi also remarked, 'Let the words of the Torah rather be destroyed by fire than be imparted to women' (p. Sot. 19a). See, ironically, A. Cohen, *Everyman's Talmud* (New York: Schocken Books, 1949), 179.

[59] These include Miriam in *L.A.B.* 9:10; Rebecca in *Jub.* 35:6; Glaphyra in *J.W.* 2.114–116 and *Ant.* 17.349–353; Stratonica in *Ap.* 1.206–207; Pilate's unnamed wife in Gosp Matt 27:19.

asherah priestess of the ancient Israelite polytheistic cult, writing as
Juvenal did in the second century C.E. from a Roman provenance.[60]
But how could a woman be *magna sacerdos arboris*?

B. Brooten has uncovered inscriptional evidence of women's leadership roles from the 1st c. B.C.E. through the 6th c. C.E. and has arrived
at a quite different portrait than that preserved in rabbinic evidence:
women are called 'president of the synagogue,' 'leader,' 'elder,' 'mother
of the synagogue,' and even 'priestess.'[61] Although Juvenal's Jewess may
be a 'high priestess,' I think it is even more likely he uses the phrase
as a functional one: she acts as a sacred intermediary in her capacity as dream interpreter. The 'arboris' might refer to her activity being
located outside, that is, not within of sanctioned buildings such as the
synagogue. Her 'tremens' is then perhaps a state of ecstasy rather than
a disease.[62]

Fourth, the passage suggests that women engaged not only in interpreting dreams, but also in interpreting the law (*interpres legume Soly-
marum*). At face-value this is a shocking claim, yet the information curiously squares with other passages we have seen that link the interpretation of Scripture with the interpretation of dreams (*J.W.* 3.351–354;
Dan 1:17; *4QNahum Pesher* frag. 3, col. IV [*4QpNah*] *4Q169*). Finally, it
should not be missed that this surprising portrait is presented in mock-
ery by Juvenal as entirely typical and familiar.

Juvenal may be grossly misinformed, or he may reflect to some
extent a popular level of unsanctioned religious and/or commercial
activity in which women sometimes interpreted dreams, perhaps in a
community without rabbinic authority. Since the vast majority of Jewish
women were illiterate;[63] it could simply be the case that Jewish dream

---

[60] For the ancient Asherah cult see J.M. Hadley, *Cult of Asherah in ancient Israel and Judah: evidence for a Hebrew Goddess* (New York: Cambridge University Press, 2000).
[61] B. Brooten has also refuted baseless claims these were merely honorific titles. Brooten, *Women Leaders in the Ancient Synagogue: Inscriptional Evidence and Background Issues* (Brown Judaic Studies 35; Chico, CA: Scholars Press, 1982), 7–29; also J. Plaskow, *Standing Again at Sinai: Judaism from a Feminist Perspective* (San Francisco; HarperSanFrancisco, 1990), 43–50.
[62] Shaking is a common cross-cultural manifestation of ecstasy. See Lewis, *Ecstatic Religion*, 39.
[63] Women were systematically denied literacy in ancient and early Jewish society, even well into the Middle ages. In discussing Jewish life in Egypt from the tenth through the thirteenth centuries, S.D. Goiten states: 'The educational gap between male and female was the ultimate source and manifestation of the repression of womanhood in civilized societies,' *A Mediterranean Society* (3 vols.; Berkeley: University of California Press, 1978), 356.

interpretation was traditionally so closely associated with the interpretation of Scripture (whether oral or written) and priestly intermediation that Juvenal combines all three in his portrait of the Jewess dream interpreter.

Summary of Social Settings

Although any extrapolation from literature to ancient social location must remain tentative, my previous investigation has amassed some literary, historical, sociological and archaeological evidence that the authors of early Jewish dreams were male priests and/or scribes familiar with a temple milieu, including the practices of sacrifice, dream incubation, and dream interpretation, and furthermore that they were involved in the reading and interpretation of Scripture. My conclusions do not extend to party affiliation or to divisions within priestly and Levitical families. Since motifs in the early Jewish dream texts function either to confer or to maintain social authority for priests and/or scribes, the social classes of the authors are somewhat indeterminable, although their aspirations for religious prestige and social power are clear. However, given that Juvenal's portrait of popular dream interpretation by women is wholly lacking in the early Jewish dream sources, I am inclined towards assuming the male authors of the dream texts represent a traditional, elite base of religious power. At the least, the construction of a worldview oriented around the heavenly *hekhal*, as well as the exaltation of pseudepigraphic heroes who are often priest-scribes (or priest-scribe-prophets), speaks to an authorship that saw itself as the proper intermediary in a chain of intermediaries acting between divinity and humanity, although it is difficult to know how much of the dreams are wish-fulfillment and how much reflect social reality.

It is my hope that these tentative conclusions spur further study on the social roles of priests and scribes in early Judaism, particularly in relation to dreaming. Future avenues of analysis might entail: more detailed investigation of the various competing priestly dream traditions, priestly lineages and corresponding sacred spaces established in the early Jewish dream texts; further archaeological, sociological and prosopographic investigations of the practice of dream incubation by Hellenistic Jews; and a reappraisal of the Qumran community in terms of scribal activity, including dream interpretation.

Three: Apocalypses and Dream Texts

Although dreams occur in various genres in early Jewish literature, including histories, gospels, poetry, testaments, autobiographies, and re-tellings of biblical stories, numerous dream texts in this study are apoc-alypses, including: *1 En.* 1–36, 85–90, Dan 7–12, *2 Bar.*, *4 Ezra*, *2 En.*, *T. Levi*, *T. Abr.* and *Ladd. Jac.*[64] In fact, if the whole of *Jubilees* is con-sidered to be an apocalypse, and not just chapter 23,[65] every early Jew-ish apocalypse contains a dream or a vision, and around half contain a dream.[66] Thus, the relationship of 'apocalypse' and 'eschatological dream' is close and contiguous in the early Jewish materials[67] and neces-sitates careful evaluation.

The SBL Genres Project has arrived at the following definition that has become standard in many subsequent works: 'Apocalypse is a genre of revelatory literature with a narrative framework, in which a rev-elation is mediated by an otherworldly being to a human recipient, disclosing a transcendent reality which is both temporal, insofar as it envisages eschatological salvation, and spatial insofar as it involves another, supernatural world.'[68] A genre is an externally imposed cate-gory that is useful since it recognizes the trans-individual features that a group of texts displays.[69] In fact, the pervasive presence of dreams

---

[64] J.J. Collins, 'Jewish Apocalypses,' in *Semeia 14*, esp. 28, and A.Y. Collins, 'Early Christian Apocalypses,' in *Semeia 14*, esp. 104. Although no or few sectarian writings from Qumran are typically classed as apocalypses, they are widely viewed as evincing an apocalyptic outlook. See for example Collins, *Apocalyptic Imagination*, 147, 175.

[65] In *Semeia 14* J.J. Collins initially only counts *Jubilees* 23 as an apocalypse, but later concludes the overall generic framework of the book is an apocalypse, *Apocalyptic Imagination*, 83. While chapter 23 has no dream, there are dreams or dream-reports in *Jubilees* 4:19, 14:1, 32:1, 32:16, 32:21, 35:6, 39:16, 40:1, and 41:24.

[66] J.J. Collins, 'Jewish Apocalypses,' 28.

[67] This is also true for the Qumran scrolls, which include some fragments of apoc-alypses known from the pseudepigrapha as well as numerous dream texts amongst the 'sectarian' writings. See J. VanderKam, 'Apocalyptic Tradition in the Dead Sea Scrolls and the Religion of Qumran,' in *Religion in the Dead Sea Scrolls* (eds. J.J. Collins and R.A. Kugler; Grand Rapids, MI: Eerdmans, 2000), 113–134 and J.J. Collins, *Apocalypti-cism in the Dead Sea Scrolls* (London: Routledge, 1997), esp. 9–10.

[68] J.J. Collins, 'Introduction: Towards the Morphology of a Genre,' in *Semeia* 14:1–20, 9.

[69] Of course, genres are not exclusive categories and depending on the definition, overlap with form. For example, G.W.E. Nickelsburg has showed that, in addition to apocalypse, the genres and forms of *1 Enoch* include rewritten biblical narrative, prophetic call narrative, cosmic journeys, a prophetic oracle, dream visions, historical reviews and epistle (in chapters 92–105). Nickelsburg, *1 Enoch*, 28–34 and 117–118.

and visions in apocalypses suggests that they may be even more integral to the Jewish apocalypse than the SBL Genres Project definition
recognizes.[70]

Some individual dream units come rather close to fulfilling the SBL
definition of apocalypse. Dreams are narrative revelations in which
messages are either mediated by the LORD, the voice of the LORD,
or angels, or in which divinely-sent symbols communicate a message,
which is often interpreted by a divine being. All of these patterns fit the
definition of *a revelation mediated by an otherworldly being to a human recipient*. In addition, many dreams—and not just dreams in apocalypses—
disclose a transcendent reality that is both *spatial* and *temporal*. For example, in a dream in *Ezekiel the Tragedian* Moses sees heaven, earth and
the underworld and learns of events past, present and future. Non-
apocalypses from Qumran, such as *4Q Apocr. Jac.*, also picture otherworldly realms in which angels dwell.

The relationship between dreams and apocalypses is particularly
complex when the dream unit is large and fairly contiguous in extent
with the text as a whole. For instance, the apocalypses *1 En.* 12–36
and 85–90, Dan 7–12, 4 Ezra, and *T. Levi* are not simply narratives
that contain isolated dreams and visions; rather, in each case dreams
and visions structure much of the apocalypse's plot and govern much
of the logic of the narrative. As Rowland in particular has noted,[71]
the bulk of these texts concern issues related to dreaming or visions,
such as establishing the reasons for dreaming or recording the setting,
transmission, content and interpretation of dreams and visions.[72]

It is the case, then, that some dreams and some early Jewish apocalypses overlap in both extent and content, with most remaining apoca-

---

[70] In this project, I limit myself to the early Jewish materials, but a consideration of
genre in terms of the relation of dreams and visions to Christian, Gnostic and Graeco-
Roman apocalypses is also worth an investigation. While approximately 93% of early
Jewish apocalypses and 83% of early Christian apocalypses contain dreams or visions,
less than a third of Gnostic apocalypses do. See A.Y. Collins, 'The Early Christian
Apocalypses' in *Semeia 14*, 61–122, 104–105; also F. Fallon, 'The Gnostic Apocalypses'
in *Semeia 14*, 123–158, 148–149. Also, of those Graeco-Roman texts that H. Attridge
identifies as apocalypses, roughly half contain dreams or visions while the other half
involve revelations to or from dead people, 'Greek and Latin Apocalypses,' in *Semeia
14*, 159–186. Both the absence of dreams and visions in the Gnostic material and
the correlation of dreams with death in the Graeco-Roman apocalypses bear further
study.

[71] Rowland, *Open Heaven*, 214–240.

[72] For instance, many early Jewish dreams, like apocalypses, involve a setting of
perceived oppression. See Collins, *Apocalyptic Imagination*, 9, 38, 41.

lypses containing at least one dream or vision. Earlier I argued that the fluid space engendered by the dream form, which allows for the suspension of the normal constraints of spatial, temporal, ontological and perceptual reality, may have facilitated the articulation of the apocalyptic worldview itself. In fact, in his early definition of 'apocalypticism,' P.D. Hanson noted something similar, stating: '... the partial suspension of spatial and temporal categories enabled the apocalyptic communities to celebrate proleptically these new possibilities in their communal life.'[73] Kellner has further argued that is precisely the ambiguity of pictorial symbols (*die Vieldeutigkeit des Bildes*) that makes possible the expression of apocalyptic ideas.[74] Indeed, symbolic dreams, which are viewed with some suspicion in other cultures,[75] do figure prominently in all the apocalypses that contain dreams (*1 Enoch* 1–36, 85–90, Daniel 7–12, *2 Baruch*, *4 Ezra*, *2 Enoch*, *Testament of Levi*, *Testament of Abraham* and *Ladder of Jacob*).[76] Thus, I propose that a catalyst for the articulation of an apocalyptic construction of reality in early Judaism is the combination of polyvalent symbols in tandem with dream forms that imply that the limits of reality—whether spatial, temporal, ontological or perceptual—may be overcome.

Attending to the role of dreams and visions in apocalypses speaks to another knotty problem bearing on wisdom themes. G. von Rad's thesis that the origins of apocalypticism originate from the wisdom traditions has been rightly refuted,[77] yet he did call attention to the presence of non-eschatological wisdom elements in apocalypses.[78] More

---

[73] P.D. Hanson's recognition of the role of a 'symbolic universe' and its deconstruction are vitally important to my thesis, but his early definition of 'apocalypticism' is unsatisfactory since it presupposes that a unitary movement exists around texts, acting over and against dominant society: 'A system of thought produced by visionary movements; builds upon a specific eschatological perspective in generating a symbolic universe opposed to that of the dominant society.' P.D. Hanson, 'Apocalypticism,' *IDB Supplement* (3rd printing; eds. K. Crim et al; Nashville: Abingdon, 1982), 28–34.

[74] W. Kellner, *Der Traum vom Menschensohn: die politisch-theologische Botschaft Jesu* (München: Kösel, 1985), 29–30.

[75] Oppenheim, *Interpretation*, 207. There are notably few symbolic dreams in Latin literature in comparison with message dreams and in ancient Near Eastern sources women almost exclusively are the dreamers of symbolic dreams.

[76] Hanson, 'Apocalypticism,' 28–34.

[77] G. von Rad, *Theologie des Alten Testaments* (vol. 2; 4th ed.; Munich: Kaiser, 1965), 315–330; idem, *Wisdom in Israel* (Nashville: Abingdon, 1972), 263–283; for a listing of critics see Collins, 'Apocalyptic Literature,' in *EJMI*, 355–356.

[78] M. Stone carried this observation further in 'Lists of Revealed Things in the Apocalyptic Literature,' in *Magnalia Dei: The Mighty Acts of God: Essays on the Bible and*

recent scholarship has likewise recognized that 'Jewish wisdom and apocalypticism cannot be cleanly separated from one another.'[79] I suggest that increased awareness of the mode, and not just the content, of revelation in apocalypses is one key to unraveling the relationship of sapiential and eschatological elements in apocalypses. The earliest Jewish apocalypse (*1 En.* 1–36) and at least half of other ancient Jewish apocalypses transmit revelation via dreams, the quintessential function of which is the transmission of extraordinary knowledge to dreamers.

C. Rowland and J. Carmignac have offered intriguing definitions of apocalypses and apocalypticism that recognize the importance of dreams and sapiential elements to the genre. For instance, Rowland summarizes the essence of 'apocalyptic' by stating: '… apocalyptic, therefore, is a type of religion whose distinguishing feature is a belief in direct revelation of the things of God which was mediated through dream, vision or divine intermediary.'[80] Also, over two decades ago Carmignac tantalizingly suggested the origin of apocalyptic literature in the Hebrew Bible lay in dreams.[81] Unfortunately, both Rowland and Carmignac minimize the centrality of eschatology, as is evident from this statement by Rowland: 'It must, therefore, be questioned whether … eschatology can so easily be used as the characteristic feature of the hope for the future in the apocalypses.'[82]

In fact, since dreams facilitate the suspension of both spatial and temporal axes, sapiential and eschatological revelations may co-exist

---

Archaeology in Memory of G. Ernest Wright (eds. F.M. Cross, W.E. Lemke, and P.D. Miller; Garden City, NY: Doubleday, 1976), 414–452.

[79] This recognition resulted in the formation of the Wisdom and Apocalypticism in Early Judaism and Early Christianity Consultation (and later a Group) of the Society of Biblical Literature. See the early papers by G.W.E. Nickelsburg, 'Wisdom and Apocalypticism in Early Judaism: Some Points for Discussion,' and the respondent remarks by Sarah Tanzer in *George W.E. Nickelsburg in Perspective*, 1.267–300. Shortly before, J.J. Collins came to similar conclusions in the case of Q. See 'Wisdom, Apocalypticism, and Generic Compatibility,' in *In Search of Wisdom: Essays in Memory of John G. Gammie* (eds. L.G. Perdue, B.B. Scott, W.J. Wiseman; Louisville, KY: Westminster/John Knox, 1993), 165–185.

[80] Rowland, *Open Heaven*, 14, 17.

[81] J. Carmignac, 'Description du phénomène de l'Apocalyptique dans l'Ancien Testament,' in *Apocalypticism in the Mediterranean World and the Near East: Proceedings of the International Colloquium on Apocalypticism Uppsala, August 12–17, 1979* (ed. D. Hellholm; Tübingen: J.C.B. Mohr, 1983), 163–170.

[82] Rowland, *Open Heaven*, 29; also J. Carmignac, 'Les Dangers de l'Eschatologie,' *NTS* 17 (1981): 365–390.

in a single dream narrative, with dreams in apocalypses being distinguishable from those in non-apocalypses by their greater accent on eschatology.[83] Whereas dreams in *1 Enoch* 1–36, 85–90, Daniel 7–12, *2 Baruch*, *4 Ezra*, *Testament of Levi*, and perhaps *Ladder of Jacob* clearly relate eschatological secrets, dreams in non-apocalypses such as *L.A.B.*, *2 Maccabees*, and Josephus are non-eschatological in content, even when they feature future temporal elements in the life of the dreamer or Israel. In the cases of *2 Enoch* and *Testament of Abraham*, the dreams are not eschatological in nature, but the dreams foreshadow or trigger ascents to heaven that serve to transmit both eschatological and cosmological knowledge of the workings of the universe.

Another distinguishing factor is that in the apocalypses alone dreamers *as well as readers* learn details of the eschatological future (in 'historical apocalypses') and/or the contents of heaven (in 'otherworldly journeys').[84] In non-apocalypses, readers do not share in dream knowledge. For example, in *Ezek. Trag.*, which is not an apocalypse, Moses learns of otherworldly spheres (heaven, earth and the underworld) and possibly learns eschatology as well (past, present and future). However,

---

[83] Neither dream types, complexity nor the presence of priestly and scribal themes distinguish dreams in apocalypses from non-apocalypses. (1) All types of divinely-sent dreams appear in the non-apocalypses as well as in apocalypses. The latter comprise the following types of dreams: message dreams (4 Ezra 3:1–5:14, 5:21–6:17, 6:35–7:2; *2 En.* 69:1–70:11, 70:3–13; 71:27–72:11), an auditory message dream component (*1 En.* 13:8, 14:24–16:4; *Jub.* 14:1–4), a *Wecktraum* (*2 En.* 1:3–10), symbolic dreams (*1 En.* 83:3–10, 85:3–90:38, Dan 7:1–28, 8:1–27b, *2 Bar.* 36:1–11 and 52:7–53:12, 4 Ezra 11:1–12:3 and 13:1–14, *Jub.* 29:17–40:4 and *T. Abr.* 7:1–15), and combinations of dream types that provide access to otherworldly realms (*1 En.* 13:7–36:4, *T. Levi* 2:4–5:7, 8:1–9:3, 4 Ezra 9:26–10:59, *Jub.* 27:21–24 and *Ladd. Jac.*). (2) Although it might be said with some truth that the dreams in apocalypses are more complex than those in non-apocalypses, some notable exceptions occur. *Testament of Abraham* 7:1–15 is a relatively simple dream, but the dreams in *T. Naph.* and *T. Jos.* are complex in their own ways. (3) The apocalypses containing dreams evince some priestly themes, but as I have shown repeatedly, many non-apocalypses with dreams also share priestly concerns (e.g. Josephus, *T. Naph*, *T. Jos.*, *L.A.B.*). As for scribal imagery, it is also the case that all the apocalypses containing dreams, except for *Ladder of Jacob*, possess abundant scribal imagery in which humans or angels write or read, including: (*1 En.* 13:4, 14:4, 7, 33:4, 83:10, 89:70–71, 89:76–77, 90:20; *2 En.* 19:5, 22:11, 23:3–6; Dan 7:1, 10, 8:26?, 12:4; *Jub.* 4:17–19, 32:20–26; 4 Ezra 14:6, 14:37–48; *2 Bar.* 77:11–20, 78:1–86:1; *T. Levi* 1:1?, 8:17; *T. Abr. A* 12:7–13:10, *T. Abr. B* 10:8–16, 11:1–4, *T. Abr. Romanian* 30–32). However, a few non-apocalypses also contain scribal-related imagery *within dreams*, including *T. Naph.* 5:8, 1QGen. Apocry., 4QEn. 4QBook of Giants, and 4QApocry. Jac. In 4QVisions of Amram the dreamer wakes up from sleep and writes down his vision.

[84] See the seminal article by Collins, 'Jewish Apocalypses,' in *Semeia 14*.

the reader is not made privy to the content of these revelations.[85] Other borderline cases may be clarified by this distinction. Mordecai's dream in Greek Additions to Esther may have some eschatological content in describing a cosmic war involving heaven and earth (11:6–7).[86] If dreams are revelations sent from an otherworldly mediator, and if the dragons represent heavenly figures, the categorization of this text could be as an apocalypse. Yet, since the eschatological facet of the dream symbols remains uninterpreted, eschatological secrets are not explicitly communicated *to the reader*.

The *Book of Jubilees* as a whole is another marginal text for which attention to audience reception and the role of dreams in revelation may help clarify its difficult position in relation to the definition of apocalypse. Chapter 23, which does not contain a dream, is manifestly eschatological and generally considered an apocalypse.[87] Several dreams in the rest of the book, which as a whole is not typically deemed an apocalypse, also share an eschatological worldview. For instance, *Jub.* 4:19 refers to Enoch's dreams of 'what was and what will be … as it will happen among the children of men in their generations until the day of judgment,' and *Jub.* 32:21, in which Jacob dreams of an angel who descends from heaven and gives him heavenly tablets to read so that 'he knew everything which was written in them, which would happen to him and to his sons during all the ages.' However, the details of those eschatological revelations are not communicated *to the readers* except in chapter 23.

By contrast, those texts that are commonly recognized as apocalypses readily impart knowledge of the structure and appearance of the universe to both the dreamers and the readers. Enoch tours the heavenly Temple as well as remote regions of the earth (*1 En.* 12–36), and each sight is carefully related to the audience, insofar as Enoch can express the wondrous appearance of the sacred realms that he sees. Similarly, the *Testament of Levi* describes each level of heaven and its contents which Levi witnesses during his ascent (*T. Levi* 2–5), as well as some

---

[85] However, caution must be exercised since the play is only preserved as quotations in Eusebius, Clement of Alexandria and Pseudo-Eustathius. Robertson, *Ezekiel the Tragedian*, 803.

[86] Nickelsburg notes the dream has 'a cosmic dimension,' *Jewish Literature*, 173.

[87] *Jubilees* 23 is manifestly an apocalypse, but *Jubilees* as a whole is 'a borderline case for the apocalyptic genre,' with Collins concluding it should be counted. Collins, *Apocalyptic Imagination*, 83.

scenes in the heavenly sanctuary (*T. Levi* 8–10). Daniel describes his dream vision of the heavenly throne-room/Temple[88] and the divine beings he sees therein (Dan 7), and Ezra narrates scenes from his symbolic dream of the hiding place of the eschatological 'Man from the Sea,' including the appearance of sea, mountain and sky (4 Ezra 13). Thus, the distinction between texts commonly recognized as apocalypses and non-apocalypses continues to be a useful one, and seems in part to turn on the issue of the transmission of dream knowledge to the reader.

To sum up: it is my hope that this project will add to future discussions of apocalypticism on the following six points.

First, the pervasive presence of dreams and visions in apocalypses suggests that they may be even more integral to the Jewish apocalypse than the SBL Genres Project definition recognizes.

Second, this has important implications for the rise of apocalypticism or apocalyptic thinking. At this juncture, I suggest that Carmignac's initial suspicions were correct and that the expression of the apocalyptic worldview originates in a sense within the dream tradition.[89] I attribute this to the artistic freedom the dream form provides in erasing spatial and temporal boundaries of reality, allowing for the articulation of the apocalyptic construction of reality while also providing a means of transcending it. I suggest that the dream form itself catalyzed the production of this worldview in a way that more limiting forms, such as the prophetic oracle or wisdom poem, could not.

Third, I hope to have clearly shown that dreams in apocalypses as well as in non-apocalypses subscribe to an overarching priestly and scribal worldview that appears to translate into some measure of social prestige and/or power. This should caution against conclusions that apocalypticism was necessarily the outlook of a tiny, uniform, disenfranchised group within Jewish society.

Fourth, I propose that a reconsideration of certain apocalypses *as varieties of dream texts* may mitigate the tension between what appears to

---

[88] Collins argues the throne-room vision in Daniel 7 differs from biblical throne-room visions and instead closely parallels the heavenly throne-room/Temple in *1 Enoch* 14, although the location of the throne-room is not specified in Daniel. He notes that direct literary dependence cannot be excluded, given that both contain a river of fire, clothing white as snow and an entourage of ten thousand times ten thousand. Collins, *Daniel*, 300.

[89] Carmignac, 'Description du phénomène,' 168–169.

be two sub-types of apocalypse or even two distinct genres, namely, the historical apocalypse and the apocalypse containing an otherworldly journey.[90] The definition of 'apocalypse' should never drive our reading of the texts; the opposite should always be the case. The group of dream texts that are also apocalypses comprises both the 'historical' type (Dan 7–12, *2 Baruch*, 4 Ezra, *1 Enoch* 85–90) as well as the 'otherworldly journey' type of apocalypse[91] (*1 Enoch* 1–36, *T. Abraham*, *T. Levi*), since dreams transcend both temporal and spatial norms and thus explain the presence of both sub-genres.

Fifth, this study suggests that 'apocalypses' do in fact cohere as a genre and that dreams and visions play a vital role in transmitting eschatological (and/or otherworldly secrets) to dreamers as well as to readers. Thus, efforts to redefine apocalypse and apocalypticism should take into account the role of the reader as a receiver of extraordinary knowledge and should not discount the importance of eschatology. A worthy study might be an evaluation of the Qumran texts in terms of the extent to which eschatological revelation is communicated to or otherwise known by *the reader*.

Sixth, since so many apocalypses contain dreams and almost all of the remainder contain visions, we should use terms such as 'ascent' only with marked caution. Ancient dreams bridge the liminal threshold of reality as a state of sleep consciousness in which perceptions are real and in which dream objects can become material objects. Similarly, through the dreamer's experience, some early Jewish dream texts blend the spatial, temporal and ontological dimensions of reality: heaven with earth,[92] past with future, angel with human.[93] Ultimately, early Jewish dreams facilitate *the transcendence or erasure of distinctions between planes of existence* without necessarily employing the imagery of spatial ascent or journey. Within this larger group of dream texts, the apocalypses still distinguish themselves through accents on the eschatological dimension

---

[90] Collins raises the issue of whether we should speak of historical apocalypses and apocalypses containing otherworldly journeys as two genres, 'Introduction,' in *Semeia 14*, 16.

[91] Collins, 'Jewish Apocalypses,' in *Semeia 14*, 21–59, 30–44.

[92] It is this collapsing of dimensions through transcendence that is in view when Gnostic and/or mystical texts describe joining the upper to the lower and the outer to the inner. See for example *Ladder of Jacob* 7, a later Christian mystical addition.

[93] See Segal, *Two Powers in Heaven*, 188; Charlesworth, 'The Portrayal of the Righteous,' 135–152; Himmelfarb, *Ascent to Heaven*; and Fletcher-Louis, *All the Glory of Adam*.

of reality (sometimes along with the spatial and ontological ones) and on communicating otherworldly *realia* (both temporal and spatial) to the audience.

Four: Jewish Mysticism and Oneiric Experiences

By now it should come as no surprise that numerous mystical or proto-mystical themes are evident in early Jewish dream texts. Scholem and Gruenwald have argued that the roots of early Jewish mysticism reach well back into the pseudepigraphic literature, beginning with *1 Enoch* 1–36, with Gruenwald labeling Enoch's dream-report 'the oldest Merkavah vision we know of from the literature outside of the canonical Scriptures'[94] Nickelsburg comes to a similar conclusion:

> This paradox—that a rare righteous person can penetrate into the presence of the inaccessible God—is also a mark of Jewish Merkavah mystical literature. *1 Enoch* 14 stands at an important transitional point between prophetic and mystical traditions.[95]

The dream ascents of seers like Enoch (*1 En.*, *4QEn.*, *2 En.*), Levi (*T. Levi Greek*, *4Q Aram. Levi*) and Naphtali (*T. Naph.*) to the heavenly *hekhal* appear to prefigure the journey described in *Hekhalot* texts of the *yored merkabah* to the same location. By contrast, while agreeing that the Ezekiel *merkabah* tradition significantly influences the *Book of the Watchers*, M. Himmelfarb distinguishes between these motifs in apocalyptic literature and the *Hekhalot* texts, seeing no direct trajectory.[96]

However, the image of ascent is not the only connection between later mystical texts and early Jewish dream texts. The angel that helps Jacob to memorize and perfectly reproduce knowledge from heavenly tablets revealed in a dream (*Jub. 32*) shares much with later Sar ha-Torah traditions in *Hekhalot* literature.[97] Moreover, other oneiric means of accessing divine realities, such as the descent of the heavenly Zion in 4 Ezra 9 and the descent of numerous angelic dream messengers who appear and converse with dreamers, often as a result of prayer

---

[94] Gruenwald, *Apocalyptic and Merkavah Mysticism*, 36.

[95] Nickelsburg, 'Enoch, Levi and Peter,' 581; see also Collins, *Apocalyptic Imagination*, 54.

[96] Himmelfarb, *Ascent to Heaven*, 7.

[97] For the Sar ha-Torah tradition see especially Swartz, *Scholastic Magic*; R. Lesses, *Ritual Practices to Gain Power*), esp. 52–61, 273; and J. Davila, *Descenders to the Chariot*, esp. 204–213.

or other rituals, also strongly gesture towards later mystical texts. The recent works by J. Davila and R. Lesses have brilliantly clarified that rituals and adjurations to gain control of angels are major if not central components of the *Hekhalot* literature.[98]

The earliest Hellenistic Jewish dream text, *1Enoch* 13:7–16:4 (or 36:4), aptly illustrates the pervasive similarities between early dream texts and later *Hekhalot* literature. Whether or not there is a single direct trajectory to *Merkabah* mysticism, there is a definite collocation of rituals and images that are clearly developed in that direction. For instance, the *Book of the Watchers* contains descriptions of rituals that resemble later *Merkabah* mystical practices. At the beginning of his dream, Enoch is not lying down in the typical posture for ANE, biblical, Greek and Roman dreams. Rather, he is sitting, which is characteristic of *Merkabah* mystics.[99] Enoch's location by the waters is probably influenced by the tradition of Ezekiel by the Chebar river (Ezek 1:1), but this setting is so frequently emphasized in the *Hekhalot* literature that Gruenwald and M. Idel posit a connection between *Merkabah* mysticism and water divination.[100] When Enoch recites the petition of the sons of heaven, which appears to induce sleep and the ensuing revelation, one thinks readily of the lengthy trance-inducing recitations of hymns and prayers are also a characteristic feature of the *Hekhalot* texts.[101]

In addition, *1Enoch* 14:9–12 develops specific images from Ezekiel in the same way as do later *Hekhalot* texts:

---

[98] Scholem identified mystical ascent as the constitutive element of the *Hekhalot* texts, while Halperin challenged this assumption by centering the *Sar ha Torah* material, in which the practitioner receives Torah knowledge effortlessly through the adjuration of an angel. Schäfer tried to balance the importance of adjurations in the literature, while not discounting the importance of the ascent material. Scholem, *Major Trends*; idem, *Jewish Gnosticism, Merkabah Mysticism*; Halperin, *The Merkabah in Rabbinic Literature* (New Haven, Conn.: American Oriental Society, 1980); idem, *Faces of the Chariot*; Schäfer, *Hidden and Manifest God*. More recently, in *Ritual Practices to Gain Power* R. Lesses has done an in-depth study of the adjurations, and has proposed that ritual practices to gain power include adjurations for the ritual learning of Torah as well as for ascents and descents. Similarly, J. Davila has argued in *Descenders to the Chariot* that the theme of using ritual means to gain control of angels is the main thrust of the literature, which thus includes adjurations of all sorts, the Sar ha Torah material, angelic revelations, and guidance/protection for heavenly ascents.

[99] In the Greek recension, however, Enoch is standing. The mystic in *Hekh. Zut.* section 424 is sitting with his head between his knees, in the fashion of Elijah in 1 Kings 18:42.

[100] In Halperin, *Faces of the Chariot*, 231–232.

[101] Scholem, *Major Trends*, 57–63.

> And I went in until I drew near to a wall built of hailstones;
> and tongues of *fire* were encircling them all around;
> and they began to frighten me.
> And I went into the tongues of *fire*, and I drew near to a great house
>   built of hailstones;
> and the walls of this house were like stone slabs;
> and they were all of snow, and the floor was of snow;
> And *the ceiling was like shooting stars and lightning flashes*;
> and among them were *fiery cherubim*, and *their heaven was water*;
> and a *flaming fire* encircled its walls, and the doors blazed with *fire*.
>
> (*1 Enoch* 14:9–12; cf. Ezek 1–2)

1 Enoch 14 juxtaposes *hailstones, building stones, fire, cherubim and water*, and rivers of fire (14:19). In a similar fashion, *Hekhalot Zuṭarti* lists *hailstones, stones of broom fire, beryl stones, rows of angels*, and *rivers of fire* as items located between the *cherubim* and the divine throne.[102] *1 Enoch's* descriptions of stone walls as white as snow and a heaven made of water are also reminiscent of several *Hekhalot* traditions that describe the white marble stones of the *hekhal* flashing so brightly that the *yored merkabah* mistakes it for 'thousands upon thousands of waves of water.'[103]

Finally, *1 Enoch* and *Hekhalot* texts share thematic motifs of a terrified seer who swoons, the vision of the Godhead who sits on the throne surrounded by angels, and a seer who is actively involved in his vision rather than the passive recipient of revelation.[104] Most importantly, unlike Ezekiel, both the *Hekhalot* literature and *1 Enoch* 1–36 depict an ascent to the heavenly temple[105] that culminates in a vision of the Glory of God.[106] Thus, *1 Enoch* appears to be an important link between Ezekiel and the *Merkabah* mystical traditions,[107] since in some ways *1 Enoch* more closely resembles later *Hekhalot* texts than does Ezekiel itself.

---

[102] *Hekh. Zut.* section 356; Schäfer, *Hidden and Manifest*, 63. D. Halperin traces the motif of water in heaven and fiery angels to Psalm 104:1–4 as well, and notes several rabbinic midrashim on the subject, Halperin, *Faces of the Chariot*, 83–84.

[103] In his translation of *1 Enoch*, E. Isaac translates these stones as 'white marble,' *OTP* 1:5–90.

[104] Gruenwald, *Apocalyptic and Merkabah*, 36–37; Nickelsburg, 'Enoch, Levi and Peter,' 578–580.

[105] Gruenwald, *Apocalyptic and Merkabah*, 36–37; Nickelsburg, 'Enoch, Levi and Peter,' 578.

[106] See *1 Enoch* 14:15, 18–20, 21, 24; P. Schäfer, *Hidden and Manifest*, 12, 124 and elsewhere.

[107] Scholem, *Major Trends*, 43; Gruenwald, *Apocalyptic and Merkavah Mysticism*, 36; Nickelsburg, 'Enoch, Levi and Peter,' 578; idem, *1 Enoch*, 259–260.

Thus, I suggest that the examples of shared rituals, images and themes in *1 Enoch* and the *Hekhalot* texts are not merely 'parallelomania,' but rather evidence that the roots of *merkabah* mysticism do reach as far back in early Judaism as *1 Enoch*, as Scholem and Gruenwald have posited. Dreams provide the means for transcending multiple axes of reality through a variety of formulas, including heavenly ascent, theurgic descent, adjuration of angels and ontological transformation, themes which have close affinities with a mystical worldview.

Conclusion

In ancient texts, dreamers lie down, dream, and awaken in a fashion that follows conventional cross-cultural patterns established for millennia. However, within this standard formal frame, any imaginable dream may take shape. Various authors of Hellenistic Judaism press 'dream logic' in new ways, creating worlds in which dreamers are no longer bound by any limits of ordinary reality. That is, dreams construct universes by interweaving spatial, temporal, ontological and perceptual dimensions of reality in an overarching matrix, while simultaneously deconstructing these axes by providing dreamers with access to divine spheres.

Dream texts in early Judaism often envision or presuppose the ultimate tier of reality as the heavenly *hekhal*, and accordingly, they are permeated by scribal and priestly concerns. As Clifford Geertz has so aptly demonstrated, religious symbols are particular to certain cultures, and they reflect as well as solidify social organization.[108] Thus, we may glean insights into the social history of early Judaism and early Christianity from the preponderance of scribal and priestly images pervading Jewish dreams in the Hellenistic and Roman eras.

On the level of audience reception, dream texts also had a social dimension. Since the dreamers in Hellenistic Jewish texts are pseudepigraphic heroes of Israelite history, ancient Jewish readers likely did not read the texts dispassionately, but rather identified to varying degrees with their ancestors, sharing in the traditional benefits of dreams. Fictional characters and actual audiences alike received extraordinary

---

[108] Geertz, *The Interpretation of Cultures*, 3–32.

knowledge of the nature of reality, experienced a degree of psychological healing and consolation, and were assured of divine sanction for
themselves and their community.

Thus, dreams such as Daniel's vision of the throne room of the
Ancient of Days or Enoch's ascent to the heavenly Palace-Temple
where he sees the enthroned Glory of God were much more than the
Freudian wish-fulfillments of a culture. Rather, such symbolic orderings
of the universe reified Jewish self-identity and asserted Jewish authority over and against the prevailing Hellenistic and Roman rulers and
societies. Early Jewish dreams revealed to their ancient audiences that
beyond the dim prospects of the mundane world lay other, unknown
realms, the ordering of which reflects the sovereignty of the heavenly
Palace-Temple. From here the God of Israel rules, unfolding a plan for
the Universe in which Israel's dreamers and their descendants play key
roles.

BIBLIOGRAPHY

Primary Sources

Aeschylus. *The Complete Greek Tragedies: Aeschylus.* Vol. 1. Edited by D. Grene and R. Lattimore. Translated by R. Lattimore. Chicago: University of Chicago Press, 1974.

Andersen, F.I. (trans.). '*2 Enoch.*' *OTP* 1:91–221. Edited by Charlesworth.

Apollonius of Rhodes. *Argonautica.* In *The Voyage of the Argo: The Argonautica.* Translated by E.V. Rieu. London: Penguin, 1959. Repr. 1971.

Aristophanes. Translated by B.B. Rogers. 3 vols. Loeb Classical Library. Cambridge, MA: Harvard University Press, 1979–1982.

Aristophanes, *Frogs.* Translated by G. Murray. London: George Allen & Unwin Ltd., 1908. Repr. 1946.

Aristotle. *On the Soul, Parva Naturalia, On Breath.* Vol. 8. Translated by W.S. Hett. Cambridge, MA: Harvard University Press, 1975.

Artemidorus, Daldianus. *The Interpretation of Dreams: Oneirocritica.* Translated by R. White. Noyes Classical Studies. Park Ridge: Noyes, 1975.

Biblia Hebraica Stuttgartensia. Stuttgart: Deutsche Bibelgesselschaft, 1967. Repr. 1990.

Bidawid, R.J. (ed.). *4 Esdras. The Old Testament in Syriac According to the Peshitta Version.* Part IV, fasc. 3. Leiden: E.J. Brill, 1973.

Box, G.H. (trans.). '4 Ezra.' In *The Apocrypha and Pseudepigrapha of the Old Testament in English,* 542–624. Edited by R.H. Charles. Vol. 2. Oxford: Clarendon, 1913.

Brock, S. (ed.). Testamentum Iobi. / Apocalypsis Baruchi Graece / ed. J.-C. Picard. *Pseudepigrapha Veteris Testamenti Graece* 2. Leiden: E.J. Brill, 1967.

Campbell, D.A. (trans.). *Greek Lyric: Sappho, Alcaeus.* Vol. 1. Cambridge, MA: Harvard University Press, 1982.

———. (trans.). *Greek Lyric: Anacreon, Anacreontea, Choral Lyric from Olympus to Alcman.* Vol. 2. Cambridge, MA: Harvard University Press, 1988.

Charles, R.H. (ed.). *The Ethiopic Version of the Hebrew Book of Jubilees.* Oxford. 1895.

———. (ed.). *The Ethiopic Version of the Book of Enoch: Edited from Twenty-Three Mss. together with the Fragmentary Greek and Latin Versions.* Oxford: Clarendon, 1906.

———. (ed.). *The Greek Versions of the Testaments of the Twelve Patriarchs.* Oxford: Oxford University Press, 1908.

———. (trans.). *The Testaments of the Twelve Patriarchs: Translated from the Editor's Greek Texts.* London: Blackwell, 1908.

———. (trans.). *The Book of Enoch.* Oxford: Clarendon, 1912.

———. (trans.). *The Apocrypha and Pseudepigrapha of the Old Testament in English.* 2 vols. Oxford: Clarendon, 1913.

Charlesworth, J.H. (ed.). *The Old Testament Pseudepigrapha.* 2 vols. Garden City: Doubleday, 1983, 1985.

Cicero. *De Republica, De Legibus.* Translated by C.W. Keyes. London: William Heinemann, 1928.

———. *De Senectute, De Amicitia, De Divinatione.* Translated by W.A. Falconer. London: William Heinemann, 1923.

Collins, J.J. *Daniel: A Commentary on the Book of Daniel.* Hermeneia. Minneapolis: Fortress, 1993.

Dedering, S. (ed.). *Apocalypse of Baruch. The Old Testament in Syriac According to the Peshitta Version.* Part IV, fasc. 3. Leiden: E.J. Brill, 1973.

De Jonge, M. 'The Testaments of the Twelve Patriarchs.' In *The Apocryphal Old Testament,* 526–537. Edited by H.F.D. Sparks. Oxford: Clarendon, 1984.

———. (ed.). *The Testaments of the Twelve Patriarchs: A Critical Edition of the Greek Text.* Leiden: E.J. Brill, 1978.

Diels, H. (ed.). *Die Fragmente der Vorsokratiker, griechisch und deutsch.* Berlin: Weidmann, 1952.

Diodorus of Sicily. Vol. 12. Translated by F.R. Walton. London: Heinemann, 1967.

Edelstein, L. and E. Edelstein (eds.). *Asclepius: A Collection and Interpretation of the Testimonies.* 2 vols. Ancient Religion and Mythology. Baltimore: Johns Hopkins University Press, 1945. Repr. New York: Garland, 1975.

Euripides. 4 vols. Translated by A.S. Way. Cambridge, MA: Harvard University Press, 1912. Repr. 1942.

Gelston, A. (ed.). *Dodekapropheten, Daniel-Bel-Draco. The Old Testament in Syriac According to the Peshitta Version.* Part III, fasc. 4. Leiden: Brill, 1980.

Graves, R. *The Twelve Caesars: Gaius Suetonius Tranquillus.* Baltimore, MD: Penguin, 1957.

Grensemann, H. *Die hippokratische Schrift: 'Über die heilige Krankheit.'* Berlin: Walter de Gruyter & Co., 1968.

Harrington, D.J. (ed.). *The Hebrew Fragments of Pseudo-Philo's Liber Antiquitatum Biblicarum: Preserved in the Chronicles of Jerahmeel.* Missoula, MT: Society of Biblical Literature, 1974.

———. (trans.). *Pseudo-Philon Les Antiquités Bibliques.* Translated by J. Cazeaux. 2 vols. Paris: Les Éditions du Cerf, 1976.

———. (trans.). 'Pseudo-Philo.' In *OTP* 2:297–378. Edited by Charlesworth.

Herodotus. Translated by A.D. Godley. 4 vols. Loeb Classical Library. Cambridge, MA: Harvard University Press, 1971.

Hesiod, Homeric Hymns and Homerica. Translated by H.G. Evelyn-White. London: William Heinemann, 1929.

Hippocrates. *Du Regime.* Edited and translated by R. Joly, with S. Byl, ed. Berlin: Akademie, 1984.

Homer. *The Iliad.* 2 vols. Translated by A.T. Murray. London: William Heinemann, 1925.

———. *The Odyssey.* 2 vols. Translated by A.T. Murray. London: William Heinemann, 1927.

Kavvadias, P. (ed.). *Fouilles d'Épidaure*. Athens: Vlastos, 1891.

Kee, H.C. 'Testaments of the Twelve Patriarchs.' In *OTP* 1:776–828. Edited by Charlesworth.

Kirk, G.S., and J.E. Raven. *The Presocratic Philosophers: A Critical History with a Selection of Texts*. Cambridge: Cambridge University Press, 1963.

Kisch, G. *Pseudo-Philo's Liber Antiquitatum Biblicarum*. Notre Dame, IN: University of Notre Dame, 1949.

Klijn, A.F.J. (trans.). '*2 Baruch*.' In *OTP* 1:615–652. Edited by Charlesworth.

———. (ed.). *Der Lateinische Text der Apokalypse des Esra*. Berlin: Akademie, 1983.

Knibb, Michael. (ed.). *Ethiopic Book of Enoch: A New Edition In Light of the Aramaic*. 2 vols. Oxford: Clarendon. 1978.

LiDonnici, L. *The Epidaurian Miracle Inscriptions: Text, Translation and Commentary*. Society of Biblical Literature Texts and Translations 36. Graeco-Roman Religion Series 11. Atlanta: Scholars Press, 1995.

Lunt, H.G. (trans.). '*Ladder of Jacob*.' In *OTP* 2:401–411. Edited by Charlesworth.

Macrobius, Ambrosius Aurelius. *Commentary on the Dream of Scipio*. Translated by H. Stahl. New York: Columbia University Press, 1952.

Martínez, F. G and E.J.C. Tigchelaar (eds.). *The Dead Sea Scrolls Study Edition*. 2 vols. Leiden: Brill, 1997–1998.

Metzger, B.M. (trans.). 'The Fourth Book of Ezra.' In *OTP* 1:516–569. Edited by Charlesworth.

Nickelsburg, G.W.E. *1 Enoch: A Commentary on the Book of 1 Enoch, Chapters 1–36; 81–108*. Hermeneia. Minneapolis, Fortress, 2001.

Oppenheim, L. *The Interpretation of Dreams in the Ancient Near East: With a Translation of an Assyrian Dream-Book*. Transactions of the American Philosophical Society, vol. 46, pt. 3. Philadelphia: American Philosophical Society, 1956.

Ovid. *Metamorphoses*. Translated by R. Humphries. Bloomington: Indiana University Press, 1999.

Oxford Annotated Apocrypha, RSV. Edited by B.M. Metzger. New York: Oxford University Press, 1965. Repr. 1977.

Pennington, A. (trans.). 'Ladder of Jacob.' In *The Apocryphal Old Testament*, 453–464. Edited by H.F.D. Sparks. Oxford: Clarendon, 1984. Repr. 1990.

Pindar. *Olympian Odes, Pythian Odes*. Edited and translated by W.H. Race. Cambridge, MA: Harvard University Press, 1997.

Pritchard, J. (ed.). *Ancient Near Eastern Texts Relating to the Old Testament*. 3rd ed. Princeton: Princeton University Press, 1970.

Ramsay, G.G. (ed.). *Juvenal and Persius*. London: William Heinemann, 1928.

Robertson, R.G. (trans.). 'Ezekiel the Tragedian.' In *OTP* 2:803–819. Edited by Charlesworth.

Sanders, E.P. (trans.). 'Testament of Abraham.' In *OTP* 1:871–902. Edited by Charlesworth.

Snell, B. (trans.). 'Ezekiel the Tragedian.' *Tragicorum Graecorum Fragmenta*. Vol. 1, 288–301. Göttingen: Vandenhoeck & Ruprecht, 1971.

Sophocles. *Ajax, Electra, Oedipus Tyrannus*. Edited and translated by Hugh Lloyd-Jones. Cambridge, MA: Harvard University Press, 1994.

——. *Antigone, Women of Trachis, Philoctetes, Oedipus at Colonus*. Edited and translated by H. Lloyd-Jones. Cambridge, MA: Harvard University Press, 1994.

Sparks, H.F.D. (ed.). *The Apocryphal Old Testament*. Oxford: Clarendon, 1984. Repr. 1990.

Spittler, R.P. (trans.). 'Testament of Job.' In *OTP* 1:828–868. Edited by Charlesworth.

Stahl, W.H. (ed.). *Macrobius: Commentary on the Dream in Scipio*. New York: Columbia University Press, 1952. Repr. 1990.

Stone, M.E. (ed.). *The Testament of Abraham: The Greek Recensions*. Texts and Translations 2. Pseudepigrapha Series 2. Missoula, MN: Society of Biblical Literature, 1972.

——. (trans.). *Fourth Ezra: A Commentary on the Book of Fourth Ezra*. Hermeneia. Edited by F.M. Cross. Minneapolis: Fortress, 1990.

—— and J.C. Greenfield, 'Aramaic Levi Document.' In *DJD XXII: Qumran Cave 4, XVII Parabiblical Texts, Pt. 3*, 1–72. Discoveries in the Judean Desert. Edited by E. Tov et al. Oxford: Clarendon, 1996.

Suetonius. 2 vols. Translated by J.C. Rolfe. London: William Heinemann, 1920.

——. *The Twelve Caesars: Gaius Suetonius Tranquillus*. Translated by R. Graves. Baltimore: Penguin, 1957.

Tanakh. Philadelphia: Jewish Publication Society, 1988.

Theophrastus, Herodas, Cercidas and the Choliambic Poets: Characters, Mimes. Edited and translated by J. Rusten, I.C. Cunningham and A.D. Knox. Cambridge, MA: Harvard University Press, 1929. Repr. 1993.

Tisserant, E. 'Fragments syriaques du Livre des Jubilés.' *Revue biblique* 30 (1921) 55–86, 206–232.

Uhlig, Siegbert. (ed.). *Das äthiopische Henochbuch*. Jüdische Schriften aus hellenistisch-römischer Zeit 5/6. Gütersloh: MOHN, 1984.

Vaillant, A. (ed. and trans.). *Le livre des secrets d'Hénoch: Texte slave et traduction française*. Paris: 1952. Repr. 1976.

VanderKam, J.C. (ed.). *The Book of Jubilees: A Critical Text.* Lovanii: Peeters, 1989.

Virgil. *The Aeneid*. Translated by C.D. Lewis. Garden City, N.Y.: Doubleday Anchor, 1952.

Volten, A.D.F. (ed.). *Demotische Traumdeutung. Analecta Aegyptiaca* 3. Kopenhagen: Einar Munksgaard, 1942.

Warmington, E.H. (ed.). *Remains of Old Latin: Ennius and Caecilius*. Vol. 1. Loeb Classical Library. Cambridge, MA: Harvard University Press, 1935. Repr. 1956.

Wintermute, O.S. (trans.). 'Jubilees.' In *OTP* 2:35–142. Edited by Charlesworth.

Secondary Sources

Abusch, T. 'Ascent to the Stars in a Mesopotamian Ritual.' In *Death, Ecstasy, and Otherworldly Journeys*, 15–39. Edited by J.J. Collins and M. Fishbane. Albany: State University of New York, 1995.

Ackerman, S. 'The Deception of Isaac, Jacob's Dream at Bethel, and Incubation on an Animal Skin.' In *Priesthood and Cult in Ancient Israel*, 92–120. Edited by G.A. Anderson and S.M. Olyan. Sheffield: JSOT Press, 1991.

Aicher, P. 'Ennius' Dream of Homer.' *American Journal of Philology* 110 (Summer 1989) 227–232.

Aleshire, S.B. *The Athenian Asklepieion: The People, their Dedications, and the Inventories*. Amsterdam: J.C. Gieben, 1989.

Alexander, F. 'Dreams in Pairs and Series.' *International Journal of Psychoanalysis* 6 (1925, repr. 1953) 446–457.

Amory, A. 'Omens and Dreams in the *Odyssey*.' Ph.D. Diss., Harvard University, 1958.

——. 'The Gates of Horn and Ivory.' In *Yale Classical Studies 20: Homeric Studies* 3–57. Edited by G.S. Kirk and A. Parry. New Haven: Yale University Press, 1966.

Anderson, C.A. 'The Dream-Oracles of Athena, *Knights* 1090–1095.' *Transactions of the American Philological Association* 121 (1991) 149–155.

Anz, W. *Zur Frage nach dem Ursprung des Gnostizismus: Ein religionsgeschichtlicher Versuch*. TU 15.4. Leipzig: Hinrichs, 1897.

Argall, R.A., B.A. Bow, and R.A. Werline (eds.). *For a Later Generation: The Transformation of Tradition in Israel, Early Judaism and Early Christianity*. Harrisburg, PA: Trinity, 2000.

Attridge, H. 'Greek and Latin Apocalypses.' In *Apocalypse: The Morphology of a Genre*, 159–186. *Semeia 14*. Edited by J.J. Collins. Missoula, MT: Scholars Press, 1979.

Baird, R. and A. Bloom. *Indian and Far Eastern Religious Traditions*. New York: Harper & Row, 1971.

Bar, S. *A Letter that Has Not Been Read: Dreams in the Hebrew Bible*. Cincinnati: Hebrew Union College Press, 2001.

Barfield, O. 'Dream, Myth and Philosophical Double Vision.' In *Myths, Dreams and Religion*, 211–224. Edited by J. Campbell. New York: Dutton, 1970.

Barton, J. 'Form Criticism: Old Testament.' In *Anchor Bible Dictionary* 2:838–841. 6 vols. Edited by D.N. Freedman. New York: Doubleday, 1992.

——. *Oracles of God: Perceptions of Ancient Prophecy in Israel after the Exile*. London: Darton, Longman & Todd, 1986.

Becker, J. *Untersuchungen zur Entstehungsgeschichte der Testamente der Zwölf Patriarchen*. Leiden: Brill, 1970.

Benedetti, G. 'Über die Objektivität des Traumverstehens.' In *Traum und Träumen: Traumanalysen in Wissenschaft, Religion und Kunst*, 10–31. Edited by T. Wagner-Simon and G. Benedetti. Götttingen: Vandenhoeck & Ruprecht, 1984.

Bentzen, A. *Daniel*. Handbuch zum Alten Testament 19. 2nd ed. Tübingen: Mohr, 1952.

Ben Zvi, E. *Micah*. Forms of the Old Testament Literature XXIB. Grand Rapids, MI: Eerdmans, 2000.

Berchman, R.M. 'Arcana Mundi: Magic and Divination in *De Somnis* of Philo of Alexandria.' *SBL Seminar Papers, 1987*, 403–428. Society of Biblical Literature Seminar Papers 26. Edited by K.H. Richards. Atlanta: Scholars Press, 1987.

———. (ed.). *Mediators of the Divine: Horizons of Prophecy, Divination, Dreams and Theurgy in Mediterranean Antiquity*. Atlanta: Scholars Press, 1998.

Berger, P. and T. Luckman. *The Social Construction of Reality: A Treatise in the Sociology of Knowledge*. Garden City, N.Y.: Anchor Books, 1967.

Berlin, N. 'Dreams in Roman Epic: The Hermeneutics of a Narrative Technique.' Ph.D. diss., University of Michigan, 1994.

Betz, H.D. 'Zum Problem des religionsgeschichtlichen Verständnisses der Apokalyptik.' *Zeitschrift für Theologie und Kirche* 63 (1966) 391–409.

———. 'Magic and Mystery in the Greek Magical Papyri.' In *Magika Hiera: Ancient Greek Magic and Religion*, 244–259. Edited by C.A. Faraone and D. Obbink. NewYork: Oxford University Press, 1991.

———(ed.). *The Greek Magical Papyri in Translation: Including the Demotic Spells*. 2nd ed. Chicago: University of Chicago Press, 1996.

Bickerman, E. *The Jews in the Greek Age*. Cambridge, MA: Harvard University Press, 1988.

———. 'The Historical Foundations of Postbiblical Judaism.' In *Emerging Judaism: Studies on the Fourth and Third Centuries B.C.E.*, 9–48. Edited by M.E. Stone and D. Satran. Minneapolis: Fortress, 1989.

Bietenhard, H. *Die himmlische Welt im Urchristenturm und Spätjudentum*. Tübingen: J. C.B. Mohr (Paul Siebeck), 1951.

Bilde, P. *Flavius Josephus between Jerusalem and Rome: His Life, his Works and their Importance*. Journal for the Study of the Old Testament: Supplement Series 2. Sheffield: JSOT, 1988.

Bilu, Y. and H. Abramovitch. 'In search of the saddiq: visitational dreams among Moroccan Jews in Israel.' *Psychiatry* 48:1 (Feb. 1985) 83–92.

Blum, E. '*Formgeschichte*—A Misleading Category? Some Critical Remarks.' In *The Changing Face of Form Criticism for the Twenty-First Century*, 32–45. Edited by M. Sweeney and E. Ben Zvi. Grand Rapids, MI: Eerdmans, 2003.

Bogaert, P.M. *L'Apocalypse syriaque de Baruch*. Sources chretiennes 144–145. 2 vols. Paris: Cerf, 1969.

Boorer, S. 'Kaleidoscopic Patterns and the Shaping of Experience.' In *Changing Face of Form-Criticism*, 199–216. Edited by Sweeney and Ben Zvi.

Booth, M. *Opium: A History*. London: Simon & Schuster, 1996.

Borger, R. 'Die Beschwörungsserie BĪT MĒSERI und die Himmelfahrt Henochs.' *Journal of Near Eastern Studies* 33 (1974) 183–196.

Botterweck, J. and H. Ringgren (eds.). *Theological Dictionary of the Old Testament*. 5 vols. Translated by S. Willis and G. Bromiley. Grand Rapids: Eerdmans, 1974–1990.

Böttrich, C. *Weltweisheit, Menschheitsethik, Urkult: Studien zum slavischen Henochbuch*. Wissenschaftliche Untersuchungen zum Neuen Testament 2. Tübingen: Mohr-Siebeck, 1992.

———. *Das slavische Henochbuch*. Jüdische Schriften aus hellenistisch-römischer Zeit V.7. Gütersloh: Gütersloh Verlaghaus, 1996.

Bouché-Leclerq, A. *Histoire de la divination dans l'antiquité*. 4 vols. Paris: Bruxelles, 1879–1881.

Bousset, W. *Die Himmelreise der Seele*. Darmstadt: Wissenschaftliche Buchgesellschaft, 1960.

Bow, B.A. *The Story of Jesus' Birth: A Pagan and Jewish Affair*. Ph.D. diss., The University of Iowa, 1995.

Brainard, F.S. 'Defining "Mystical Experience."' *Journal of the American Academy of Religion* 64 (1996) 359–393.

Brandenburger, E. *Die Verborgenheit Gottes im Weltgeschehen: Das literarische und theologische Problem des 4. Esrabuches*. Zürich: Theologischer, 1981.

Brayer, M. 'Psychosomatics, Hermetic Medicine, and Dream Interpretation in the Qumran Literature.' *Jewish Quarterly Review* 60 (1970) 213–230.

Breech, E. 'These fragments I have shored against my ruins: the Form and Function of 4 Ezra.' *Journal of Biblical Literature* 92 (1973) 267–274.

Brelich, A. 'The Place of Dreams in the Religious World Concept of the Greeks.' In *The Dream and Human Societies*, 293–301. Edited by G.E. von Grunebaum and R. Callois. Berkeley: University of California Press, 1966.

Bremmer, J. *Greek Religion*. Oxford: Oxford University Press, 1994.

Brooke, G. 'Qumran Pesher: Towards the Redefinition of a Genre.' *Revue de Qumran*, num. 10, tome 10, fasc. 4 (1981): 483–504.

Brooten, B. *Women Leaders in the Ancient Synagogue: Inscriptional Evidence and Background Issues*. Brown Judaic Studies 35. Chico, CA: Scholars Press, 1982.

Brown, F. with S.R. Driver and C.A. Briggs. *A Hebrew and English Lexicon of the Old Testament*. Oxford: Clarendon, 1906. Repr. 1951.

Brown, R.E. *The Birth of the Messiah: A Commentary on the Infancy Narratives in the Gospels of Matthew and Luke*. New York: Doubleday, 1993.

Büchsenschütz, B. *Traum und Traumdeutung im Altertum*. Wiesbaden: Dr. Martin Sändig oHG, 1967.

Bulkley, K. 'The Evil Dreams of Gilgamesh: An Interdisciplinary Approach to Dreams in Mythological Texts.' In *The Dream and the Text: Essays on Literature and Language*, 159–177. Edited by C.S. Rupprecht. Albany: SUNY, 1993.

Burkert, W. *Greek Religion*. Translated by J. Raffan. Cambridge: Harvard University Press, 1985.

Buss, M.J. *Biblical Form Criticism in Context*. Journal for the Study of the Old Testament: Supplement Series 274. Sheffield: Sheffield Academic Press, 1999.

Butrica, J.L. 'Propertius 3.3.7–12 and Ennius.' *Classical Quarterly* 33.2 (1983) 464–468.

Buxton, R.G.A. *Imaginary Greece: The Contexts of Mythology*. Cambridge: Cambridge University Press, 1994.

Byl, S. 'Quelques idées grecques sur le rêve, d'Homère à Artémidore.' *Les Études Classiques* XVII, 2 (1979) 107–123.

Campbell, A.F. 'Form Criticism's Future.' In *The Changing Face of Form Criticism for the Twenty-First Century*, 19–20. Edited by M.A. Sweeney and E. Ben Zvi. Grand Rapids, MI: Eerdmans, 2003.

Cancik, H. 'Idolum and Imago: Roman Dreams and Dream Theories.' In *Dream Cultures: Explorations in the Comparative History of Dreaming*, 169–188. Edited by D. Shulman and G. Stroumsa. New York: Oxford University Press, 1999.

Caquot, A. 'Les songes et leur interpretátion selon Canaan et Israel.' In *Les*

Songes et leur interpretation, 99–124. Edited by S. Sauneron. *Sources Orientales*, vol. 2. Paris: Seuil, 1959.

——. 'Sur les quatre Bêtes de Daniel VII,' *Semitica* 5 (1955), 10–12.

Carmignac, J. 'Les Dangers de l'Eschatologie.' *New Testament Studies* 17 (1981) 365–390.

——. 'Description du phénomène de l'Apocalyptique dans l'Ancien Testament.' In *Apocalypticism in the Mediterranean World and the Near East: Proceedings of the International Colloquium on Apocalypticism Uppsala, August 12–17, 1979*, 163–170. Edited by D. Hellholm. Tübingen: J.C.B. Mohr, 1983.

Cederstrom, E.R. 'A Study of the Nature and Function of Dreams in Greek Tragedy.' Ph.D. diss., Bryn Mawr, 1971.

Charlesworth, J.H. 'The Portrayal of the Righteous as an Angel.' In *Ideal Figures in Ancient Judaism*, 135–152. Edited by G.W.E. Nickelsburg and J.J. Collins. Ann Arbor, MI: Scholars Press, 1980.

Civil, M. 'The Song of the Plowing Oxen.' In *Kramer Anniversary Volume*, 83–95. Edited by Barry Eichler. *Alter Orient und Altes Testament* 25. Kevelaer/ Neukirchen-Vluyn: Verlag Butzon und Bercker/Neukirchener Verlag, 1976.

Clark, R.J. 'Trophonius.' *Transactions of the American Philological Association* 99 (1968) 63–75.

——. *Catabasis: Vergil and the Wisdom-Tradition*. Amsterdam: B.R. Grüner, 1979.

Clarke, H. *Vergil's Aeneid and Fourth ('Messianic') Eclogue in the Dryden Translation*. University Park: Pennsylvania State University Press, 1989.

Clay, J.S. *The Politics of Olympus: Form and Meaning in the Major Homeric Hymns*. Princeton, N.J.: Princeton University Press, 1989.

Clifford, R.J. *The Cosmic Mountain in Canaan and the Old Testament*. Harvard Semitic Monographs 4. Cambridge, MA: Harvard University Press, 1972.

Cohen, A. *Everyman's Talmud*. New York: Schocken Books, 1949.

Collins, A.Y. 'Early Christian Apocalypses.' In *Apocalypse: The Morphology of a Genre*, 61–122. *Semeia 14*. Edited by J.J. Collins. Missoula, MT: Scholars Press, 1979.

——. 'The Seven Heavens in Jewish and Christian Apocalypses.' In *Death, Ecstasy, and Otherworldly Journeys*, 57–92. Edited by J.J. Collins and M. Fishbane. Albany: State University of New York, 1995.

——. *Cosmology and Eschatology in Jewish and Christian Apocalypticism*. Leiden: Brill, 1996.

Collins, J.J. 'The Symbolism of Transcendence in Jewish Apocalyptic.' *Biblical Research* 19 (1974) 5–22.

——. 'Introduction: Towards the Morphology of a Genre.' In *Apocalypse: The Morphology of a Genre*, 1–20. *Semeia 14*. Edited by J.J. Collins. Missoula, MT: Scholars Press, 1979.

——. 'Jewish Apocalypses.' In *Apocalypse: The Morphology of a Genre. Semeia 14*, 21–59. Missoula, MT: Scholars Press, 1979.

——. 'Testaments.' In *Jewish Writings of the Second Temple Period: Apocrypha, Pseudepigrapha, Qumran Sectarian Writings, Philo, Josephus*, 325–356. Edited by M.E. Stone. Assen: Van Gorcum, 1984.

——. 'Apocalyptic Literature.' In *Early Judaism and its Modern Interpreters*, 345–

370. Edited by R. Kraft and G.W.E. Nickelsburg. Philadephia: Fortress, 1986.

———. 'The Testamentary Literature in Recent Scholarship.' In *Early Judaism and its Modern Interpreters*, 268–286. Edited by R.A. Kraft and G.W.E. Nickelsburg. Atlanta: Scholars Press, 1986.

———. 'Wisdom, Apocalypticism, and Generic Compatibility.' In *In Search of Wisdom: Essays in Memory of John G. Gammie*, 165–185. Edited by L.G. Perdue, B.B. Scott, W.J. Wiseman. Louisville, KY: Westminster/John Knox, 1993.

———. *Daniel: A Commentary on the Book of Daniel*. Hermeneia. Edited by F.M. Cross. Minneapolis: Fortress, 1993.

———. 'A Throne in the Heavens.' In *Death, Ecstasy, and Otherworldly Journeys*, 41–56. Edited by Collins and Fishbane.

———. *Apocalypticism in the Dead Sea Scrolls*. London: Routledge, 1997.

———. *Seers, Sybils and Sages in Hellenistic-Roman Judaism*. Leiden: Brill, 1997.

———. *The Apocalyptic Imagination: An Introduction to Jewish Apocalyptic Literature*. 2nd ed. Grand Rapids, MI: Eerdmans, 1998.

———. (ed.). *Apocalypse: The Morphology of a Genre*. Semeia 14. Missoula, MT: Scholars Press, 1979.

———. and M. Fishbane (eds.). *Death, Ecstasy, and Otherworldly Journeys*. Albany: State University of New York, 1995.

———. and R.A. Kugler (eds.). *Religion in the Dead Sea Scrolls*. Grand Rapids, MI: Eerdmans, 2000.

Conzelmann, H. *Acts of the Apostles: A Commentary on the Acts of the Apostles*. Translated by J. Limburg, A.T. Kraabel and D.H. Juel. Philadephia: Fortress, 1987.

Crahay, R. *La littérature oraculaire chez Hérodote*. Paris: Société d'Édition 'Les Belles Lettres,' 1956.

Cross, F.M. *Canaanite Myth and Hebrew Epic*. Cambridge, MA: Harvard University, 1973.

Cryer, F.H. *Divination in Ancient Israel and its Near Eastern Environment: A Socio-Historical Investigation*. JSOT Supp. 142. Sheffield: Sheffield Academic Press, 1994.

Culianu, I.P. *Expériences de l'extase: Extase, ascension et récit visionnaire de l'Hellénisme au moyen âge*. Paris: Payot, 1984.

Cumont, F. *Astrology and Religion among the Greeks and Romans*. New York: Dover, 1960.

Dan, J. 'Mysticism in Jewish History, Religion and Literature.' In *Studies in Jewish Mysticism: Proceedings of Regional Conferences Held at the University of California, Los Angeles and McGill University in April, 1978*, 1–14. Edited by J. Dan and F. Talmage. Cambridge, MA: Association for Jewish Studies, 1982.

Dauphin, C. *Israel Exploration Journal* 29 (1979): 235–236; 31 (1981): 117–119; 34 (1984): 271–274.

———. 'Dor, Byzantine Church, 1983.' *Israel Exploration Journal* 34 (1984): 271–274.

———. 'Dora-Dor: A Station for Pilgrims in the Byzantine Period on their Way to Jerusalem.' In *Ancient Churches Revealed*, 90–97. Edited by Y. Tsafrir. Jerusalem: Israel Exploration Society, 1993.

——. 'From Apollo to Asclepius to Christ: Pilgrimage and Healing at the Temple and Episcopal Basilica of Dor.' *Studium Biblicum Franciscanum Liber Annus XLIX* (1999): 397–430.

Davila, J. *Descenders to the Chariot: The People behind the Hekhalot Literature*. Leiden: Brill, 2000.

Day, J. *God's Conflict with the Dragon and the Sea: Echoes of a Canaanite Myth in the Old Testament*. Cambridge: Cambridge University Press, 1985.

De Jonge, M. *The Testaments of the Twelve Patriarchs: A Study of their Text, Composition and Origin*. Assen: Van Gorcum, 1953. Repr. 1975.

——. *Jewish Eschatology, Early Christian Christology and the Testaments of the Twelve Patriarchs: Collected Essays of Marinus de Jonge*. Leiden: Brill, 1991.

——. 'Levi in Aramaic Levi and in the Testament of Levi.' In *Pseudepigrapha Perspectives: The Apocrypha and Pseudepigrapha in Light of the Dead Sea Scrolls: Proceedings of the International Symposium of the Orion Center for the Study of the Dead Sea Scrolls and Associated Literature, 12–14 January, 1997*, 71–90. Studies on the Texts of the Desert of Judah XXXI. Edited by E.G. Chazon and M. Stone. Leiden: Brill, 1999.

——. (ed.). *Studies on the Testaments of the Twelve Patriarchs: Text and Interpretation*. Studia in Vetris Testamenti Pseudepigraphica 3. Leiden: Brill, 1975.

Dean-Otting, M. *Heavenly Journeys: A Study of the Motif in Hellenistic Jewish Literature*. Frankfurt am Main: Peter Lang, 1984.

Dehandschutter, B. 'Le rêve dans l'apocryphe de la Genèse.' In *La Littérature Juivre entre Tenach et Mischna*, 1–14. Edited by W.C. Van Unnik. Leiden: Brill, 1974.

Delcor, M. *Le Testament d'Abraham*. Leiden: Brill, 1973.

Dement, W. *The Promise of Sleep*. New York: Dell, 1999.

Deubner, L. *De Incubatione capita quattuor*. Leipzig: In aedibus B.G. Teubneri, 1900.

Devereux, G. *Dreams in Greek Tragedy: An Ethno-Psychoanalytic Study*. Berkeley: University of California Press, 1976.

Dodds, E.R. *Greeks and the Irrational*. Berkeley: University of California Press, 1968.

——. *Pagan and Christian in an Age of Anxiety*. New York: Norton, 1970.

Douglas, M. *Purity and Danger: An Analysis of the Concepts of Pollution and Taboo*. London: Routledge & Kegan Paul, 1966.

——. *Leviticus as Literature*. Oxford: Oxford University Press, 1999.

Dupont-Sommer, A. 'Le Testament de Lévi (XVII–XVIII) et la secte juive de l'Alliance.' *Semitica* 4 (1954) 33–53.

Easterling, P. and J. Muir (eds.). *Greek Religion and Society*. Cambridge: Cambridge University Press, 1985.

Edmunds, L. (ed.). *Approaches to Greek Myth*. Baltimore, MD: Johns Hopkins University Press, 1990.

Edwards, R.A. *Matthew's Story of Jesus*. Philadelphia: Fortress, 1985.

Ehrlich, E. *Der Traum in Alten Testament. Beihefte zur Zeitschrift für die Alttestamentliche Wissenschaft* 73. Berlin: Alfred Töppelmann, 1953.

——. 'Der Traum im Talmud.' In *Zeitschrift für die neutestamentliche Wissenschaft* 47 (1956) 133–145.

Ehrman, B. *The New Testament: A Historical Introduction to the Early Christian Writings.* 2nd ed. New York: Oxford University Press, 2000.

Eitrem, S. 'Dreams and Divination in Magical Ritual.' In *Magika Hiera: Ancient Greek Magic and Religion*, 175–187. Edited by C.A. Faraone and D. Obbink. New York: Oxford University Press, 1991.

Fallon, F. 'The Gnostic Apocalypses.' In *Apocalypse: The Morphology of a Genre, 123–158. Semeia 14.* Edited by J.J. Collins. Missoula, MT: Scholars Press, 1979.

Faraone, C.A. and D. Obbink (eds.). *Magika Hiera: Ancient Greek Magic and Religion.* New York: Oxford University Press, 1991.

Farnell, L.B. *The Cults of the Greek States.* 5 vols. New Rochelle: Caratzas Brothers, 1895. Repr. 1977.

Feen, R.H. 'Nedyia {sic!} as Apocalypse: A Study of Cicero's *Dream of Scipio.*' *Journal of Religious Studies* 9 (Spring 1981) 28–34.

Ferguson, J. 'Divination and Oracles: Rome.' In *Civilization of the Ancient Mediterranean: Greece and Rome* 2:951–958. Edited by M. Grant and R. Kitzinger. New York: Charles Scribner's Sons, 1988.

———. 'Magic.' In *Civilization of the Ancient Mediterranean* 2:881–886. Edited by Grant and Kitzinger.

Festinger, L. *A Theory of Cognitive Dissonance.* Stanford, CA: Stanford University Press, 1962.

Fishbane, M. *Biblical Interpretation in Ancient Israel.* Oxford: Clarendon, 1985.

Flannery-Dailey, F. 'Standing at the Heads of Dreamers: A Study of Dreams in Antiquity.' Ph.D. diss., The University of Iowa, 2000.

———. 'Review of *A Letter that Has Not Been Read.*' *Journal of Biblical Literature* 121:3 (Fall, 2002) 536–537.

Fletcher-Louis, C. *All the Glory of Adam: Liturgical Anthropology in the Dead Sea Scrolls.* Leiden: Brill, 2002.

Foley, H. *Homeric Hymn to Demeter: Translation, Commentary and Interpretive Essays.* Princeton, NJ: Princeton University Press, 1994.

Forman, R. (ed.). *The Problem of Pure Consciousness: Mysticism and Philosophy.* New York: Oxford University Press, 1990.

Fossum, J. *The Name of God and the Angel of the Lord: Samaritan and Jewish Concepts of Intermediation and the Origin of Gnosticism.* Wissenschaftliche Untersuchungen zum Neuen Testament 35. Tübingen: Mohr-Siebeck, 1985.

Foucart, G. 'Dreams and Sleep: Egyptian.' *Encyclopedia of Religion and Ethics* 5:34–37. 13 vols. Edited by J. Hastings, J. Selbie and L. Gray. New York: Scribners, 1922–1928.

Fredriksen, P. *Jesus of Nazareth: King of the Jews.* New York: Vintage, 1999.

Freedman, D.N. (ed.). *Anchor Bible Dictionary.* 6 vols. New York: Doubleday, 1992.

Freud, S. *The Interpretation of Dreams.* 8th ed. Translated by J. Strachey. New York: Basic Books, 1965. First German Edition, *Die Traumdeutung.* Leipzig and Vienna: Franz Deuticke, 1900.

Friedrich, J. 'tešhaniia.' In *Kurzgefaßtes Hethitisches Wörterbuch.* Heidelberg: Carl Winter Universitätsverlag, 1991.

Frisch, P. *Die Träume bei Herodot.* Meisenheim am Glan: Anton Hain, 1968.

Frymer-Kensky, T. *In the Wake of the Goddesses: Women, Culture and the Biblical Transformation of Pagan Myth.* New York: Fawcett Columbine, 1992.

Gafni, I. 'The Historical Background.' In *Jewish Writings of the Second Temple Period: Apocrypha, Pseudepigrapha, Qumran Sectarian Writings, Philo, Josephus.* Edited by M.E. Stone. Philadelphia: Fortress Press, 1984.

Gallop, D. 'Dreaming and Waking in Plato.' In *Essays in Ancient Greek Philosophy,* 187–201. Edited by J. Anton and G. Kustas. Albany: State University of New York, 1971.

———. *Aristotle on Sleep and Dreams: A Text and Translation with Introduction, Notes and Glossary.* Warminster, England: Aris & Phillips, 1996.

Gantz, T. *Early Greek Myths: A Guide to Literary and Artistic Sources.* Baltimore: Johns Hopkins University Press, 1993.

Garland, R. *Introducing New Gods: The Politics of Athenian Religion.* Ithaca, NY: Cornell University Press, 1992.

Gaster, T. 'Dreams: In the Bible.' *Encyclopedia Judaica* 6:208–211. 16 vols. Jerusalem: Keter, 1971.

Geertz, C. *The Interpretation of Cultures.* New York: Basic Books, 1973.

Ginzberg, L. *Legends of the Jews.* 7 vols. Philadelphia: Jewish Publication Society, 1909–1938.

Glare, P.G.W. (ed.). *Oxford Latin Dictionary.* 8th ed. Oxford: Clarendon, 1982. Repr. 1983.

Glasson, T.F. *Greek Influence in Jewish Eschatology.* London: SPCK, 1961.

Gnuse, R. 'A Reconsideration of the Form-Critical Structure in 1 Samuel 3: An Ancient Near Eastern Dream Theophany.' *Zeitschrift für alttestamentliche Wissenschaft* 94 (1982) 379–390.

———. *The Dream Theophany of Samuel: Its Structure in Relation to Ancient Near Eastern Dreams and its Theological Significance.* Lanham, MD: University Press of America, 1984.

———. 'Dream Genre in the Matthean Infancy Narratives,' in *Novum Testamentum* XXXII, 2 (1990): 97–120.

———. 'Dreams in the night—scholarly mirage or theophanic formula?: The dream report as a motif of the so-called elohist tradition.' *Biblische Zeitschrift,* 39.1 (1995) 28–53.

———. *Dreams and Dream Reports in the Writings of Josephus: A Traditio-Historical Analysis.* Leiden: E.J. Brill, 1996.

Goiten, S.D. *A Mediterranean Society.* 3 vols. Berkeley: University of California Press, 1978.

Goldstein, J. *1 Maccabees: A New Translation with Introduction and Commentary.* Anchor Bible 41. New York: Doubleday, 1976.

———. *2 Maccabees: A New Translation with Introduction and Commentary.* Anchor Bible 41A. New York: Doubleday, 1984.

Goodman, M. Review of E.P. Sanders' *Judaism: Practice and Belief, 63 BCE–66 CE. Scottish Journal of Theology* 47, 1 (1994) 89–119.

Grabbe, L. *Judaism from Cyrus to Hadrian.* 2 vols. Minneapolis: Fortress, 1992.

Graf, F. 'Prayer in Magical and Religious Ritual.' In *Magika Hiera: Ancient Greek Magic and Religion,* 188–213. Edited by C.A. Faraone and D. Obbink. New York: Oxford University Press, 1991.

———. *Greek Mythology: An Introduction.* Baltimore, Johns Hopkins University Press, 1993.

Grant, F.D. *Hellenistic Religion: The Age of Syncretism.* New York: Liberal Arts Press, 1953.

Grant, M. and R. Kitzinger (eds.). *Civilization of the Ancient Mediterranean: Greece and Rome.* Vol. 2. New York: Charles Scribner's Sons, 1988.

Grottanelli, C. 'On the Mantic Meaning of Incestuous Dreams.' In *Dream Cultures*, 143–168. Edited by Shulman and Stroumsa.

Gruenwald, I. *Apocalyptic and Merkavah Mysticism.* Leiden: Brill, 1980.

———. *From Apocalypticism to Gnosticism: Studies in Apocalypticism, Merkavah Mysticism and Gnosticism.* Frankfurt am Main: Peter Lang, 1988.

———. 'Reflections on the Nature and Origins of Jewish Mysticism.' In *Gershom Scholem's Major Trends in Jewish Mysticism: 50 Years Later*, 25–38. Edited by P. Schäfer and J. Dan. Tübingen: J.C.B. Mohr, 1993.

Grunebaum, G.E. von, and R. Callois (eds.). *The Dream and Human Societies.* Berkeley: University of California Press, 1966.

Guillaume, A. *Prophecy and Divination Among the Hebrews and Other Semites.* London: Hodder and Stoughton, 1938.

Gunkel, H. *Genesis.* 3rd ed. Translated by M.E. Biddle. Macon, GA: Mercer University Press. Repr. 1997.

———. *Die Psalmen.* 5th ed. Göttingen: Vandenhoeck & Ruprecht, 1968.

——— and J. Begrich. *Einleitung in die Psalmen.* 2nd ed. Göttingen: Vandenhoeck & Ruprecht, 1966.

Gurney, O.R. 'The Babylonians and Hittites.' In *Oracles and Divination*, 142–173. Edited by M. Loewe and C. Blacker. Boulder: Shambhala, 1981.

Hadley, J.M. *Cult of Asherah in ancient Israel and Judah: evidence for a Hebrew Goddess.* New York: Cambridge University Press, 2000.

Haenchen, E. *The Acts of the Apostles.* Philadelphia: Westminster, 1971.

Halliday, W.R. *Greek Divination: A Study of its Methods and Principles.* Chicago: Argonaut Inc., 1913. Repr. 1967.

Halperin, D. *The Merkabah in Rabbinic Literature.* New Haven, CT: American Oriental Society, 1980.

———. 'Heavenly Ascension in Ancient Judaism: The Nature of the Experience.' In *SBL Seminar Papers 1987*, 218–232. Society of Biblical Literature Seminar Papers 26. Atlanta: Scholars Press, 1987.

———. *The Faces of the Chariot: Early Jewish Responses to Ezekiel's Vision.* Tübingen: J.C.B. Mohr, 1988.

Hamilton, M. *Incubation: Or the Cure of Disease in Pagan Temples and Christian Churches.* London: W.C. Henderson and Son, 1906.

Hanson, J.S. 'Dreams and Visions in the Graeco-Roman World and Early Christianity.' In *Religion. Aufstieg und Niedergang der Römischen Welt, II: Principat* 23.2, 1395–1427. Edited by W. Haase. Berlin: Walter de Gruyter, 1980.

Hanson, P.D. 'Apocalypticism.' In *Interpreter's Dictionary of the Bible*: *Supplementary Volume*, 28–34. 3rd printing. Edited by K. Crim et al. Nashville: Abingdon, 1982.

———. (ed.). *Visionaries and their Apocalypses.* Philadelphia: Fortress, 1983.

Haran, M. 'Priestly Vestments.' *Encyclopedia Judaica* 13:1063–1069.

——— and M. Stern. 'Priests and Priesthood.' *Encyclopedia Judaica* 13:1069–1090. 16 vols. Jerusalem: Keter and Macmillan, 1971–1972.

Hardie, P. *Virgil*. Oxford: Oxford University Press, 1998.

Harnisch, W. *Verhängnis und Verheißung der Geschichte: Untersuchungen zum Zeit und Geschichtsverständnis im 4. Buch Esra und in der syr. Baruchapokalypse*. Göttingen: Vandenhoeck & Ruprecht, 1969.

———. 'Die Ironie der Offenbarung: Exegetische Erwägungen zur Zionvision im 4 Buch Esra.' In *SBL Seminar Papers 1981*, 79–104. Society of Biblical Literature Seminar Papers 20. Edited by K.H. Richards. Chico, CA: Scholars Press, 1981.

———. 'Der Prophet als Widerpart und Zeuge der Offenbarung Erwägungen zur Interdependenz von Form und Sache im IV. Buch Esra.' In *Apocalypticism in the Mediterranean World and the Near East: Proceedings of the International Colloquium on Apocalypticism, Uppsala, August 12–17, 1979*, 461–493. Edited by D. Hellholm. Tübingen: J.C.B. Mohr, 1983.

Harrington, D.J. *The Maccabean Revolt: Anatomy of a Biblical Revolution*. Wilmington: Glazier, 1988.

Hartman, L. *Asking for a Meaning*. Sweden: CWK Gleerup Lund, 1979.

Harvey, P. *Oxford Companion to Classical Literature*. Oxford: Clarendon, 1937. Repr. 1962.

Hasan-Rokem, G. 'Communication with the Dead in Jewish Dream Culture.' In *Dream Cultures: Explorations in the Comparative History of Dreaming*, 213–232. Edited by D. Shulman and G. Stroumsa. New York: Oxford University Press, 1999.

Hausmann, U. *Kunst und Heiltum: Untersuchungen zu den Griechischen Asklepiosreliefs*. Potsdam: Eduard Stichnote, 1948.

Hay, D.M. 'Politics and Exegesis in Philo's Treatise on Dreams.' *SBL Seminar Papers 1987*, 429–438. Society of Biblical Literature Seminar Papers 26. Edited by K.H. Richards. Atlanta: Scholars Press, 1987.

Hellholm, D. 'The Problem of Apocalyptic Genre and the Apocalypse of John.' In *SBL Seminar Papers 1982*, 157–198. Society of Biblical Literature Seminar Papers 21. Edited by K.H. Richards. Chico, CA: Scholars Press, 1982.

———. (ed.). *Apocalypticism in the Mediterranean World and the Near East: Proceedings of the International Colloquium on Apocalypticism, Uppsala, August 12–17, 1979*. Tübingen: J.C.B. Mohr, 1983.

Hengel, M. *Judaism and Hellenism: Studies in their Encounter in Palestine during the Early Hellenistic Period*. 2 vols. J. Bowden, trans. Philadelphia: Fortress, 1974.

———. 'Judaism and Hellenism Revisited.' In *Hellenism in the Land of Israel)*, 6–37. Christianity and Judaism in Antiquity 13. Edited by J.J. Collins and G.E. Sterling. Notre Dame, IN: University of Notre Dame Press, 2001.

Herzog, R. *Die Wunderheilungen von Epidauros*. Philologus Suppl. 22.3. Leipzig: Dieterich, 1931.

Hewitt, J.W. 'The Major Restrictions of Access to Greek Temples.' *Transactions of the American Philological Society* 40 (1909) 83–91.

Hillman, J. *The Dream and the Underworld*. New York: Harper & Row, 1978.

Himmelfarb, M. *Tours of Hell: An Apocalyptic Form in Jewish and Christian Literature.* Philadelphia: University of Pennsylvania Press, 1983.

———. 'Apocalyptic Ascent and the Heavenly Temple.' *SBL Seminar Papers 1987,* 210–217. Society of Biblical Literature Seminar Papers 26. Edited by K.H. Richards. Atlanta: Scholars Press, 1987.

———. *Ascent to Heaven in Jewish and Christian Apocalypses.* New York: Oxford University Press, 1993.

———. 'The Practice of Ascent in the Ancient Mediterranean World.' In *Death, Ecstasy, and Other Worldly Journeys,* 123–137. Edited by Collins and Fishbane.

———. 'The Wisdom of the Scribe, the Wisdom of the Priest, and the Wisdom of the King.' In *For a Later Generation: The Transformation of Tradition in Israel, Early Judaism and Early Christianity,* 89–99. Edited by R.A. Argall, B.A. Bow, R.A. Werline. Harrisburg, PA: Trinity Press International, 2000.

Horsley, R. *The Liberation of Christmas: The Infancy Narratives in Social Context.* New York: Crossroad, 1989.

Huffmon, H. 'Prophecy in the Mari Letters.' *Biblical Archaeologist* 31:4 (1968) 101–124.

Hultgård, A. *L'eschatologie des Testaments des Douze Patriarches. Composition de l'ouvrage texts et traductions.* 2 vols. Acta Universitatus Upsaliensis. Historia Religionum 7. Uppsala: Almqvist & Wiksell, 1982.

Hundt, J. *Der Traumglaube bei Homer.* Greifswald: Hans Dallmeyer, 1935.

Huskey, Samuel J. 'Ovid's *Tristia* I and III: An Intertextual Katabasis.' Ph.D. diss., The University of Iowa, 2002.

Hutchinson, G.O. *Hellenistic Poetry.* Oxford: Clarendon, 1988.

Jansen, H.L. *Die Henochgestalt.* Oslo: Dybwed, 1939.

Jayne, W.A. *The Healing Gods of Ancient Civilizations.* New Haven: Yale University Press, 1925.

Jeremias, J. *Jerusalem in the Time of Jesus.* London: SCM Press, 1969. English trans. of 3rd rev. German ed. 1967. 1st German ed. 1923–1937.

Jirku, A. 'Ein Fall von Inkubation im Alten Testament.' *Zeitschrift für die alttestamentliche Wissenschaft* 33 (1913) 151–153.

Jocelyn, H.D. *The Tragedies of Ennius: The Fragments Edited with an Introduction and Commentary.* Cambridge: Cambridge University Press, 1967.

Johnson, A.R. *The Cultic Prophet in Ancient Israel.* 2nd ed. Cardiff: University of Wales Press, 1962.

Kabisch, R. *Das vierte Buch Esra auf seine Quellen untersucht.* Göttingen: Vandendoeck & Ruprecht, 1889.

Katz, S. 'Language, Epistemology and Mysticism.' In *Mysticism and Philosophical Analysis,* 22–74. Edited by S. Katz. New York: Oxford University Press, 1978.

———. 'On Mysticism.' *Journal of the American Academy of Religion* 56 (1988) 751–761.

Kellner, W. *Der Traum vom Menschensohn: die politisch-theologische Botschaft Jesu.* München: Kösel, GmbH und Co., 1985.

Kenney, E.J. (ed.). *Cambridge History of Classical Literature.* 2 vols. Cambridge: Cambridge University Press, 1982–1985.

Kerényi, K. *Asklepios: Archetypal Image of the Physician's Existence.* Translated by P. Manheim. Bollingen Series LXV.3. N.Y.: Pantheon Books, 1959.

Kessels, A.H.M. 'Ancient Systems of Dream-Classification.' *Mnemosyne* 22 (1969) 389–424.

———. *Studies on the Dream in Greek Literature*. Utrecht: HES Publishers, 1978.

Kim, H.C.P. 'Form Criticism in Dialogue with Other Criticisms.' In *Changing Face of Form Criticism*, 85–106. Edited by Sweeney and ben Zvi.

King, S. 'Two Epistemological Models for the Interpretation of Mysticism.' *Journal of the American Academy of Religion* 56 (1988) 257–279.

Kingsbury, J.D. *Matthew*. Philadelphia: Fortress, 1986.

Kittel, G., G.W. Bromiley, and G. Friedrich (eds.). *Theological Dictionary of the New Testament*. 8 vols. Grand Rapids, MI: Eerdmans, 1964–1976.

Knierim, R.P. 'Old Testament Form Criticism Reconsidered,' *Interpretation* 27 (1973) 435–468.

———. 'Criticism of Literary Features, Form, Tradition and Redaction.' In *The Hebrew Bible and Its Modern Interpreters*, 123–166. Edited by D.A. Knight and G.M. Tucker. Minneapolis: Fortress, 1985.

Knight, D.A. and G.M. Tucker (eds.). *The Hebrew Bible and Its Modern Interpreters*. Minneapolis: Fortress, 1985.

Koch, K. *The Rediscovery of Apocalyptic*. Studies in Biblical Theology 2/22. Naperville, IL: Allenson, 1972.

———. 'Is Daniel Also among the Prophets?' *Interpretation* 39 (1985) 117–130.

Kraemer, R.S. *Her Share of the Blessings: Women's Religions among Pagans, Jews and Christians in the Graeco-Roman World*. New York: Oxford University Press, 1992.

———. *Joseph and Aseneth: A Late Antique Tale of the Biblical Patriarch and his Egyptian Wife, Reconsidered*. New York: Oxford University Press, 1998.

Kraft, R. and G.W.E. Nickelsburg (eds.). *Early Judaism and its Modern Interpreters*. Atlanta: Scholars Press, 1983.

Kragelund, P. 'Epicurus, Priapus and the Dreams in Petronicus.' *Classical Quarterly*. 39, 2 (1989) 436–450.

Kramer, K.P. with J. Larkin. *Death Dreams: Unveiling Mysteries of the Unconscious Mind*. New York: Paulist Press, 1993.

Kramer, S. 'Epic of Gilgamesh.' In *American Schools of Oriental Research Bulletin*. 94:6, n. 11.

Kugler, R. *From Patriarch to Priest: The Levi-Priestly Tradition from Aramaic Levi to Testament of Levi*. Society of Biblical Literature Early Judaism and its Literature 9. Atlanta: Scholars Press, 1996.

———. *Testaments of the Twelve Patriarchs*. Guides to the Apocrypha and Pseudepigrapha. Edited by M.A. Knibb. Sheffield: Sheffield Academic Press, 2001.

Kuntz, J.K. *The Self-Revelation of God*. Philadelphia: Westminster, 1967.

Kvanvig, H. *Roots of Apocalyptic: The Mesopotamian Background of the Enoch Figure and of the Son of Man. Wissenschaftliche Monographien zum Alten und Neuen Testament*. Vol. 61. Neukirchen-Vluyn: Neukirchener, 1988.

Lambdin, T.O. *Introduction to Classical Ethiopic (Ge'ez)*. Harvard Semitic Studies 24. Atlanta: Scholars Press, 1978.

Lang, A. and A.E. Taylor, 'Dreams and Sleep: Introductory, Greek.' *Encyclopedia of Religion and Ethics* 5:28–32. 13 vols. Edited by J. Hastings, J. Selbie and L. Gray. New York: Scribners, 1922–1928.

Lange, A. 'The Essene Position on Magic and Divination.' In *Legal Texts and Legal Issues: Proceedings of the Second Meeting of the International Organization for Qumran Studies*, 377–436. Edited by M. Bernstein, F.G. Martínez and J. Kampen. Leiden: Brill, 1997.

Latacz, J. 'Funktionen des Traums in der antiken Literatur.' In *Traum und Träumen: Traumanalysen in Wissenschaft, Religion und Kunst*, 10–31. Edited by T. Wagner-Simon and G. Benedetti. Göttingen: Vandenhoeck & Ruprecht, 1984.

Lebram, J.C.H. *Das Buch Daniel*. Zürich: Theologische Verlag, 1984.

Leibovici, M. 'Les songes et leur interprétation à Babylone.' In *Les songes et leur Interprétation*, 63–86. Edited by S. Sauneron. *Sources Orientales* 2. Paris: Seuil, 1959.

Lennig, R. 'Traum und Sinnestäuschung bei Aischylos, Sophokles, Euripides.' Ph.D. diss., Universität Tübingen, 1969.

Lenski, G.E. *Power and Privilege: A Theory of Social Stratification*. New York: Mc-Graw, 1966.

Lesses, R. *Ritual Practices to Gain Power: Angels, Incantations, and Revelation in Early Jewish Mysticism*. Harvard Theological Studies 44. Harrisburg, PA: Trinity, 1998.

Levenson, J.D. *Sinai and Zion: An Entry into the Jewish Bible*. San Francisco: HarperSanFrancisco, 1985.

Lewis, I.M. *Ecstatic Religion: A Study of Shamanism and Spirit Possession*. London: Routledge, 1971. Repr. 1989.

Licht, J. 'An Analysis of Baruch's Prayer (*Syr. Bar.* 21).' *Journal of Jewish Studies* 33 (Spr.-Aut., 1982) 327–331.

Liddell, H.G., R. Scott, and H.S. Jones. *A Greek-English Lexicon*. 9th ed. with revised supplement. Oxford, 1996.

LiDonnici, L. 'Epidaurian Miracle Cures.' *SBL Seminar Papers 1988*, 272–276. Society of Biblical Literature Seminar Papers 27. Edited by D.J. Lull. Atlanta: Scholars Press, 1988.

———. *The Epidaurian Miracle Inscriptions: Text, Translation and Commentary*. Society of Biblical Literature Texts and Translations 36. Graeco-Roman Religion Series 11. Atlanta: Scholars Press, 1995.

Lieshout, R.G.A. van. *Greeks on Dreams*. Utrecht, the Netherlands: HES, 1980.

Lindblom, J. 'Theophanies in Holy Places in Hebrew Religion.' *Hebrew Union College Annual* 32 (1961) 91–106.

———. *Prophecy in Ancient Israel*. Philadelphia: Muhlenberg, 1962. Repr. 1965.

———. *Gesichte und Offenbarungen: Vorstellungen von göttlichen Weisungen und übernatürlichen Erscheinungen im ältesten Christentum*. Lund: Gleerup, 1968.

Lindner, H. *Die Geschichtsauffassung des Flavius Josephus im Bellum Judaicum*. Leiden: Brill, 1972.

Lloyd, G.E.R. *Magic, Reason and Experience: Studies in the Development of Greek Science*. Cambridge: Cambridge University Press, 1979.

Loewe, M. and C. Blacker (eds.). *Oracles and Divination*. Boulder: Shambhala, 1981.

Long, B. 'Prophetic Call Traditions and Reports of Visions.' *Zeitschrift für die Alttestamentliche Wissenschaft* 84 (1972) 494–500.

Longenecker, B. 'Locating 4 Ezra: A Consideration of its Social Setting and Functions.' *Journal for the Study of Judaism in the Persian, Hellenistic and Roman Period* 28 (Aug. 1997) 271–293.

Loretto, F. 'Träume und Traumglaube in den Gesichtswerken der Griechen und Romer.' Ph.D. diss., Graz, 1956.

Luck, G. *Arcana Mundi: Magic and the Occult in the Greek and Roman Worlds.* Baltimore: Johns Hopkins University Press, 1985.

Luck, U. 'Das Weltverständnis in der jüdischen Apokalyptik dargestellt am äthiopischen Henoch und am 4 Esra.' *Zeitschrift für Theologie und Kirche* 73 (1976) 283–305.

Lüdemann, G. *Early Christianity according to the Traditions in Acts: A Commentary.* London: SCM, 1989.

Luz, U. *Matthew 1–7: A Commentary.* Translated by W.C. Linss. Minneapolis: Ausburg, 1985.

MacAlister, S. 'Gender as Sign and Symbolism in Artemidoros' *Oneirokritika*: Social Aspirations and Anxieties.' *Helios* 19:1–2 (1992) 140–160.

MacDermot, V. *The Cult of the Seer in the Ancient Middle East.* Berkeley: University of California Press, 1971.

Mack, B.L. and Murphy, R.E. 'Wisdom Literature.' In *Early Judaism and its Modern Interpreters*, 371–396. Edited by R. Kraft and G.W.E. Nickelsburg. Philadephia: Fortress, 1986.

Mack, S. *Ovid.* New Haven: Yale University Press, 1988.

Magnus, H. *Abhandlungen zur Geschichte du Medicin.* Vol. 1. Breslau, 1902.

Malamat, A. 'A Forerunner of Biblical Prophecy: The Mari Documents.' In *Ancient Israelite Religion: Essays in Honor of Frank Moore Cross*, 33–52. Edited by P. D. Miller, P.D. Hanson and S.D. McBride. Philadelphia: Fortress, 1987.

Marinatos, N. and R. Hagg. *Greek Sanctuaries: New Approaches.* London: Routledge, 1993.

Marsh, J. *The Fulness of Time.* New York: Harper & Brothers, 1952.

Martin, L. *Hellenistic Religions: an Introduction.* N.Y.: Oxford University, 1987.

———. 'Artemidorus: Dream Theory in Late Antiquity.' *Second Century* 8 (1991) 97–108.

Mason, S. 'Priesthood in Josephus and the "Pharisaic Revolution."' *Journal of Biblical Literature* 107,4 (1988) 657–661.

———. *Flavius Josephus on the Pharisees: A Composition-Critical Study.* Leiden: Brill, 1991.

McKenzie, S.L. and S.R. Haynes. *To Each Its Own Meaning: Biblical Criticisms and Their Application.* Louisville, KY: Westminster John Knox, 1999.

Meier, C.A. *Antike Incubation und Moderne Psychotherapie: Mit vier Kunst- drucktafeln und einer Abbildung im Text.* Zürich: Rascher & Cie.aG, 1949.

———. 'The Dream in Ancient Greece and Its Use in Temple Cures (Incubation).' In *The Dream and Human Societies*, 303–320. Edited by G.E. von Grunebaum and R. Callois. Berkeley: University of California Press, 1966.

Meier, J.P. *Matthew. New Testament Message: A Biblical-Theological Commentary.* Vol. 3. Wilmington, DE: Michael Glazier, 1980.

———. 'The Gospel of Matthew.' *Anchor Bible Dictionary* 4:622–641. Edited by D. N. Freedman. New York: Doubleday, 1992.

Meijer, P.A. 'Philosophers, Intellectuals, and Religion in Hellas.' In *Faith, Hope and Worship: Aspects of Religious Mentality in the Ancient World*, 216–263. Edited by H.S. Versnel. Leiden: Brill, 1981.

Melugin, R.F. 'Recent Form Criticism Revisted in an Age of Reader Response.' In *The Changing Face of Form Criticism*, 46–64. Edited by M. Sweeney and E. Ben Zvi. Grand Rapids, MI: Eerdmans, 2003.

Merkur, D. 'The Visionary Practices of Jewish Apocalyptists.' In *Psychoanalytic Study of Society*. Vol. 14: 119–148. Edited by L.B. Boyer and S.A. Grolnick: Hillsdale, NJ: The Analytic Press, 1989.

———. *Gnosis: An Esoteric Tradition of Mystical Visions and Unions.* Albany: State University of New York, 1993.

Messer, W.S. *The Dream in Homer and Greek Tragedy.* New York: Columbia University Press, 1918.

Meyers, C.A. and E.M. Meyers. *Haggai, Zechariah 1–8: A New Translation with Introduction and Commentary.* Anchor Bible. Garden City, NY: Doubleday, 1987.

Mikalson, J.D. *Athenian Popular Religion.* Chapel Hill: University of North Carolina Press, 1983.

Miller, J.M. and J. Hayes. *A History of Ancient Israel and Judah.* Philadelphia: Westminster, 1986.

Miller, P.C. *Dreams in Late Antiquity: Studies in the Imagination of a Culture.* Princeton: Princeton University Press, 1994.

Miller, P.D., P.D. Hanson and S.D. McBride (eds.). *Ancient Israelite Religion: Essays in Honor of Frank Moore Cross.* Philadelphia: Fortress, 1987.

Monson, J. 'The Ain Dara Temple: Closest Solomonic Parallel.' *Biblical Archaeology Review* (May-June 2000) 22–35.

Moorsel, G. van. *The Mysteries of Hermes Trismegistus: A Phenomenological Study in the Process of Spiritualisation in the Corpus Hermeticum and Latin Asclepius.* Utrecht: Drukkerij en Uitgeverij V/H Kemink en zoon N.V., 1955.

Morray-Jones, C.R.A. 'Transformational Mysticism in the Apocalyptic-Merkabah Tradition.' *Journal of Jewish Studies* 43 (1992) 1–31.

———. 'Paradise Revisited (2 Cor 12:1–12): The Jewish Mystical Background of Paul's Apostolate, Part 1: The Jewish Sources' and 'Part 2: Paul's Heavenly Ascent and Its Significance.' *Harvard Theological Review* 86 (1993): 177–217, 265–292.

Muilenberg, J. 'Form Criticism and Beyond.' *Journal of Biblical Literature* 88 (1969) 1–18.

Mundle, W. *Das religiöse Problem des IV. Esrabuches. Zeitschrift für die alttestamentliche Wissenschaft* 47 (1929) 222–249.

Murphy, F. *The Structure and Meaning of 2 Baruch.* Society of Biblical Literature Dissertation Series 78. Atlanta: Scholars Press, 1984.

———. *Pseudo-Philo: Rewriting the Bible.* New York: Oxford University Press, 1993.

Muss-Arnolt, W. (ed.). *A Concise Dictionary of the Assyrian Language.* 2 vols. Berlin: Reuther and Reichard, 1905.

Mussies, G. 'Joseph's dream (Matt 1,18–23) and Comparable Stories.' In *Text *and Testimony: Essays on New Testament and Apocryphal Literature in Honour of A. F.J. Klijn*, 177–186. Edited by T. Baarda, A. Hilhorst, G.P. Luttikhuizen, A.S. van der Woude. Kampen: Iutgeversmaatschappij J.H. Kok, 1988.

Nagy, G. *Greek Mythology and Poetics*. Ithaca: Cornell University Press, 1990.

Neusner, J. *Judaism: The Evidence of the Mishna*. Chicago: University of Chicago Press, 1981.

Newsom, C.A. 'Angels.' In the *Anchor Bible Dictionary* 1:248–253. Edited by D.N. Freedman. New York: Doubleday, 1992.

Nickelsburg, G.W.E. *Resurrection, Immortality, and Eternal Life in Intertestamental Judaism*. Harvard Theological Studies 26. Cambridge: Harvard University Press, 1972.

———. 'Good and Bad Leaders in Pseudo-Philo's *Liber Antiquitatum Biblicarum*.' In *Ideal Figures in Ancient Judaism*, 49–65. Edited by G.W.E. Nickelsburg and J. J. Collins. Chico, CA: Scholars Press, 1980.

———. 'Enoch, Levi, and Peter: Recipients of Revelation in Upper Galilee.' *Journal of Biblical Literature* 100:4 (1981) 575–600.

———. *Jewish Literature between the Bible and the Mishnah*. Philadelphia: Fortress, 1981.

———. *Faith and Piety in Early Judaism*. Philadelphia: Fortress, 1983.

———. 'Social Aspects of Palestinian Jewish Apocalypticism.' In *Apocalypticism in the Mediterranean World and the Near East: Proceedings of the International Colloquium on Apocalypticism, Uppsala, August 12–17, 1979*, 641–654. Edited by D. Hellholm. Tübingen: J.C.B. Mohr, 1983.

———. 'The Bible Rewritten and Expanded.' In *Jewish Writings of the Second Temple Period: Apocrypha, Pseudepigrapha, Qumran Sectarian Writings, Philo, Josephus*, 89–156. Edited by M.E. Stone. Assen: Van Gorcum, 1984.

———. 'Stories of Biblical and Early Post-Biblical Times.' In *Jewish Writings of the Second Temple Period*, 33–88. Edited by Stone. Assen: Van Gorcum, 1984.

———. 'The Apocalyptic Construction of Reality in 1 Enoch.' In *Mysteries and Revelations: Apocalyptic Studies since the Uppsala Colloquium*, 50–64. Journal for the Study of the Pseudepigrapha Supplement Series 9. Edited by J.J. Collins and J. Charlesworth. Sheffield: JSOT Press, 1991.

———. *1 Enoch: A Commentary on the Book of 1 Enoch, Chapters 1–36; 81–108*. Hermeneia. Edited by Klaus Baltzer. Minneapolis, Fortress, 2001.

———. 'Wisdom and Apocalypticism in Early Judaism: Some Points for Discussion.' In *George W.E. Nickelsburg in Perspective: An Ongoing Dialogue of Learning*, 1:279–283. 3 vols. Edited by J. Neusner and A.J. Avery-Peck. Leiden: Brill, 2003.

Niditch, S. *The Symbolic Vision in Biblical Tradition*. Harvard Semitic Monographs 30. Chico, CA: Scholars Press, 1980.

———. 'The Visionary.' In *Ideal Figures in Ancient Judaism*, 153–179. Septuagint and Cognate Studies 12. Edited by G.W.E. Nickelsburg and J.J. Collins. Chico, CA: Scholars Press, 1980.

———. *Ancient Israelite Religion*. New York: Oxford University Press, 1997.

Nilsson, M.P. *Geschichte der griechische Religion*. 2 vols. München: C.H. Beck, 1941–1950.

Olmo Lete, G. del and J. Sanmartín. *Diccionario de la Lengua Ugarítica*. Barcelona: Editorial AUSA, 1996.

Oppenheim, L. *The Interpretation of Dreams in the Ancient Near East: With a Translation of an Assyrian Dream-Book*. Transactions of the American Philosophical Society. Vol. 46, part 3. Philadelphia: American Philosophical Society, 1956.

————. *Ancient Mesopotamia*. Chicago: University of Chicago Press, 1964.

————. 'Mantic Dreams in the Ancient Near East.' In *The Dream and Human Societies*, 341–350. Edited by G.E. von Grunebaum and R. Callois. Berkeley: University of California Press, 1966.

————. 'New Fragments of the Assyrian Dream-Book.' *Iraq* 31 (1969) 153–165.

Orton, D. *The Understanding Scribe: Matthew and the Apocalyptic Ideal*. Journal for the Study of the New Testament Supplement Series 25. Sheffield: Sheffield Academic Press, 1989.

Otto, W. *The Homeric Gods: Spiritual Significance of Greek Religion*. Translated by M. Hadas. N.Y.: Pantheon, 1955.

Parrot, A. *Ziqqurats et Tour de Babel*. Paris: Michel, 1949.

————. *The Arts of Assyria*. New York: Golden, 1961.

Parsifal-Charles, N. *The Dream: 4000 Years of Theory and Practice*. 2 vols. West Cornwall: Locust Hill Press, 1986.

Patte, D. *The Gospel According to Matthew: A Structural Commentary on Matthew's Faith*. Philadelphia: Fortress, 1987.

Payne Smith, J. (ed.). *A Compendious Syriac Dictionary*. Winona Lake, IN: Eisenbrauns, 1998.

Pedersen, J. *Israel, Its Life and Culture*. 2 vols. London: Oxford University Press, 1926.

Perrot, C., P.M. Bogaert, with D.J. Harrington. *Pseudo-Philon: Les Antiquités Bibliques*. Vol. 2. Paris: Cerf, 1976.

Pesch, R. *Die Apostelgeschichte*. 2.Teilband, Apg. 13–28. Zürich: Benziger, 1986.

Petersen, D.L. *The Roles of Israel's Prophets*. Journal for the Study of the Old Testament: Supplement Series 17. Sheffield: JSOT Press, 1981.

————. Review of seven volumes of *Forms of the Old Testament Literature* through 1992. *Recherches de science religieuse* 18, 1 (Jan 1992) 29–33.

Philonenko, M. *Les interpolations chrétiennes des Testaments des Douze Patriarches et les manuscrits de Qoumrân*. Paris: Presses universitaires de France, 1960.

Plaskow, J. *Standing Again at Sinai: Judaism from a Feminist Perspective*. San Francisco: HarperSanFrancisco, 1990.

Pollard, J. 'Dreams and Oracles: Greece.' In *Civilization of the Ancient Mediterranean: Greece and Rome*. Vol. 2: 941–950. Edited by M. Grant and R. Kitzinger. New York: Charles Scribner's Sons, 1988.

Porteous, N.W. *Daniel: A Commentary*. Philadelphia: Westminster, 1965.

Porter, J.R. 'Ancient Israel.' In *Oracles and Divination*, 191–214. Edited by M. Loewe and C. Blacker. Boulder: Shambhala, 1981.

Porter, P. *Metaphors and Monsters: A Literary-Critical Study of Daniel 7 and 8*. ConB 20. Lund: Gleerup, 1983.

Pratt, L. 'Odyssey 19.535–550: On the Interpretation of Signs in Homer.' *Classical Philology* 89 (April 1994) 147–152.

Priest, J.F. 'Myth and Dream in Hebrew Scripture.' In *Myths, Dreams and Religion*, 48–67. Edited by J. Campbell. New York: Dutton, 1970.

Rad, G. von. *Genesis*. Translated by J.F. Marks. Philadelphia: Westminster, 1961.

———. *Theologie des Alten Testaments*. Vol. 2. 4ᵗʰ ed. Munich: Kaiser, 1965.

———. *Wisdom in Israel*. Nashville: Abingdon, 1972.

Rajak, T. *Josephus: The Historian and His Society*. Philadelphia: Fortress, 1983.

Rankin, A.V. 'Penelope's Dreams in Books XIX and XX of the *Odyssey.*' *Helicon* 2 (1962) 617–624.

Ray, J.D. 'Ancient Egypt.' In *Oracles and Divination*, 174–190. Edited by M. Loewe and C. Blacker. Boulder: Shambhala, 1981.

Reckford, K.J. 'Catharsis and Dream Interpretation in Aristophanes' *Wasps.*' *Transactions of the American Philological Association* vol. 10, 7 (1977) 283–312.

Resch, A. *Der Traum im Heilsplan Gottes: Deutung und Bedeutung des Traumes im Alten Testament*. Greiburg: Herder, 1964.

Reventlow, H.G. *Das Amt des Propheten bei Amos*. Göttingen: Vandenhoeck & Ruprecht, 1962.

Richardson, M.E.J. (ed.). *The Hebrew and Aramaic Lexicon of the Old Testament*. 2 vols. Leiden: Brill, 2001.

Richter, W. 'Traum und Traumdeutung im AT.' *Biblische Zeitschrift* 7 (1963) 202–220.

———. *Exegese als Literaturwissenschaft: Entwurf einer alttestamentlichen Literaturtheorie und Methodologie*. Göttingen: Vandenhoeck & Ruprecht, 1971.

Ringgren, H. *Religions of the Ancient Near East*. Translated by J. Sturdy. Philadelphia: Westminster, 1973.

Robert, C. *Die antiken Sarkophagenreliefs III,1* (1897).

Roberts, J.J.M. 'The Ancient Near Eastern Environment.' In *The Hebrew Bible and Its Modern Interpreters*, 75–122. Edited by D.A. Knight and G.M. Tucker. Minneapolis: Fortress, 1985.

Roddy, N. *The Romanian Version of the Testament of Abraham: Text, Translation, and Cultural Context*. Early Judaism and Its Literature 19. Atlanta, GA: Society of Biblical Literature, 2001.

Roloff, J. *Die Apostelgeschichte*. Göttingen: Vandenhoeck & Ruprecht, 1981.

Rosenthal, L. 'Die Josephsgeschichte, mit den Büchern Ester und Daniel verglichen.' *Zeitschrift für die alttestamentliche Wissenschaft* 15 (1895) 278–284.

Rousseau, G.S. 'Dream and Vision in Aeschylus' *Oresteia.*' *Arion* 2 (1963) 101–136.

Rowland, C. *The Open Heaven: A Study of Apocalyptic in Judaism and Early Christianity*. London: SPCK, 1982.

Russell, D.S. *Between the Testaments*. Philadelphia: Muhlenberg Press, 1960.

———. *The Method and Message of Jewish Apocalyptic*. Philadelphia: Westminster, 1964.

———. *Divine Disclosure: An Introduction to Jewish Apocalyptic*. Minneapolis: Fortress, 1992.

Russell, J.S. *The English Dream Vision: Anatomy of a Form*. Columbus, OH: Ohio State University Press, 1988.

Saldarini, A.J. *Pharisees, Scribes and Sadducees in Palestinian Society*. Grand Rapids, MI: Eerdmans, 2001.

Sanders, E.P. *Paul and Palestinian Judaism: A Comparison of Patterns of Religion.* Philadelphia: Fortress, 1977.

——. 'The Genre of Palestinian Apocalypses.' In *Apocalypticism in the Mediterranean World and the Near East: Proceedings of the International Colloquium on Apocalypticism, Uppsala, August 12–17, 1979,* 447–459. Edited by D. Hellholm. Tübingen: Mohr-Siebeck, 1983.

——. *Judaism: Practice and Belief 63 BCE–66 CE.* Philadelphia: Trinity, 1992.

Sandford, J.A. *Gottes vergessene Sprache.* Zürich: Rascher & Cie. AG, 1966.

Sandmel, S. 'Parallelomania.' *Journal of Biblical Literature* 81 (1962) 1–13.

Sasson, J. 'Mari Dreams.' *Journal of the American Oriental Society* 103 (1983) 283–293.

Satran, D. 'Daniel: Seer, Philosopher, Holy Man.' In *Ideal Figures in Ancient Judaism,* 33–48. Edited by G.W.E. Nickelsburg and J.J. Collins. Ann Arbor, MI: Scholars Press, 1980.

Sauneron, S. 'Les songes et leur interprétation dans l'Égypte Ancienne.' In *Les songes et leur interprétation,* 17–62. Edited by S. Sauneron. *Sources Orientales* 2. Paris: Seuil, 1959.

——. (ed.). *Les songes et leur interprétation. Sources Orientales* 2. Paris: Seuil, 1959.

Sayce, A.H. 'Dreams and Sleep: Babylonian.' *Encyclopedia of Religion and Ethics* 5:33–34. 13 vols. Edited by J. Hastings, J. Selbie and L. Gray. New York: Scribners, 1922–1928.

Sayler, G.B. *Have the Promises Failed? A Literary Analysis of 2 Baruch.* Society of Biblical Literature Dissertation Series 72. Chico, CA: Scholars Press, 1984.

Schäfer, P. *Hekhalot-Studien.* Tübingen: J.C.B. Mohr (Paul Siebeck), 1988.

——. *Hidden and Manifest God: Some Major Themes in Early Jewish Mysticism.* Translated by A. Pomerance. Albany: State University of New York Press, 1992.

Schams, C. *Jewish Scribes in the Second-Temple Period.* Journal for the Study of the Old Testament Supplement Series 291. Sheffield: Sheffield Academic Press, 1998.

Schmidtke, F. 'Träume, Orakel und Totengeister als Kunder der Zukunft in Israel und Babylonien.' *Biblische Zeitschrift* 11 (1967) 240–246.

Scholem, G. *Jewish Gnosticism, Merkabah Mysticism, and Talmudic Tradition.* New York: Jewish Theological Seminary of America, 1960.

——. *Major Trends in Jewish Mysticism.* New York: Schocken, 1941. Repr. 1995.

Schürer, E. *The History of the Jewish People in the Age of Jesus Christ.* 3 vols. Edited by G. Vermes. F. Millar, M. Black and M. Goodman. Edinburgh: T&T Clark, 1979; 1st English trans. of German, 1885–1891.

Schwartz, S. *Josephus and Judaean Politics.* Leiden: Brill, 1990.

Scullard, H.H. *Festivals and Ceremonies of the Roman Republic.* Ithaca, Cornell University Press, 1981.

Segal, A.F. *Two Powers in Heaven: Early Rabbinic Reports about Christianity and Gnosticism.* Leiden: E.J. Brill, 1977.

——. 'Heavenly Ascent in Hellenistic Judaism, Early Christianity and their Environment.' *Aufstieg und Niedergang der römischen Welt* II.23.2 (1980), 1333–1394.

——. 'Paul and the Beginning of Jewish Mysticism.' In *Death, Ecstasy, and*

Otherworldly Journeys, 93–122. Edited by J.J. Collins and M. Fishbane. Albany: State University of New York, 1995.

Seow, C.L. 'The Syro-Palestinian Context of Solomon's Dream.' *Harvard Theological Review* 77 (April 1984) 141–152.

Seybold, K. 'Der Traum in der Bibel.' In *Traum und Träumen: Traumanalysen in Wissenschaft, Religion und Kunst*, 32–54. Edited by T. Wagner-Simon and G. Benedetti. Götttingen: Vandenhoeck & Ruprecht, 1984.

Shear, J. 'On Mystical Experiences as Support for the Perennial Philosophy.' *Journal of the American Academy of Religion* 62 (1994) 319–342.

Shenhav, E. 'Shuni.' *Excavations and Surveys in Israel* 7–8 (1988/1989) 166–168.

———. 'Shuni.' In *The New Encyclopedia of Archaeological Excavations in the Holy Land*, 4:1382–1384. 4 vols. Edited by E. Stern. Jerusalem, 1993.

Shoulson, J.S. 'Daniel's Pesher: A Proto-Midrashic Reading of Genesis 40–41.' *Essays in Literature* 20 (Spring 1993) 111–128.

Shulman, D. and G. Stroumsa (eds.). *Dream Cultures: Explorations in the Comparative History of Dreaming*. New York: Oxford University Press, 1999.

Skutsch, O. *The Annals of Q. Ennius*. Oxford: Clarendon, 1985.

Sleep Research Society, *Basics of Sleep Behavior*. UCLA and Sleep Research Society, 1993, 21–32.

Slingerland, H.D. *The Testaments of the Twelve Patriarchs: A Critical History of Research*. Missoula, MT: Scholars, 1977.

Smith, H. 'Is there a Perennial Philosophy?' *Journal of the American Academy of Religion* 55 (1987) 553–566.

Soares Prabhu, G.M. *The Formula Quotations in the Infancy Narrative of Matthew: An Enquiry into the Tradition History of Mt 1–2*. Rome: Biblical Institute, 1976.

Sourvinou-Inwood, C. *'Reading' Greek Culture: Texts and Images, Rituals and Myths*. Oxford: Clarendon, 1991.

Speiser, E.A. *Genesis*. The Anchor Bible. Garden City, NY: Doubleday, 1964.

Stone, M.E. 'The Concept of the Messiah in IV Ezra.' In *Religions in Antiquity: E. R. Goodenough Memorial*, 295–312. Edited by J. Neusner. Studies in the History of Religions 14. Leiden: Brill, 1968.

———. 'Lists of Revealed Things in the Apocalyptic Literature.' In *Magnalia Dei: The Mighty Acts of God*, 414–454. Edited by F.M. Cross, W.E. Lemke and P.D. Miller, Jr. Garden City, NY: Doubleday, 1976.

———. 'Apocalyptic Literature.' In *Jewish Writings of the Second Temple Period: Apocrypha, Pseudepigrapha, Qumran Sectarian Writings, Philo, Josephus*, 383–442. Edited by M.E. Stone. Assen: Van Gorcum, 1984.

———. 'Enoch, Aramaic Levi, and Sectarian Origins.' *Journal for the Study of Judaism in the Persian, Hellenistic, and Roman Periods* 19 (1988) 159–170.

———. *Features of the Eschatology of 4 Ezra*. Atlanta: Scholars Press, 1989.

———. *Fourth Ezra: A Commentary on the Book of Fourth Ezra*. Hermeneia. Edited by F.M. Cross. Minneapolis: Fortress, 1990.

———. (ed.). *Jewish Writings of the Second Temple Period: Apocrypha, Pseudepigrapha, Qumran Sectarian Writings, Philo, Josephus*. Assen: Van Gorcum, 1984.

——— and D. Satran (eds.). *Emerging Judaism: Studies on the Fourth and Third Centuries B.C.E.* Minneapolis: Fortress, 1989.

Strecker, G. *Der Weg der Gerechtigkeit: Untersuchung zur Theologie des Matthäus.* Göttingen: Vandenhoeck & Ruprecht, 1962.

Suter, D. 'Mapping the First Book of Enoch: Geographical Issues in George Nickelsburg's Commentary.' In *George W.E. Nickelsburg in Perspective: An Ongoing Dialogue of Learning*, 2:387–394. 3 vols. Edited by J. Neusner and A. J. Avery-Peck. Leiden: Brill, 2003.

Swartz, M.D. *Scholastic Magic: Ritual and Revelation in Early Jewish Mysticism.* Princeton, NJ: Princeton University Press, 1996.

Sweeney, M.A. 'Form Criticism.' In *To Each Its Own Meaning: Biblical Criticisms and Their Application*, 58–89. Edited by S.L. McKenzie and S.R. Haynes. Louisville, KY: Westminster John Knox, 1999.

—— and E. Ben Zvi (eds.). *The Changing Face of Form Criticism for the Twenty-First Century.* Grand Rapids, MI: Eerdmans, 2003.

Tabor, J.D. *Things Unutterable: Paul's Ascent to Paradise in its Graeco-Roman, Judaic and Early Christian Contexts.* Lanham, MD: University Press of America, 1986.

Tanzer, S. Respondent remarks. In *George W.E. Nickelsburg in Perspective: An Ongoing Dialogue of Learning*, 1.267–300. 3 vols. Leiden: Brill, 2003.

Tcherikover, V. *Hellenistic Civilization and the Jews.* New York: Atheneum, 1970.

Thompson, A.L. *Responsibility for Evil in the Theodicy of IV Ezra: A Study Illustrating the Significance of Form and Structure for the Meaning of the Book.* Missoula, MT: Scholars Press, 1977.

Thrämer, E. 'Health and Gods of Healing.' *Encyclopedia of Religion and Ethics* 6:540–556. 13 vols. Edited by J. Hastings, J. Selbie and L. Gray. New York: Scribners, 1922–1928.

Tomlinson, R.A. *Epidauros.* New York: Granada, 1983.

Tucker, G. 'Prophecy and the Prophetic Literature.' In *The Hebrew Bible and Its Modern Interpreters*, 325–368. Edited by D.A. Knight and G.M. Tucker. Minneapolis: Fortress, 1985.

Turcan, R. *Cults of the Roman Empire.* Oxford: Blackwell, 1996.

Turner, J.H. *Societal Stratification: A Theoretical Analysis.* New York: Columbia University Press, 1984.

VanderKam, J.C. *Textual and Historical Studies in the Book of Jubilees.* Harvard Semitic Monographs 14. Missoula, MT: Scholars Press, 1977.

——. 'Enoch Traditions in *Jubilees* and Other Second-Century Sources.' *SBL Seminar Papers 1978*, 1:229–251. Society of Biblical Literature Seminar Papers 13. Edited by P.J. Achtemeier. Missoula, MT: Scholars Press, 1978.

——. 'The Putative Author of the *Book of Jubilees*.' *Journal of Semitic Studies* 26 (1981) 209–217.

——. *Enoch: A Man for All Generations.* Columbia, SC: University of South Carolina, 1995.

Van Straten, F.T. 'Gifts for the Gods.' In *Faith, Hope and Worship: Aspects of Religious Mentality in the Ancient World*, 65–151. Edited by H.S. Versnel. Leiden: Brill, 1981.

Vermaseren, M.J. *Mithras: The Secret God.* Translated by T. Megaw and V. Megaw, New York: Barnes and Noble, 1963.

Versnel, H.S. (ed.). *Faith, Hope and Worship: Aspects of Religious Mentality in the Ancient World.* Leiden: Brill, 1981.

Vielhauer, P. 'Apocalypses and Related Subjects.' In *New Testament Apocrypha*, vol. 2:581–607. 2 vols. Edited by E. Hennecke and W. Schneemelcher. Philadelphia: Westminster, 1965.

Vieyra, M. 'Les songes et leur interprétation chez les Hittites.' In *Les songes et leur interprétation*, 87–98. Edited by Sauneron. *Sources Orientales* 2. Paris: Seuil, 1959.

Vigano, L. 'Literary Sources for the History of Palestine and Syria: The Ebla Tablets.' *Biblical Archaeologist* 47 (1984) 6–16.

Vinagre, M.A. 'Die griechische Terminologie der Traumdeutung.' *Mnemosyne* 49 (June 1996) 247–282.

Wagner-Simon, T. 'Der Heiltraum.' In *Traum und Träumen: Traumanalysen in Wissenschaft, Religion und Kunst*, 67–80. Edited by T. Wagner-Simon and G. Benedetti. Göttingen: Vandenhoeck & Ruprecht, 1984.

Walde, C. 'Dream Interpretation in a Prosperous Age.' In *Dream Cultures: Explorations in the Comparative History of Dreaming*, 121–142. Edited by D. Shulman and G. Stroumsa. New York: Oxford University Press, 1999.

Walton, A. *The Cult of Asklepios*. Cornell Studies in Classical Philology 3. Ithaca: Cornell University Press, 1894.

Watson, D.F. 'Angels: New Testament.' In *Anchor Bible Dictionary* 1:253–255. Edited by D.N. Freedman. New York: Doubleday, 1992.

Weber, G. 'Traum und Alltag in hellenistischer Zeit' *Zeitschrift für Religions- und Geistesgeschichte* 50, 1 (1998) 22–39.

Weber, M. *Economy and Society*. New York: Bedminster Press, 1968.

Weinfeld, M. 'Ancient Near Eastern Patterns in Prophetic Literature,' *Vetus Testamentum*. Vol. XXVII, Fasc. 2, 178–195.

Weiser, A. *Die Apostelgeschichte 1,11. OTK* 5; Gütersloh and Würzburg, 1981. Repr. 1985.

Westermann, C. *Basic Forms of Prophetic Speech*. Philadelphia: Westminster, 1967.

———. *Joseph: Eleven Bible Stories on Genesis*. Minneapolis: Fortress, 1996.

White, R. *Artemidorus: The Interpretation of Dreams*. Park Ridge, N.J: Noyes Press, 1975.

———. 'Techniques in Early Dream Interpretation.' *SBL Seminar Papers 1976*, 323–325. Society of Biblical Literature Seminar Papers. Edited by G. MacRae. Missoula, MT: Scholars Press, 1976.

Widengren, G. *The Ascension of the Apostle and the Heavenly Book*. Uppsala: Uppsala Universitets Årsskrift, 1950.

Wijsenbeeck-Wijler, H. *Aristotle's Concept of Soul, Sleep and Dreams*. Amsterdam: Hakkert, 1978.

Wikenhauser, A. 'Die Traumsgeschichte des Neuen Testament in religionsgeschichtlicher Sicht.' In *Pisciculi: Studien zur Religion und Kultur des Altertums*, 320–333. Edited by T. Klouser and A. Rücker. Münster: Aschendorff, 1939.

———. 'Doppelträume.' *Biblica* 29 (1948) 100–111.

Wilkinson, L.P. 'Cicero and the relation of oratory to literature.' In *Cambridge History of Classical Literature* Vol. 2: 264–265. Cambridge: Cambridge University Press, 1982.

Wilson, R.R. *Prophecy and Society in Ancient Israel*. Philadelphia: Fortress, 1980.

Wolfson, E. 'Mysticism and the Poetic-Liturgical Compositions from Qum-ran.' *Jewish Quarterly Review* 85 (1994) 185–202.

Wood, K. 'The Dreams of Joseph in Light of Ancient Near Eastern Divinatory Practice.' M.A. Thesis, University of Georgia, 1994.

Xella, P. 'Eschmun von Sidon: Der phönizische Asklepios.' In *Mesopotamia Ugaritica Biblica: Festschrift für Kurt Bergerhof zur Vollendung seines 70. Lebensjahres am 7. Mai 1992*, 481–498. Neukirchen-Vluyn: Neukirchener Verlag and Ver-lag Butzon and Bercker Kevelaer, 1993.

Zeitlin, S. 'Dreams and their Interpretation from the Biblical Period to the Tannaitic Time: An Historical Study,' *Jewish Quarterly Review* 66 (July 75) 1–18.

INDEX OF SUBJECTS

INDEX OF AUTHORS

INDEX OF PRIMARY TEXTS

SUPPLEMENTS

TO THE

JOURNAL FOR THE STUDY OF JUDAISM

79. Burkes, S.L. *God, Self, and Death*. The Shape of Religious Transformation in the Second Temple Period. 2003. ISBN 90 04 12954 5

80. Neusner, J. & A.J. Avery-Peck (eds.). *George W.E. Nickelsburg in Perspective*. An Ongoing Dialogue of Learning (2 vols.). 2003. ISBN 90 04 12987 1 (set)

81. Coblentz Bautch, K. *A Study of the Geography of 1 Enoch 17–19*. "No One Has Seen What I Have Seen". 2003. ISBN 90 04 13103 5

82. García Martínez, F., & G.P. Luttikhuizen. *Jerusalem, Alexandria, Rome*. Studies in Ancient Cultural Interaction in Honour of A. Hilhorst. 2003. ISBN 90 04 13584 7

83. Najman, H. & J.H. Newman (eds.). *The Idea of Biblical Interpretation*. Essays in Honor of James L. Kugel. 2004. ISBN 90 04 13630 4

84. Atkinson, K. *I Cried to the Lord*. A Study of the Psalms of Solomon's Historical Background and Social Setting. 2004. ISBN 90 04 13614 2

85. Avery-Peck, A.J., D. Harrington & J. Neusner. *When Judaism and Christianity Began*. Essays in Memory of Anthony J. Saldarini. 2004. ISBN 90 04 13659 2 (Set), ISBN 90 04 13660 6 (Volume I), ISBN 90 04 13661 4 (Volume II)

86. Drawnel, H. *The Aramaic Levi Document*. Text, Translation, and Commentary. 2004. ISBN 90 04 13753 X

87. Berthelot, K. *L'«humanité de l'autre homme» dans la pensée juive ancienne*. 2004. ISBN 90 04 13797 1

88. Bons, E. (ed.) «*Car c'est l'amour qui me plaît, non le sacrifice …*». Recherches sur Osée 6:6 et son interprétation juive et chrétienne. 2004. ISBN 90 04 13677 0

89. Chazon, E.G., D. Satran & R. Clements. (eds.) *Things Revealed*. Studies in Honor of Michael E. Stone. 2004. ISBN 90 04 13885 4.

90. Flannery-Dailey, F. *Dreamers, Scribes, and Priests*. Jewish Dreams in the Hellenistic and Roman Eras. 2004. ISBN 90 04 12367 9.

ISSN 1384-2161